Lecture Notes of the Institute for Computer Sciences, Social Informatics and Telecommunications Engineering

670

The LNICST series publishes ICST's conferences, symposia and workshops.
LNICST reports state-of-the-art results in areas related to the scope of the Institute.
The type of material published includes

- Proceedings (published in time for the respective event)
- Other edited monographs (such as project reports or invited volumes)

LNICST topics span the following areas:

- General Computer Science
- E-Economy
- E-Medicine
- Knowledge Management
- Multimedia
- Operations, Management and Policy
- Social Informatics
- Systems

Congan Xu · Guan Gui · Zhicheng Dong ·
Xuefei Ma

Editors

Mobile Multimedia Communications

18th EAI International Conference,
MobiMedia 2025
Lhasa, China, August 15–17, 2025
Revised Selected Papers

 Springer

Editors
Congan Xu
Naval Aeronautical University
Yantai, China

Zhicheng Dong
Tibet University
Lhasa, China

Guan Gui
Nanjing University of Posts
and Telecommunications
Nanjing, China

Xuefei Ma
Harbin Engineering University
Harbin, China

ISSN 1867-8211　　　　　　　　ISSN 1867-822X (electronic)
Lecture Notes of the Institute for Computer Sciences, Social Informatics
and Telecommunications Engineering
ISBN 978-3-032-16822-1　　　　ISBN 978-3-032-16823-8 (eBook)
https://doi.org/10.1007/978-3-032-16823-8

This Springer imprint is published by the registered company Springer Nature Switzerland AG
The registered company address is: Gewerbestrasse 11, 6330 Cham, Switzerland

If disposing of this product, please recycle the paper.

Preface

We are delighted to introduce the proceedings of the 18th European Alliance for Innovation (EAI) International Conference on Mobile Multimedia Communications MOBIMEDIA 2025. Hosted by Xizang University of Lhasa, China, the conference was held from August 15 to 17, 2025. This conference brings together researchers from academia, industry, and research institutes to discuss innovations in content analysis, media access, QoE, cloud solutions, security, and more. The theme of MOBIMEDIA 2025 was "Cutting-Edge Advancements in Mobile Multimedia Processing Amid the Rapid Growth of 5G".

The technical program of MOBIMEDIA 2025 consisted of 26 full papers, including two invited papers, in oral presentation sessions at the main conference tracks. These papers were selected from 70 submissions. Each submission was reviewed following a double-blind process with a minimum of three reviews per paper. The conference hosted four insightful keynote speeches covering intelligence theory, underwater communication security, intelligent sensing, and visual restoration. Hongkai Xiong presented "Intelligence and Mathematics: Posteriori and Priori," discussing the foundational relationship between mathematical principles and intelligent systems, and how priori knowledge and posteriori data jointly drive AI development. Guangjie Han delivered "Multi-Dimensional Dynamic Trust Management Mechanism in Underwater Acoustic Sensor Networks," introducing intrusion detection, fuzzy-based trust calculation, cloud-theory trust evaluation, and machine-learning-based trust prediction to enhance the security and reliability of UASNs. Professor Yiguang Liu gave a talk on "Information Probing and Intelligent Sensing for Special Environments," analyzing visible/infrared/SAR signal characteristics, multi-wave probing mechanisms, and single-photon probing, with applications in challenging aerospace sensing scenarios. Professor Xi Peng presented "All-in-One Visual Restoration Fundamental Models," summarizing unified frameworks for image and video restoration that address multiple degradations simultaneously, and highlighting blind restoration and open-set restoration as emerging research directions. These keynote presentations collectively offered a concise overview of current frontiers in smart sensing, secure underwater communication, visual computing, and intelligent systems.

Coordination with the general chair, Nyima Tashi, and general co-chairs, Yun Lin, Xianchao Zhang, Xiaohu Tang, and Lantu Guo, was essential for the success of the conference. We sincerely appreciate their constant support and guidance. It was also a great pleasure to work with such an excellent organizing committee team for their hard work in organizing and supporting the conference. In particular, the Technical Program Committee, led by our TPC Chairs, Guan Gui, Zhicheng Dong, Congan Xu, and Xuefei Ma, completed the peer-review process of technical papers and made a high-quality technical program. We are also grateful to Conference Manager, Stella Dao for her support, and to all the authors who submitted their papers to the MOBIMEDIA 2025 conference and workshops.

We strongly believe that MOBIMEDIA provides a good forum for all researchers, developers, and practitioners to discuss all science and technology aspects that are relevant to mobile multimedia. We also expect that future MOBIMEDIA conferences will be as successful and stimulating, as indicated by the contributions presented in this volume.

Guan Gui
Zhicheng Dong
Congan Xu
Xuefei Ma

Organization

Organizing Committee

General Chair

Nyima Tashi   Tibet University, China

General Co-chairs

Yun Lin   Harbin Engineering University, China
Xianchao Zhang   Jiaxin University, China
Xiaohu Tang   Southwest Jiaotong University, China
Lantu Guo   China Research Institute of Radiowave
                                Propagation, China

TPC Chairs

Guan Gui   Nanjing University of Posts and
                                Telecommunications, China
Zhicheng Dong   Tibet University, China
Congan Xu   Naval Aeronautical University, China
Xuefei Ma   Harbin Engineering University, China

Sponsorship and Exhibit Chairs

Zhengwei Xu   Hohai University, China
Zhenyu Na   Dalian Maritime University, China
Meiyu Wang   Hangzhou Dianzi University, China

Local Chairs

Yanxia Zhou	Tibet University, China
Liang Kou	Hangzhou Dianzi University, China
Yu Han	Harbin Engineering University, China

Workshops Chairs

Ping Lan	Tibet University, China
Chao Li	Riken Center for Advanced Intelligence Project, Japan
Xingru Huang	Hangzhou Dianzi University, China

Publicity and Social Media Chairs

Dun Pu	Tibet University, China
Qi Xuan	Zhejiang University of Technology, China
Yu Wang	Nanjing University of Posts and Telecommunications, China

Publications Chairs

Zhicheng Dong	Tibet University, China
Qingling Gao	Harbin Engineering University, China
Qian Wang	Zhejiang University of Technology, China

Web Chairs

Gadeng Luosang	Tibet University, China
Qianyun Zhang	Beijing University of Aeronautics and Astronautics, China
Qinghe Zheng	Shandong Management University, China

Technical Program Committee

Zhuoran Cai	Yantai University, China
Zhuangzhi Chen	Zhejiang University of Technology, China

Lei Chen	Georgia Southern University, USA
Chenyuan Feng	EURECOM, France
Daquan Feng	Shenzhen University, China
Qingling Gao	Harbin Engineering University, China
Xingru Huang	Hangzhou Dianzi University, China
Hao Huang	Nanjing University of Posts and Telecommunications, China
Liang Kou	Hangzhou Dianzi University, China
Chao Li	RIKEN-AIP, Japan
Peihan Qi	Xidian University, China
Yu Wang	Nanjing University of Posts and Telecommunications, China
Guodong Wang	Massachusetts College of Liberal Arts, USA
Shihao Wang	Fondazione Bruno Kessler, Italy
Jinming Wen	McGill University, Canada
Jingjin Wu	BNU-HKBU United International College, China Zhiqiang Wu, Wright State University, USA
Wei Xiang	La Trobe University, Australia
Zhengwei Xu	Hohai University, China
Dongwei Xu	Zhejiang University of Technology, China
Haoran Zha	Harbin Engineering University, China
Qinghe Zheng	Shandong Management University, China
Tianyi Zhou	Institute of High Performance Computing, Singapore
Ruolin Zhou	University of Massachusetts Dartmouth, USA

Contents

Algorithms, Architecture, Applications of 5G/6G

Flexible Architecture in AI-Enabled Software-Defined Networks

Wireless Body Area Network (WBAN)

Computational Framework and Structure for Big Data

Real-Time Stream Data Mining

AI for Communication

Algorithms, Architecture, Applications of 5G/6G

Digital Cancellation of Passive Intermodulation Interference for Fast Time-Varying Channels

Wang Yulong[1,2(✉)], Tian Lu[1], Zhao Siheng[1], Xu Zhan[1], Meng Anqi[1], and Zhi Ruxin[1]

[1] Key Laboratory of Modern Measurement and Control Technology, Ministry of Education, Beijing Information Science and Technology University, Beijing, China
yulong.wang@bistu.edu.cn
[2] Beijing Information Science and Technology University, Beijing, China

Abstract. Passive intermodulation (PIM) interference has become a key problem to restrict the performance of high-sensitivity communication systems, especially under fast time-varying channels. To address this problem, this paper proposes an extended model-based PIM interference cancellation method. Zadoff-Chu(ZC) sequences are designed as training sequences in transmitters. The channel model is decomposed into a linear combination of time-varying basis functions, which can be the discrete basis expansion model (BEM).The time-invariant basis coefficients are extracted by using the least-squares estimation. The reconstructed PIM interfererence signals are eliminated in receivers to achieve efficient suppression. The experimental validation shows that under the Rayleigh fast time-varying channel with a maximum Doppler shift $650\,\mathrm{Hz}$, the proposed method can significantly improve the PIM interference suppression performance by more than $10\,\mathrm{dB}$ of signal-to-interference ratio (SIR) gain for bit error rate (BER) of 10^{-2}. The results show that this method can significantly improve the PIM interference suppression performance in fast time-varying scenarios, which provides an effective solution for the anti-PIM design of 6G air-to-space integrated networks.

Keywords: Passive intermodulation · Interference cancellation · Basis expansion model · Fast time-varying channel

1 Introduction

PIM interference is a persistent nonlinear distortion issue in high-frequency high-power communication systems, originating from signal distortion caused by nonlinear passive components in communication systems [1]. As unmanned aerial vehicle(UAV) communication systems evolve towards high dynamicity and

Supported by National Natural Science Foundation of China under Grant 62201070.

C. Xu et al. (Eds.): MobiMedia 2025, LNICST 670, pp. 3–16, 2026.
https://doi.org/10.1007/978-3-032-16823-8_1

reliability, communication equipment faces severe instantaneous power fluctuations and Doppler frequency shifts. This causes traditional PIM suppression methods, based on static or quasi-static channel assumptions, to suffer severe performance degradation due to model mismatches [2]. Particularly noteworthy is that in dynamic communication scenarios involving airborne platforms and mobile terminals, the high-speed relative motion between transceivers and scatterers induces fast time-varying channels with dual selectivity in time and space [3]. Traditional channel estimation methods based on fixed pilot intervals become ineffective in this scenario due to outdated information, leading to significant degradation in PIM interference signal reconstruction accuracy [4]. With increasingly scarce spectrum resources in modern wireless communication systems, such intermodulation interference issues have become a critical challenge requiring urgent resolution for achieving high-reliability transmission in high-power application scenarios with significant dynamic characteristics, such as UAV systems.Therefore, as shown in Fig. 1, this paper focuses on achieving high-precision PIM interference cancellation under fast time-varying channels in UAV communications.

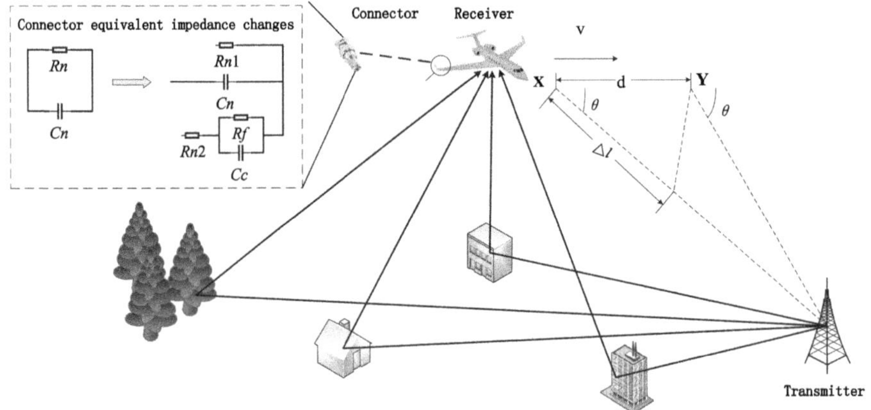

Fig. 1. PIM interference in UAV communication systems.

Research on PIM interference suppression can be divided into two major technical approaches, which are passive and active methods. Passive suppression strategies reduce nonlinear effects through physical means such as material process improvement and structural optimization, but their performance is limited by the inherent characteristics of the devices and lacks dynamic adaptability [5].In contrast, active digital cancellation technology reconstructs and cancels interference through signal processing algorithms, and has become the core direction of current research [6]. In recent years, many innovative achievements have emerged in this field. Waheed addressed the problem of harmonic distortion in the receive band caused by the nonlinear characteristics of passive components in frequency-division duplex simultaneous transmit and receive systems, and achieved interference suppression by establishing a nonlinear distortion model and generating digital cancellation signals [7]. Lampu proposed a low-complexity digital cancellation scheme based on physical modeling for airborne PIM interference caused by external objects in frequency-division duplex multiple-input multiple-output systems, and achieved efficient interference suppression in four-carrier dual-transmit dual-receive MIMO RF measurements [8]. Liu proposed a novel multi-band Wiener-Hammerstein model for the interference problem caused by PIM in multi-band frequency-division duplex systems, and verified the effectiveness of this model in multi-band PIM cancellation through simulation experiments involving four NR band carrier components and different transmit powers [9]. Luo proposed a novel wideband PIM model based on frequency division methods and modified Gaussian distribution to address the challenge of spectrum regeneration quantification for wideband PIM signals. This model enables more accurate spectrum regeneration estimation within selected channels, providing theoretical and experimental support for PIM interference characteristic analysis and suppression [10]. In addition, Stanislav proposed a multi-PIM source simulation framework based on physical modeling for airborne PIM interference caused by external metal objects in MIMO systems. Simulation results show that the performance of artificial PIM cancellation is consistent with real experiments [11]. Although the above studies have made significant progress in specific scenarios, research on PIM suppression methods for UAV communication systems under fast time-varying channels is a key problem.

Joint interference suppression methods based on channel estimation have attracted increasing attention. The core idea is to achieve parametric characterization of the PIM generation path through accurate channel modeling. Traditional channel estimation methods such as least squares (LS) and minimum mean square error [12] perform well in slow time-varying scenarios, but require frequent insertion of pilot sequences in fast time-varying channels, resulting in a significant decrease in spectral efficiency [13]. To address this, the academic community has proposed using BEM to decompose time-varying channels into a linear combination of a finite number of basis functions, thereby transforming the estimation of time-varying parameters into the solution of time-invariant coefficients [14]. Typical basis functions include complex exponential basis (CE-BEM) [15], polynomial basis (P-BEM) [16], and discrete prolate spheroidal basis (DPS-BEM) [17]. Among them, DPS-BEM has been proven to approximate the time-varying characteristics of channels in high-speed mobile scenarios with a lower order due to its comprehensive advantages in energy concentration and orthogonality [18]. Recently, the introduction of basis expansion models into PIM interference suppression methods for large-scale MIMO systems has gradually attracted scholars' attention, but the research is still limited to the assumption of time-invariant channels and has not addressed the core contradiction in fast time-varying scenarios.

To address the above challenges, this study proposes a PIM interference cancellation method based on the DPS-BEM. By decomposing the time-varying channel into a linear combination of basis functions and time-invariant coefficients, and combining with segmented training sequence design, dynamic estimation of fast time-varying channel parameters and high-precision reconstruction of PIM interference signals are achieved.

The remainder of this paper is organized as follows. Section 2 introduces the system model. Section 3 presents the proposed PIM interference reconstruction and cancellation method. Section 4 conducts simulation experiments and result analysis to evaluate the performance of the proposed solution. Finally, Section 5 concludes the paper.

2 System Model

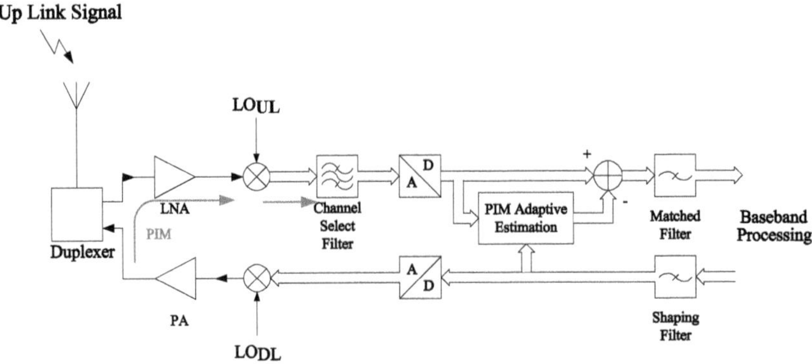

Fig. 2. Diagram of system model.

In UAV communication systems, the system model for PIM cancellation can usually be simplified as shown in Fig. 2. In this example, the PIM interference signal is generated at the antenna port of the transmitter; however, in reality, the PIM interference signal can occur in any passive component between the transmitter output and the antenna.

In the adaptive estimation section of the PIM interference signal, we consider constructing a system framework for PIM interference cancellation based on the DPS-BEM. The model achieves efficient interference suppression in fast time-varying channels through segmented signal design, linear decomposition of channel parameters, and iterative reconstruction of interference, as shown in Fig. 3.

First, We consider dividing the transmitted signal into multiple transmitted signal segments, with training sequences prepended to each segment. A transmitted signal segment and its prepended training sequence form a signal group, with

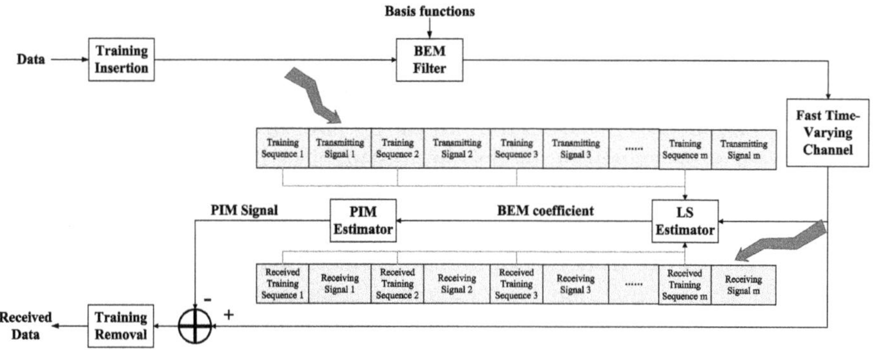

Fig. 3. System diagram of PIM interference cancellation.

each group assigned a basis function. The receiving end obtains received signals comprising multiple received sequences corresponding one-to-one with the training sequences, and multiple received signal segments corresponding one-to-one with the transmitted signal segments. The received signal can be expressed as:

$$s_{rPIM} = \boldsymbol{Ah} + s_n, \tag{1}$$

where s_n denotes noise, $\boldsymbol{s_{rPIM}} = [\boldsymbol{s_{r1}}^T, \boldsymbol{s_{r2}}^T, \ldots, \boldsymbol{s_{rm}}^T$, where s_n represent the m-th received signal segment, $\boldsymbol{h} = [\boldsymbol{h_1}^T, \boldsymbol{h_2}^T, \ldots, \boldsymbol{h_m}^T]^T$, where $\boldsymbol{h_m}$ indicate the channel impulse response during the transmission of the m-th training sequence, $\boldsymbol{A} = [\boldsymbol{A_1}^T, \boldsymbol{A_2}^T, \ldots, \boldsymbol{A_m}^T]^T$,where $\boldsymbol{A_m}$ correspond to the Toeplitz matrix formed by the m-th training sequence, with T denoting transposition.

3 PIM Interference Reconstruction and Cancellation Method

In the previous section, we discussed the fundamentals of the system model. In this section, we first select appropriate basis functions from different candidate basis functions. Then, based on the chosen basis function model, we divide the to-be-transmitted signal into multiple transmission signal segments, prepending training sequences before each transmission signal segment. Based on the DPS-BEM expansion model, we compute the time-invariant basis coefficient estimates for each transmitted signal segment. Subsequently, we calculate the received signal segment samples corresponding to each transmitted signal segment. Based on the time-invariant basis coefficient estimates of the transmitted signal segments and their corresponding received signal segment samples, we compute the PIM interference signal for each received signal segment. Finally, by subtracting the PIM interference signal of each received signal segment from the received signals, we achieve PIM interference cancellation.

3.1   Choice of Base Extension Model

Selection of Basis Expansion Models Affects Channel Estimation Accuracy.In experiments, the appropriate basis expansion model must be selected through comprehensive consideration of the specific environment and other factors.Different basis expansion models are distinguished by their employed basis functions. Several common types include.

Complex Exponential Basis Expansion Model (CE-BEM) The Complex Exponential Basis Expansion Model employs complex exponentials as its basis functions, with its theoretical foundation rooted in Fourier series. The expression for lthe basis functions is as follows:

$$B_m\left(n\right) = e^{\frac{-j2\pi n\left(m-M/2\right)}{N}},\tag{2}$$

where $n \in [0, N-1]$, $M \in [0, M-1]$, M represents the number of basis functions. In time-varying channel modeling, the Complex Exponential Basis Expansion Model constructs a linear parameter system for time-domain channels through $1/N$ quantized sampling of the Doppler frequency domain.This model does not rely on channel statistical characteristics and demonstrates notable universality in engineering practice, making it one of the most widely used models in time-varying channel modeling.The finite-dimensional basis function space construction method adopted by the CE-BEM essentially constitutes a time-domain truncation operation on the original time-varying channel sequence.This operation inevitably induces two issues: first, spectral leakage effects caused by frequency-domain energy diffusion; second, time-domain oscillations triggered by Gibbs oscillation phenomena.These two nonlinear distortion effects exhibit spatial accumulation characteristics during channel estimation, ultimately leading to significant estimation deviations at truncation boundaries of time-domain channel impulse responses.

Polynomial Basis Expansion Model (P-BEM) The Polynomial Basis Expansion Model employs polynomials as basis functions, utilizing linear combinations of polynomials to fit time-varying channels.Its theoretical foundation lies in Taylor series, with the basis function expression being:

$$B_m\left(n\right) = \left(n - \frac{N}{2}\right)^m.\tag{3}$$

The Polynomial Basis Expansion Model is a relatively fundamental basis expansion model that can directly reflect signal variation rates through polynomial coefficients.Low-order polynomial parameter estimations exhibit low computational complexity, making them suitable for real-time channel estimation tasks.For example, in urban cellular scenarios where user terminals have low movement speeds and channel time-varying characteristics are gradual, a 3rd-order polynomial can effectively fit channel variations. However, the Polynomial Basis Expansion Model shows high sensitivity to Doppler frequency shifts, and high-order polynomial models are prone to overfitting.

Discrete Karhunen-Loève Basis Expansion Model (DKL-BEM)) The Discrete Karhunen-Loève Basis Expansion Model is a statistical characteristic-based orthogonal expansion method for optimal dimensionality reduction representation of discrete random signals or data. Its core concept involves constructing adaptive orthogonal basis functions through eigen decomposition of the data covariance matrix, thereby capturing signal energy predominantly in the most compact manner.Let R_l be the normalized time-domain autocorrelation matrix of the L-th path channel:

$$R_l = E\left\{h_l h_l^H\right\}, \tag{4}$$

Perform singular value decomposition on R_l:

$$R_l = U_l \Lambda_l V_l^H = U_l \begin{bmatrix} \lambda_{0,l} & & & \\ & \lambda_{1,l} & & \\ & & \ddots & \\ & & & \lambda_{N-1,l} \end{bmatrix} V_l^H, \tag{5}$$

where V_l is the diagonal matrix composed of eigenvalues of matrix R_l arranged in descending order.Taking the first M columns of the U_l matrix as M basis functions,then the basis function matrix can be expressed as:

$$B = U_l(:, 1:M). \tag{6}$$

The Discrete Karhunen-Loève Basis Expansion Model requires prior knowledge of channel statistical characteristics during modeling.In simulations, the Jakes model is typically employed to characterize channel autocorrelation characteristics, i.e.:

$$R_l = E\left\{h_l(n) h_l^H(m)\right\} = \sigma_l^2 J_0\left[2\pi(n-m) f_{\max} T_s\right], \tag{7}$$

where σ_l^2 denotes the power of the L-th path, and $J_0(\bullet)$ represents the zero-order Bessel function.

The Discrete Karhunen-Loève Basis Expansion Model captures maximum signal energy with minimal basis functions, achieves minimal reconstruction error, exhibits low autocorrelation for analytical simplification, and its basis functions determined by data statistics outperform fixed bases.Its drawbacks include high computational complexity and significant dependency of basis function quality on sample covariance matrix accuracy.

Discrete Prolate Spheroidal Basis Expansion Model (DPS-BEM) The DPS-BEM Expansion Model is a signal representation based on discrete prolate spheroidal sequences, designed for optimal energy concentration representation of finite-duration band-limited signals.Its time-domain autocorrelation matrix is given by:

$$R_l = E\left\{h_l(n) h_l^H(m)\right\} = \sigma_l^2 \frac{\sin\left[2\pi(n-m) f_{\max} T_s\right]}{\pi(n-m)}. \tag{8}$$

The DPS-BEM Expansion Model is a signal representation based on discrete prolate spheroidal sequences, designed to optimally concentrate energy for finite-duration band-limited signals. This model requires no data-driven training and significantly reduces variance and bias in conventional periodogram methods through multitaper spectral analysis, offering simpler implementation.

To select appropriate basis expansion models for channel estimation, this section first compares the estimation accuracy of different models. Experimental results are evaluated using mean squared error (MSE) metrics, with the MSE expression defined as:

$$MSE = \frac{1}{N} \sum_{n=0}^{N-1} E \left\{ |h_l(n) - \sum_{m=0}^{M-1} b_{lm} B_m(n)|^2 \right\}, \tag{9}$$

where $h_l(n)$ represents the actual channel time-domain impulse response, $B_m(n)$ and b_{lm} denote basis functions and expansion coefficients respectively. The simulation adopts a symbol rate of 300K, sampling frequency of 2.4MHz, carrier frequency of 2GHz, and employs Rayleigh fading channels for fast time-varying scenarios.The simulation compares the impact of Doppler frequency shifts across different basis expansion models. Results are shown in the following figure, with terminal velocity as the x-axis and MSE of estimation results as the y-axis. The figure demonstrates that CE-BEM and P-BEM exhibit significantly lower estimation accuracy than DPS-BEM and DKL-BEM. DPS-BEM outperforms DKL-BEM in precision. Considering that DKL-BEM requires assuming channel statistical characteristics during channel estimation, DPS-BEM is selected for subsequent experiments based on practical considerations (Fig. 4).

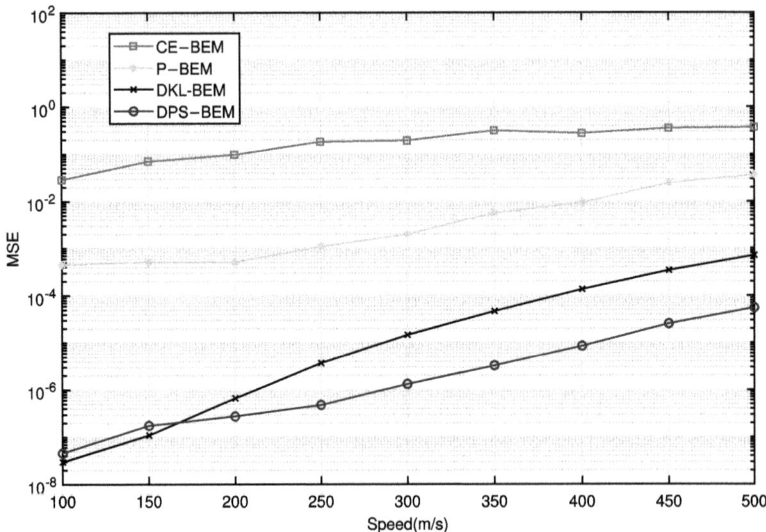

Fig. 4. Channel estimation performance on different basis expansion models.

The number of basis functions also impacts channel estimation performance, but this influence is nonlinear. Simply increasing or decreasing the number of basis functions does not linearly improve channel estimation accuracy, as there exists a well-defined optimal range for this parameter. Insufficient basis functions lead to inaccurate estimation results, while excessive numbers not only significantly increase computational complexity, but also tend to induce overfitting, causing oscillation in estimation results that degrades system robustness and estimation precision. The simulation results shown in the following figure demonstrate the impact of different basis function quantities on channel estimation performance. Minimal performance degradation is observed when using 4 or 5 basis functions. Therefore, we select 4 basis functions for subsequent experiments (Fig. 5).

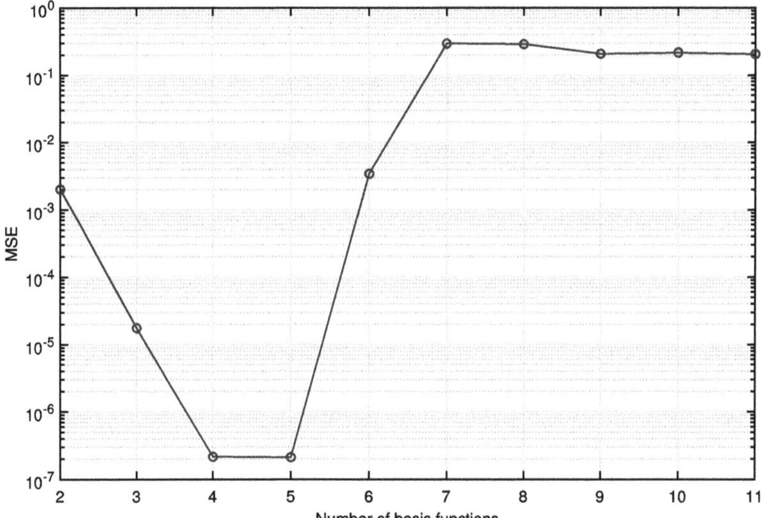

Fig. 5. Channel estimation performance on different numbers of basis functions.

3.2   Base Coefficient Estimation and PIM Reconstruction

First, using the basis function of the signal group containing each transmitted signal segment, we sample positions corresponding to the received sequence of the training sequence within that signal group, obtaining multiple received sequence sampling values, such as:

$$\boldsymbol{B_m} = [B_m(1), ..., B_m(N)]. \tag{10}$$

Subsequently, each training sequence is multiplied with its corresponding received sequence sampling values to obtain the coefficients of each basis function. The received signal $s_{r\,PIM}$ can then be expressed as follows:

$$s_{rPIM} = diag\left\{\boldsymbol{AbB} + s_n\right\}$$

$$= diag\left\{\boldsymbol{A}\begin{pmatrix} b_{k,1} & \cdots & b_{k,m} \\ \vdots & \ddots & \vdots \\ b_{-k+1,1} & \cdots & b_{-k+1,m} \end{pmatrix}\begin{pmatrix} B_1 \\ \vdots \\ B_m \end{pmatrix} + s_n\right\}$$

$$= \begin{pmatrix} A_{1,:}B_1\left(1\right) & \cdots & A_{1,:}B_1\left(1\right) \\ \vdots & \ddots & \vdots \\ A_{n,:}B_1\left(N\right) & \cdots & A_{n,:}B_1\left(N\right) \end{pmatrix}\begin{pmatrix} b_1 \\ \vdots \\ b_m \end{pmatrix} + s_n$$

$$= \overline{\boldsymbol{A}}\boldsymbol{b}' + s_n \tag{11}$$

where $\boldsymbol{A_n}$ denotes the n-th row sequence of A, $\boldsymbol{B_m} = [B_m(1),\ldots,B_m(N)]$ represents the sampling value of the m-th basis function in the training sequence, and $\boldsymbol{b_m} = [b_{k,m},\ldots,b_{-k+1,m}]$ indicates the coefficient of the m-th basis function, $\boldsymbol{b}' = [b_1^T,\ldots,b_m^T]^T$.

Subsequently, each received sequence is subjected to least squares estimation with the coefficients of the basis function in the corresponding training sequence's signal group, yielding time-invariant basis coefficient estimates $\hat{b}'$ for the transmitted signal segments. In this process, the cost function is defined as:

$$J(\hat{\boldsymbol{b}}') = \left\|s_{rPIM} - \overline{\boldsymbol{A}}\boldsymbol{b}'\right\|^2$$

$$= \left(s_{rPIM} - \overline{\boldsymbol{A}}\boldsymbol{b}'\right)^H \left(s_{rPIM} - \overline{\boldsymbol{A}}\boldsymbol{b}'\right) \tag{12}$$

$$= s_{rPIM}{}^H s_{rPIM} - s_{rPIM}{}^H \overline{\boldsymbol{A}}\hat{\boldsymbol{b}}' - \hat{\boldsymbol{b}}'{}^H \overline{\boldsymbol{A}}{}^H \overline{\boldsymbol{A}}\hat{\boldsymbol{b}}'$$

among them, $\hat{\boldsymbol{b}}'$ represents the time-invariant basis coefficient estimates of the transmitted signal segment, $J(\hat{\boldsymbol{b}}')$ denotes the cost function, S_{rPIM} stands for the received signal, $\boldsymbol{A} = [\boldsymbol{A_1}^T, \boldsymbol{A_2}^T,\ldots,\boldsymbol{A_m}^T]^T$, where $\boldsymbol{A_m}$ indicate the Toeplitz matrix formed by the m-th training sequence. The employed training sequence is a ZC sequence, $\bar{A}$ represents the augmented matrix of matrix A, T denotes transpose, and H signifies conjugate.

By setting the partial derivative of the above cost function with respect to $\hat{\boldsymbol{b}}'$ to zero, we obtain:

$$\frac{\partial \boldsymbol{J}(\hat{\boldsymbol{b}})}{\partial \hat{\boldsymbol{b}}} = -2\left(\overline{A}{}^H s_{rPIM}\right)^* + 2\left(\overline{A}{}^H \overline{A}\hat{b}\right)^* = 0. \tag{13}$$

From Equation (5), we can get $\overline{A}{}^H s_{rPIM} = \overline{A}{}^H \overline{A}\hat{b}$, then the least squares estimate solution of the basis coefficient $\hat{b}'$ is:

$$\widehat{\boldsymbol{b}}' = \left(\overline{A}{}^H \overline{A}\right)^{-1} \overline{A}{}^H s_{rPIM}. \tag{14}$$

3.3   PIM Interference Cancellation

From the calculations in the previous section, we obtained time-invariant basis coefficient estimates for the transmitted signal segments. In this section, we perform PIM interference signal reconstruction and cancellation. Since the basis function coefficients within each data segment of the model remain constant, we multiply the time-invariant basis coefficient estimates of each transmitted signal segment with the sampled values of its corresponding received signal segment to derive fitted channel parameters at the location of that received signal segment. Subsequently, we estimate the order of PIM products within the receiving frequency band, construct required matrices, and multiply the transmitted signal segment with the fitted channel parameters at its corresponding received signal segment location to obtain the estimated PIM interference signal for that received signal segment. This can be expressed using the following formula:

$$y = \overline{A}\widehat{b}'.\tag{15}$$

After completing PIM interference signal reconstruction, PIM interference cancellation is achieved by subtracting the reconstructed interference signal of each received signal segment from the received signal.

4   Measurements and Results

To evaluate the effectiveness of the proposed basis expansion model-based PIM interference cancellation, this section conducts simulation tests on the proposed algorithm using the MATLAB simulation platform. The reconstruction of PIM interference signals employs dual-carrier signals in simulations. For computational simplification, the PIM signal model adopts a power series model, which calculates that the PIM products falling into the receiving frequency band are 7th-order, 9th-order, and 11th-order products. The basis expansion model employs DPS-BEM.All parameters used in the experiment are shown in Table 1.

Table 1. Experimental simulation parameters

Parameter	Value
Modulation mode	BPSK
Carrier frequency	1.95GHz
Maximum Doppler shift	650Hz
Basis expansion model	DPS-BEM
Number of basis functions	4
Training sequence	ZC sequence

Figure 6 shows the system's uncoded BER versus signal-to-noise ratio (SNR) curve after applying the proposed PIM cancellation algorithm, with a SIR of

−10 dB. The figure demonstrates that after subtracting the PIM signals reconstructed using the basis expansion model, the system's BER shows significant reduction. Considering the SNR gain at a BER of 10^{-2}, the gain exceeds 4 dB, proving the method's effectiveness in mitigating PIM impacts on communication systems. Figure 7 presents the system BER versus SIR curves with and without the proposed PIM cancellation algorithm at an SNR of 0 dB. When evaluating the SIR gain at a BER of 10^{-2}, the SIR improvement exceeds 10 dB.

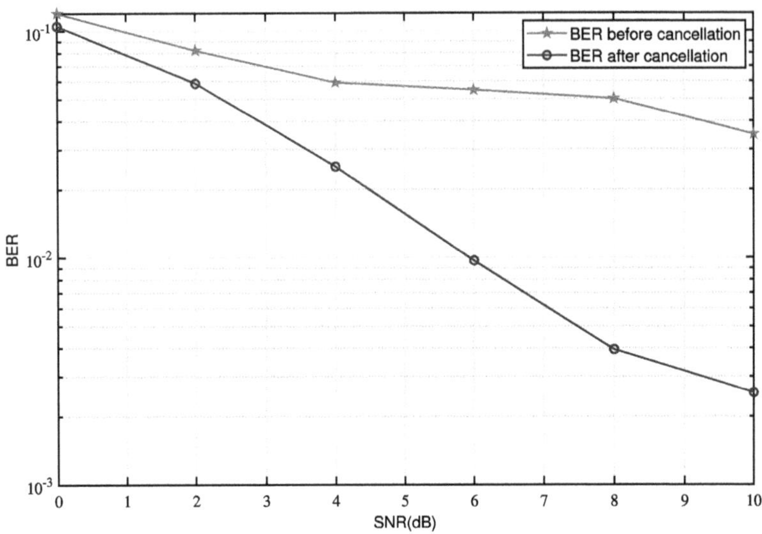

Fig. 6. BER performance of PIM cancellation algorithm under SIR = −10 dB.

This section verifies the performance of the DPS-BEM-based PIM interference cancellation algorithm through simulations. The experiment employs dual-carrier signals and a power series PIM model, targeting 7th/9th/11th-order PIM products within the receiving band for reconstruction. Key system parameters include BPSK modulation, Rayleigh fading channel, 1.95 GHz carrier frequency, 650 Hz maximum Doppler shift (see Table 1 for details). Simulation results demonstrate: Under −10 dB SIR conditions, the proposed algorithm significantly reduces the system's BER, achieving over 4 dB SNR gain at a BER of 10^{-2}; Furthermore, at 0 dB SNR, the corresponding SIR gain reaches above 10 dB for the same BER level. Both experimental results jointly prove that this basis expansion model approach effectively suppresses PIM interference in fast time-varying channels, markedly enhancing communication system reliability.

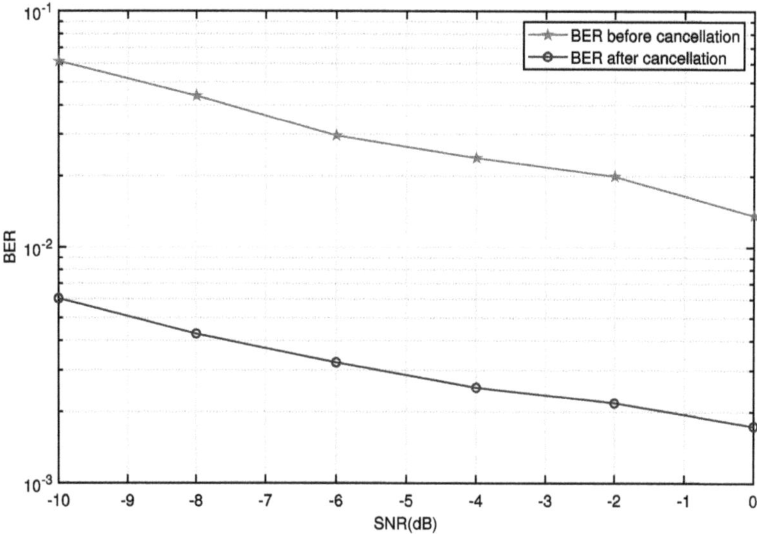

Fig. 7. BER performance of PIM cancellation algorithm under SIR = 0 dB.

5 Conclusion

PIM interference suppression in fast time-varying channels constitutes a critical challenge for high-frequency evolution of integrated space-air-ground networks. This paper proposes a PIM interference cancellation method based on the DPS-BEM. Through segmented signal design, time-invariant basis coefficient estimation, and iterative interference reconstruction, it effectively addresses performance limitations caused by channel estimation failures in traditional approaches under fast time-varying channels. Specifically, ZC training sequences are inserted into transmitted signals in segments. Combined with DPS-BEM decomposition of fast time-varying channels into linear combinations of time-varying basis functions and time-invariant coefficients, least squares estimation extracts time-invariant coefficients to achieve high-precision PIM interference signal reconstruction and cancellation. Simulation results under Rayleigh fast time-varying channels (maximum Doppler 650 Hz) demonstrate: When SIR is -10 dB, the proposed method achieves SNR gain exceeding 4 dB at a BER of 10^{-2}; At 0 dB SNR, SIR gain reaches over 10 dB for the same BER level. Experiments further validate the method's suppression capability against 7th/9th/11th-order PIM products in the receiving band, significantly enhancing communication system reliability. By employing a low-complexity time-invariant coefficient estimation framework, this approach overcomes traditional adaptive filtering's insufficient convergence speed and neural networks' high computational complexity, providing theoretical support and technical pathways for high-dynamic anti-interference design in integrated space-air-ground networks. It holds significant application value for 6G high-frequency communications and low Earth orbit satellite dense networking scenarios. Future research will optimize basis function selection strategies and explore scalability enhancements in multi-carrier scenarios.

References

1. Wilkerson, J.R., et al.: Passive intermodulation distortion in antennas. IEEE Trans. Antennas Propagation **63**(2), 474–482 (2014)
2. Haider, M.F., et al.: Predistortion-based linearization for 5G and beyond millimeter-wave transceiver systems: a comprehensive survey. IEEE Commun. Surveys Tutor. **24**(4), 2029–2072 (2022)
3. Chowdhury, M.Z., et al.: Optical wireless hybrid networks: trends, opportunities, challenges, and research directions. IEEE Commun. Surveys Tutor. **22**(2), 930–966 (2020)
4. Yang, L., et al.: On the performance of RIS-assisted dual-hop UAV communication systems. IEEE Trans. Veh. Technol. **69**(9), 10385–10390 (2020)
5. Zhang, K., Li, T., Jiang, J.: Passive intermodulation of contact nonlinearity on microwave connectors. IEEE Trans. Electromagn. Compat. **60**(2), 513–519 (2017)
6. Waheed, M.Z., et al.: Passive intermodulation in simultaneous transmit-receive systems: modeling and digital cancellation methods. IEEE Trans. Microwave Theory Tech. **68**(9), 3633–3652 (2020)
7. Waheed M.Z., et al.: Modeling and digital suppression of passive nonlinear distortion in simultaneous transmit–Receive systems. In: 56th Asilomar Conference on Signals, Systems, and Computers. IEEE (2022)
8. Lampu, V., et al.: Air-induced passive intermodulation in FDD MIMO systems: algorithms and measurements. IEEE Trans. Microwave Theory Tech. **71**(1), 373–388 (2022)
9. Liu, J., et al.: Digital cancellation of multi-band passive inter-modulation based on Wiener-Hammerstein model. Dig. Commun. Netw. **10**(4), 1189–1197 (2024)
10. Luo, J., et al.: Modeling of spectral regrowth effects of passive intermodulation with broadband signal excitation. IEEE Microw. Wireless Technol, Lett (2024)
11. Krikunov, S., Zemlyakov, V., Ivanov, A.: Physical modelling and cancellation of external passive intermodulation in FDD MIMO. In: IEEE International Multi-conference on Engineering, Computer and Information Sciences (SIBIRCON). IEEE (2024)
12. Haykin, S.S.: Adaptive filter theory. Pearson Educ, India (2002)
13. Yang, Y., et al.: Deep learning-based channel estimation for doubly selective fading channels. IEEE Access **7**, 36579–36589 (2019)
14. Sayed, A.H.: Adaptive Filters. John Wiley and Sons (2011)
15. Veeresh, A.C., et al.: Multiuser/MIMO doubly selective fading channel estimation using TM training and CE-BEM. TENCON 2019–2019 IEEE Region 10 Conference (TENCON). IEEE (2019)
16. Lu, T.I.A.N., et al.: Adaptive suppression of passive intermodulation in digital satellite transceivers. Chin. J. Aeronaut. **30**(3), 1154–1160 (2017)
17. Yang S., et al.: BEM based fast time-varying channel estimation method for 5G integrated satellite systems. In: IEEE 22nd International Conference on Communication Technology (ICCT). IEEE (2022)
18. Zhou Z., et al.: Two-stage joint BEM-OTFS channel estimation algorithm based sparse bayesian learning algorithm. In: IEEE 15th International Conference on Advanced Infocomm Technology (ICAIT). IEEE (2023)

Localized Statistical Channel Modeling by Exploiting Joint and Block Sparsity

Linzhi Zhang[1] and Ye Xue[2][✉]

[1] Xi'an Jiaotong-Liverpool University, Suzhou, China
`linzhizhang777@gmail.com`
[2] Shenzhen Research Institute of Big Data (SRIBD), Shenzhen, China
`xueye@cuhk.edu.cn`

Abstract. Precise characterization of localized channel behaviors plays a vital role in the optimization of 5G cellular networks. However, many existing approaches either overlook fine-grained geographic variations or impose excessive computational burdens. To overcome these issues, this work introduces a localized statistical channel model (LSCM) that adapts to the propagation characteristics of a specific region. In contrast to CIR-based approaches, the LSCM framework reconstructs the channel using only reference signal received power (RSRP) measurements, expressed in a linear form with respect to the angular power spectrum (APS). This allows this channel representation to be considered as a sparse recovery problem, so nonzero APS components correspond to the power levels and departure directions of significant propagation paths. Furthermore, we introduce a joint block non-negative orthogonal matching pursuit (JBNOMP) algorithm that leverages block-structured sparsity and shared propagation characteristics across neighboring grids. Finally, simulation studies are carried out to demonstrate the performance advantages of the proposed approach.

Keywords: Localized statistical channel modeling · Angular power spectrum · Block sparsity · Joint sparsity

1 Introduction

The expansion of 5G networks has made cellular system optimization a key factor in maintaining user quality of experience (QoE). However, because optimization is typically carried out offline, precise characterization of the wireless propagation environment is required [1,2]. Because network optimization is generally carried out offline, one key challenge is to obtain an accurate description of the wireless propagation characteristics within the BSUE coverage area. Consequently, an accurate representation of location-dependent propagation behavior is crucial for achieving effective network optimization.

C. Xu et al. (Eds.): MobiMedia 2025, LNICST 670, pp. 17–25, 2026.
https://doi.org/10.1007/978-3-032-16823-8_2

Yet most channel models widely employed in 5G system are generally developed for generic propagation scenarios rather than for network optimization purposes. They either cater to general scenarios, failing to accurately characterize the spatially varying structural features of the underlying propagation environment, or involve high computational complexity, making them impractical for efficient optimization. For instance, geometry-based stochastic models (GBSMs) have been extensively investigated [3–5]. These models are typically designed for standard propagation scenarios–such as indoor versus outdoor, or rural versus urban–and therefore cannot accurately represent the characteristics of a specific localized environment. On the other hand, deterministic modeling approaches, such as ray tracing [6], are capable of capturing fine-grained spatial channel features. However, their dependence on Maxwell's equations leads to substantial computational overhead, rendering them impractical for large-scale cellular network optimization. In addition, ray tracing requires detailed and accurate environmental maps, which are not always available in real-world deployments, further restricting its applicability [7].

To address these limitations, we propose a localized statistical channel modeling (LSCM) framework that adapts to the physical propagation conditions of the target area. Unlike conventional GBSMs that are based on the channel impulse response (CIR), the proposed LSCM utilizes only the reference signal received power (RSRP) measurements [8]. Such processing enables the efficient recovery of the angular power spectrum (APS), providing insight into the dominant multipath structure and the geographically dependent propagation characteristics. However, extracting APS information solely from RSRP data has not been previously explored and presents a nontrivial challenge.

In this work, a statistical linkage between the RSRP measurements and the APS is derived, enabling the latter to be inferred from the former. Under this formulation, recovering the APS reduces to a structured sparse reconstruction task, where the nonzero elements represent the power contributions and angular directions of the dominant propagation paths.

In standard compressed sensing frameworks, orthogonal matching pursuit (OMP) is widely adopted as a baseline method for sparse signal reconstruction [9], but its convergence properties are guaranteed only under favorable matrix conditions. Building on previous research, we make full use of the non-negativity of signal elements. Moreover, due to spatial consistency, the channel paths are similar to those of its adjacent grids, allowing us to reformulate the problem as a multiple measurement vectors (MMV) model instead of the traditional single measurement vector (SMV) approach. Additionally, we take advantage of the block sparsity of signals, which results from the physical scattering structure in the wireless environment[10]. Simulation results show that leveraging these properties leads to better performance and lower computational complexity.

2   MIMO Downlink Transmission and RSRP-Based Channel Observation

This section develops the channel model for a massive MIMO downlink system defined over the target grid and then presents the analytical form of the associated RSRP observations.

2.1   Discretized Channel Modeling in the Angle Domain

In the context of massive MIMO for 5G communications, beamforming serves as the fundamental mechanism that controls spatial signal distribution, as it allows the channel to be represented with high angular resolution in the angle domain. Therefore, we begin by examining the downlink channel model under a beamforming architecture, where the transmitted signal propagates on the BSUE downlink link through multiple multipath components.

Following the 3GPP modeling guideline [11], each propagation path is characterized by its vertical and horizontal departure angles, together with the corresponding complex gain. We consider a single-antenna UE and therefore only the angles of departure are involved, while the angles of arrival and delay profiles are not included in the model. Let the base station employ a uniform rectangular array with $N_T = N_x \times N_y$ transmit antennas. The channel impulse response (CIR) associated with antenna (x, y) is then expressed as

$$h_{x,y}(t) = \sum_{i=1}^{N_V} \sum_{j=1}^{N_H} \sqrt{\alpha_{i,j}(t)}\, g_{i,j}\, e^{-j2\pi \frac{d_x x}{\lambda} \cos\theta_i \sin\varphi_j} e^{-j2\pi \frac{d_y y}{\lambda} \sin\theta_i}$$

$$\times\, e^{-j\omega_{i,j}(t) - j\omega_{x,y}(t)}. \tag{1}$$

In the elevation and azimuth dimensions, the angle of departure is sampled into N_V and N_H discrete angular grids, respectively. For an angular pair (θ_i, φ_j) containing no valid propagation path, If no propagation component is present at angle (θ_i, φ_j), the corresponding gain term $\alpha_{i,j}(t)$ is zero. When a valid path exists at that angle, $\alpha_{i,j}(t)$ takes a positive value. Due to the limited number of dominant scattering clusters, $\alpha_{i,j}(t)$ is sparse over the angle domain.

The channel gain $\alpha_{i,j}(t)$ accounts for large-scale and small-scale propagation effects. The large-scale component reflects path loss, which depends on propagation distance, carrier frequency, and surrounding structures, and is assumed to vary slowly. The small-scale component models shadowing, typically represented as a log-normal random variable. As a result, $\alpha_{i,j}(t)$ is modeled as a log-normal random variable. The mean of $\alpha_{i,j}(t)$ reflects the large-scale path loss, while its covariance captures the spatial correlation induced by shadowing.

The term $\omega_{i,j}(t)$ accounts for the phase variations introduced by reflection, diffraction, and scattering along different angular directions. In contrast, $\omega_{x,y}(t)$ reflects phase offsets among antenna elements, which arise from hardware-related imperfections. Following [11], we assume that $\omega_{i,j}(t)$ is uniformly distributed over $[-\pi, \pi]$, whereas $\omega_{x,y}(t)$ follows a zero-mean Gaussian distribution with variance σ^2.

2.2 RSRP-Based Measurement Model

Within the LSCM framework, the channel is probed via the received power of multiple beamformed signals. In a 5G downlink setting, these measurements are typically extracted from SSB-based beams or CSI-RS sounding beams transmitted by the base station. We denote the precoder of the m-th beam by $\mathbf{W}^{(m)} \in \mathbb{R}^{N_x \times N_y}$, where each element is given as $w_{x,y}^{(m)} = e^{j\phi_{x,y}^{(m)}}$. Let $\mathbf{H} \in \mathbb{C}^{N_x \times N_y}$ denote the CIR matrix corresponding to the BSUE downlink link, where each element is given by $h_{x,y}(t)$ in (1). The precoding matrix of the m-th beam is denoted by $\mathbf{W}^{(m)}$, with entries $w_{x,y}^{(m)} = e^{j\phi_{x,y}^{(m)}}$. The RSRP for beam m at time t is formulated as

$$\mathrm{rsrp}_m(t) = P \left| \mathrm{tr}\left(\mathbf{H}^T \mathbf{W}^{(m)} \right) \right|^2 = P \left| \sum_{x,y} h_{x,y}(t) w_{x,y}^{(m)} \right|^2. \tag{2}$$

Here, P denotes the transmit power. A larger value of $\mathrm{rsrp}_m(t)$ corresponds to a stronger received signal, and thus reflects a better channel condition.

Because $h_{x,y}(t)$ involves the random terms $\omega_{x,y}(t)$, $\omega_{i,j}(t)$, and $\alpha_{i,j}(t)$, the value of $\mathrm{rsrp}_m(t)$ also becomes a random quantity. Theorem 1 provides an analytical relation linking the mean RSRP values to the angular-domain channel power coefficients $\alpha_{i,j}(t)$, which enables inferring angular propagation characteristics from RSRP measurements.

Theorem 1 (Statistical Correspondence Between RSRP and APS). Let $\mathrm{RSRP}_m \triangleq \mathbb{E}\left[\mathrm{rsrp}_m(t)\right]$ and $X_{i,j} \triangleq \mathbb{E}\left[\alpha_{i,j}(t)\right]$. Then,

$$\mathrm{RSRP}_m = \sum_{i=1}^{N_V} \sum_{j=1}^{N_H} A_{i,j}^{(m)} X_{i,j}, \tag{3}$$

where

$$A_{i,j}^{(m)} = P g_{i,j}^2 \left(N_x N_y (1 - e^{-\sigma^2}) \right.$$

$$\left. + e^{-\sigma^2} \sum_{x,y} \sum_{x',y'} \cos\left(\psi_{i,j,x,y}^{(m)} - \psi_{i,j,x',y'}^{(m)} \right) \right), \tag{4}$$

$$\psi_{i,j,x,y}^{(m)} = 2\pi \frac{d_x x}{\lambda} \cos\theta_i \sin\varphi_j + 2\pi \frac{d_y y}{\lambda} \sin\theta_i - \phi_{x,y}^{(m)}. \tag{5}$$

Proof. The detailed derivation can be found in the Appendix of [12].

3 LSCM and JBNOMP

In this section, we reformulate the expectation of the RSRP measurements and the channel gain into a vectorized representation, which serves as the foundation of the proposed LSCM framework. Leveraging this model, we design a joint block non-negative orthogonal matching pursuit (JBNOMP) algorithm to estimate the angular power spectrum (APS) directly from RSRP observations.

3.1 Vectorized Mapping Between RSRP and Angular Power Statistics

Theorem 1 establishes that the expectation of the RSRP measurements, RSRP_m, is linearly related to the expected channel gain, $X_{i,j}$, through the coefficient $A_{i,j}^{(m)}$. This implies that if $X_{i,j}$ can be recovered from RSRP_m, then the angular power spectrum (APS) of the channel can be obtained. The quantities $X_{i,j}$ represent the average channel gain associated with the tilt angle θ_i and azimuth angle φ_j, respectively.

For convenience in vectorized representation, the set of angular gains $X_{i,j}$ for $i = 1, \ldots, N_V$ and $j = 1, \ldots, N_H$ is arranged into a vector.

$$\boldsymbol{x} = [X_{1,1}, X_{1,2}, \ldots, X_{1,N_H}, X_{2,1}, \ldots, X_{N_V,N_H}]^\top, \tag{6}$$

where $\boldsymbol{x}$ has length $N = N_V N_H$. Since only a limited number of propagation paths exist in practice, many angular components are absent and $X_{i,j} = 0$ at those angles; hence, $\boldsymbol{x}$ is sparse.

Assume that M beams are used for measurement, and define the vector of their RSRP expectations as

$$\boldsymbol{y} = [\mathrm{RSRP}_1, \mathrm{RSRP}_2, \ldots, \mathrm{RSRP}_M]^\top. \tag{7}$$

Similarly, for each beam m, we arrange the coefficients $A_{i,j}^{(m)}$ into a vector

$$\boldsymbol{a}^{(m)} = \left[A_{1,1}^{(m)}, A_{1,2}^{(m)}, \ldots, A_{1,N_H}^{(m)}, A_{2,1}^{(m)}, \ldots, A_{N_V,N_H}^{(m)} \right]^\top. \tag{8}$$

The coefficient matrix $\mathbf{A} \in \mathbb{R}^{M \times N}$ is obtained by arranging all these vectors $\mathbf{a}^{(1)}, \mathbf{a}^{(2)}, \ldots, \mathbf{a}^{(M)}$ as its rows:

$$\mathbf{A} = \left[\mathbf{a}^{(1)}, \mathbf{a}^{(2)}, \ldots, \mathbf{a}^{(M)} \right]^\top. \tag{9}$$

With these definitions, the relationship in Theorem 1 can be written compactly as

$$\boldsymbol{y} = \boldsymbol{A}\boldsymbol{x}. \tag{10}$$

3.2 The Designed JBNOMP Algorithm

Due to the slow spatial variation of dominant multipath components across adjacent grids, the corresponding APS vectors exhibit joint sparsity across adjacent spatial locations, we consider a joint modeling problem involving L adjacent grids. The observation model for the l-th grid is given by:

$$\boldsymbol{y}_l = \boldsymbol{A}\boldsymbol{x}_l, \quad l = 1, 2, \ldots, L, \tag{11}$$

JBNOMP effectively exploits both block sparsity and joint sparsity, enhancing computational efficiency while maintaining high accuracy.

We begin by merging x_l and y_l into matrices $\mathbf{X} \in \mathbb{R}^{N \times L}$ and $\mathbf{Y} \in \mathbb{R}^{M \times L}$. Since N is pre-partitioned into N/d blocks, the algorithm leverages structural sparsity to avoid computationally expensive element-wise selection. Instead, it first identifies the most correlated block, enabling a fast yet effective initial selection:

$$\omega^k = \arg \max_{1 \leq l \leq N/d} \|\mathbf{A}_{[l]}^T \mathbf{r}^{k-1}\|_F \tag{12}$$

To further refine selection precision, an additional parameter b is introduced to filter out irrelevant columns within the selected block, ensuring robustness against noise and redundancy. Specifically, a finer selection is performed within the initially chosen block:

$$i^k = \arg \max_{i \in S} \|\mathbf{A}_s^T \mathbf{r}^{k-1}\|_F, \tag{13}$$

$$\text{where } S = \{d(\omega^k - 1), d(\omega^k - 1) + 1, \ldots, d(\omega^k - 1) + b\} \tag{14}$$

Algorithm 1 Joint Block Non-negative OMP (JBNOMP)

Require: Measurement matrix $\mathbf{Y} \in \mathbb{R}^{m \times l}$, sensing matrix $\mathbf{A} \in \mathbb{R}^{m \times n}$,
1: maximum iterations K, residual threshold ϵ, window size d, block size b
Ensure: Recovered signal $\mathbf{X}^*$
2: Initialize: $k \leftarrow 0$, $\mathbf{r}^0 \leftarrow \mathbf{Y}$, $T^0 \leftarrow \emptyset$
3: **while** $\|\mathbf{r}^k\|_F \geq \epsilon$ **and** $k < K$ **do**
4:     $k \leftarrow k + 1$
5:     $\omega^k \leftarrow \arg \max_{1 \leq l \leq n/d} \|\mathbf{A}_l^\top \mathbf{r}^{k-1}\|_F$
6:     $S \leftarrow \{d(\omega^k - 1), \ldots, d(\omega^k - 1) + b\}$
7:     $i^k \leftarrow \arg \max_{i \in S} \|\mathbf{A}_i^\top \mathbf{r}^{k-1}\|_F$
8:     $h^k \leftarrow \{i^k, i^k + 1, \ldots, i^k + b\}$
9:     $T^k \leftarrow T^{k-1} \cup h^k$
10:     $\mathbf{x}^k \leftarrow \arg \min_{\mathbf{z} \geq 0} \|\mathbf{Y} - \mathbf{A}_{T^k} \mathbf{z}\|_F$
11:     $\mathbf{r}^k \leftarrow \mathbf{Y} - \mathbf{A}_{T^k} \mathbf{x}^k$
12: **end while**
13: **return** $\mathbf{X}^* \leftarrow \arg \min_{\mathbf{z} \geq 0} \|\mathbf{Y} - \mathbf{A}_{T^k} \mathbf{z}\|_F$

This two-stage selection strategy not only reduces computational complexity but also improves reconstruction accuracy, making the algorithm particularly effective for high-dimensional sparse recovery problems. By balancing efficiency and precision, it outperforms conventional approaches that rely on exhaustive search or less structured sparsity constraints.

4 Simulation and Discussion

To evaluate the performance of JBNOMP and WNOMP, we consider two key metrics: the normalized recovery error and computational time. These metrics provide insights into the accuracy and efficiency of both algorithms.

The normalized recovery error is used to measure the accuracy of the recovered sparse signal and is computed using the Frobenius norm:

$$E_{\text{rec}} = \frac{\|\mathbf{X}_{\text{recovered}} - \mathbf{X}_{\text{true}}\|_F}{N \times L} \tag{15}$$

The computational efficiency of each algorithm is assessed based on the average execution time across multiple trials:

$$T_{\text{avg}} = \frac{\sum_{i=1}^{R} t_i}{R} \tag{16}$$

where t_i denotes the execution time of the i-th trial, and R represents the total number of trials. A lower T_{avg} implies better computational efficiency.

Figure 1 presents the normalized recovery error versus SNR for JBNOMP and WNOMP. It is evident that JBNOMP consistently achieves lower recovery error than WNOMP across all tested SNR levels. At low SNR values (e.g., -5 dB), JBNOMP demonstrates significant robustness to noise, maintaining a much lower recovery error than WNOMP. As the SNR increases, the recovery error decreases for both algorithms, which aligns with the expectation that a higher SNR leads to improved signal reconstruction. However, even at high SNR levels (e.g., 15 dB), JBNOMP continues to outperform WNOMP, confirming its advantage in achieving higher accuracy.

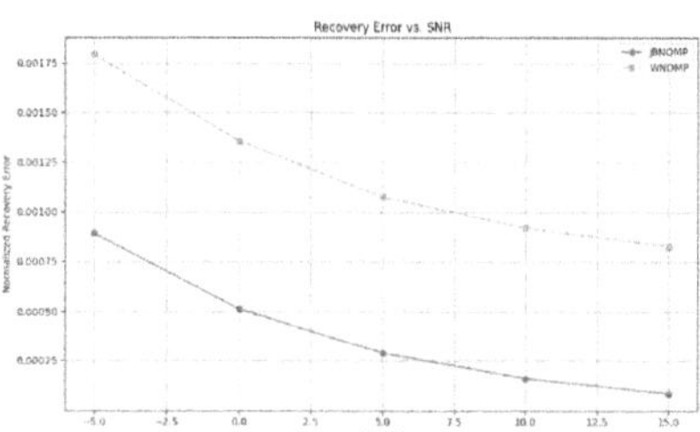

Fig. 1. Normalized recovery error versus SNR for JBNOMP and WNOMP

The computational time of both algorithms is illustrated in Fig. 2. JBNOMP consistently requires significantly less computation time than WNOMP, demonstrating its efficiency. The computational cost of JBNOMP remains stable across different SNR levels, whereas WNOMP requires much longer execution time. The reduction in computational complexity of JBNOMP can be attributed to its structured block selection approach, which effectively limits the search space

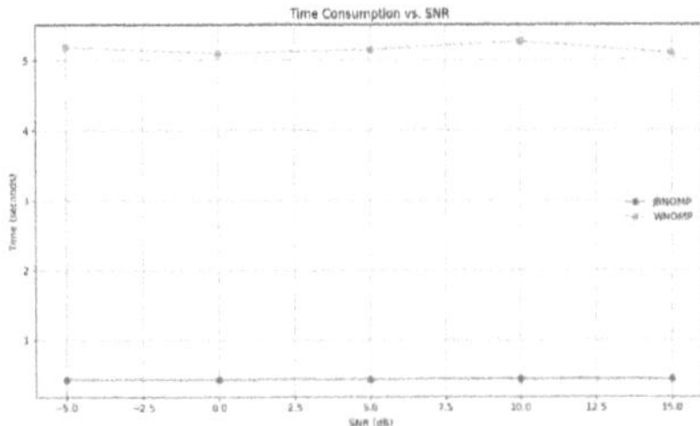

Fig. 2. Computational time versus SNR for JBNOMP and WNOMP

and enhances efficiency. This makes JBNOMP more suitable for real-time and large-scale applications where computational speed is critical.

The results demonstrate that JBNOMP achieves superior performance in both accuracy and efficiency. It provides lower recovery error compared to WNOMP while significantly reducing computational cost.

5   Conclusion

This work introduces a localized statistical channel model (LSCM) that captures environment-specific propagation characteristics. The model utilizes the expectations of the RSRP values obtained from different beams to reconstruct a high-resolution angular-domain representation of the multipath structure. The resulting APS distribution remains consistent with that of the actual wireless environment. To enable accurate APS recovery, we propose a joint block non-negative orthogonal matching pursuit (JBNOMP) algorithm that leverages inter-grid joint sparsity and intra-grid block sparsity. Simulation results reveal that JBNOMP offers fertile advantages.

References

1. Dreifuerst, R.M., Daulton, S., Qian, Y., Varkey, P., Balandat, M., Kasturia, S., Tomar, A., Yazdan, A., Ponnampalam, V., Heath, R.W.: Optimizing coverage and capacity in cellular networks using machine learning. In: Proceeding IEEE ICASSP, pp. 8138–8142 (2021)
2. Li, W., L'opez-P'erez, D., Geng, X., Bao, H., Song, Q., Chen, X.: A zeroth-order continuation method for antenna tuning in wireless networks. In: Proceeding IEEE ICC, pp. 1–6 (2021)
3. Wu, S., Wang, C.-X., Alwakeel, M.M., You, X., et al.: A general 3-D nonstationary 5G wireless channel model. IEEE Trans. Commun. **66**(7), 3065–3078 (2017)
4. Wang, C.-X., Bian, J., Sun, J., Zhang, W., Zhang, M.: A survey of 5G channel measurements and models. IEEE Commun. Surv. Tutor. **20**(4), 3142–3168 (2018)
5. Bian, J., Wang, C.-X., Gao, X., You, X., Zhang, M.: A general 3D non-stationary wireless channel model for 5G and beyond. IEEE Trans. Wireless Commun. **20**(5), 3211–3224 (2021)

6. Hussain, S., Brennan, C.: Efficient preprocessed ray tracing for 5G mobile transmitter scenarios in urban microcellular environments. IEEE Trans. Antennas Propagat. **67**(5), 3323–3333 (2019)
7. Rodriguez, A.C.S., Haider, N., He, Y., Dutkiewicz, E.: Network optimisation in 5G networks: a radio environment map approach. IEEE Trans. Veh. Technol., **69**(10), 12 043–12 (2020)
8. Park, C.S., Park, S.: Analysis of RSRP measurement accuracy. IEEE Commun. Lett. **20**(3), 430–433 (2016)
9. Tropp, J.A., Gilbert, A.C.: Signal recovery from random measurements via orthogonal matching pursuit. IEEE Trans. Inf. Theory **53**(12), 4655–4666 (2007)
10. Liu, A., Lau, V.K.N., Dai, W.: Exploiting burst-sparsity in massive MIMO with partial channel support information. IEEE Trans. Wireless Commun. **15**(11), 7820–7830 (2016)
11. 3GPP, "Study on channel model for frequencies from 0.5 to 100 GHz (Release 16). Technical Report (TR) 38.901, Jan. 2020, version 16.1.0
12. Zhang, S., Ning, X., Zheng, X., Shi, Q., Chang, T.-H., Luo, Z.-Q.: A Physics-based and data-driven approach for localized statistical channel modeling. IEEE Trans. Wireless Commun. **23**(6), 5409–5424 (2024). https://doi.org/10.1109/TWC.2023.3326209

Vision-Assisted Beam Prediction with 3D Convolutional Network and Efficient Channel Attention Mechanism

Shaohui Pan[1], Zhuoran Cai[1(✉)], and Yu Wang[2]

[1] Yantai University, Yantai, China
m18769632286@163.com, caizhuoran@ytu.edu.cn
[2] Nanjing University of Posts and Telecommunications, Nanjing, China
yuwang@njupt.edu.cn

Abstract. In millimeter wave (mm Wave) and massive multiple input multiple output (MIMO) systems, beam selection can enhance channel capacity and reduce bit error rate. However, existing beam selection methods for MIMO systems rely on traditional optimization techniques, which may not be feasible for real-time data transmission. Therefore, this paper proposes a vision-aided beam prediction method based on a three-dimensional convolutional neural network (3D CNN) and efficient channel attention (ECA) mechanism. First, 3D CNN is used to extract features from image data. Then, ECA assigns larger weights to critical image features, enhancing the representation capability of specific regions in the image. Finally, a multilayer perceptron (MLP) is employed to predict the optimal beam index. Experimental results on real-world data demonstrate that this method significantly improves prediction accuracy and stability compared to existing methods.

Keywords: Beam prediction · Millimeter wave communication · Efficient channel attention · 3D convolutional neural network

1 Introduction

In the field of wireless communications, beam prediction technology has become a key element in ensuring efficient and fast data transmission. The global deployment of fifth-generation (5G) communication technology networks and the active research on sixth-generation (6G) communication technology have highlighted the importance of beam prediction in improving network performance, optimizing signal clarity, and enhancing system processing capabilities [1–3].

Millimeter wave and terahertz (THz) frequency band communications are key drivers of the high data rate requirements of 5G, 6G and beyond. However, these systems require the deployment of large antenna arrays and the use of narrow beams at the transmitter and receiver to ensure that the received signal has sufficient power. Selecting the best beam is usually accompanied by

C. Xu et al. (Eds.): MobiMedia 2025, LNICST 670, pp. 26–34, 2026.
https://doi.org/10.1007/978-3-032-16823-8_3

high training overhead, which makes it difficult for millimeter wave/terahertz communication systems to support highly mobile wireless applications such as virtual/augmented reality and connected vehicles. Therefore, researchers are exploring new methods to overcome the high overhead of beam training and realize highly mobile millimeter wave/terahertz communication systems.

Over the past decade, the development of mmWave beam training and channel estimation techniques has attracted extensive attention. Researchers and practitioners have focused on key areas such as constructing adaptive beamforming codebooks to adapt to changing environments [4], developing accurate beam tracking techniques [5], and leveraging efficient compressed sensing techniques combined with channel sparsity to simplify the channel estimation process [5–7]. Although these advances have made some progress in reducing the overhead in beam training and channel estimation, the cost reduction is still limited. In particular, in complex systems equipped with large-scale antenna arrays, especially those that need to respond quickly to mobility and are highly sensitive to latency, traditional methods are clearly insufficient.

To address the shortcomings of traditional techniques, the emergence of machine learning schemes provides an effective approach for mmWave/THz beam prediction by incorporating prior observations and auxiliary information into the prediction process [8]. Given that mmWave/THz communication systems rely heavily on direct line-of-sight (LOS) links, a comprehensive understanding of the location of the device and its surroundings (e.g., building layout, moving scatterers) is essential for accurate beam selection. With detailed environmental perception information, such as the user's precise location and orientation [9], Sub-6GHz channel information [10], RGB images [11,12], LiDAR point cloud data [13,14], and radar measurement data [15], the beam management strategy can be significantly optimized and the complexity and overhead of beam training can be reduced. This approach of leveraging perception data not only helps achieve accurate beam positioning, but also narrows the range of potential beam pointing options.

In this context, 3D CNN [16] and attention mechanisms have been gradually applied to beam prediction to further improve the accuracy and efficiency of prediction. As a powerful machine learning model, 3D CNN is widely used to process three-dimensional data with a time dimension. In mmWave/THz beam management, 3D CNN can effectively process and analyze time series data, such as moving scatterers in dynamic environments and time-varying channel characteristics. By utilizing its deep convolutional layer structure, 3D CNN can automatically learn complex feature representations from raw input data, thereby providing more accurate and reliable beam prediction results. In addition, the introduction of the attention mechanism can make the model more focused on extracting key information, thereby enhancing its expressiveness and accuracy when processing high-dimensional data and dynamic environmental changes. By weighting the important parts of the input data, the attention mechanism can improve the accuracy and response speed of beam prediction.

Therefore, this paper proposes a vision-assisted beam prediction method based on 3D CNN and ECA attention mechanism. First, the 3D CNN is used to effectively capture the rich spatial and temporal information in the image data and generate high-dimensional feature representation. Then, ECA is used to assign larger weights to key image features to improve the representation ability of specific areas of the image. Finally, the optimal beam index is predicted by MLP.

2   Problem Description

The task of beam prediction is to determine the index d of the optimal beamforming vector f_d in the candidate beam codebook $\mathcal{F} = \{f_d\}_{d=1}^{D}$ to maximize the beam gain, where D is the total number of beamforming vectors. Mathematically, the beam selection problem can be expressed as:

$$\hat{d} = \arg \max_{d \in \{1,2,\ldots,D\}} \left| h_u^T f_d \right|^2 , \tag{1}$$

where, h_u represents the channel between the base station and user u, and $\hat{d}$ represents the optimal beam index.

To solve this problem, we designed a machine learning model to predict the optimal beam index. Specifically, our goal is to find a model function Φ_Θ with parameter Θ that uses image data $I = [I_1, I_2, \ldots, I_n]$ to predict the optimal beam index $\hat{d} \in \{1, 2, \ldots, D\}$. The mathematical representation of this model function is as follows:

$$\Phi_\Theta : \left\{ [I_1, I_2, \ldots, I_n] \right\} \to \left\{ \hat{d} \right\}. \tag{2}$$

3   The Proposed Beam Prediction Method

3.1   Overview

The model based on 3D CNN and ECA mechanism proposed in this paper is shown in Fig. 1. First, 3D CNN is used to extract features from image data. Then, the ECA module is introduced to assign larger weights to key image features to improve the representation ability of specific areas of the image. Finally, the optimal beam index is predicted by MLP.

3.2   3D Convolutional Neural Networks

3D CNN is a deep learning model specifically designed to process volumetric data or temporal dynamic sequence data. Traditional 2D convolutional neural networks are very effective in analyzing spatial information in images, and 3D CNN further expands this capability by capturing spatial and temporal features in videos, medical images, and other 3D data. The operation of the 3D CNN is illustrated in Fig. 2.

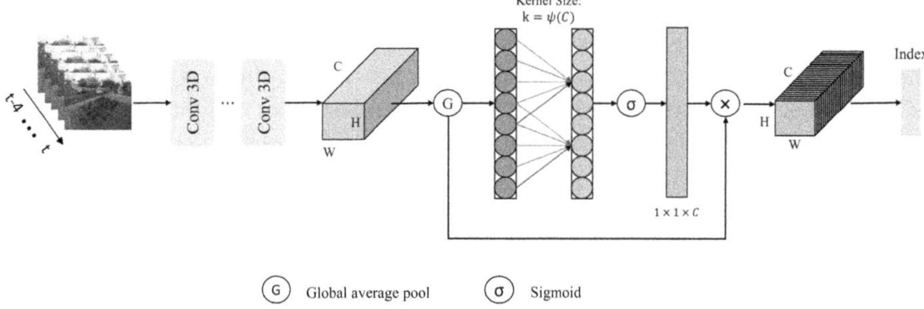

Fig. 1. Architecture of the proposed beam prediction model based on 3D CNN and ECA.

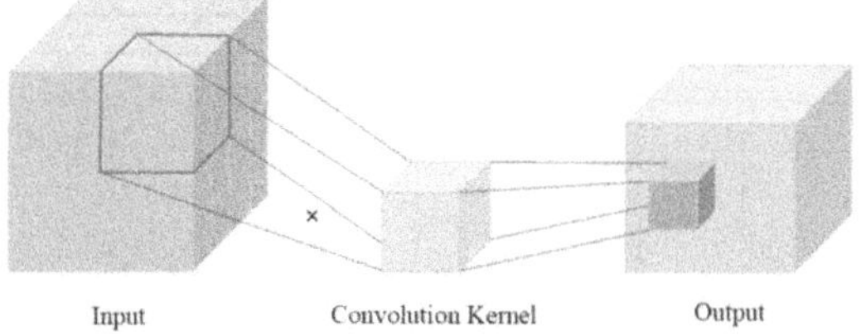

Fig. 2. 3D CNN operation.

3D convolution takes $X \in \mathbb{R}^{W \times H \times C}$ as input, slides the convolution kernel in its three dimensions, and generates a feature map by calculating the sum of the dot products of the 3D convolution kernel and the input data. After each convolution operation, activation and batch normalization are performed, and the generated feature map is used as the input of the next convolution layer. The calculation formula for the neuron ν_{lj}^{xyz} at position (x, y, z) of the j-th feature map of the l-th convolution layer is:

$$\nu_{lj}^{xyz} = f \left(\sum_{m=0}^{M_l-1} \sum_{h=0}^{H_l-1} \sum_{w=0}^{W_l-1} \sum_{r=0}^{R_l-1} k_{ljm}^{hwr} \nu_{(l-1)m}^{(x+h)(y+w)(z+r)} + b_{lj} \right), \tag{3}$$

where, H_l, W_l and R_l represent the length, width and time dimension of the three-dimensional convolution kernel respectively, M_l represents the number of convolution kernels in the l-th layer, k_{ljm}^{hwr} represents the value of the m-th three-dimensional convolution kernel at the position (h, w, r) in the j-th layer, b_{lj} represents the bias of the l-th layer connected to the j-th three-dimensional feature data, and $f(\cdot)$ represents the activation function.

3.3   Efficient Channel Attention Mechanism

The attention mechanism originated from the study of the human visual system and focuses on local information. Channel attention aims to assign weights to the signals of each channel to indicate the relevance of the channel to key information. This paper uses ECA to learn the interdependence between channels within the network, so as to effectively capture the key information of image features. ECA assigns larger weights to key features and smaller weights to irrelevant features through the method of local cross-channel interaction strategy without dimensionality reduction and adaptive selection of one-dimensional convolution kernel size, thereby improving the network's sensitivity to the main features and achieving significant performance improvement. The ECA structure is shown in Fig. 3.

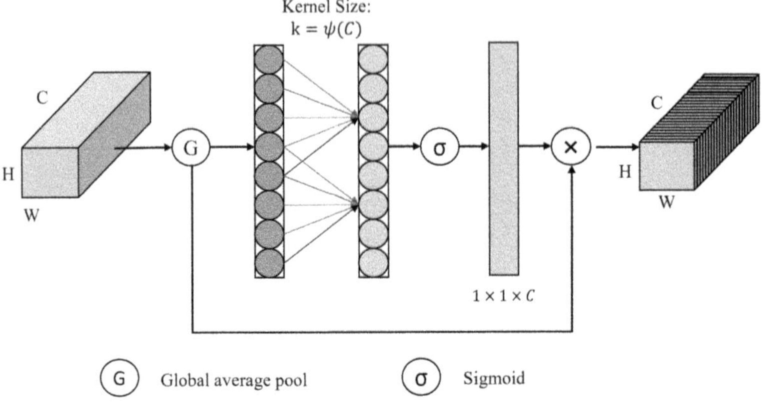

Fig. 3. The structure of ECA.

Given an input feature map $T \in \mathbb{R}^{W \times H \times C}$, ECA first computes the global average pooling across spatial dimensions to obtain the output y:

$$y_c = \frac{1}{W \times H} \sum_{i=1}^{W} \sum_{j=1}^{H} T_{i,j,c}. \tag{4}$$

Next, the convolution kernel size k for the 1D convolution is adaptively determined by:

$$k = \psi(C) = \left| \frac{\log_2 C}{y} + \frac{g}{\gamma} \right|_{\text{odd}}, \tag{5}$$

where $|t|_{\text{odd}}$ denotes the nearest odd integer to t, and γ and g are hyperparameters, typically set to 2 and 1, respectively.

The attention weights ω are then generated by applying a 1D convolution followed by a sigmoid activation:

$$\omega = f_\sigma \left(f_{\text{Conv1D}_k}(y) \right). \tag{6}$$

Finally, the refined feature map $\hat{T}$ is obtained by rescaling the original feature map T with the attention weights ω via channel-wise multiplication:

$$\hat{T} = \omega_c \cdot T. \tag{7}$$

4   Experimental Results and Analysis

4.1   Dataset

The dataset used in this paper comes from the open source platform DeepSense6G [17], which can provide high-quality data. The settings of the experimental parameters are shown in Table 1.

Table 1. Main parameter settings for experiments

Parameter	Value
Dataset split ratio	8:1:1
Epochs	150
Batch size	8
Python version	3.7.13
PyTorch version	1.13.1
Optimizer	AdamW
Learning rate	0.0001
Platform	NVIDIA GeForce RTX 3080Ti GPU

4.2   Experimental Results Analysis

This experiment uses distance-based accuracy (DBA) score and Top-k accuracy as evaluation indicators, among which DBA score is the main performance comparison indicator. The specific format is as follows:

$$S_{DBA} = \frac{1}{3} \sum_{k=1}^{3} Y_k, \tag{8}$$

where, Y_k, $K \in \{1, 2, 3\}$ is

$$Y_k = 1 - \frac{1}{N} \sum_{n=1}^{N} \min_{1 \le j \le K} \left[\min \left(\frac{|\hat{d}_{n,j} - d_n|}{\Delta}, 1 \right) \right] \tag{9}$$

where, d_n is the true beam index of sample n, and Δ is the regularization factor, which is usually set to 5. The benchmark models for comparison include 3D CNN, a network combining 2D CNN and ECA, and a network combining 3D CNN and Shuffle Attention Networks (SA-Net).

The experimental results are shown in Table 2. As shown in Table 2, the proposed method performs best in most evaluation indicators in comprehensive scenarios. Specifically, the Top-1 accuracy of the proposed method is 0.4864, which is 1.9%, 4.2% and 1.0% higher than 3D CNN, 2D CNN + ECA and 3D

CNN + SA-Net respectively, indicating its advantage in predicting the optimal beam index. The Top-2 accuracy is significantly better than other models, and is 3.5% higher than the second-best model 3D CNN + SA-Net. The DBA index is 0.8922, which is slightly higher than 3D CNN and 3D CNN + SA-Net, but the improvement is only 0.3%, indicating that its performance in beam alignment stability is similar to other advanced methods. In addition, the scene data, such as the Top-1 accuracy of Scenario34 of 0.4591 is lower than that of 3D CNN + SA-Net of 0.4759, indicating that the proposed method still has room for optimization in specific complex scenarios. In specific complex dynamic obstruction scenarios, ECA emphasizes important features by assigning higher weights to channels but neglects spatial positional relationships, leading to a reduction in accuracy to some extent.

Table 2. Experimental results of the proposed model compared to other benchmark models

Model	Scenario	Top-1	Top-2	Top-3	DBA
3D CNN	Scenario32	0.4932	0.7313	0.8469	0.8938
	Scenario33	0.4757	0.6772	0.8009	0.8744
	Scenario34	0.4663	0.7211	0.8413	0.8969
	Overall	0.4773	0.7084	0.8284	0.8891
2D CNN + ECA	Scenario32	0.4830	0.7312	0.8299	0.8938
	Scenario33	0.4757	0.6845	0.8228	0.8777
	Scenario34	0.4423	0.6947	0.8317	0.8878
	Overall	0.4667	0.7013	0.8284	0.8860
3D CNN + SA-Net	Scenario32	0.4863	0.7449	0.8333	0.8948
	Scenario33	0.4830	0.7112	0.8180	0.8773
	Scenario34	0.4759	0.6971	0.8462	0.8971
	Overall	0.4818	0.7156	0.8462	0.8895
Our proposed	Scenario32	0.4864	0.7483	0.8673	0.8939
	Scenario33	0.4830	0.7330	0.8252	0.8837
	Scenario34	0.4591	0.7404	0.8678	0.8989
	Overall	**0.4864**	**0.7404**	**0.8524**	**0.8922**
Our proposed - ECA	Scenario32	0.4821	0.7358	0.8311	0.8923
	Scenario33	0.4781	0.7293	0.8197	0.8815
	Scenario34	0.4541	0.7352	0.8298	0.8941
	Overall	0.4714	0.7334	0.8268	0.8893

5 Conclusion

This paper proposes a vision-assisted beam prediction method based on 3D CNN and ECA mechanism. First, 3D CNN is used to extract features from image data. Then, the ECA module is introduced to assign larger weights to key image features to improve the representation ability of specific areas of the image. Finally, the optimal beam index is predicted by a multi-layer perceptron. Since the image data used contains information in the time dimension, our model has better learning and expression capabilities than CNN and other methods. Experiments on real data have shown that this method has significantly improved prediction accuracy and stability over existing methods.

References

1. Xue, Q., et al.: A survey of beam management for mmWave and THz communications towards 6G. IEEE Commun. Surv. Tutor. **26**(3), 1520–1559 (2024)
2. Gui, G., et al.: 6G: opening new horizons for integration of comfort, security, and intelligence. IEEE Wireless Commun. **27**(5), 126–132 (2020)
3. Xu, Y., et al.: A survey on resource allocation for 5G heterogeneous networks: current research, future trends, and challenges. IEEE Commun. Surv. Tutor. **23**(2), 668–695 (2021)
4. Zhang, Y., et al.: Reinforcement learning of beam codebooks in millimeter wave and terahertz MIMO systems. IEEE Trans. Commun. **70**(2), 904–919 (2022)
5. Jayaprakasam, S., et al.: Robust beam-tracking for mmWave mobile communications. IEEE Commun. Lett. **21**(12), 2654–2657 (2017)
6. Alkhateeb, A., et al.: Channel estimation and hybrid precoding for millimeter wave cellular systems. IEEE J. Sel. Top. Signal Process. **8**(5), 831–846 (2014)
7. Heath, R.W., et al.: An overview of signal processing techniques for millimeter wave MIMO systems. IEEE J. Sel. Top. Signal Process. **10**(3), 436–453 (2016)
8. Alkhateeb, A., et al.: Machine learning for reliable mmWave systems: blockage prediction and proactive handoff. In: Proceedings of IEEE Global Conference on Signal and Information Processing (GlobalSIP), Anaheim, CA, USA, pp. 1055–1059 (2018)
9. Morais, J., et al.: Position-aided beam prediction in the real world: how useful GPS locations actually are? In: Proceedings of IEEE International Conference on Communications (ICC), Rome, Italy, pp. 1824–1829 (2023)
10. Alrabeiah, M., Alkhateeb, A.: Deep learning for mmWave beam and blockage prediction using sub-6 GHz channels. IEEE Trans. Commun. **68**(9), 5504–5518 (2020)
11. Alrabeiah, M., et al.: Millimeter wave base stations with cameras: vision-aided beam and blockage prediction. In: Proceedings of IEEE 91st Vehicular Technology Conference (VTC Spring), Antwerp, Belgium, pp. 1–5 (2020)
12. Charan, G., et al.: Vision-position multi-modal beam prediction using real millimeter wave datasets. In: Proceedings of IEEE Wireless Communications and Networking Conference (WCNC), Austin, TX, USA, pp. 2727–2731 (2022)
13. Jiang, S., et al.: LiDAR aided future beam prediction in real-world millimeter wave V2I communications. IEEE Wireless Commun. Lett. **12**(2), 212–216 (2023)
14. Marasinghe, D., et al.: LiDAR aided wireless networks beam prediction for 5G. In: Proceedings of IEEE 96th Vehicular Technology Conference (VTC-Fall), London, UK, pp. 1–7 (2022)
15. Demirhan, U., Alkhateeb, A.: Radar aided 6G beam prediction: deep learning algorithms and real-world demonstration. In: Proceedings of IEEE Wireless Communications and Networking Conference (WCNC), Austin, TX, USA, pp. 2655–2660 (2022)

16. Zhou, Q., et al.: Multi-modal fusion for millimeter-wave communication systems: a spatio-temporal enabled approach. Neurocomputing **555**, 126604 (2023)
17. Alkhateeb, A., et al.: DeepSense 6G: a large-scale real-world multi-modal sensing and communication dataset. IEEE Commun. Mag. **61**(9), 122–128 (2023)

Time-Varying Channel Estimation Using Tobit-Extended Kalman Filter: Handling Censored Data Challenges

Jiaming Dong[1], Haotian Zhou[2], Qi Wang[2], Xingyu Fan[2(✉)], and Peng Yin[2]

[1] China Mobile Chengdu Institute of Research and Development, Chengdu, China
[2] Defence Industry Secrecy Examination and Certification Center, Beijing, China
william_fan@aliyun.com

Abstract. This study investigates the challenge of time-varying channel estimation under censored data conditions, a prevalent issue in communication systems caused by sensor saturation or detection constraints. Such censoring effects, typically manifested as signal clipping or discontinuous measurements, can introduce significant estimation errors that adversely affect subsequent signal demodulation and channel equalization processes. To address this problem, we propose a Tobit Extended Kalman Filter (TEKF) algorithm that integrates the Tobit censored measurement model with Extended Kalman Filtering. The TEKF enables unbiased and computationally efficient estimation for channels with censored data outputs, making it particularly suitable for complex propagation environments. Numerical simulations demonstrate that the TEKF consistently outperforms Extended Kalman Filter methods in estimation accuracy, providing a reliable approach for recovering channel characteristics from censored communication signals.

Keywords: Varying channel estimation · Kalman filters · Tobit measurement model

1 Introduction

In wireless communication systems, signal transmission is inherently susceptible to channel distortions caused by noise, interference, and multipath propagation [1]. The time-varying nature of wireless channels, exacerbated by user mobility and Doppler shifts in high-speed scenarios, leads to rapid fluctuations in channel characteristics such as amplitude, phase, and delay [2]. These dynamic variations introduce estimation errors that critically impair channel equalization and symbol detection accuracy, degrading overall system performance. Traditional channel estimation algorithms often assume quasi-static channels, which fail to capture the dynamic behavior of time-varying systems [3]. To address this limitation, Kalman filtering emerges as a robust method for real-time channel estimation. By recursively estimating channel states through a "predict-measure-update" mechanism, Kalman filters adapt efficiently to temporal variations without relying on historical data [3], effectively mitigating distortions in complex communication environments.

C. Xu et al. (Eds.): MobiMedia 2025, LNICST 670, pp. 35–43, 2026.
https://doi.org/10.1007/978-3-032-16823-8_4

Early work by Dai et al. introduced a Kalman interpolation filter for LTE downlink channel estimation in high-mobility scenarios, laying the foundation for adaptive tracking of time-varying channels [4]. Subsequent studies expanded this framework: Soni and Mishra provided a comprehensive review of Kalman filter-based channel equalizers, emphasizing their potential in mitigating intersymbol interference under quasistatic assumptions [5]. The extension to nonlinear systems began with Rashmi and Sarvagya, who employed the Extended Kalman Filter (EKF) for channel estimation in superposition-coded modulation, demonstrating superior performance over conventional methods in non-Gaussian noise environments [6].

In practical engineering applications, signal censoring effects, typically manifested as signal clipping or discontinuous measurements, frequently occur due to abrupt environmental variations, limitations in receiver dynamic range, or detection threshold constraints. These censored data severely degrade the performance of Kalman filter-based channel estimation. Prior studies have explored related challenges, for example, Sinopoli et al. treated the censored measurement data as intermittent measurements, where the absence of measurement updates in Kalman filtering introduces state estimation bias [7]. A critical challenge in applying Kalman filters to truncated measurements lies in the non-Gaussian nature of measurement noise near censored data, which violates the zero-mean Gaussian noise assumption inherent to standard Kalman filters. To address this limitation, Allik et al. proposed the Tobit Kalman Filter (TKF), which explicitly models censored measurements within the recursive filtering framework, enabling complete state estimation under truncation constraints [8]. TKF has gained extensive engineering applications: it enables tracking of hidden state vectors for human skeletal motion analysis [9], provides robust estimation of missile guidance capture areas under saturated measurements [10], and effectively resolves beacon tracking with censored measurements along with communication encryption challenges in wireless communications [11, 12].

2 Research Problem

To formalize the censored data problem in time-varying channels, we begin by defining the output samples of the time-varying channel as:

$$h_n = Ah_{n-1} + w(n-1),$$
$$y(n)^* = B\left(\sum_{k=0}^{K-1} h_n(k)x(n-k)\right) + v(n). \tag{1}$$

The first expression characterizes the time-varying channel. In slow-fading channels, the channel coefficients do not vary rapidly across samples but instead exhibit high temporal correlation between successive variations. We model this temporal evolution using a first-order Gauss-Markov autoregressive model, h_n represents the impulse response of the time-varying multipath channel, expressed as $h_n = [h_n(0), h_n(1), ..., h_n(K-1)]$, with K denoting the number of taps in the multipath channel, $w(n)$ is the state noise of the time-varying channel, A corresponds to the time-varying coefficient matrix of the multipath channel.

The second expression describes the observation model of the time-varying multipath channel. The observation model may exhibit complex nonlinear characteristics due to various factors such as noise and hardware nonlinearity. Let $B(\cdot)$ denote the nonlinear channel output observation function, and $v(n)$ represent the observation noise. The censored data can be modeled as:

$$y(n) = \begin{cases} y(n)^*, & y(n)^* < \tau, \\ \tau, & y(n)^* \geq \tau. \end{cases} \tag{2}$$

$y(n)^*$ is the latent observation, which is recorded as censored data τ when it exceeds the threshold τ. The $w(n)$ and $v(n)$ are zero-mean Gaussian random vectors with covariance matrices $Q \in \mathbb{R}^{n \times n}$ and $R = \sigma^2$, respectively, where σ is the standard deviation of the measurement noise. However, when the noise distribution on $y(n)$ contains censored data, the noise becomes correlated with the observations, violating the assumptions of the Kalman filter and leading to degraded channel estimation performance [8]. To achieve unbiased and reliable estimation of time-varying channels in communication systems under censored data conditions, this paper proposes a Tobit Extended Kalman Filter (TEKF) method to address the challenges of time-varying channel estimation with censored measurements.

3 The Tobit Extended Kalman Filter

The application of the Kalman filter in channel estimation is primarily divided into two phases: the prediction phase and the update phase. In the prediction phase, the a priori state estimate and its covariance matrix are obtained by leveraging prior knowledge of the channel model. In the update phase, the Kalman gain is calculated to minimize the covariance of the posterior state estimate, which is then updated using observed measurements. This iterative process forms a semi-blind recursive feedback framework.

For the time-varying channel model outputs in Eqs. (1) and (2), the presence of censored data and nonlinear time-varying channel conditions violates the independent Gaussian noise assumption inherent to the Kalman filter. As a result, critical components such as the Kalman gain and state covariance deviate from theoretical expectations, leading to biased state and covariance estimations. Therefore, it is necessary to rederive the recursive equations for both the prediction and update phases to address these non-ideal conditions.

To more comprehensively account for the impact of censored measurement data on the statistical properties of the Kalman filter, we introduce a Bernoulli variable $p(n)$ to reformulate the observation equation as:

$$y(n) = p(n)y(n)^* + (I - p(n))\tau,$$
$$Prob\{p(n) = 1\} = \bar{p}(n), Prob\{p(n) = 0\} = 1 - \bar{p}(n), \tag{3}$$

where $Prob\{\cdot\}$ is the probability distribution, $\bar{p}(n)$ and $p(n)$ are Bernoulli random variables, treated as known non-negative constants, . The variable $\bar{p}(n)$ characterizes the censoring phenomenon of the observed value $y(n)$ through its probability distribution.

38   J. Dong et al.

First, during the prediction phase, the a priori state estimation covariance $\psi_{n|n-1}$, generated from the state Eq. (1), must be provided:

$$\psi_{n|n-1} = E\left[\left(h_n - \hat{h}_{n|n-1}\right)\left(h_n - \hat{h}_{n|n-1}\right)^T\right], \tag{4}$$

where $\hat{h}_{n|n-1} = A\hat{h}_{n-1}$ represents the estimate of the channel impulse response at time $n-1$, based on all state estimation information up to time $n-1$. Leveraging the Taylor expansion approximation and the Gaussian independence property of the state noise, Eq. (4) can be expressed as:

$$\begin{aligned}
\psi_{n|n-1} &\approx E\left[A\left(h_{n-1} - \hat{h}_{n|n-1}\right)\left(h_{n-1} - \hat{h}_{n|n-1}\right)^T A^T + w(n-1)w(n-1)^T\right] \\
&= A\psi_{n-1|n-1}A^T + Q(n-1),
\end{aligned} \tag{5}$$

where Q is the state noise covariance matrix. Based on the state equation's estimation of $\hat{h}_{n|n-1}$, the Kalman filter corrects the state estimate in the update phase using the current observation $y(n)$ and the Kalman gain $K(n)$. The Kalman gain is determined to minimize the posterior state estimation covariance $\psi_{n|n}$, and the state update equation can be expressed as:

$$\hat{h}_{n|n} = \hat{h}_{n|n-1} + K(n)(y(n) - \hat{y}(n|n-1)). \tag{6}$$

By combining Eqs. (3) and (6), the posterior estimation covariance can be expanded as:

$$\begin{aligned}
\psi_{n|n} &= E\left[\left(h_n - \hat{h}_{n|n}\right)\left(h_n - \hat{h}_{n|n}\right)^T\right] \\
&= \psi_{n|n-1} + E\left[\left(h_n - h_{n|n-1}\right)(y(n) - \hat{y}(n|n))^T K(n)^T\right] \\
&\quad - K(n)E\left[(y(n) - \hat{y}(n|n))\left(h_n - h_{n|n-1}\right)^T\right] \\
&\quad + K(n)E\left[(y(n) - \hat{y}(n|n))(y(n) - \hat{y}(n|n))^T\right]K(n)^T.
\end{aligned} \tag{7}$$

To determine the Kalman gain $K(n)$ that minimizes the posterior estimation covariance $\psi_{n|n}$, we take the partial derivative of $\psi_{n|n}$ with respect to $K(n)$ and set it to zero, yielding the expression for $K(n)$:

$$\begin{aligned}
K(n) &= E\left[\left(h_n - h_{n|n-1}\right)(y(n) - \hat{y}(n|n))^T\right] \\
&\quad \times E\left[(y(n) - \hat{y}(n|n))(y(n) - \hat{y}(n|n))^T\right]^{-1},
\end{aligned} \tag{8}$$

Where the first $E[\cdot]$ represents the cross-covariance between the observation error and the current channel impulse response error, denoted as $R_{\tilde{x}\tilde{y}}$. The second $E[\cdot]$ corresponds to the variance of the observation error, denoted as $R_{\tilde{y}\tilde{y}}$. To explicitly characterize the impact of the time-varying nonlinear observation equation and censored data on the gain weights, further explicit derivations of $R_{\tilde{x}\tilde{y}}$ and $R_{\tilde{y}\tilde{y}}$ are performed through Taylor expansion and noise distribution properties.

$$\begin{aligned}
R_{\tilde{x}\tilde{y}} &= E\left[\left(h_n - h_{n|n-1}\right)((p(n)(B(h_n x(n)) + v(n))) + (I - p(n))\tau - \hat{y}(n|n))^T\right] \\
&= E\left[h_n h_n^T b_n^T p(n)\right] + E[h_n v(n)] + E\left[h_n \tau^T (I - p(n))\right] - E\left[h_n \hat{y}(n|n)^T\right] \\
&\quad - E\left[h_{n|n-1} h_n^T b_n^T p(n)\right] - E\left[h_{n|n-1} v(n)^T p(n)\right] - E\left[h_{n|n-1}\tau^T (I - p(n))\right] \\
&\quad + E\left[h_{n|n-1}\hat{y}(n|n)^T\right],
\end{aligned} \tag{9}$$

Where $b_n = \left.\frac{\partial B}{\partial h_n}\right|_{h_n=\hat{h}_{n|n-1}}$, denotes the linearized observation matrix obtained from the Taylor expansion approximation of the nonlinear observation equation. In practical applications, the prior estimate of the channel response at time n-1 is typically used to compute the censoring probability $1 - E[p(n)]$ at time n. To address this, Assumption 1 is proposed: $E[p(n)]$ can be approximated by replacing h_n with the prior estimate $h_{n\,|\,n-1}$. Under this assumption, the distribution of $p(n)$ no longer depends on the true h_n, implying that $p(n)$ and h_n are mutually independent. Consequently, Eq. (9) can be simplified as:

$$R_{\tilde{x}\tilde{y}} = \psi_{n|n-1} b_n^T E\big[p(n)\big]. \tag{10}$$

Similarly, based on the linearized observation matrix b_n and the independence property of noise, substituting Eq. (3), the covariance $R_{\tilde{y}\tilde{y}}$ can be expanded as:

$$R_{\tilde{y}\tilde{y}} = E\big[p(n)\big]b_n\psi_{n|n-1}b_n^T E\big[p(n)\big] + E\Big[p(n)\big(y(n) - E[y(n)|y(n) < \tau]\big) \\ \big(y(n) - E[y(n)|y(n) < \tau]\big)^T p\big(n\big)^T\Big], \tag{11}$$

where $E[y(n)|\,y(n) < \tau]$ represents the expected value of the observation output under non-censored data conditions. For simplicity, Assumption 2 is introduced: the observation noise covariance matrix $R = E[v(n)v(n)^T]$ is diagonal. Consequently, Eq. (11) can be simplified as:

$$R_{\tilde{y}\tilde{y}} = E\big[p(n)\big]b_n\psi_{n|n-1}b_n^T E\big[p(n)\big] + E\big[p(n)(y(n) - Var(y(n)|y(n) < \tau))\big]. \tag{12}$$

Further, substituting the derived Kalman gain $K(n) = R_{\tilde{x}\tilde{y}}R_{\tilde{y}\tilde{y}}^{-1}$ into Eq. (7), the update expression for the posterior estimation covariance can be obtained as:

$$\psi_{n|n} = \big(I - E\big[p(n)\big]K(n)b_n\big)\psi_{n|n-1}. \tag{13}$$

In summary, the complete recursive formula for the Tobit Extended Kalman filter is:

$$\begin{aligned} h_{n|n-1} &= Ah_{n-1|n-1} + w(n - 1), \\ \psi_{n-1|n-1} &= A\psi_{n-1|n-1}A^T + Q(n - 1), \\ \hat{h}_{n|n} &= \hat{h}_{n|n-1} + K_n(y(n) - \hat{y}(n|n - 1)), \\ \psi_{n|n} &= \big(I - E\big[p(n)\big]K(n)b_n\big)\psi_{n|n-1}. \end{aligned} \tag{14}$$

In the recursive formula, the expected value of the observation $\hat{y}(n|n - 1)$, the variance $Var(y(n)|\,y(n) < \tau)$, and $E[p(n)]$ can all be obtained from the regression model in the Tobit marginal effect [8]:

$$y(n|n - 1) = \Phi\Big(\tfrac{B(h_n x(n))-\tau}{\sigma}\Big)[B(h_n x(n)) + \sigma\lambda((\tau - B(h_n x(n)))/\sigma)] \\ + \Phi\Big(\tfrac{\tau - B(h_n x(n))}{\sigma}\Big)\tau, \tag{15}$$

$$Var(y(n)|y(n) < \tau) = \\ \sigma^2\Big[1 - \lambda\Big(\tfrac{\tau - B(h_n x(n))}{\sigma}\Big) \cdot \Big[\lambda\Big(\tfrac{\tau - B(h_n x(n))}{\sigma}\Big) - \Big(\tfrac{\tau - B(h_n x(n))}{\sigma}\Big)\Big]\Big], \tag{16}$$

$$E[p(n)] = \Phi\left(\frac{B(h_n x(n)) - \tau}{\sigma}\right), \tag{17}$$

where $\lambda = \frac{\phi(\alpha)}{[1-\Phi(\alpha)]}$, $\Phi(\cdot)$ and $\phi(\cdot)$ denote the cumulative distribution function and probability density function of a Gaussian random variable with mean $B(h_n x(n))$, respectively.

4 Experimental Results

This chapter presents simulation studies for the Tobit Extended Kalman Filter (TEKF). The first simulation considers a nonlinear motion model with censored measurement data and additive noise, while the second simulates a nonlinear time-varying channel model with censored measurements and additive noise. EKF and TEKF are respectively employed for estimation in these simulations, and the advantages and disadvantages of each method are analyzed.

4.1 Estimation of Nonlinear Motion Model

In the simulation, a motion model with nonlinear damping was constructed to verify the adaptability of the proposed method to nonlinear models. The state equation and observation equation are as follows:

$$\begin{aligned} x(n) &= x(n-1) + \left(\frac{x(n-1)}{1+x(n-1)^2}\right) + w(n), \\ y(n) &= \ln(x(n)) + v(n). \end{aligned} \tag{18}$$

In the equations, $x(n)$ represents the target's motion position, and $y(n)$ denotes the observed value of the target's motion position in the logarithmic domain, the observation noise $v(n)$ has $\sigma = 1$, the state noise covariance $Q = 10^{-3}$, and the censoring limit is $\tau = 0.1$. The initial conditions are $x(0) = 8$ and $\Psi_0 = 1$. Estimations are performed using both the EKF and TEKF.

As shown in Fig. 1, in the positions of censored data at the front segment of the observations, the TEKF can consistently converge to the true values. The estimates generated by the EKF exhibit deviations at the time points of front-segment censored data, but the EKF can gradually converge to the true state values at subsequent time points with uncensored data. The different performances of the two filters for censored and uncensored data also confirm that when the state values are far from the censored data region, the TEKF and EKF are nearly equivalent.

4.2 Nonlinear Time-Varying Channel Model

In this simulation, the nonlinear time-varying channel model has the following state equation and observation equation:

$$\begin{aligned} h_n &= Ah_{n-1} + w(n), \\ y(n)^* &= \sin\left(\sum_{k=0}^{K-1} h_n(k)x(n-k)\right) + v(n), \end{aligned} \tag{19}$$

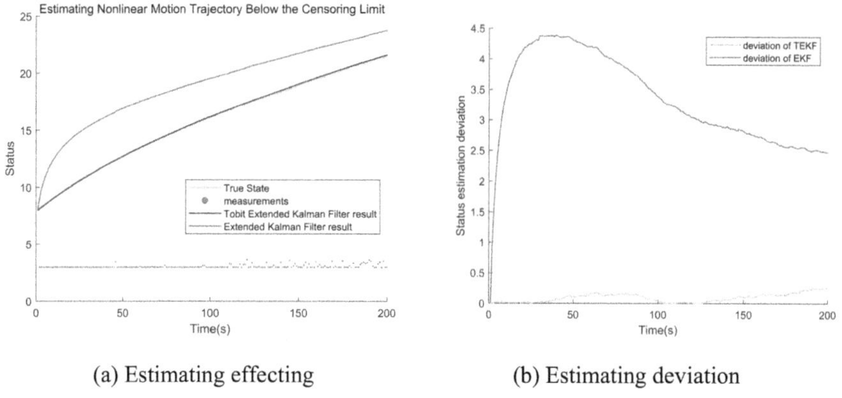

(a) Estimating effecting   (b) Estimating deviation

Fig. 1 Nonlinear motion estimation: estimation of TEKF and EKF.

where $A = \begin{bmatrix} 0.997 & 0 \\ 0 & 0.999 \end{bmatrix}$, $x(n)$ is a BPSK modulated signal with an amplitude of 1. And the number of tapped-delays $K = 2$ for the time-varying channel model is set. The observation noise $v(n)$ has $\sigma = 0.1$, the state noise covariance $Q = 10^{-3}$, and the censoring limit is $\tau = 0.5$. The initial conditions are $h_0 = [1; 0.9]$ and $\Psi_0 = 100I$. Estimations are performed using both the EKF and TEKF.

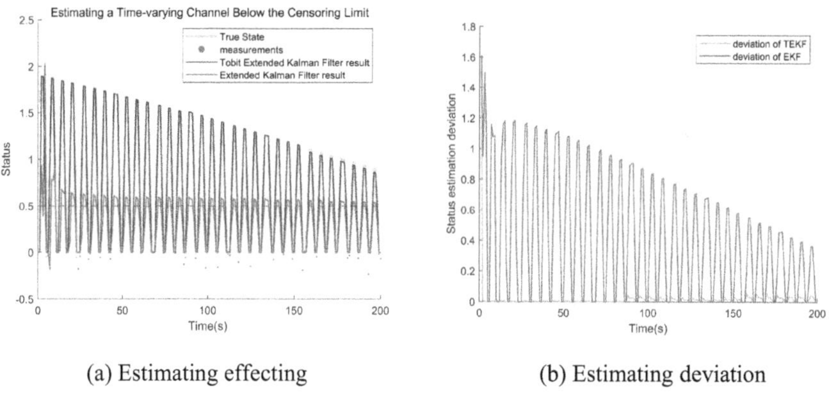

(a) Estimating effecting   (b) Estimating deviation

Fig. 2 Nonlinear time-varying channel estimation: estimation of TEKF and EKF.

As shown in Fig. 2, TEKF achieves relatively unbiased estimation results in simulations of nonlinear time-varying channels with censored data. In contrast, the estimation of EKF shows an over-dependence on the channel output measurements and fails to provide a smooth estimation when transitioning from censored to uncensored data. The TEKF method can be well applied to estimating the discontinuity in the output of the nonlinear time—varying channel caused by censored data. Moreover, since some channel output measurements are lost due to nonlinear fading and noise, it is difficult to recover the complete channel response from the obtained measurements. This results in a small deviation between the estimated channel response and the true state.

To further explore the robustness of the algorithm under high-dynamic conditions, the channel multipath effect is introduced based on the model in Sect. 4.2, and the influence of the measurement errors of the key parameters τ and Q on the algorithm performance is verified.

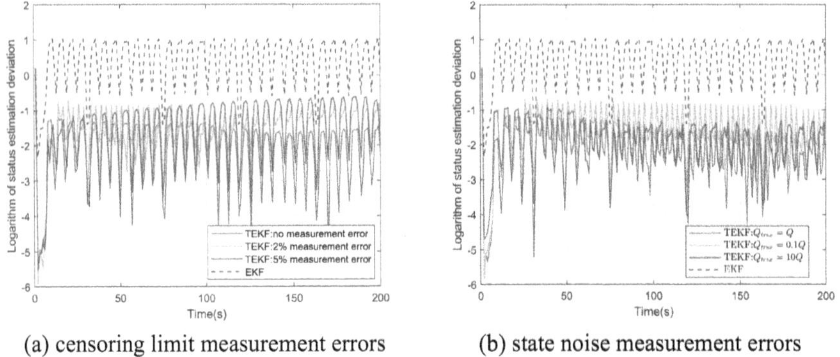

(a) censoring limit measurement errors   (b) state noise measurement errors

Fig. 3 Robustness analysis of key parameters: estimation deviation of TEKF and EKF under different conditions.

Specifically, measurement errors of the censoring limit τ are set at 2% and 5%, while fluctuations in the true value of state noise covariance Q ($0.1Q$ and $10Q$) are introduced. Logarithmic plots of channel estimation errors for both TEKF and EKF under these conditions are presented in Fig. 3, enabling an intuitive performance comparison across different scenarios. Fig. 3 demonstrates that an increase in measurement error of the censoring threshold and fluctuations in state noise covariance lead to a corresponding rise in the estimation error of the TEKF. Nevertheless, compared to the conventional EKF, the TEKF consistently delivers relatively accurate channel estimation. This underscores the robustness of TEKF against variations in noise statistics and censoring limits under high-dynamic environments.

5 Conclusion

This paper addresses the challenge of time-varying channel estimation under censored data conditions—a critical issue in modern communication systems caused by sensor saturation or detection thresholds. The proposed Tobit Extended Kalman Filter (TEKF) integrates the Tobit censored measurement model with nonlinear Extended Kalman Filtering, enabling robust estimation in time-varying channel environments characterized by censored data and nonlinear observations. By predicting censoring probabilities through prior state estimates and optimizing the Kalman gain, the TEKF mitigates bias induced by non-Gaussian noise distributions and nonlinear dynamics. Numerical simulations vividly demonstrate that the TEKF surpasses conventional Extended Kalman Filter methods in estimation accuracy, providing a powerful and reliable solution for accurately recovering channel characteristics from censored communication signals. Future research may explore further reduction of residual minor biases and investigate more complex channel scenarios with diverse measurement nonlinearities and varying levels of data censoring.

References

1. Jain, R.: Kalman filter based channel estimation. Int. J. Eng. Res. **3**(4) (2014)
2. Ma, X., Yang, F., Liu, S., Ding, W., Song, J.: Structured compressive sensing-based channel estimation for time frequency training OFDM systems over doubly Selective Channel. IEEE Wirel. Commun. Lett. **6**(2), 266–269 (2017)
3. Wu, S., Liu, X., Wei, Y., Bai, X.: Channel estimation for FBMC/OQAM with fast fading channels by Kalman filter. In: 2018 14th International Wireless Communications & Mobile Computing Conference (IWCMC), pp. 987–992. IEEE, Limassol (2018)
4. Dai, X., Zhang, W., Xu, J., Mitchell, J.E., Yang, Y.: Kalman interpolation filter for channel estimation of LTE downlink in high-mobility environments. EURASIP J. Wirel. Commun. Netw. **2012**(1) (2012)
5. Soni, P., Mishra, A.: Kalman filter based channel equalizer: a literature review. Int. J. Eng. Technol. Adv. Eng. **4**(3) (2014)
6. Rashmi, N., Sarvagya, M.: Channel estimation using extended Kalman filter for superposition coded modulation system. In: 2016 3rd International Conference on Computing for Sustainable Global Development (INDIACom), pp. 3482–3486. IEEE, New Delhi (2016)
7. Sinopoli, B., Schenato, L., Franceschetti, M., Poolla, K., Jordan, M.I., Sastry, S.S.: Kalman filtering with intermittent observations. IEEE Trans. Autom. Control. **49**(9), 1453–1464 (2004)
8. Allik, B., Miller, C., Piovoso, M.J., Zurakowski, R.: The Tobit Kalman filter: an estimator for censored measurements. IEEE Trans. Control Syst. Technol. **24**(1), 365–371 (2016)
9. Loumponias, K., Vretos, N., Tsaklidis, G., et al.: An improved Tobit Kalman filter with adaptive censoring limits. Circuits Syst. Signal Process. **39**, 5588–5617 (2020)
10. Lee, Y., Lee, S., Kim, Y., Han, Y., Park, J., Kim, G.-H.: Capture region of tactile missile equipped with semi-active laser seeker using Tobit Kalman filter. IEEE Access. **10**, 11714–11729 (2022)
11. Xiong, J., Zhan, Y., Sun, Y., Yang, L.: Design and implementation of Beacon tracking system in vehicle-mounted laser communication based on Tobit Kalman filtering algorithm. In: 2021 Asia Communications and Photonics Conference (ACP), pp. 1–3, Shanghai, China (2021)
12. Yang, S., Lin, N., Yuan, R., Hu, J.: Encryption-decryption-based Tobit recursive filtering for nonlinear systems: handling censored measurements. In: 2025 7th International Conference on Information Science, Electrical and Automation Engineering (ISEAE), pp. 584–588. Harbin, China (2025)

Flexible Architecture in AI-Enabled Software-Defined Networks

Collaborative Decision-Making Methods for Non-stationary Communication Environments

Qin Liu[1] , Weiwei Gao[2], Changbo Hou[1](✉) , Bin Wang[1] , and Xiangyu Wu[1]

[1] Harbin Engineering University, Harbin 150001, China
`houchangbo@hrbeu.edu.cn`
[2] Naval Aeronautical University, Qingdao 266000, China

Abstract. With the rapid advancement of artificial intelligence, multi agent reinforcement learning (MARL) has been widely adopted for tasks such as unmanned vehicle formation, robot cooperation, resource scheduling, and collaborative decision-making due to its strong capability to model real world scenarios. However, packet loss in non-stationary communication environments remains a primary obstacle to effective multi agent coordination. To address this issue, this paper introduces a communication mechanism within the QMIX framework and proposes a packet loss information reconstruction technique. By learning the loss function between real messages and predicted messages, it is used to predict messages lost due to unstable communication environments, thereby enhancing the robustness of the model. Experimental results on the SMAC benchmark demonstrate that our approach achieves an average improvement of approximately 5%~15% in collaborative decision-making performance over baseline algorithms and exhibits marked gains in communication resilience. Provide practical and feasible solutions for future research methods related to multi agent systems.

Keywords: Multi-agent Reinforcement Learning · Non-stationary Communication Environments · Packet Loss Information Reconstruction

1 Introduction

In 2017, the State Council promulgated the New Generation Artificial Intelligence Development Plan [1], which calls for major breakthroughs in fundamental theory by 2025 and for significant achievements in the intelligent economy and intelligent society by 2030.

In 2022, OpenAI introduced Chat GPT, capable of sustaining continuous conversations with users, automatically generating text, and performing text summarization and analysis, thereby advancing toward commercialization and signifying a breakthrough in AI's perceptual capabilities [2, 3]. As decision-making remains another focal direction for AI, it continues to face numerous challenges. Early AI decision techniques relied excessively on manual design and were ill-equipped to handle complex decision scenarios. Reinforcement Learning (RL) enables agents to learn through continual interaction

© ICST Institute for Computer Sciences, Social Informatics and Telecommunications Engineering 2026
Published by Springer Nature Switzerland AG 2026. All Rights Reserved
C. Xu et al. (Eds.): MobiMedia 2025, LNICST 670, pp. 47–57, 2026.
https://doi.org/10.1007/978-3-032-16823-8_5

with the environment, selecting actions based on the observed state to maximize cumulative rewards. It is typically formulated as a Markov Decision Process (MDP) [4]. Deep learning offers powerful computational and storage capabilities and has achieved remarkable success across various domains. In particular, Deep Mind [5] introduced the Deep Q-Network (DQN) algorithm, which combines reinforcement learning with deep neural networks to create deep reinforcement learning (DRL), thereby unifying perception, learning, and decision-making within an end-to-end framework from input to action. Applying DRL to the game of Go led to the development of Alpha Zero, which defeated the world Go champion [6]. Subsequently, numerous researchers have focused on this area, introducing techniques such as Deep Recurrent Q-Networks (DRQN) [7], dueling network architectures [8], prioritized experience replay [9], and Double DQN [10] to address the shortcomings of the original DQN algorithm and improve its performance.

In fact, whether in military or civilian domains, typically involving multiple agents that participate concurrently, influence one another, and collaborate to accomplish tasks. In such systems, agents operate under partial observability and engage in fully cooperative, fully competitive, or mixed cooperative competitive interactions to achieve their objectives; this paradigm is known as a Multi-Agent System (MAS). To address these complex challenges, researchers have combined deep reinforcement learning with multi-agent systems to propose Multi-Agent Deep Reinforcement Learning (MDRL) [11], developing algorithms, protocols, and frameworks for applications such as unmanned vehicle formations [12], robotic cooperation [13], resource scheduling [14], and collaborative decision-making [15], thereby demonstrating strong prospects for real-world deployment. Currently, the predominant training paradigm in MDRL is Centralized Training with Decentralized Execution (CTDE). However, owing to the partial observability inherent in a Multi-Agent System (MAS), each agent can only perceive local information rather than the global state, which impedes efficient coordination among agents. Communication-based Multi-agent Deep Reinforcement Learning (CMDRL) is an effective mechanism that assumes agents exchange essential information to facilitate cooperation. Researchers have developed various multi-agent communication protocols—such as CommNet [16] and IC3Net [17] and others [18], enabling each agent to make decisions based on its own partial observations combined with messages received from peers. These methods achieve collective task completion within an MAS and demonstrate strong collaborative capabilities.

This paper focuses on the robustness of inter agent communication in multi-agent deep reinforcement learning. A consistency regularization mechanism is introduced to generate prediction messages based on the historical and current information of other agents. By learning the loss function between real and predicted messages, the lost messages of the agents are recovered, thereby improving the robustness of the model.

2 Problem

2.1 Problem Formulation

In this paper, we model the multi agent collaborative decision-making problem as a Partially Observable Markov Decision Process. The system is formally described by the tuple $G = N, S, U, P, Z, O, \gamma, R$, where N is the set of agents; $s \in S$ is the set of global states; U is the set of joint actions; $a_i \in U$ denotes the action selected by agent i in a given state s_i; $P(s'|s, u) : S \times U^N \times S \to [0, 1]$ is the state transition probability; $z_i \in Z$ denotes the partial observation of agent i in a given state s_i, where z_i as determined by the observation function $O(s, i) : S \times N \to Z$; $\gamma \in [0, 1]$ is the discount factor; $r(s, u) : S \times U^N \to R$ is the joint reward function shared by all agents. The objective of the system is to find a joint policy $\pi(\tau, a)$ that maximizes the global value function $Q_{tot}^{\pi}(\tau, a)$, agent i policy is $\pi_i(u_i|\tau_i) : \tau \times U \to [0, 1]$, where $\tau_i \in \tau := (Z \times U)^*$ is the action observation history available to agent i.

2.2 QMIX Algorithm

In a multi agent system, each agent receives an observation o_i from the environment, selects an action a_i, and subsequently obtains the next observation o_{i+1} along with the corresponding reward r_i^t. Each agent learns its individual action value function $Q_i(\tau_i^t, a_i^t)$ while jointly learning the optimal joint action value function $Q_{tot}(\tau, a)$. The QMIX algorithm employs mixing network to aggregate the individual agents value functions, integrating global state information under the CTDE framework to enhance its performance:

$$\arg_u maxQ_{tot}(\tau, u) = \begin{pmatrix} \arg_{u1} maxQ_1(\tau_1, u_1) \\ \arg_{u2} maxQ_2(\tau_2, u_2) \\ \cdots \\ \arg_{uN} maxQ_N(\tau_N, u_N) \end{pmatrix} \tag{1}$$

The QMIX algorithm computes a non-linear decomposition of the joint state action value function, mapping it into a higher-dimensional space with enhanced representational capacity:

$$Q_{tot}(\tau, u) = f_s(Q_1(\tau_1, u_1), Q_2(\tau_2, u_2), \cdots, Q_N(\tau_N, u_N)) \frac{\partial f_s}{\partial Q_i} \geq 0 \tag{2}$$

The learning objective of QMIX is to minimize the loss function.

$$\sum_i (Q_{tot}(o, a|\theta) - y_i)^2 \tag{3}$$

$$y_i = r + \gamma \max_{a'} \cdot Q_{tot}(o', a'|\theta^-) \tag{4}$$

3 Collaborative Decision-Making Methods for Non-stationary Communication Environments

QMIX does not have an embedded communication mechanism between intelligent agents. Multi agent systems have local observability and cannot obtain global environmental information for collaborative decision-making. To remedy this, we introduce a communication mechanism and construct an inter-agent communication framework (see Fig. 1), whereby agents learn to exchange essential information.

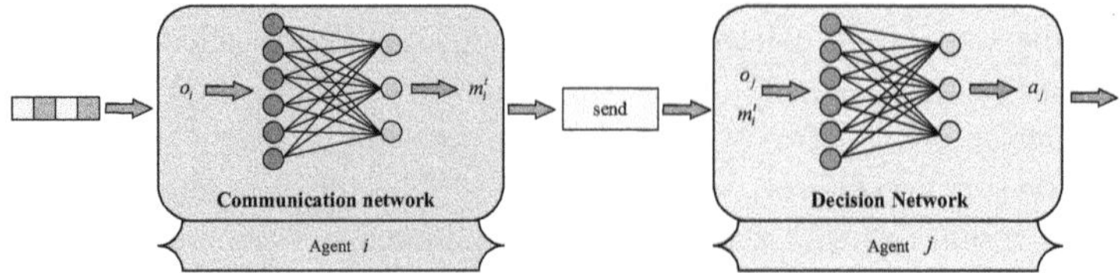

Fig. 1. Inter-agent communication framework

3.1 Information Fusion and Decision Network

In this work, we construct an information fusion and decision network as the communication mechanism within the QMIX algorithm (see Fig. 2). Each agent local observation is broadcast through the network, and agents make decisions based on their own local observations together with the messages received from other agents.

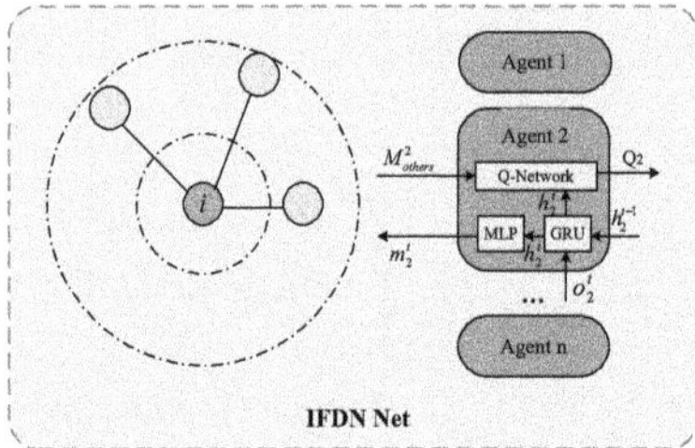

Fig. 2. Information fusion and decision network

The observation encoder employs GRU. At each time step t, agent i feeds x_t its current observation o_i together with the previous hidden state h_{t-1} into the GRU. Within the GRU, the reset gate computes r_t the dependencies needed to capture temporal dynamics by determining how the new input and past memory are combined to form a candidate hidden state $\tilde{h}_t$; simultaneously, the update gate regulates z_t the extent to which historical state information is retained in the current state, thereby updating the memory to produce the current hidden state h_t.

Through the GRU, each agent processes its entire history of observations and actions to produce the final hidden state at the current time step, which serves as the encoder output.

$$h_i^t = f_{obs}\left(o_i^t, h_i^{t-1}\right) \tag{5}$$

The message encoder is implemented as a MLP takes the encoded output h_i^t from the observation encoder as its input. Features a_1 are first extracted via a fully connected layer followed by a rectified linear unit $ReLU(.)$ activation. The activated features a_1 are then fed through a second fully connected layer to produce the agent message m_i^t at the current time step. The message encoder broadcasts these encoded messages m_i^t to the other agents in the system, enabling information fusion that informs each agent decision-making.

$$a_1 = \mathrm{Re}\,LU\left(h_i^t W_1 + b_1\right) \tag{6}$$

$$m_i^t = f_{msg}\left(h_i^t\right) = a_1 W_2 + b_2 \tag{7}$$

Where, W_1 and W_2 are weight matrices, and b_1 and b_2 are bias terms.

The Q-network of the individual decision network takes each agent own observation h_i^t together with the messages m_j^t received from other agents as input and computes the action value function $Q_i\left(o_i, m_j^t, a_i\right)$ for each of the agent available actions a_i. During both the training and testing phases, agents perform exploration and action selection according to $\varepsilon - greedy$ policies, optimize the loss function based on the action value estimates, and select the action with the highest estimated value $Q_i\left(o_i, m_j^t, a_i\right)$.

$$L\left(\theta_q, \theta_{gen}\right) = \sum_{t-1}^{T}\left[\left(y_t^{tot} - Q_{tot}\left(\tau, u, s; \theta_q\right)\right)^2\right] \tag{8}$$

3.2 Packet Loss Information Reconstruction Technique

We integrate a consistency regularization criterion into the information fusion and decision network (Sect. 3.1) to construct a message generation module that enables an agent experiencing packet loss to predict missing messages based on both current and historical communications from other agents in the system (see Fig. 3).

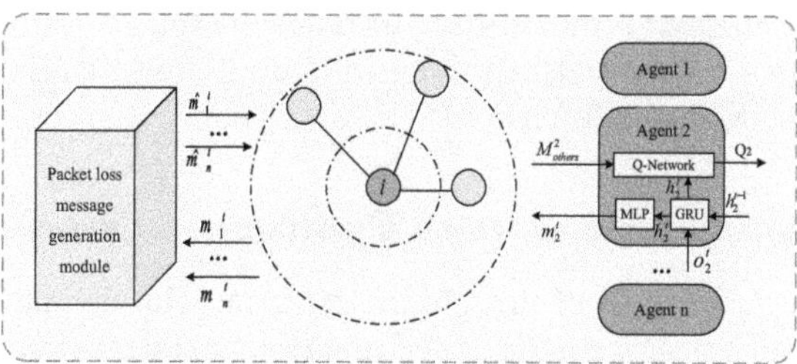

Fig. 3. Message generation module architecture

In the information fusion and decision network, agent i is able to receive messages M_{others}^i from other agents within the system, lead to partial message losses m_t, which are realized by p_{loss} independently discarding message packet blocks according to a specified probability (see Fig. 4).

Assume that a message m_j^t transmitted from agent j to agent i is lost. The message generation module then employs a prediction function implemented to produce a substitute message $\hat{m}_j^t$ based on the available current and historical information, and the loss

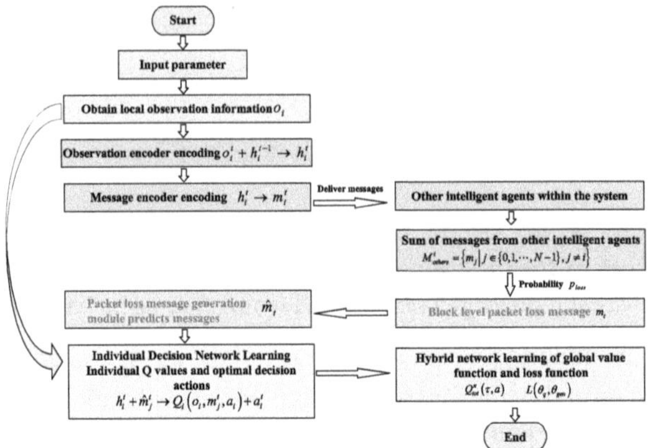

Fig. 4. Flow chart of packet loss message reconstruction module

function $L(\theta_{gen})$ for the message generation module is constructed using consistency regularization.

$$M_{others}^i = \{m_j | j \in \{0, 1, \cdots, N - 1\}, j \neq i\} \tag{9}$$

$$\hat{m}_j^t = f_{N-1}\left(m_j^{t-1}\right) \tag{10}$$

$$f_{N-1}(x) = W_2^{N-1} \cdot \mathrm{Re}\,LU\left(W_1^{N-1} \cdot x + b_1^{N-1}\right) + b_2^{N-1} \tag{11}$$

$$L\left(\theta_{gen}\right) = \sum i(m_t - \hat{m}_t)^2 \tag{12}$$

The network is trained via the defined loss function $L(\theta_{gen})$ to minimize the distance between the lost messages m_t and their reconstructed substitutes m_t, enabling the module to approximate the original information.

3.3 Communication-Integrated QMIX Algorithm with Consistency Criterion

The loss function $L(\theta_q, \theta_{gen})$ of the QMIX algorithm with the introduction of communication and consistency criteria is the ability of multi-agent systems to achieve collaborative task completion in unstable communication environments after multiple rounds of iterative learning (Fig. 5).

$$L\left(\theta_q, \theta_{gen}\right) = \sum_{t-1}^{T}\left[\left(y_{tot}^t - Q_{tot}\left(\tau, u, s; \theta_q\right)\right)^2 + \lambda L\left(\theta_{gen}\right)\right] \tag{13}$$

$$y_{tot}^t = r_t + \gamma \max_{u'} Q_{tot}\left(\tau', u', s'; \theta_q\right) \tag{14}$$

The detailed implementation procedure of the overall algorithm is shown in Table 1.

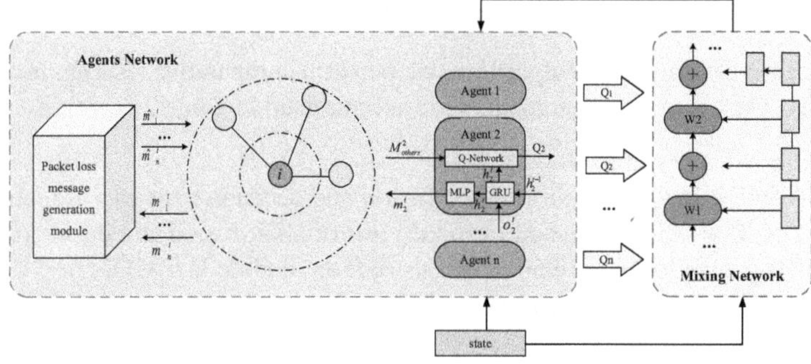

Fig. 5. QMIX algorithm with integrated communication and consistency criterion

Table 1. Pseudocode of the algorithm

Input: Agent i local observations o_i, messages received from other agents in the system o_j, initialized historical state information h_i^0, packet-loss probability p_{loss}.

1 Encode observations using the observation encoder $o_i^t + h_i^{t-1} \rightarrow h_i^t$;

2 Encode using the message encoder $h_i^t \rightarrow m_i^t$, transmit them to the other agents;

3 Receive messages from other agents $M_{others}^i = \{m_j | j \in \{0, 1, \cdots, N-1\}, j \neq i\}$;

4 Drop message m_t blocks at the block level with probability p_{loss};

5 The message generation module predicts the messages lost due to packet loss $\hat{m}_t$;

6 The individual decision network learns each agent Q-values and the optimal action

$h_i^t + \hat{m}_j^t \rightarrow Q_i\left(o_i, m_j^t, a_i\right) + a_i^t$;

7 The mixing network learns the global value function
$Q_{tot}^\pi(\tau, a)$ and optimizes the loss function $L(\theta_q, \theta_{gen})$;

Output: The optimal joint policy $\pi(\tau, a)$ of the multi-agent system.

4 Results and Analysis

4.1 Experimental Environment

In SMAC, allied agents learn policies to perform actions and engage enemy units, while enemy units are controlled by built-in environment algorithms to provide an adversarial challenge, and we therefore choose it as the testbed for our experiments.

In the SMAC environment, each agent action space is discrete. An agent local observability is determined by its attack range and the positions and health values of nearby units. The system joint reward is defined as the total damage dealt by our agents to the enemy, and the overall objective is to defeat all enemy units while minimizing damage to our own. We evaluate our algorithm in the 3 m and 3s_vs_5z battle scenarios.

4.2 Baseline Algorithms and Implementation Details

To validate the efficacy of our algorithm, we perform comparative tests against baseline algorithms. The agent hyperparameters are summarized in Table 2:

1. QMIX: Basic algorithm.
2. IFDN+QMIX: In QMIX, information fusion and decision networks are introduced.
3. CR-IFDN+QMIX: Our method introduce information fusion and decision network, as well as packet loss information reconstruction module in QMIX.
4. VBC+QMIX: An communication model based on variance control in QMIX.

Table 2. Agent parameter list

Parameter	Value
Learning rate	0.0005
Discount factor	0.99
Experience sample size	64
Replay buffer size	1000000
Target network update interval	200
Initial exploration rate	1.0
Final exploration rate	0.05
Exploration rate decay rate	10000
Hidden layer dimension	64
Message dimension	32
Packet-loss probability	0.4
Regularization weight	0.01

4.3 Ablation Experiment

The experiments were performed in the 3 m and the more complex 3s_vs_5z. We conducted eight independent training runs with the same number of timesteps, averaged the results to obtain the mean win rate, and compared these to evaluate the impact of communication quality differences on the agent collaborative performance.

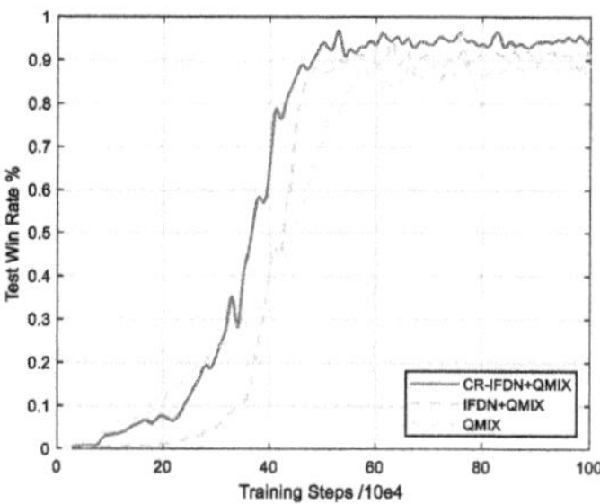

Fig. 6. Comparison of average win rate in the 3 m

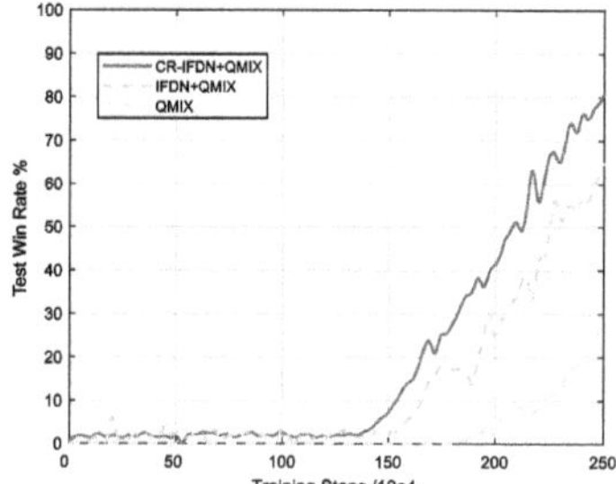

Fig. 7. Comparison of average win rate in the 3s_vs_5z

Table 3. Experimental analysis of the average winning rate in Ablation experiments

Map	CR-IFDN+QMIX	IFDN+QMIX	QMIX
3s_vs_5z	80.3%	64.7%	29.0%
3 m	93.4%	91.8%	88.6%

As shown in Fig. 7 and Table 3, in the more complex 3s_vs_5z, CR-IFDN+QMIX algorithm exhibits a marked advantage in collaborative decision-making. Both IFDN+QMIX and QMIX suffer from limited agent observability, making it difficult for their policies to defeat the enemy and obtain rewards within the finite training timesteps. Our model enables agents to access rich, reliable global state information via reconstructed communications, thereby accelerating convergence and achieving higher win rates. In the simpler 3 m, all three algorithms eventually attain high training win rates; however, as Fig. 6 illustrates, our method achieves faster convergence and greater stability.

4.4 Comparative Experiment

To further validate the effectiveness of the algorithm, the experiment will compare the improved algorithm with the VBC+QMIX algorithm. The VBC algorithm allows agents to communicate using only valid information during execution. This experiment is trained in the scenario corridor, with 20 rounds of testing conducted every 10000 time steps. The winning rate of each round is recorded, and the experimental results are averaged to output the average winning rate (Fig. 8).

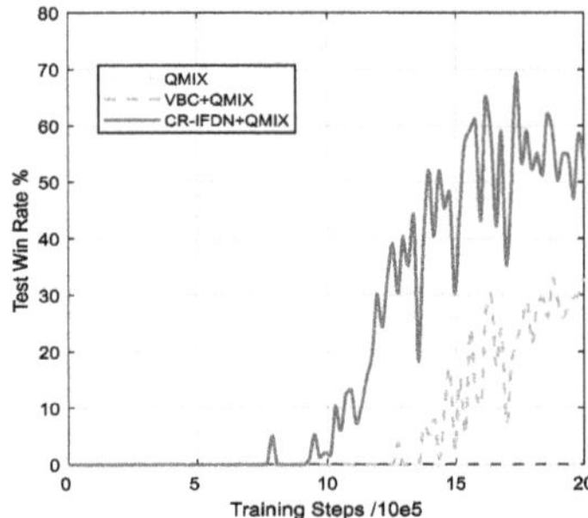

Fig. 8. Comparison of average win rate in the corridor

The experimental results indicate that the scene is complex and difficult to converge, and the QMIX algorithm failed to train an effective model. The average win rate of the VBC+QMIX algorithm has slightly improved, but it has not converged to a very good effect. The improved performance of the algorithm in this article is better, and it can complete tasks with a higher probability and achieve victory.

5 Conclusion

In multi agent reinforcement learning, two major challenges are limited cooperative capability and non stationary communication environments. We introduces a communication mechanism to construct an information fusion and decision network, and proposes a packet loss reconstruction technique to enhance the QMIX algorithm. Comparative experiments in the SMAC environment demonstrate that our method maintains robust inter agent communication under high packet loss rates in complex adversarial scenarios, resulting in a stable communication channel and an approximately 5%~15% improvement in collaborative decision making performance over baseline algorithms. Future work will focus on further improving communication efficiency.

References

1. Rudolph, J., Tan, S., Tan, S.: ChatGPT: bullshit Spewer or the end of traditional assessments in higher education. J. Appl. Learn. Teach. **6**(1) (2023)
2. Liebrenz, M., Schleifer, R., Buadze, A., et al.: Generating scholarly content with ChatGPT: ethical challenges for medical publishing. Lancet Digit. Health. **5**(3), e105–e106 (2023)

3. Farhadi, A., Mirzarezaee, M., Sharifi, A., et al.: Review: domain adaptation in reinforcement learning. Front. Inf. Technol. Electron. Eng. **25**(11), 1446–1466 (2024)

4. Mnih, V., Kavukcuoglu, K., Silver, D., et al.: Human-level control through deep reinforcement learning. Nature. **518**(7540), 529–533 (2015)

5. Silver, D., Schrittwieser, J., Simonyan, K., et al.: Mastering the game of go without human knowledge. Nature. **550**(7676), 354–359 (2017)

6. Hausknecht, M.; Stone, P.: Deep recurrent G-learning for partially observable MDPs. Proceedings of the AAAI Conference on Artificial Intelligence 23(2), 4721–4734 (2015).

7. Wang, Z., Schaul, T., Hessel, M., et al.: Dueling network architectures for deep reinforcement learning. In: International Conference on Machine Learning, vol. 1995–2003, (2016)

8. Schaul, T., Quan, J., Antonoglou, I., et al.: Prioritized experience replay. In: International Conference on Learning Representations, vol. 1822, p. 06594 (2015)

9. Van Hasselt, H.; Guez, A.; Silver, D.: Deep reinforcement learning with double Q-learning. Proceedings of the AAAI Conference on Artificial Intelligence 30(1), 331–342 (2016).

10. Kraemer, L., Banerjee, B.: Multi-agent reinforcement learning as a rehearsal for decentralized planning. Neurocomputing. **190**, 82–94 (2016)

11. Qu, X., Li, C., Jiang, Y., et al.: Cooperative pursuit of unmanned surface vehicles using multi-agent reinforcement learning. J. Shanghai Jiaotong Univ. (Sci.). (prepublish), 1–8 (2025)

12. Garcia, G., Eskandarian, A., Fabregas, E., et al.: Cooperative formation control of a multi-agent Khepera IV Mobile robots system using deep reinforcement learning. Appl. Sci. **15**(4), 1777–1777 (2025)

13. Mohammadi, P., Darshi, R., Darabkhani, G.H., et al.: Multiagent energy management system design using reinforcement learning: the new energy lab training set case study. Int. Trans. Electr. Energy Syst. **2025**(1), 3574030–3574030 (2025)

14. You, C., Wu, Y., Cai, J., et al.: Dynamic subtask representation and assignment in cooperative multi-agent tasks. Neurocomputing. **628**, 129535–129535 (2025)

15. Sukhbaatar, F.R.: Learning multiagent communication with backpropagation. Adv. Neural Inf. Proces. Syst. **29**(1), 64–73 (2016)

16. Singh, A., Jain, T., Sukhbaatar, S.: Learning when to communicate at scale in multiagent cooperative and competitive tasks. In: International Conference on Learning Representations, vol. 1812, p. 09755 (2018)

17. Wang, H., Yu, Y., Jiang, Y.: Review of Progress in communication-based multi-agent reinforcement learning (part I). Sci. China Inf. Sci. **34**(1), 287–314 (2022)

18. Nguyen, D.T., Kumar, A., Lau, H.C.: Credit assignment for collective multiagent RL with global rewards. Adv. Neural Inf. Proces. Syst. **31**(2), 437–446 (2018)

Wireless Body Area Network (WBAN)

Non-intrusive In-Bed Patient Monitoring via Piezoelectric Signal Analysis and Temporal Deep Learning*

Xufeng Gu[1], Zhigang Li[1], Shunan Wu[2,3,4]([✉]), Xu Jiao[2,3,4], and Qiliang Li[3]

[1] College of Information and Communication Engineering, Harbin Engineering University, Harbin, China
`guxufeng@hrbeu.edu.cn`, `lizhigang@hrbeu.edu.cn`
[2] Peking University Nanchang Innovation Institute, Nanchang, China
`jiaoxu@wittower.com`
[3] College of Engineering, Peking University, Beijing, China
`qiliang.li@pku.edu.cn`
[4] Beijing MicroVibration DataNet Technology Co. Ltd., Beijing, China
`shunan.wu@pkuncii.cn`

Abstract. Accurate and non-intrusive patient identification is vital for ensuring safety in clinical environments, particularly in scenarios involving bedridden or unconscious individuals. This paper proposes a novel in-bed identity recognition framework based on multi-channel piezoelectric sensor arrays and deep learning. A comprehensive dataset was constructed using an 8×8 piezoelectric sensor grid, capturing 5,040 samples across 30 individuals in 168 distinct in-bed action classes covering four standard postures and multiple bed zones. Two data processing strategies were explored—image-based and time-series modeling. Experimental comparisons among AlexNet, ResNet, InceptionTime and XceptionTime demonstrated that temporal models, particularly XceptionTime, offered superior performance, achieving 98.73% average accuracy and a peak of 99.50%. Furthermore, a channel-wise averaging replacement data augmentation strategy was introduced to improve generalization under limited sample conditions, leading to performance gains of up to 9.3%. The study also investigated the influence of time window lengths, confirming that a 10-second window optimally captured temporal identity features. Overall, the proposed framework offers a robust, privacy-preserving, and real-time solution for in-bed individual recognition. Future work will focus on expanding recognition capabilities to include unregistered individuals and integrating the system into broader smart healthcare infrastructures.

Keywords: Individual Recognition · Deep learning · Time series data augmentation

---

*This research was funded by the Peking University Nanchang Innovation Institute.

C. Xu et al. (Eds.): MobiMedia 2025, LNICST 670, pp. 61–73, 2026.
https://doi.org/10.1007/978-3-032-16823-8_6

1 Introduction

With the global aging population accelerating, healthcare systems face growing challenges in managing elderly patients with chronic diseases. Among these challenges, accurate patient identification is critical to ensuring safety and preventing medical errors. The China Hospital Association Patient Safety Goals (2025 Edition) explicitly states that correct patient identification should be a top priority. However, in clinical practice, various interfering factors continue to contribute to patient misidentification, leading to incorrect diagnoses, treatment plans, pathology assessments, or specimen labeling, often with serious consequences. According to a 2018 report by the Joint Commission on Accreditation of Healthcare Organizations, 409 out of 3,326 reported medical incidents (12.3%) between 2014 and 2017 were directly related to patient identification errors [1]. Such incidents are especially hazardous in high-risk environments like intensive care units and operating rooms, where patients may be sedated or unconscious.

Mainstream biometric identification technologies—such as fingerprinting [2], facial recognition [3], and voice recognition [4] have seen widely commercialized but face limitations. These methods are vulnerable to spoofing (e.g., mold forgery or voice synthesis) and are often impractical in bedridden scenarios. Although iris recognition [5] offers high precision, its high cost and operational complexity hinder its deployment in everyday clinical settings.

In contrast, piezoelectric sensor-based identity recognition offers a promising alternative. These systems non-invasively capture human vibration signals (e.g., from respiration or heartbeat), requiring no active cooperation from the subject while offering inherent anti-spoofing characteristics due to individual-specific mechanical signatures. As research interest in this area grows, several promising developments have emerged. For instance, Pouyan et al. [6] constructed the first open-source sleep posture dataset using dual pressure sensing pads in 2017, achieving over 80% individual recognition accuracy under three bed rest postures with convolutional neural networks, validating the feasibility of this technological approach. Kaczmarek et al. [7] introduced "Assentication," a posture-based identification technique that achieved 94.2% accuracy with 16 sensors. In 2019, Davoodnia et al. [8] proposed an intelligent mattress-based method using multi-task deep convolutional networks, nearing 100% accuracy on the Pmat-Data dataset. Other innovations include Konings et al.'s [9] capacitance sensing floors paired with bidirectional long short-term memory networks (BLSTM) (98.12% accuracy), Davoodnia et al.'s [10] multi-task learning approach linking pressure features with BMI and identity (>95% accuracy), and Zhang et al.'s [11] contrastive learning method using a high-density pressure array, reaching 87.96% accuracy.

Building on these advancements, this study proposes a deep-learning-based identity recognition framework tailored to bedridden individuals. The system integrates an array-based piezoelectric sensor network with advanced temporal modeling techniques. Additionally, to address the challenges posed by limited sample sizes in practical settings, a novel data augmentation strategy is introduced to improve model generalization. The objective is to achieve accurate, real-time, and non-invasive identification that is both clinically viable and privacy preserving. This approach provides a new technological direction for applications in elderly care institutions, long-term care wards, and home monitoring environments. Compared to vision-based surveillance methods, it eliminates the risk of privacy leakage while assisting medical staff in accurately tracking the in-bed behavior of target individuals, thereby significantly improving monitoring efficiency and the quality of personalized care.

2   Dataset Construction

2.1   Data Acquisition Device

This study is conducted based on a data acquisition system developed by Beijing MicroVibration DataNet Technology Corporation, the SleepMatrix® noncontact sleep monitoring system, which uses an array of piezoelectric sensors. The hardware architecture of the system is illustrated in Fig. 1.

The data acquisition device is divided into two functional units: the acquisition module and the data processing module. The acquisition module is composed of ceramic piezoelectric sensors, which convert external vibration signals into electrical signals. As shown in Fig. 1, the sensors are arranged in an 8×8 layout, with each of the 8 horizontal piezoelectric sensor strips evenly embedded with 8 sensors, enabling 64-channel data collection.

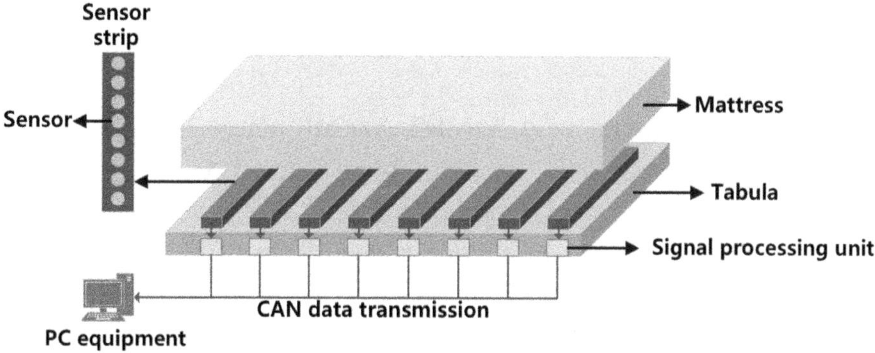

Fig. 1. Design and configuration of piezoelectric sensor arrays for data acquisition.

The data processing module uses the STM32F103 chip as the main control unit. This module handles signal amplification, signal sampling, and analog to digital conversion. It ultimately produces digital signals at a sampling frequency 40 Hz. These digital signals are then assembled into data frames and transmitted to the host computer via the CAN communication protocol for further processing and storage.

The device is easy to deploy, adaptable to various environments, and capable of collecting physiological information without requiring any active cooperation from the subject. It provides a comfortable and comprehensive technological solution for real-time monitoring of bedridden individuals.

2.2 Data Collection Scheme

The dataset constructed in this study comprises 30 subjects. In the data-acquisition protocol, the basic lying-posture dimension categorizes an individual's in-bed posture into four core postures—supine, prone, left lateral, and right lateral—while the spatial-position dimension divides the bed area into three zones: left side, center, and right side. Integrating these two dimensions yields 12 primary categories. During collection, hand and foot movements were further refined and combined with the 12 primary categories to produce 168 distinct action classes—i.e., 168 samples per subject. Ultimately, a piezoelectric dataset of $30 \times 168 = 5040$ samples was assembled; whose structural distribution is shown in Table 1.

Table 1. Multi-channel piezo signal data set labeling scheme.

In-bed status	Supine	Left lateral	Right lateral	Prone	Total
Center	12	16	16	12	
Right side	12	16	16	12	
Left side	12	16	16	12	
Total	36	48	48	36	168

3 Data Processing and Model Architecture Design

3.1 Dimension Reduction Based on Peak-to-Peak Value

To visualize the spatial pressure distribution of the sensor network, the time series data must be reconstructed into 8×8 grayscale images that mirror the sensors' physical layout. A classic dimensionality reduction technique for time series data is PCA [12], but owing to the specific characteristics of the dataset used here, a peak to peak valuebased reduction method yields a clearer representation of the in-bed subject's pressure distribution. The precise operations of this method are given by Eqs. 1 and 2

$$V_{ppj} = \max(A'_{.j}) - \min(A'_{.j}) \tag{1}$$

$$V_{pp} = [V_{pp1}, V_{pp2}, \dots, V_{pp64}] \tag{2}$$

Here, $A \in \mathbf{R}^{400 \times 64}$ denotes the original data matrix, and A_{ij} is the element in the ith and jth column of A. V_{ppj} represents the peak-to-peak value of the jth sensor over 400 sampling points, and the resulting feature vector $V_{pp} \in \mathbf{R}^{64}$ characterizes the pressure distribution. Figure 2 shows the heatmaps of the in bed pressure distributions reconstructed by this method for two different subjects.

Fig. 2. Pressure distribution maps of different individuals lying supine at the center of the bed.

3.2   Image-Based Individual Recognition Network

In this study, a convolutional neural network model for individual identification was built based on the classic residual neural network architecture (Res-Net18) [13], as illustrated in Figs. 3 and 4.

Since the data dimension (8 × 8) is relatively small, in constructing this model, compared with the original ResNet18 architecture, it reduces the number of residual blocks and decreases both the convolutional kernel sizes and strides in the convolutional layers, thereby mitigating the risk of overfitting during training.

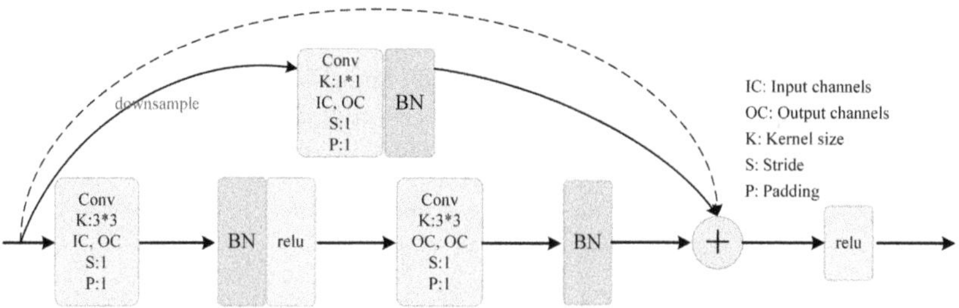

Fig. 3. Residual block architecture.

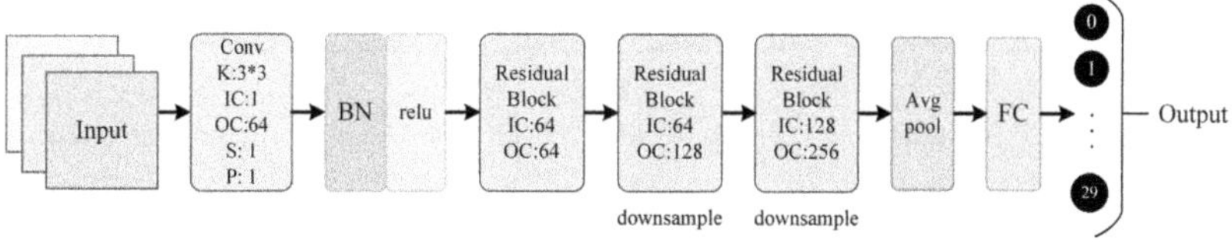

Fig. 4. ResNet architecture.

3.3 Individual Identification Network Based on Time Series

Temporal deep learning uses models to analyze chronological numerical sequences. Since the emergence of relevant datasets [14], this technique has demonstrated significant advantages in fields requiring long term feature modeling, such as modulation recognition [15] and signal recognition [16].

The rationale for this technical approach lies in the inherently multichannel time series nature of the piezoelectric signals. As shown in Fig. 5, signals from the same sensor differ between subjects in identical postures. Compared to static feature extraction, time series modeling better captures the dynamic, identity-specific information in the data.

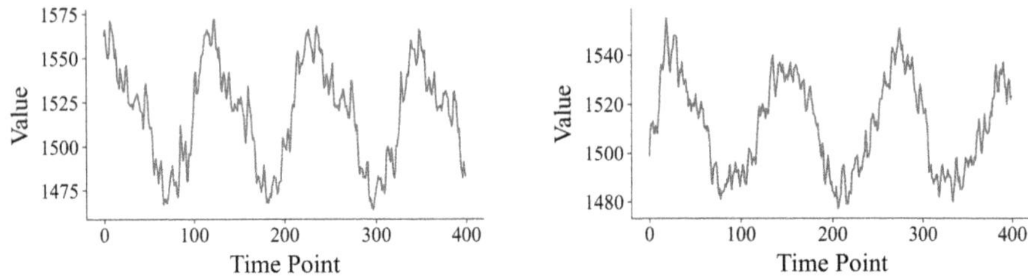

Fig. 5. The piezo signals collected by different individuals.

In this study, we built a deep learning model for processing multichannel time series data based on the XceptionTime architecture [17]. During its construction, the model's structure was optimized to match the dimensionality of our dataset, with particular emphasis on expanding the channel dimension to better accommodate the 64 channel time series inputs. The resulting model architecture is illustrated in Figs. 6 and 7.

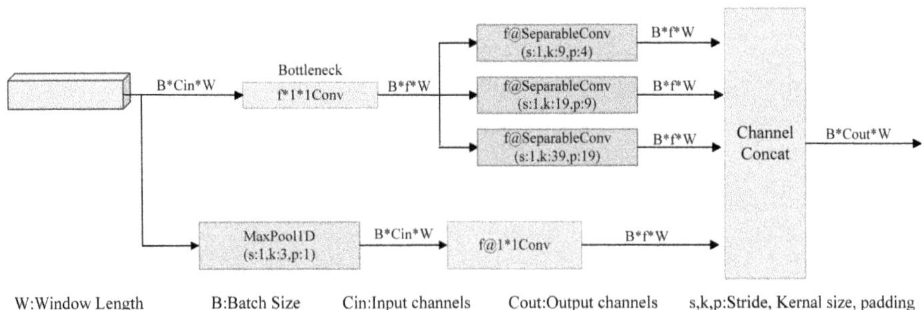

Fig. 6. XceptionTime module.

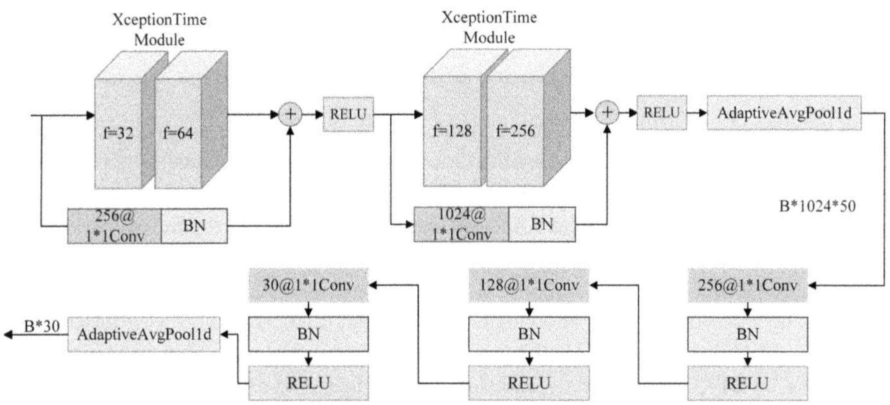

Fig. 7. XceptionTime architecture.

3.4 Channel-Wise Averaging Replacement Data Augmentation Strategy

In the actual collection scene, the number of collected samples may be limited, and the model is easy to be overfitting when the size of the training sample data is small. Therefore, it is a simple and effective method to expand the number of samples in the training set.

Suppose the dataset is $X \in \mathbf{R}^{B \times C \times T}$ where B is the batch size, $C = 64$ is the number of channels and $T = 400$ is the time series length. For each sample x, a Bernoulli mask is generated:

$$M_{b,c,t} = \begin{cases} 0 & \text{Drop with probability } p = 0.3 \\ 1 & \text{Retain with probability } 1 - p \end{cases} \tag{3}$$

Zero out dropped channels while preserving original values of retained channels:

$$x_{valid} = x \odot M \tag{4}$$

Calculate average value over surviving channels:

$$\mu = \frac{\Sigma_{c=1}^{C} x_{valid}}{\Sigma_{c=1}^{C} M} \tag{5}$$

Replace the discarded channels with mean values while retaining all the other channels:

$$x_{augmented} = \begin{cases} \mu \; if \; M = 0 \\ x \; if \; M = 1 \end{cases} \tag{6}$$

During training, augmented data are combined with the original data to expand the training set, which is then fed into the deep learning model for training.

4 Experiment and Result Analysis

4.1 Model Performance Under Different Data Processing Strategies

This section aims to identify the optimal model architecture for individual identification. In addition to our baseline model, we built two classic deep learning architectures for comparative experiments: AlexNet [18] for image-based processing and InceptionTime [19] for time-series analysis. This comprehensive evaluation assesses the recognition performance of different models and data processing strategies in our task.

For the training setup, the dataset was split into training, validation, and test sets in a ratio of 3:1:1. During model training, we set the maximum number of epochs to 240, batch size to 128, and learning rate to 0.001. The model with the lowest validation loss was retained, and the final evaluation metric was the mean test accuracy across five training runs.

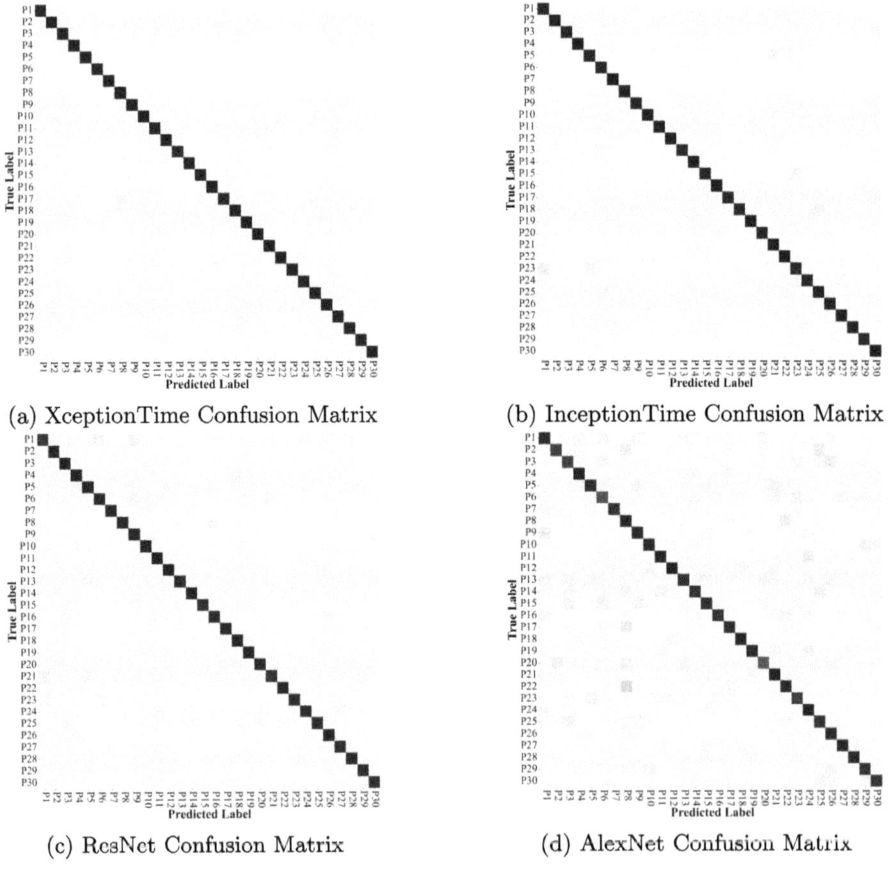

(a) XceptionTime Confusion Matrix

(b) InceptionTime Confusion Matrix

(c) ResNet Confusion Matrix

(d) AlexNet Confusion Matrix

Fig. 8. Confusion matrices of different model.

Figure 8 presents the confusion matrices of all four models on the test set. The XceptionTime matrix displays the most distinct diagonal pattern, demonstrating its superior classification capability among the compared architectures.

Table 2. Model test accuracy.

Model type	Time series neural networks		Image neural networks	
	XceptionTime	InceptionTime	ResNet	AlexNet
Mean accuracy (%)	**98.73 ± 0.44**	93.49 ± 1.92	91.01 ± 0.52	79.25 ± 1.12
Peak accuracy (%)	**99.50**	95.54	91.76	81.08

Experimental results are presented in Table 2. The results show that, compared with image-based models, time-series models deliver superior recognition performance. This indicates that the rhythmic patterns of respiration and heartbeat embedded in the data provide more distinctive identity-related information than static pressure distributions. Among the four models evaluated, XceptionTime performed best, achieving an average test accuracy of 98.73% over five independent runs and a peak accuracy of 99.50%. These gains suggest that its use of depthwise separable convolutions and adaptive average pooling layers helps the network better capture long-term temporal features and thus boosts recognition performance. In contrast, InceptionTime achieved an average accuracy of 93.49%; although its multi-scale parallel convolutions capture features at different temporal resolutions, its ability to extract long-term dependencies is somewhat weaker. The ResNet model reached an average accuracy of 91.01%, significantly outperforming AlexNet, which indicates that residual connections facilitate more effective spatial feature extraction from the 8×8 image representations. AlexNet ranked last with an accuracy of 79.25%, reflecting that its shallow convolutional and fully connected architecture lacks sufficient capacity to extract informative features from such low-dimensional image data.

4.2 Time Window Impact Analysis

In time-series classification tasks, the length of the time window significantly influences model performance. Building on the results of Experiment 1, this study systematically investigates how different time window lengths affect the recognition accuracy of XceptionTime and InceptionTime, aiming to identify the optimal window size for model training.

The original dataset was collected using a fixed 10-second window. To evaluate the impact of window length, we segmented the time-series data into subsequences of varying durations (1 s, 2 s, 5 s, and 10 s) and trained the models accordingly. All other training configurations remained consistent with Experiment 1. The experimental results are presented in Fig. 9.

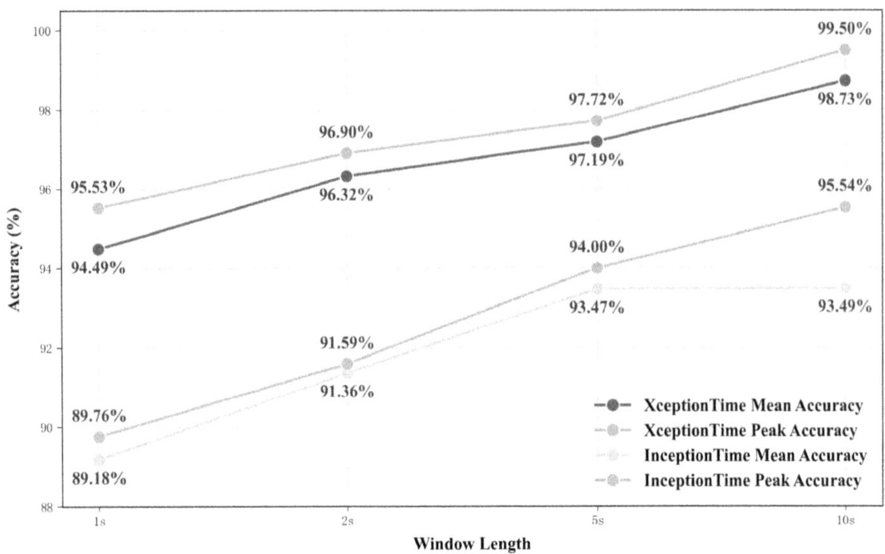

Fig. 9. Model performance under different time window lengths.

The experimental results demonstrate that, across both sequence model architectures, there is a strong positive correlation between time window length and identification accuracy. Specifically, when the window length is extended from 1 s to 10 s, the mean recognition accuracy of the XceptionTime model improves by 4.24%. This improvement can be attributed to the fact that longer windows more fully capture the subject's extended physiological signatures (e.g., cardiac and respiratory rhythms), enabling the model to learn more discriminative long term temporal patterns. These findings further corroborate the observation made in the first experiment—that the respiratory and cardiac rhythms embedded in the data possess high identity discriminative power. Consequently, our results offer a quantitative basis for selecting time window configurations in practical deployments.

4.3   Data Augmentation Performance Under Limited Samples

To address the potential limitation of sample collection in practical deployment scenarios, this study simulates a data-scarce environment by controlling the number of training samples. Specifically, for each subject, n samples are selected from each of the 12 postural categories (4 postures × 3 bed positions), forming a training set of 12 × n samples per person. A fixed validation strategy is employed, where 5 samples are retained for each category and evenly split into a validation set and a test set, resulting in 30 validation and 30 test samples per subject.

To further mitigate the risk of overfitting, a dynamic learning rate mechanism is adopted: if the validation loss does not decrease for 20 consecutive epochs, the learning rate is halved. To evaluate the generalizability of the channel-wise averaging data augmentation strategy, five independent experiments are conducted on both the XceptionTime and InceptionTime models. The evaluation metrics remain consistent with previous experiments, and the results are presented in Table 3.

Table 3. Test accuracy under different sample sizes.

Model	Setting	12	24	36	48	60
XceptionTime	Base	61.97 ± 0.49	85.38 ± 0.56	90.17 ± 0.63	93.91 ± 0.41	95.35 ± 0.38
	Aug	71.27 ± 1.83	88.98 ± 1.01	93.00 ± 0.54	95.71 ± 0.50	96.40 ± 0.23
InceptionTime	Base	47.13 ± 0.94	68.60 ± 0.59	76.35 ± 1.51	83.73 ± 1.27	85.64 ± 0.61
	Aug	56.98 ± 1.25	79.37 ± 1.89	86.33 ± 1.07	90.95 ± 0.09	92.39 ± 1.07

The results demonstrate that the channel-wise averaging data augmentation technique plays a crucial role in enhancing model performance, particularly in low-sample scenarios. For the XceptionTime model, which was tested under a data-scarce condition with only 12 samples per subject, the application of this technique led to a notable improvement in recognition accuracy, increasing by 9.3%. This suggests that channel-wise averaging effectively mitigates the challenges posed by limited data, enhancing the model's ability to generalize and perform more reliably in real-world applications where data may be scarce.

5   Conclusion

This study introduces a novel, non-contact framework for in-bed individual identification using multi-channel piezoelectric signals combined with deep learning techniques. A comprehensive dataset was constructed, covering four common lying postures across various bed zones, enabling robust identity recognition under diverse conditions. Comparative analysis of model architectures revealed that time-series-based models, particularly XceptionTime, significantly outperformed image-based approaches, achieving a peak accuracy of 99.50% and a mean accuracy of 98.73%. To optimize model performance, the effect of time window length was investigated, confirming that a 10-second window best captured identity-relevant temporal features. Moreover, to address real-world limitations in data collection, a channel-wise averaging replacement augmentation strategy was proposed. This technique effectively enhanced recognition accuracy under data-scarce conditions, with improvements of up to 9.3% for the XceptionTime model. The proposed framework not only ensures high accuracy and real-time identification but also maintains patient comfort and privacy, making it highly applicable in clinical and eldercare environments. Future research will explore unknown identity detection and system integration into smart healthcare infrastructures.

References

1. De Rezende, H.A., Melleiro, M.M., Shimoda, G.T.: Interventions to reduce patient identification errors in the hospital setting: a systematic review protocol. JBI Evid. Synth. **17**(1), 37–42 (2019)
2. Ali, M.M., Mahale, V.H., Yannawar, P., Gaikwad, A.: Overview of fingerprint recognition system. In: 2016 International Conference on Electrical, Electronics, and Optimization Techniques (ICEEOT), pp. 1334–1338. IEEE (2016)
3. Duan, W., et al.: A review of cross-age facial recognition based on discriminative models. In: International Conference on Intelligent Computing, pp. 262–273. Springer (2024)
4. Sarbast, H.: Voice recognition based on machine learning classification algorithms: a review. Indones. J. Comput. Sci. **13**(3) (2024)
5. Yin, Y., He, S., Zhang, R., Chang, H., Zhang, J.: Deep learning for iris recognition: a review. Neural Comput. Appl. 1–49 (2025)
6. Pouyan, M.B., Birjandtalab, J., Heydarzadeh, M., Nourani, M., Ostadabbas, S.: A pressure map dataset for posture and subject analytics. In: 2017 IEEE EMBS International Conference on Biomedical & Health Informatics (BHI), pp. 65–68. IEEE (2017)
7. Kaczmarek, T., Ozturk, E., Tsudik, G.: Assentication: user de-authentication and lunchtime attack mitigation with seated posture biometric. In: International Conference on Applied Cryptography and Network Security, pp. 616–633. Springer (2018)
8. Davoodnia, V., Etemad, A.: Identity and posture recognition in smart beds with deep multitask learning. In: 2019 IEEE International Conference on Systems, Man and Cybernetics (SMC), pp. 3054–3059. IEEE (2019)
9. Konings, D., Alam, F., Faulkner, N., de Jong, C.: Identity and gender recognition using a capacitive sensing floor and neural networks. Sensors **22**(19), 7206 (2022)
10. Davoodnia, V., Slinowsky, M., Etemad, A.: Deep multitask learning for pervasive BMI estimation and identity recognition in smart beds. J. Ambient Intell. Humaniz. Comput. **14**(5), 5463–5477 (2023)
11. Zhang, Y., et al.: Contrastive learning-based user identification with limited data on smart textiles. In: 2024 IEEE International Conference on Systems, Man, and Cybernetics (SMC), pp. 2820–2825. IEEE (2024)
12. Lin, Y., Zhu, X., Zheng, Z., Dou, Z., Zhou, R.: The individual identification method of wireless device based on dimensionality reduction and machine learning. J. Supercomput. **75**(6), 3010–3027 (2019)
13. Wu, S., Zhong, S., Liu, Y.: Deep residual learning for image recognition. Multimed. Tools Appl. 1–17 (2017)
14. Ya, T., et al.: Large-scale real-world radio signal recognition with deep learning. Chin. J. Aeronaut. **35**(9), 35–48 (2022)
15. Tu, Y., Lin, Y., Hou, C., Mao, S.: Complex-valued networks for automatic modulation classification. IEEE Trans. Veh. Technol. **69**(9), 10085–10089 (2020)
16. Lin, Y., Tu, Y., Dou, Z., Chen, L., Mao, S.: Contour stella image and deep learning for signal recognition in the physical layer. IEEE Trans. Cogn. Commun. Network. **7**(1), 34–46 (2020)
17. Rahimian, E., Zabihi, S., Atashzar, S.F., Asif, A., Mohammadi, A.: XceptionTime: independent time-window XceptionTime architecture for hand gesture classification. In: ICASSP 2020—2020 IEEE International Conference on Acoustics, Speech and Signal Processing (ICASSP), pp. 1304–1308. IEEE (2020)

18. Krizhevsky, A., Sutskever, I., Hinton, G.E.: ImageNet classification with deep convolutional neural networks. Adv. Neural Inf. Process. Syst. **25** (2012)
19. Ismail Fawaz, H., et al.: InceptionTime: finding AlexNet for time series classification. Data Min. Knowl. Discov. **34**(6), 1936–1962 (2020)

Computational Framework
and Structure for Big Data

A Privacy-Preserving Federated Learning Framework with Adaptive Client Clustering for Healthcare AI

Yexuan Hu[1], Yan Sun[1], Shunan Wu[2,3,4]($\boxtimes$), Qiliang Li[3], and Zhaoming Li[1]

[1] College of Information and Communication Engineering, Harbin Engineering University, Harbin, China
[2] Peking University Nanchang Innovation Institute, Nanchang, China
[3] College of Engineering, Peking University, Beijing, China
[4] Beijing MicroVibration DataNet Technology Co. Ltd., Beijing, China
`shunan.wu@pkuncii.cn`

Abstract. This paper proposes FedCLUS, a privacy-preserving FL framework with dynamic client clustering to address data heterogeneity and data privacy challenges in medical domains. By leveraging pseudo-data generated through a Conditional WGAN-GP, the server estimates model similarity and clusters clients accordingly. This enables adaptive and personalized model aggregation without sharing sensitive patient data. The approach improves clustering accuracy, model robustness and performance under non-IID conditions. Experimental results on a sleep posture classification task demonstrate that FedCLUS outperforms existing FL methods in both accuracy and privacy protection across varying privacy budgets and gradient clipping settings, offering a scalable and secure solution for healthcare applications.

Keywords: Federated learning · Generative adversarial networks · Pseudo-data · Client clustering · Differential privacy

1 Introduction

AI-driven electronic healthcare systems confront two core challenges: the data silo dilemma and model create risks. Containing substantial sensitive patient information, medical data create barriers to secure sharing among healthcare institutions while maintaining privacy protections. Current research indicates distributed learning techniques provide viable solutions for overcoming data silos [1]. Federated Learning (FL), for instance, enables collaborative training of deep learning models using multi-source medical data while preserving participant privacy through two fundamental mechanisms [2,3]: prohibition of raw

This research was funded by the Peking University Nanchang Innovation Institute.

C. Xu et al. (Eds.): MobiMedia 2025, LNICST 670, pp. 77–90, 2026.
https://doi.org/10.1007/978-3-032-16823-8_7

data exchange between data holders [4] and central server processing limited to model parameter updates without accessing local node-specific data [5].

Although FL has shown promise in medical applications such as posture recognition, its real-world deployment is hindered by the non-IID nature of decentralized medical data. This heterogeneity reduces the adaptability of global models to local contexts, often resulting in degraded performance [6,7]. Empirical evidence shows that under non-IID conditions, clients—particularly those with large datasets—may derive minimal benefits from the global model, which can perform worse than locally trained models [8]. This undermines a core incentive of FL: improved performance through collaboration.

To mitigate this, Wang et al. [9] proposed a restricted data-sharing strategy, achieving approximately a 30% accuracy improvement on the CIFAR-10 dataset by sharing just 5% of global data. However, this approach is unsuitable for healthcare due to strict privacy regulations. To address these limitations, this paper proposes a dynamic parameter clustering approach in federated learning, where clients are dynamically grouped into clusters based on similarity metrics. The proposed methodology resolves three critical limitations:

- **Enhanced similarity parameter:** Using pseudo-data to estimate model similarity more reliably than parameter distance metrics.
- **Privacy-preserving design:** Leveraging GAN-generated pseudo-data which are shared by the server, protecting sensitive patient information.
- **Adaptive clustering mechanism:** Dynamically grouping clients based on server-side similarity estimation, enhancing clustering accuracy and model personalization.

Experimental results validate that the proposed approach performs effectively in privacy-constrained settings, providing a robust solution to the tension between model performance and privacy preservation in healthcare FL.

2   Related Works

In references [10,11], Xie et al. and Briggs et al. proposed a multi-model federated learning strategy wherein the traditional single global model was replaced with multiple global models. These models are assigned to client groups formed based on local model similarity, with each group training its FL model independently. While this method can better capture intra-group data characteristics generalization, it inherently limits cross-group knowledge sharing, thereby reducing the generalization capability of the overall FL system and hindering the convergence to a globally optimal model. To address weight fluctuation and improve model personalization, Fraboni et al. [12] introduced a client clustering approach that grouped participants based on model similarity metrics, such as weight distributions or output responses. This clustering reduces the variance in parameter aggregation and improves local model expressiveness. However, their method involves frequent exchange of local model parameters during training, which can significantly increase the risk of privacy leakage—especially in sensitive domains like healthcare, where patient data confidentiality is employed [13,14]. In another line of work, Liu et al. proposed FedPFA [15], which employs a one-shot clustering strategy. Clients first train sparse representation models locally and transmit the resulting low-dimensional vectors to the central server. The server then performs clustering based on the similarity of these sparse vectors and initiates training within the assigned clusters. Although this technique reduces communication overhead and limits parameter exposure, it suffers from a lack of adaptability. Once formed distribution, the static clusters cannot accommodate changes in client behavior or data distribution over time, leading to suboptimal grouping—particularly in environments with high data and client heterogeneity.

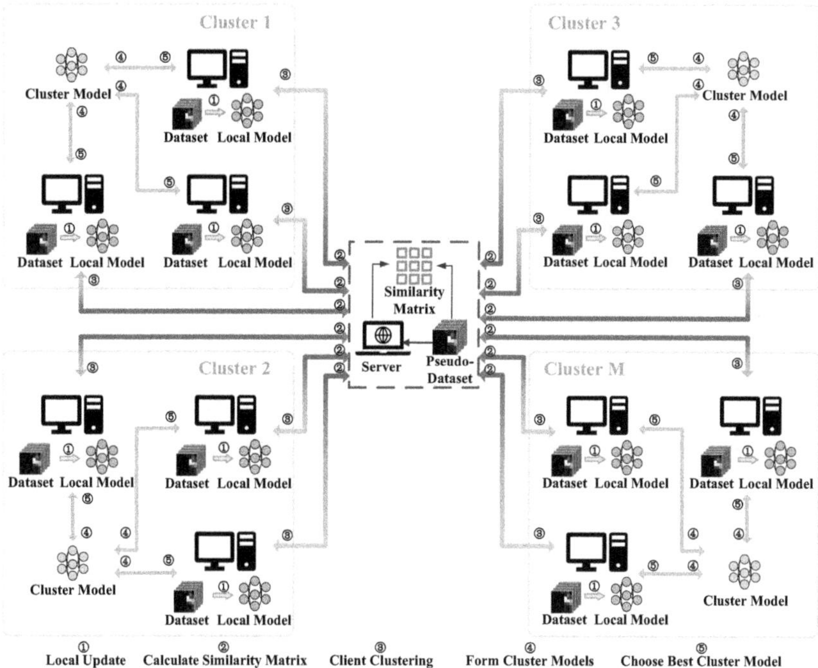

Fig. 1. Overall framework diagram.

3   Scheme Overview

3.1   Overall Framework of Our Method

The framework designed in this paper is illustrated in Fig. 1. The entire process is divided into five stages:

(1) **Pseudo-Data Generation:** In a trusted server environment, the server trains a generative adversarial network (GAN) on a real dataset to produce a pseudo-dataset that retains the underlying data distribution without revealing actual client data.
(2) **Model Initialization and Local Training:** Initial global model weights are broadcast to all clients, which subsequently perform local updates on their private datasets and transmit the revised parameters back to the server.
(3) **Similarity Measurement:** Using the server-generated pseudo-dataset, the server evaluates the updated client models by passing the pseudo-data through them and calculating a similarity measurement matrix based on their outputs.
(4) **Client Clustering and Intra-Cluster Aggregation:** Based on the similarity matrix, clients are dynamically grouped into clusters. Within each cluster, federated averaging (FedAvg) is applied to generate updated cluster-specific models.
(5) **Model Selection and Iteration:** Each client evaluates the performance of the available cluster models and selects the best-performing one for the next training round. This process repeats until a convergence or stopping condition is met.

3.2　Pseudo-Data Generation Based on Generative Adversarial Networks

The main models used for image data generation in machine learning are Generative Adversarial Networks (GANs) and Variational Autoencoders (VAEs). Since GANs can generate more realistic image samples with higher detail quality, they are more commonly used for image data generation in the field of medical imaging. For the generation of pseudo-data for posture images, we have constructed a generative model that combines Conditional Generative Adversarial Networks (cGAN) with a Wasserstein Generative Adversarial Network with Gradient Penalty (WGAN-GP).

Wasserstein Distance and WGAN-GP The Wasserstein distance (also known as Earth-Mover distance) is a metric for measuring the difference between two probability distributions, defined as Eq. 1:

$$W(P_r, P_g) = \inf_{\gamma \in \Pi(P_r, P_g)} \mathbb{E}_{(x,y) \sim \gamma}[\|x - y\|] \tag{1}$$

Here, P_r and P_g represent the real data distribution and the generated pseudo-data distribution, respectively, and $\Pi(P_r, P_g)$ denotes the set of joint distributions between them. Compared to the Jensen-Shannon (JS) divergence used in traditional GANs, the Wasserstein distance can still provide an effective gradient even when the distributions do not overlap, thereby addressing the mode collapse issue. The core idea of WGAN is to approximate the Wasserstein distance by maximizing the output difference of the discriminator D, and then optimize the quality of the generated data by minimizing the loss of the generator G. The loss function $\mathcal{L}_{WGAN}$ is Eq. 2.

$$\mathcal{L}_{WGAN} = \min_{G} \max_{D \in 1\text{-Lipschitz}} \mathbb{E}_{x \sim P_r}[D(x)] - \mathbb{E}_{z \sim P_z}[D(G(z))] \tag{2}$$

By imposing the Lipschitz continuity constraint on the discriminator, WGAN achieves more stable training. In practice, this constraint is typically enforced using techniques such as weight clipping or gradient penalty. WGAN-GP replaces weight clipping with gradient penalty, enforcing the gradient norm of the discriminator to be close to 1. Its loss function $\mathcal{L}_D$ is given by Eq. 3.

$$\mathcal{L}_D = \underbrace{\mathbb{E}_{\tilde{x} \sim P_g}[D(\tilde{x})] - \mathbb{E}_{x \sim P_r}[D(x)]}_{\text{Wasserstein Loss}} + \lambda \cdot \underbrace{\mathbb{E}_{\hat{x} \sim P_{\hat{x}}}[(\|\nabla_{\hat{x}} D(\hat{x})\|_2 - 1)^2]}_{\text{Gradient Penalty}} \tag{3}$$

Here, the interpolated sample $\hat{x}$ is defined as $\epsilon x + (1 - \epsilon)\tilde{x}(\epsilon \sim U[0,1])$, and λ is the penalty coefficient.

Integrated Conditional WGAN-GP (cWGAN-GP) Framework This paper develops a GAN architecture through the synergistic integration of the conditional generation mechanism from cGAN with the enhanced training stability of WGAN-GP.

Generator G: Takes input noise $z \sim P_z$ and conditional label y, and generates data $G(z|y)$.

Discriminator D: Evaluates the authenticity of data x under the condition y, and outputs a scalar score.

Loss functions $\mathcal{L}_D$ and $\mathcal{L}_G$ are defined as Eqs. 4 and 5.

$$\mathcal{L}_D = \mathbb{E}[D(G(z|y)|y)] - \mathbb{E}[D(x|y)] + \lambda \cdot \mathbb{E}[(\|\nabla_{\hat{x}} D(\hat{x}|y)\|_2 - 1)^2] \tag{4}$$

$$\mathcal{L}_G = -\mathbb{E}[D(G(z|y)|y)] \tag{5}$$

3.3 Client Clustering

This work presents a client clustering method that operates without prior knowledge of local data distributions. We employed a pre-trained stable image generation model to create a server-hosted pseudo-dataset that preserves the latent distribution of real data while reducing original patient information.

After each local model completes one round of training, the server inputs the pseudo-dataset into each client's local model for prediction. The last layer of the model outputs a matrix $O_i = F_i(D_{pseudo}, \theta^t_{i,c_t})$, which is a one-hot matrix of size $J \times K$, where J is the number of pseudo-dataset samples on the server, and K is the dimension size of the output tensor from the last linear layer of the model. The client indices $i = 1, ..., n$, and θ^t_{i,c_t} represent the best cluster model found by the i-th client during the t-th $(t > 1)$ communication round from current cluster models θ^t_{c,c_t}. The method for finding the best cluster model θ^t_{i,c_t} which achieves minimum test loss is given by the following Eq. 6:

$$\theta^t_{i,c_t} = argmin L_i(D^{test}_i; \theta^t_{c,c_t}) \tag{6}$$

The server constructs an $n \times n$ adjacency matrix M using O_i, where M represents the similarity measurement matrix. $M_{p,q}$ measures the similarity between client p and client q, thus M is a symmetric matrix. The calculation of $M_{p,q}$ involves converting the one-hot matrices O_p and O_q into predicted label index tensors $pred_p$ and $pred_q$, respectively. Then, the Hamming distance between $pred_p$ and $pred_q$ is computed to measure the proportion of difference between the predicted labels. The similarity is inversely proportional to the size of the Hamming distance.

$$pred_p = [argmax O^1_p, argmax O^2_p, ..., argmax O^{nsamples}_p] \tag{7}$$

$$Hamming(O_p, O_q) = \sum_{k=1}^{nsamples} \mathbb{I}\left(pred^k_p \neq pred^k_q\right) \tag{8}$$

where O^i_p and $pred^k_p$ severally represent the i-th row of matrix O_p and the k-th row of tensor $pred_p$. To map the Hamming distance to the range $[0, 1]$, the normalized similarity $M_{p,q}$ is defined as Eq. 9:

$$M_{p,q} = sim(O_p, O_q) = 1 - \frac{Hamming(O_p, O_q)}{nsamples} \tag{9}$$

Let $\mathbb{I}(\cdot)$ denote the indicator function, which returns 1 when the specified condition holds true and 0 otherwise. The variable $nsamples$ refers to the total number of data points within the globally accessible dataset.

In this framework, client clustering for each communication round can be conducted either by applying a fixed threshold or by adopting a more adaptive similarity-based ranking strategy to determine the clustering arrangement.

3.4   Classification Network Structure

We trained a sleep posture recognition classifier with an 8×8 pressure matrix using the network structure shown in Fig. 2. The pressure matrix is based on the SleepMatrix® noncontact sleep monitoring system developed by Beijing MicroVibration DataNet Technology Corporation. The data is classified through two 5×5 convolutional layers and two linear layers, ultimately mapping to probabilities for 12 categories. The predicted category labels are output through a Log-Softmax layer.

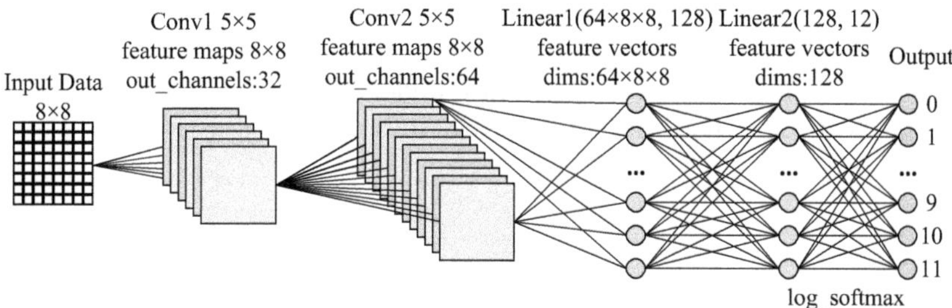

Fig. 2. Local classification network structure.

4 Experiment

4.1 Dataset

The dataset comprises 64-channel pressure recordings ($\approx$ 0.33 V range) from piezoelectric sensors as participants assumed four postures (supine, left/right lateral, prone) at three bed positions (left, center, right), yielding 12 posture–position combinations. Thirty subjects maintained each posture for 10 s, generating 5,040 raw samples. These were split into ten one-second segments per sample—totaling 50,400 segments—and converted into 8×8 pressure matrices. To emulate non-IID conditions, data were partitioned among clients via Dirichlet sampling with $\alpha = 0.1$ (α measures the sharpness of this distribution, that is, it measures how far the typical sample X in our distribution differs from its mean m, lower α yields more skewed distributions), followed by a 7:3 train–test split per client, ensuring heterogeneous local data distributions as shown in Fig. 3.

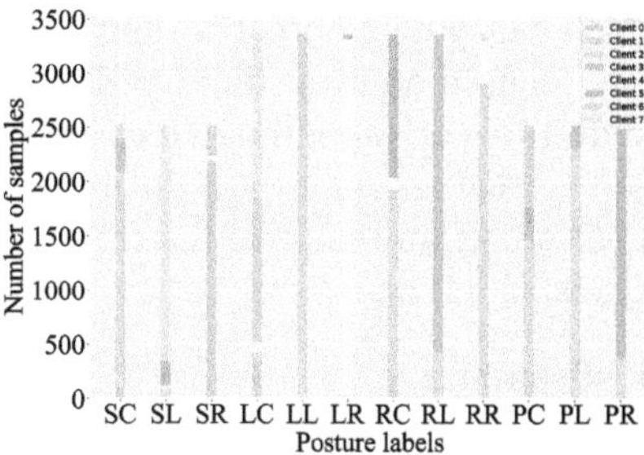

Fig. 3. Local training data distribution of each client ($\alpha = 0.1$).

4.2 Experimental Results of Generating Pseudo-Data

We utilize a publicly available dataset, which consists of data initially sampled from each client, to train the cWGAN-GP model. Both the generator and discriminator are optimized using the Adam algorithm with a learning rate of 0.0001. The training process spans 10,000 epochs. For comparative analysis, a standard WGAN-GP model is also trained under similar conditions. The training loss trajectories for the generator and discriminator are illustrated in Fig. 4(a) and (b).

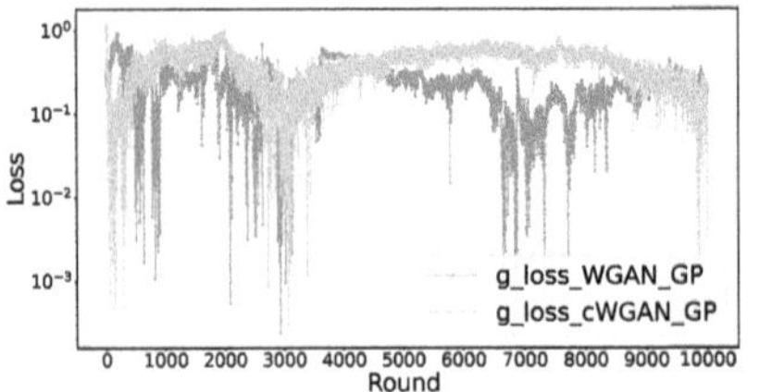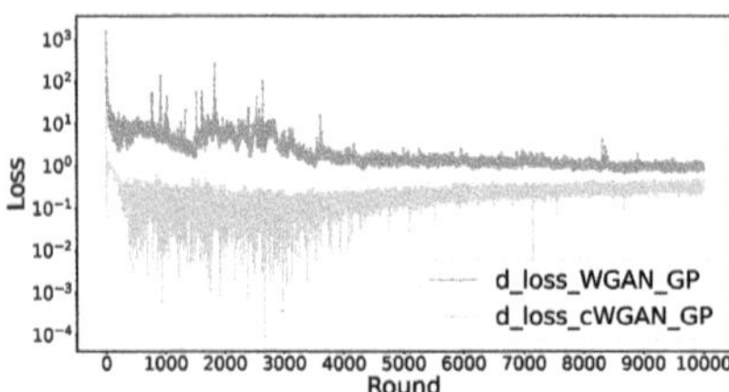

Fig. 4. Loss comparison curves for the generator (a) and the discriminator (b).

As shown, the generator loss of the cWGAN-GP designed in this paper is comparable to that of WGAN-GP, while the discriminator loss is lower than that of WGAN-GP, indicating that cWGAN-GP achieves more stable training compared to WGAN-GP. Additionally, the main advantage of cWGAN-GP over WGAN-GP is that it incorporates the benefits of cGAN, transforming the unsupervised WGAN-GP into a supervised model capable of generating corresponding data based on specified conditional labels.

To evaluate the privacy-preserving capabilities of our proposed cWGAN-GP, we conducted a Membership Inference Attack (MIA) against the discriminator network. The goal of MIA is to determine whether a given data sample was part of the model's training set. A successful attack indicates potential memorization and privacy leakage, which can pose a threat to user confidentiality.

In this experiment, we focused on attacking the discriminator $D(x, y)$, which receives both the image and its corresponding label as input. Since the discriminator is directly exposed to real training data during adversarial learning, it is the most likely component to retain sensitive information.

The attack procedure is as follows:

1. We prepare two sets of samples:
   - **Members**: samples from the training set;
   - **Non-members**: samples from the held-out test set.
2. Each sample is passed through the discriminator to obtain its output score (before activation), which is used as a feature.
3. A binary classifier (Random Forest) is trained to distinguish members from non-members based on these scores.
4. The attack performance is evaluated using four standard metrics: *Accuracy, Precision, Recall,* and *ROC-AUC*.

The attack results on the trained discriminator are summarized in Table 1.

We evaluated the semantic consistency of the pseudo-data generated by cWGAN-GP using KMeans clustering and standard unsupervised clustering metrics. As shown in Table 2, the Adjusted Rand Index (ARI) and Normalized Mutual Information (NMI) for pseudo-data (ARI: 0.7176, NMI: 0.7481) closely match those of the real dataset (ARI: 0.7119, NMI: 0.7316), with retention ratios exceeding 100%. This suggests that the pseudo-data not only preserves the underlying class structure of the real data but may even exhibit more separable cluster boundaries, potentially due to the denoising effect of the generative process. These results support the interpretability and usability of pseudo-data for downstream clustering and personalization tasks in federated learning scenarios.

Table 1. Results of membership inference attack on the discriminator

Metric	Value	Interpretation
Accuracy	0.5423	Close to random guessing
Precision	0.0319	High false positive rate
Recall	0.0340	Very few true members identified
ROC-AUC	0.3231	Indicates strong resistance to attack

Table 2. Clustering consistency (ARI and NMI) for real and fake data under different generative models

Data type	ARI		NMI	
	WGAN-GP	cWGAN-GP	WGAN-GP	cWGAN-GP
Pseudo-data	0.6358	**0.7176**	0.6623	**0.7481**
Real data	0.7119		0.7316	

4.3   Experimental Results of Federated Learning

Experimental Setup In this study, we employed eight clients for local training, each configured with 20 local epochs and a learning rate of 0.001, over a total of 200 communication rounds. To simulate a privacy-preserving federated learning environment, we integrated a Rényi Differential Privacy (RDP)-based accounting framework with a subsampled Gaussian mechanism [16], enabling evaluation of model performance under varying privacy budgets ($\varepsilon = 0.5, 1.0, 2.0, 4.0$) and gradient clipping coefficients ($c = 0.5, 1.0$). Experiments were conducted on a globally shared dataset comprising either real or synthetically generated pseudo-data, facilitating a comprehensive analysis of the privacy-utility trade-off.

To ensure formal privacy guarantees throughout the federated learning process, we adopt the subsampled Gaussian mechanism in conjunction with RDP analysis. In particular, we compute the RDP at a specified order α for each communication round and subsequently convert it into a standard (ε, δ)-differential privacy guarantee following the methodology outlined in [16].

The RDP for the subsampled Gaussian mechanism is defined as:

$$\mathcal{D}\alpha(\mathcal{M}(D) \parallel \mathcal{M}(D')) = \frac{1}{\alpha - 1} \log \mathbb{E}x \sim D \left[\left(\frac{P(x)}{Q(x)} \right)^{\alpha} \right] \tag{10}$$

where D and D' are adjacent datasets, and $P(x)$, $Q(x)$ represent the output distributions of the mechanism $\mathcal{M}$ when applied to these datasets.

To track the cumulative privacy loss across rounds, we use a moment accountant, which aggregates RDP as:

$$\mathrm{RDPtotal}(\alpha) = T \cdot \mathrm{RDPround}(\alpha) \tag{11}$$

with T denoting the total number of training rounds.

The final (ε, δ) privacy bound is derived via analytical conversion:

$$\varepsilon = \mathrm{RDP}_{\mathrm{total}}(\alpha) + \frac{1}{\alpha - 1} \log \left(\frac{1}{\delta} \right) \tag{12}$$

We then perform an optimization over $\alpha \in [2, 100]$ to obtain the tightest possible ε value.

To determine the appropriate noise multiplier σ, we utilize a binary search algorithm to identify the minimum σ that satisfies the target (ε, δ)-DP constraint, based on the following relationship:

$$q = \frac{B}{N}, \quad \sigma \geq \frac{\sqrt{2 \log(1.25/\delta)}}{\varepsilon} \tag{13}$$

where q is the sampling probability, B is the batch size per client, and N is the total number of data samples.

Parameter Sensitivity To assess how the privacy budget ε influences the performance of different federated learning algorithms, we systematically varied ε. Due to space constraints, we plotted only the resulting accuracy curves for the case of a fixed gradient clipping coefficient $c = 0.5$, as shown in Fig. 5. These curves highlight that under a highly heterogeneous data distribution ($\alpha = 0.1$), our proposed FedCLUS method not only achieves the highest overall accuracy across all tested values of ε but also exhibits markedly smoother convergence behavior. In particular, as the privacy budget tightens (i.e., ε decreases), conventional approaches such as FedAvg, FedProx [17], FedPer [18], and FedPFA [15] suffer pronounced performance degradation, with FedAvg demonstrating the slowest convergence and poorest final accuracy under stringent privacy constraints. In contrast, FedCLUS maintains stable model updates and preserves utility even when significant noise is injected, underscoring its superior resilience to privacy-induced perturbations.

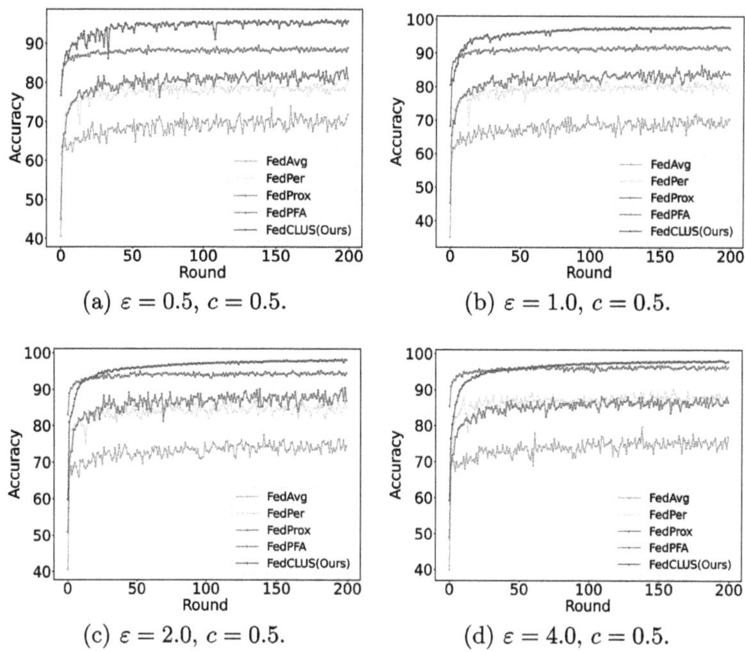

(a) $\varepsilon = 0.5$, $c = 0.5$.   (b) $\varepsilon = 1.0$, $c = 0.5$.

(c) $\varepsilon = 2.0$, $c = 0.5$.   (d) $\varepsilon = 4.0$, $c = 0.5$.

Fig. 5. Global accuracy curves under varying privacy budgets.

Next, we investigated each method's sensitivity to the gradient clipping coefficient by fixing $\varepsilon = 1.0$ and applying gradient clipping immediately after adding differential noise in every communication round. Since preliminary trials revealed that a large clipping bound ($c = 2.0$) led to unacceptable accuracy loss across all algorithms, we confined our analysis to two practical settings, $c = 0.5$ and $c = 1.0$. Figure 6 illustrates the global training accuracy for each method under these two clipping regimes. The plots reveal that tighter clipping ($c = 0.5$) generally yields more consistent, albeit slightly noisier, updates, whereas a looser bound ($c = 1.0$) can introduce larger gradient variance, leading to occasional instability in some baselines. Importantly, FedCLUS exhibits minimal sensitivity to the choice of c, converging reliably to high accuracy in both scenarios.

Table 3 and Fig. 7 further quantifies these observations by reporting the final test accuracies achieved by each algorithm across various combinations of ε and c. FedCLUS consistently attains optimal performance at $c = 0.5$, regardless of the privacy budget, confirming that this configuration strikes the best balance between gradient magnitude control and noise tolerance. While FedPFA approaches comparable accuracy under more permissive privacy settings ($\varepsilon \geq 2.0$), its effectiveness deteriorates sharply as ε is reduced, highlighting a critical vulnerability to strict privacy requirements. Finally, the last two columns of Table 3 demonstrate that whether clients share pseudo-generated data or actual local samples has a negligible impact on overall performance,

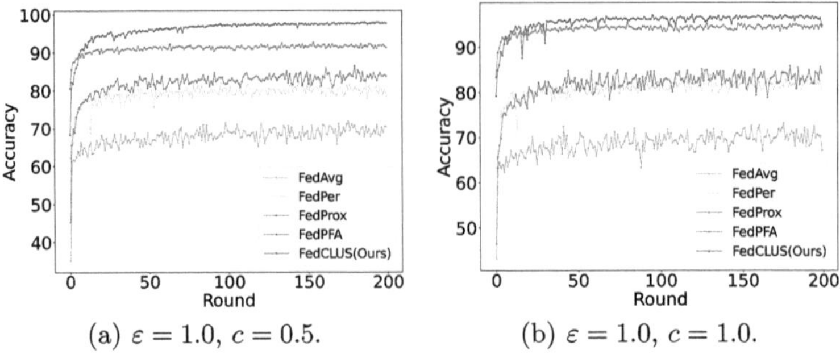

(a) $\varepsilon = 1.0$, $c = 0.5$.   (b) $\varepsilon = 1.0$, $c = 1.0$.

Fig. 6. Global accuracy curves under varying gradient clipping coefficients.

indicating that our clustering-based scheme effectively mitigates knowledge gap introduced by synthetic surrogate data.

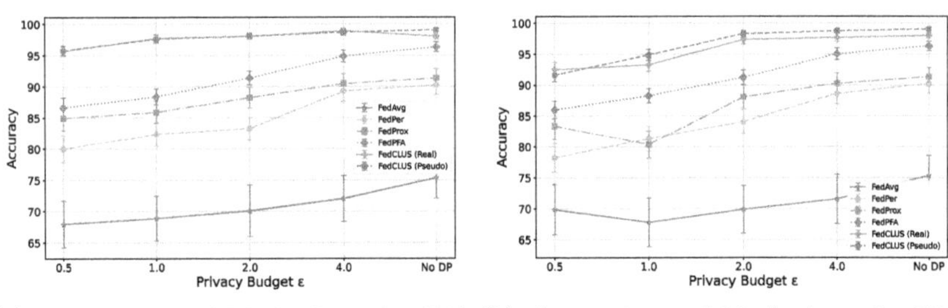

(a) Comparison of Methods under Different Privacy Budgets(Clip=0.5).

(b) Comparison of Methods under Different Privacy Budgets(Clip=1.0).

Fig. 7. Global accuracy curves under varying gradient clipping coefficients.

5   Conclusion

This paper introduces FedCLUS, a novel privacy-preserving federated learning framework for healthcare that simultaneously tackles data heterogeneity and privacy leakage. FedCLUS employs a dynamic clustering mechanism that groups clients by model behavior, using pseudo-data generated by a hybrid Conditional WGAN-GP to compute similarity metrics. Unlike traditional methods that rely solely on parameter distances or require prior knowledge of client distributions, our approach safeguards patient confidentiality by operating on high-quality synthetic samples that retain the statistical characteristics of real data. At each communication round, the server uses these pseudo-samples to simulate client updates, construct a similarity matrix, and adaptively form clusters—enhancing personalization and mitigating biases in non-IID settings. We validate FedCLUS on a sleep posture classification task, demonstrating that it consistently outperforms standard FL algorithms (FedAvg, FedProx, FedPer, and FedPFA) under

Table 3. Global model accuracy under different privacy budgets and gradient clipping coefficients (%).

Parameters		Methods					
Privacy budget ε	Gradient clip c	FedAvg	FedPer	FedProx	FedPFA	FedCLUS (real data)	FedCLUS (pseudo-data)
0.5	0.5	67.93 ± 3.72	79.98 ± 2.15	84.95 ± 1.98	86.64 ± 1.62	95.68 ± 0.83	**95.76 ± 0.67**
	1.0	69.84 ± 4.05	78.23 ± 2.33	83.39 ± 2.17	86.02 ± 1.39	**92.55 ± 1.12**	91.66 ± 1.09
1.0	0.5	68.87 ± 3.55	82.39 ± 1.89	85.89 ± 1.75	88.39 ± 1.26	**97.76 ± 0.59**	97.63 ± 0.64
	1.0	67.79 ± 3.91	81.34 ± 2.04	80.38 ± 2.22	88.29 ± 1.18	93.31 ± 1.03	**94.89 ± 0.88**
2.0	0.5	70.08 ± 4.12	83.28 ± 1.77	88.24 ± 1.63	91.39 ± 1.09	98.06 ± 0.42	**98.08 ± 0.51**
	1.0	69.89 ± 3.84	84.09 ± 1.95	88.09 ± 1.81	91.28 ± 1.17	97.35 ± 0.76	**98.30 ± 0.55**
4.0	0.5	72.03 ± 3.67	89.29 ± 1.68	90.48 ± 1.55	94.87 ± 0.95	**98.93 ± 0.37**	98.69 ± 0.49
	1.0	71.56 ± 3.98	88.65 ± 1.72	90.27 ± 1.66	95.06 ± 0.98	97.69 ± 0.68	**98.75 ± 0.43**
No differential privacy		75.35 ± 3.24	90.25 ± 1.55	91.36 ± 1.48	96.34 ± 0.78	98.03 ± 0.39	**99.07 ± 0.28**

strict privacy budgets and gradient clipping constraints. Experimental results confirm that FedCLUS maintains robust accuracy while providing strong privacy guarantees. Moreover, its scalable, flexible design makes it well suited to real-world healthcare applications, where diverse data distributions and stringent confidentiality requirements prevail. By bridging model performance and data privacy, FedCLUS offers an effective solution for optimized, personalized, and privacy-aware federated learning in sensitive domains.

References

1. Xu, J., Glicksberg, B.S., Su, C., Walker, P., Bian, J., Wang, F.: Federated learning for healthcare informatics. J. Healthc. Inform. Res. **5**, 1–19 (2021)
2. Bao, Z., Lin, Y., Zhang, S., et al.: Threat of adversarial attacks on DL-based IoT device identification. IEEE Internet Things J. **9**(11), 9012–9024 (2021)
3. Lin, Y., Zhao, H., Ma, X., et al.: Adversarial attacks in modulation recognition with convolutional neural networks. IEEE Trans. Reliab. **70**(1), 389–401 (2020)
4. Shi, J., Ge, B., Liu, Y., et al.: Data privacy security guaranteed network intrusion detection system based on federated learning. In: IEEE INFOCOM 2021-IEEE Conference on Computer Communications Workshops (INFOCOM WKSHPS), pp. 1–6. IEEE (2021)
5. Lin, Y., Tu, Y., Dou, Z., et al.: Contour stella image and deep learning for signal recognition in the physical layer. IEEE Trans. Cogn. Commun. Network. **7**(1), 34–46 (2020)
6. Fallah, A., Mokhtari, A., Ozdaglar, A.: Personalized federated learning with theoretical guarantees: a model-agnostic meta-learning approach. Adv. Neural. Inf. Process. Syst. **33**, 3557–3568 (2020)
7. Vahidian, S., Morafah, M., Lin, B.: Personalized federated learning by structured and unstructured pruning under data heterogeneity. In: IEEE ICDCS (2021)
8. Hanzely, F., Richtárik, P.: Federated learning of a mixture of global and local models. arXiv preprint arXiv:2002.05516 (2020)
9. Wang, H., Kaplan, Z., Niu, D., et al.: Optimizing federated learning on non-IID data with reinforcement learning. In: IEEE INFOCOM 2020-IEEE Conference on Computer Communications, pp. 1698–1707. IEEE (2020)
10. Long, G., Xie, M., Shen, T., et al.: Multi-center federated learning: clients clustering for better personalization. World Wide Web **26**(1), 481–500 (2023)

11. Briggs, C., Fan, Z., Andras, P.: Federated learning with hierarchical clustering of local updates to improve training on non-IID data. In: 2020 International Joint Conference on Neural Networks (IJCNN), pp. 1–9. IEEE (2020)
12. Fraboni, Y., Vidal, R., Kameni, L., et al.: Clustered sampling: low-variance and improved representativity for clients selection in federated learning. In: International Conference on Machine Learning, pp. 3407–3416. PMLR (2021)
13. Ya, T.U., Yun, L.I.N., Haoran, Z.H.A., et al.: Large-scale real-world radio signal recognition with deep learning. Chin. J. Aeronaut. **35**(9), 35–48 (2022)
14. Yin, C., Xi, J., Sun, R., et al.: Location privacy protection based on differential privacy strategy for big data in industrial internet of things. IEEE Trans. Ind. Inf. **14**(8), 3628–3636 (2017)
15. Liu, B., Guo, Y., Chen, X.: PFA: privacy-preserving federated adaptation for effective model personalization. In: Proceedings of the Web Conference 2021, pp. 923–934 (2021)
16. Mironov, I., Talwar, K., Zhang, L.: Rényi differential privacy of the sampled Gaussian mechanism. arXiv preprint arXiv:1908.10530 (2019)
17. Li, T., Sahu, A.K., Zaheer, M., et al.: Federated optimization in heterogeneous networks. Proc. Mach. Learn. Syst. **2**, 429–450 (2020)
18. Arivazhagan, M.G., Aggarwal, V., Singh, A.K., et al.: Federated learning with personalization layers. arXiv preprint arXiv:1912.00818 (2019)

DCR: Divide-and-Conquer Reasoning for Multi-choice Question Answering with LLMs

Zijie Meng[1], Yan Zhang[2], Zhaopeng Feng[1], and Zuozhu Liu[1]

[1] Zhejiang University, Jiaxing, Zhejiang, China
`zijie.22@intl.zju.edu.cn` , `zhaopeng.23@intl.zju.edu.cn`,
`zuozhuliu@intl.zju.edu.cn`
[2] Department of Electrical and Computer Engineering, National University of Singapore, Singapore, Singapore

Abstract. Large language models (LLMs) have shown impressive performance in reasoning benchmarks with the emergence of Chain-of-Thought (CoT), particularly in multi-choice question (MCQ). However, current works equally resolve questions regardless of the problem-solving difficulty, leading to an excessive focus on simple items while insufficient attention on intricate ones. To address this challenge, we propose a simple yet effective strategy, **D**ivide and **C**onquer **R**easoning (DCR), to enhance the LLMs' capability for solving MCQs, as inspired by human beings using heuristics to first categorize tasks and then handle them separately. In particular, we first divide questions into two subsets based on confidence score CS, which is estimated by statistical frequency of generated answers. Subsequently, we propose Filter Choices based Reasoning (FCR) to conquer subset with low CS. Our experiments on three tasks across nine datasets demonstrate that DCR achieves comparable accuracy to SOTA with only 54% overhead and further improves accuracy by 1.56% using 85% of the resources. The code is at https://github.com/AiMijie/DCR.

Keywords: Large language models · Chain-of-Thought · Multi-choice question

1 Introduction

Large language models (LLMs) [1,2,6,9,17,40,54–56,69] have exhibited outstanding performance on various downstream tasks by generating step by step rationales to obtain final answers without finetuning parameters, as elicited from Chain-of-Thoughts (CoT) [58]. Multiple-choice question (MCQ) is a format that incorporate a choices list with a question and prompt the model to select the gold

---

Zijie Meng and Yan Zhang: Equal contribution.

© ICST Institute for Computer Sciences, Social Informatics and Telecommunications Engineering 2026
Published by Springer Nature Switzerland AG 2026. All Rights Reserved
C. Xu et al. (Eds.): MobiMedia 2025, LNICST 670, pp. 91–111, 2026.
https://doi.org/10.1007/978-3-032-16823-8_8

answer. Owing to its simple structure, standardized results, and objective assessments, MCQ is not only widely prevalent in the real world but also extensively employed in LLMs' reasoning evaluation [19,21,48,73,74]. Consequently, the community has witnessed a surge in CoT-based works, which demonstrate outstanding performance on MCQs [14,27,28,57,68,70]. Notably, Zero-Shot-CoT [27] and Self-Consistency (SC) [57] have attracted considerable attention due to straightforward implementation and impressive efficacy. Zero-Shot-CoT stimulates the latent zero-shot reasoning abilities of LLMs by adding "Let's think step by step." into prompts, but often underperforms on complex tasks. SC samples different reasoning paths to generate multiple candidates following majority voting to derive final answer, which achieves encouraging results but introduces substantial overhead. To escape this sky-high cost, ESC [31] early-stops inference by calculating the entropy of answer distribution in a small sliding window without sacrificing SC's performance, which achieves SOTA currently. However, its accuracy ceiling is inherently limited by SC.

Therefore, to optimize the cost and performance, it is imperative to timely halt expensive sampling to reduce expenditure and further employ varied approaches for problems of differing complexity to advance accuracy. In other words, previous methods all process data uniformly regardless of the problem-solving difficulty, which means that simple questions receive unnecessarily complex and costly procedures, whereas intricate ones are not adequately addressed with basic methods. It is also natural that humans utilize heuristic strategies to categorize tasks, and then address each individually, which not only effectively resolves complex issues, but also significantly enhances efficiency [18,26]. Consequently, we apply this strategy of data partitioning followed by differential process–Divide and Conquer, which is widely deployed across numerous scenarios [4,36,47]–to LLM reasoning. In this context, we need to address two paramount challenges: (1) *What criteria should be used to divide the dataset?* (2) *How should the subsets be processed?*

For the first one, we need to explore a method to effectively classify questions based on solving difficulty. In human perception, answers with high uncertainty are often wrong, otherwise tend to be correct [60]. So we tentatively probed SC [57], where the statistical distribution of answers generated from various reasoning paths reflects a confidence score CS for the question. As shown in Fig. 3, we divided questions into two subsets based on their CS, where different subsets displays distinct accuracy and the lower CS subset demonstrates poorer performance. This suggests we can employ SC to compute CS for each problem and divide them.

Move to the second issue, we inspired from the Cannikin Law in management [16], explore more elaborately designed methods for the low confidence subsets that offer greater room for optimization, and fix other questions that are sufficiently simple for the model. Reference [45] investigated the model's sensitivity to irrelevant information within the questions, but there exists uncertainty regarding irrelevant options in choices list. To delve into this problem, we conducted preliminary studies as shown in Fig. 5, discovering a decrease in problem-solving accuracy as the number of choices increased. Following this, we removed some irrelevant options in hardly solved subsets to re-query the LLM, resulting in a universal improvement of over 20%, especially achieving staggering 75.52% on CMSQA [50], as shown in Table 7. Motivated by these findings, we introduce Filter Choices based Reasoning (FCR), which excludes abundant options by using the answers from the divide stage, to conduct inference in conquer stage.

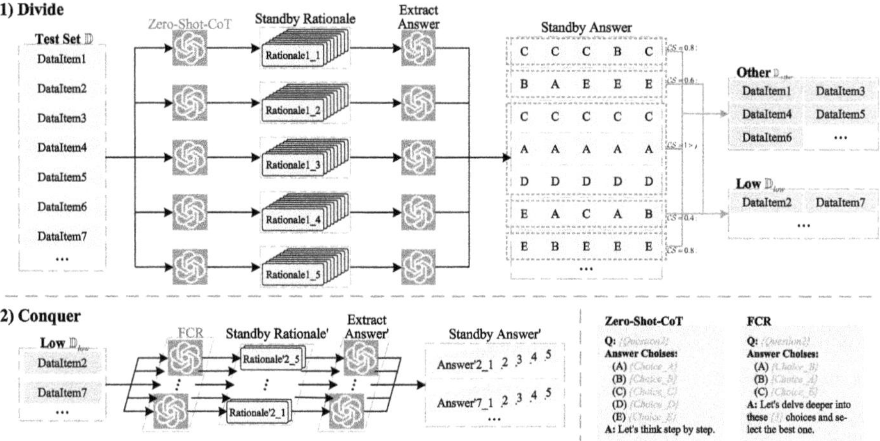

Fig. 1. Illustration of DCR. (1) Divide. We first conduct t (e.g. t=5) times inference with Zero-Shot-CoT [27] by "Let's think step by step.". Then, the dataset $\mathbb{D}$ is divided based on $\mathcal{CS}$, where DataItems with $\mathcal{CS}$ less than μ (e.g. μ=0.6) are categorized as $\mathbb{D}_{low}$, and the rest as $\mathbb{D}_{other}$. (2) Conquer. We fix $\mathbb{D}_{other}$ and propose FCR to process $\mathbb{D}_{low}$. "DataItem" includes question text and full choices list in Divide area, while involves filtered one in Conquer area. "Rationalei_j" denotes the rationale generated by j-th LLM query for i-th DataItem. "Choice_x" represents the x-th option in original DataItem. See Sect. 3.5 for the case study with a specific example.

Concretely, in this paper, we propose a simple yet effective strategy, **D**ivide and **C**onquer **R**easoning (DCR), which first categorizes questions into two subsets based on $\mathcal{CS}$ and subsequently employs FCR to improve model performance on MCQs with low $\mathcal{CS}$, as illustrated in Fig. 1. Through extensive empirical evaluation across nine datasets including arithmetic, commonsense, and logic tasks, DCR not only achieves comparable accuracy to ESC by consuming only 54% of resources, but also further improves accuracy by 1.56% with 85% overhead. Additionally, we have validated the effectiveness of DCR across various LLMs in Sect. 3.4 and the superiority of FCR over other methods in Sect. 3.4. We have also successfully adapted DCR to the cloze-style arithmetic task GSM8K [11] and symbolic reasoning task Word Sorting [48] achieving an improved performance over SC with reduced cost. In summary, our work has three major contributions: (1) To the best of our knowledge, we pioneeringly employ the Divide and Conquer at the dataset level for LLM reasoning, providing the community a fresh perspective. (2) By dividing dataset based on $\mathcal{CS}$ and conquering low $\mathcal{CS}$ subset with FCR, we optimally balance on cost and accuracy. (3) We evaluate DCR on nine datasets across three tasks, consistently yielding significant improvements.

2   Methodology

The overall framework of DCR is illustrated in Fig. 1. Given a test set of length n as $\mathbb{D} = \{(Q_1, \mathbf{C}_1), \ldots, (Q_n, \mathbf{C}_n)\}$, where Q_i denotes the i-th question and $\mathbf{C}_i$ is the corresponding choices list, we use $\mathbf{R}_i$ and $\mathbf{A}_i$ to denote its rationales and answers generated by LLMs, respectively.

2.1   Divide

With each item $(Q_i, \mathbf{C}_i), i \in \{1, \ldots, n\}$, we query the LLM for t times to obtain rationales $\mathbf{R}_i = \{r_{i,1}, \ldots, r_{i,t}\}$ and corresponding standby answers $\mathbf{A}_i = \{a_{i,1}, \ldots, a_{i,t}\}$ based on Zero-Shot-CoT[1] [27]. In particular, we set t generally equal to the length of choices list $|\mathbf{C}_i|$, considering the worst scenario where all choices could be sampled. And we conduct an analysis on different t in Sect. 3.4. We use δ to denote LLM and define the confidence score $\mathcal{CS}$ of each item as:

$$\mathcal{CS}_{(Q_i, \mathbf{C}_i)} = \max_{j \in \{1, \ldots, t\}} p(a_{i,j} | \delta(Q_i, \mathbf{C}_i)), \tag{1}$$

where $p(a_{i,j} | \delta(Q_i, \mathbf{C}_i))$ is the frequency of $a_{i,j}$ in all predicted answers. And we define it as:

$$p(a_{i,j} | \delta(Q_i, \mathbf{C}_i)) = \frac{\sum_{k \in \{1, \ldots, t\}} \mathbf{1}_{a_{i,k} = a_{i,j}}}{t}. \tag{2}$$

Intuitively, $\mathcal{CS}$ indicates the proportion of the most frequent answer among all predicted results in t times inferences, which is employed to reflect the problem-solving difficulty. Then, we can divide $\mathbb{D}$ with the following rule:

$$(Q_i, \mathbf{C}_i) \in \begin{cases} \mathbb{D}_{other}, & \text{if } \mathcal{CS}_{(Q_i, \mathbf{C}_i)} > \mu, \\ \mathbb{D}_{low}, & \text{if } \mathcal{CS}_{(Q_i, \mathbf{C}_i)} \leq \mu, \end{cases} \tag{3}$$

where $\mathbb{D}_{low}$ represents the low confidence subset containing $(Q_i, \mathbf{C}_i)$ with dispersed distribution of $\mathbf{A}_i$ and $\mathbb{D}_{other}$ includes rest items. μ is the threshold for dividing, which is specified in Sect. 3.2 and discussed in Sect. 3.4. Moreover, different from dividing the questions into two subsets, we explore a more fine-grained division in Sect. 3.4 to evaluate our rule. Next, we would fix $\mathbb{D}_{other}$ to conserve resources, while delve deeper into $\mathbb{D}_{low}$ for ongoing performance improvement.

---

[1] Fow-Shot-CoT (i.e. CoT) [58] requires substantial human labor to annotate task-specific examplars, and zero-shot gradually approaches or even surpasses few-shot as the scale of model increases [20,74]. See Table 12 in Sect. 3.5 for our verification.

2.2   Conquer

We propose Filter Choices based Reasoning (FCR) to conquer $\mathbb{D}_{low}$ in this stage, as shown in Fig. 1, where we exploit the results obtained in divide phase as alternative options for subsequent inference. Specifically, we define $\mathbf{C}'_i = uniq(\mathbf{A}_i)$, where the $uniq(\cdot)$ operation signifies deduplication of $\mathbf{A}_i = \{a_{i,1}, \ldots, a_{i,t}\}$. Then we use $(Q_i, \mathbf{C}'_i)$ to construct the new prompt and query the LLM with "Let's delve deeper into these $\{|\mathbb{C}'_i|\}$ choices and select the best one."[2]. Subsequently, through additional inference for t times, we obtain the new standby answers $\mathbf{A}'_i = \{a'_{i,1}, \ldots, a'_{i,t}\}$ for $\mathbb{D}_{low}$. Notably, our method does not merely delete options, rather it involves a synchronous modification of the option symbols (i.e. 'A', 'B', 'C', etc.) based on the number of remaining choices. Furthermore, in Sect. 3.4, we evaluate the impact of keeping different choices, conquering different subsets, and comparing FCR with other methods, to demonstrate the superiority of our conquering strategy.

Ultimately, we collect the standby answers in different stage $\{\mathbf{A}_i|(Q_i, \mathbf{C}_i) \in \mathbb{D}_{other}\}$ and $\{\mathbf{A}'_i|(Q_i, \mathbf{C}_i) \in \mathbb{D}_{low}\}$ for $\mathbb{D}_{other}$ and $\mathbb{D}_{low}$, respectively, and utilize majority voting to determine the final answer for each data item. It is evident that our full strategy requires no human intervention or manual labor, and infers t times for each data item in $\mathbb{D}_{other}$ and $2t$ for $\mathbb{D}_{low}$.

3   Experiments

3.1   Datasets and Evaluation Metrics

To evaluate the effectiveness and empirically analyse DCR, we conducted experiments on three tasks: (1) Arithmetic. AQuA (AQ.) [33] and Abstract Algebra (Alg.), High School Mathematics (Math.) from the MMLU dataset [19]. (2) Commonsense. CMSQA (CMS.) [50], OpenBookQA (OB.) [39] and ARC Challenge (ARC.) [10]. (3) Logic. RiddleSense (Rid.) [32], Logical Deduction (Logi.) from BIG-bench dataset [48] and Reclor (Rec.) [66]. The statistic is in Table 13. Additionally, we employed exact match (EM) accuracy to evaluate the performance, which is same as previous works [27,58].

3.2   Implementation Details

We primarily employed GPT-3.5-Turbo-0613 from OpenAI API[3], and conducted experiments on other opensource and blackbox LLMs in Sect. 3.4. During the divide phase, we set the temperature to 0.7, and set inference times t to 4 or 5 for different datasets, as detailed in Table 13. We divided each dataset into $\mathbb{D}_{other}$ and $\mathbb{D}_{low}$ with μ as 0.6. In the conquer stage, the temperature and inference times were consistent with previous phase. Experiments were conducted on the full dataset by default unless in Sect. 3.4 and Sect. 3.5, where we randomly sampled at most 500 items for each dataset. In addition, the final results were all obtained by averaging five random trials. Notably, considering the accuracy for ESC normally equals to or underperforms SC, we mainly compared with SC in Sect. 3.4.

---

[2] We evaluate different prompts in Sect. 3.5.

[3] https://platform.openai.com.

Table 1. Comparison of accuracy (%) between different methods.

Method	Arithmetic			Commonsense			Logic			Avg.	#Call
	AQ.	Alg.	Math.	CMS.	OB.	ARC.	Rid.	Logi.	Rec.		
SC	68.98	43.20	64.00	76.12	**87.04**	89.68	68.72	48.07	61.84	67.52	8.94
ESC	68.98	43.20	64.00	76.12	**87.04**	89.68	68.72	48.07	61.84	67.52	6.79
DCR	**71.02**	**48.60**	**66.52**	**77.97**	86.80	**89.79**	**68.81**	**50.27**	**61.96**	**69.08**	**5.79**
SC*	66.46	43.20	62.52	75.00	85.24	88.98	68.03	48.80	61.00	66.58	6.17
ESC*	68.98	42.20	64.00	76.12	84.68	88.52	68.72	48.07	60.20	66.83	6.17

"Avg." denotes average accuracy over all datasets. "#Call" indicates the average sample size (**inference times**) for each question across nine datasets. *marks the versions with similar sample size of DCR
Bold indicates the best result.

3.3 Main Results

We compared SC [57], ESC [31], and our method across nine datasets, as shown in Table 1. According to Sect. 2.2, we set $2t$ as the upperbound of inference times and defined the window size of ESC as t. Under this limitation, the #Call of original SC is 8.94 with average accuracy as 67.52%. ESC reduces #Call to 6.79 and maintains the accuracy of 67.52%. DCR further reduces #Call to 5.79 while achieves the accuracy of 69.08%, surpassing baselines with 1.56%, which demonstrates dual improvements in efficiency and performance.

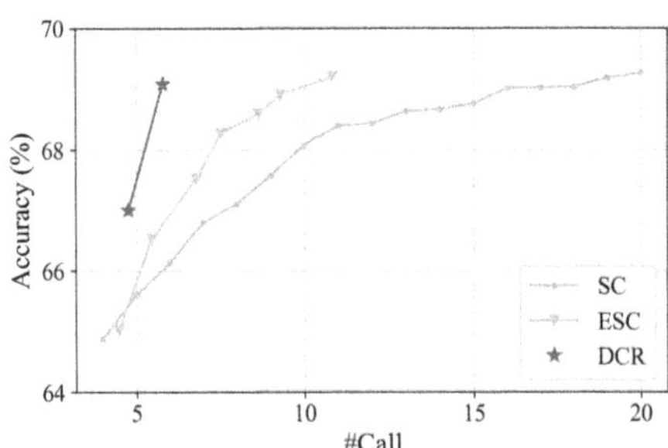

Fig. 2. The relationship between the average accuracy and #Call.

In Fig. 2, we presented the relationship between the average accuracy and #Call across different datasets. And we shown a lower cost DCR, to demonstrate the effectiveness of FCR even inferring only once (i.e. without majority voting) in the conquer stage. Notably, DCR achieves similar accuracy while consuming only 54% of the resource required by ESC and 30% required by SC. When costs are approximate, DCR consistently outperforms SC and ESC by 2.5% and 2.25%, respectively, which is also quantitatively reported in Table 1. Furthermore, we observed a diminishing performance improvement of SC and ESC as sample size increases, indicating a potential bottleneck. However, using FCR for $\mathbb{D}_{low}$ during the conquer stage may breakthrough it.

3.4   Analysis

Table 2. Accuracy (%) across different LLMs.

Setting		AQ.	CMS.
Gemma	SC	34.96 (8.00)	65.31 (6.00)
	DCR	**37.24 (7.50)**	**67.81 (5.98)**
Mistral	SC	39.29 (9.00)	71.37 (7.00)
	DCR	**43.31 (8.97)**	**73.10 (6.51)**
Palm2	SC	38.50 (6.00)	74.15 (6.00)
	DCR	**39.37 (5.21)**	**75.17 (5.53)**
Gemini	SC	**70.39** (8.00)	78.41 (6.00)
	DCR	68.74 **(7.40)**	**78.85 (5.26)**
GPT4	SC	84.17 (6.00)	84.21 (6.00)
	DCR	**85.43 (5.99)**	**85.19 (5.70)**

The number in parenthesis denotes #Call
Bold indicates the best result.

In this section, we compared SC and DCR using various models, including Gemma (gemma-7b-it) [53], Mistral (Mistral-7B-Instruct-v0.2) [22], Palm2 (text-bison-001) [1], Gemini (gemini-pro) [52] and GPT4 (gpt-4-1106-preview) [40]. As shown in Table 2, DCR generally achieves higher accuracy with lower costs, except on AQuA using Gemini. Notably, larger-scale LLMs (e.g. Gemini and GPT4) significantly outperforms other models, especially on AQuA with improvements exceeding 30%. However, this diminishes the relative advantage of DCR, such as the improvements with Mistral are 4.02% and 1.73% on two datasets, while only 1.26% and 0.98% with GPT4. Therefore, we believe that enhancing model capabilities is like addressing weaknesses, which compresses the space for optimization.

Effect of different sample size t. The Prior accuracy (i.e. accuracy in divide stage) is a key metric reflecting the effectiveness of division, where lower $\mathcal{CS}$ is expected to correlate with lower Prior accuracy. Consequently, we conducted experiment to observe the impact of varying t from 3 to 20 on Prior accuracy. As illustrated in Fig. 3, there is a clear distinction in Prior accuracy on different subsets, and only a minimal number of inferences are required to reach an oscillatory state, which supports the reasonability of setting t based on $|\mathbf{C}_i|$. Additionally, the number of different subsets size after division is also a crucial metric, as it directly impacts the overall cost of DCR. Therefore, Fig. 4 presents the sizes of

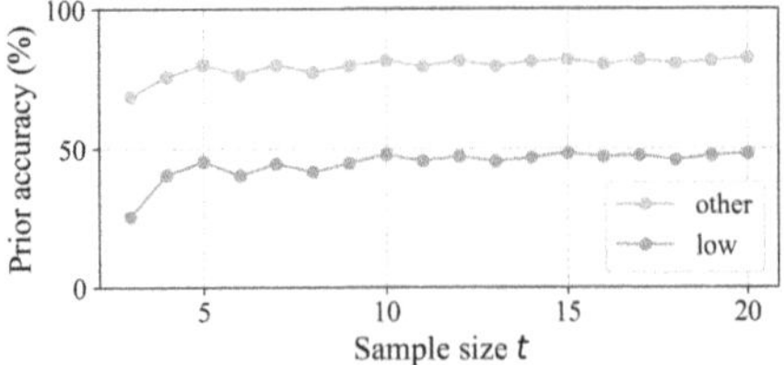

Fig. 3. Average prior accuracy on different subsets for various sample size t.

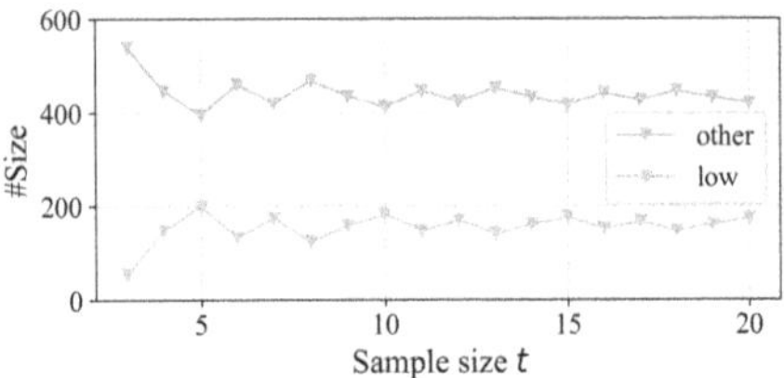

Fig. 4. The average number of different subsets size for various sample size t.

$\mathbb{D}_{other}$ and $\mathbb{D}_{low}$ across various t. Similar to Prior accuracy, the sizes of different subsets also stabilize in a fluctuating range with only minimal inferences.

Effect of different dividing threshold μ. Referring the definition of sample size t and the strategy of DCR in Sect. 2.1, we divided the dataset into four discrete subsets according to $\mathcal{CS}$ intervals: $(0.8, 1]$ for $\mathbb{D}_{high}$, $(0.6, 0.8]$ for $\mathbb{D}_{med}$, $(0.4, 0.6]$ for $\mathbb{D}_{low_t}$, and $[0, 0.4]$ for $\mathbb{D}_{low_b}$. Considering the model's high confidence on $\mathbb{D}_{high}$ ($\mathcal{CS}$ greater than 0.8), we only report Prior accuracy, which exceeds 85% in majority (7 out of 9) of datasets, as shown in Table 3. This indicates that the most questions in $\mathbb{D}_{high}$ are relatively simple and require no further process. Contrastingly, $\mathbb{D}_{med}$ demonstrate moderate Prior accuracy and achieve no improvements via FCR in three tasks. In fact, the $\mathcal{CS}$ for each item in $\mathbb{D}_{med}$ belongs to $(0.6, 0.8]$, indicating that despite the model generates diverse answers, it predominantly focuses on a specific one. This introduces a significant challenge to enhance LLM's performance by correcting its previously generated mistakes, rendering the gains through FCR as limited. In addition, comparing with original DCR, $\mathbb{D}_{low_t}$ and $\mathbb{D}_{low_b}$ comes from further dividing of the $\mathbb{D}_{low}$, where the former has higher $\mathcal{CS}$. Therefore, the average Prior accuracy of $\mathbb{D}_{low_b}$ is only 30.64%, markedly below 44.98% of $\mathbb{D}_{low_t}$, and significantly inferior to others. Meanwhile, through the conquer phase in DCR, we achieve an average accuracy improvement of 10.58% and 12.98% for $\mathbb{D}_{low_t}$ and $\mathbb{D}_{low_b}$, respectively. However, more than half of the $\mathbb{D}_{low_b}$ across various datasets contain a minimal number of data items, making it difficult to reliably report accuracy or effectively improve performance for entire dataset. Therefore, we set the threshold μ as 0.6 to conduct dataset dividing. Furthermore, we reported a visual statistical analysis about distribution of different subsets in Fig. 8 to illustrate the utility of fixing the other subsets for resource saving under current μ.

Table 3. Comparison of accuracy (%) on different confidence subsets.

Subset	Setting	Arithmetic			Commonsense			Logic			Avg.
		AQ.	Alg.	Math.	CMS.	OB.	ARC.	Rid.	Logi.	Rec.	
$\mathbb{D}_{high}$	#Size	74.60	30.40	71.80	588.80	325.80	856.20	404.40	27.60	232.60	290.24
	Prior	91.96	53.95	90.53	92.09	96.13	96.26	89.81	86.96	75.41	85.90
$\mathbb{D}_{med}$	#Size	51.20	38.20	82.40	265.60	97.00	191.20	218.40	81.00	151.40	130.71
	Prior	**79.69**	**43.46**	61.17	**72.74**	**73.61**	**75.42**	**69.60**	**60.49**	51.52	**65.30**
	FCR	74.22	35.08	**62.86**	69.95	70.31	73.95	63.00	53.58	**52.84**	61.75
$\mathbb{D}_{low_t}$	#Size	70.00	30.20	109.60	265.20	74.00	115.40	251.40	153.40	113.20	131.38
	Prior	55.71	28.48	39.60	53.24	50.27	48.87	**50.99**	35.59	42.05	44.98
	FCR	**62.86**	**49.01**	**55.47**	**61.61**	**64.05**	**65.68**	50.68	**42.11**	**48.59**	**55.56**
$\mathbb{D}_{low_b}$	#Size	58.20	1.20	6.20	101.40	3.20	2.20	146.80	38.00	2.80	40.00
	Prior	36.08	–	–	33.14	–	–	35.97	17.37	–	30.64
	FCR	**46.39**	–	–	**52.47**	–	–	**40.87**	**34.74**	–	**43.62**

"#Size" indicates the number of data items in different subsets. "Prior" denotes the accuracy of results generated in the divide stage. For $\mathbb{D}_{low_b}$, "–" refer results lacking reliability because of insufficient data
Bold indicates the best result.

Table 4. Comparison of accuracy (%) for conquering different subsets across different tasks

Conquer subset	Arithmetic	Common-sense	Logic	Avg.	#Call
$\mathbb{D}_{med}$&$\mathbb{D}_{low}$	60.79	84.36	59.39	68.18	6.78
$\mathbb{D}_{low}$	**62.05**	**84.85**	**60.35**	**69.08**	**5.79**

Bold indicates the best result.

Different number of choices. Based on the frequency of results from the Divide phase, we filtered choices lists by keeping the top2 or top3 choices, comparing FCR that retains all results. As shown in Table 6, accuracy decreases with the reduction of retained options. We considered this is mainly due to the decreased probability of the correct option appearing in the choices list (i.e. upperbound of accuracy) as fewer options are kept.

Different conquer subsets. Building upon Sect. 3.4, we retain $\mathbb{D}_{med}$ and combine $\mathbb{D}_{low_t}$ and $\mathbb{D}_{low_b}$ into $\mathbb{D}_{low}$ to compare the impact of conquering different subsets, as shown in Table 4. Conquering only $\mathbb{D}_{low}$ requires an average sample size of 5.79, which is 0.99 lower than conquering $\mathbb{D}_{med}$ and $\mathbb{D}_{low}$ together. Furthermore, conquering $\mathbb{D}_{med}$ and $\mathbb{D}_{low}$ together underperforms in all tasks, which steers us to pay more attention solely on $\mathbb{D}_{low}$ in conquer stage.

Other elimination based methods. There are also some works in the community regarding filtering choices. Specifically, PoE [35] first scores each option to identify incorrect ones and then masks these options to guide prediction based on the remaining ones. PoE-CoT [3] explores the ability of LLMs to select incorrect

Table 5. Comparison of accuracy (%) for various elimination methods.

Method	CMS.	OB.	ARC.
POE	50.03 (70.92*)	30.83 (65.28*)	41.33 (66.84*)
POE-CoT	39.66 (58.43*)	44.04 (68.13*)	39.97 (60.20*)
FCR	**54.39** (89.58*)	**52.33** (92.23*)	**58.16** (93.71*)

*Denotes the upperbound accuracy
Bold indicates the best result.

Table 6. Accuracy (%) for different number of choices.

Dataset	Top2	Top3	FCR
AQ.	69.37 (69.58*)	70.71 (82.06*)	71.02 (85.65*)
CMS.	77.20 (77.85*)	77.87 (86.85*)	77.97 (89.58*)

* is the ceiling of accuracy

options and incorporates CoT into PoE with 10-shot prompt. Therefore, we conducted comparison on $\mathbb{D}_{low}$ of three datasets as shown in Table 5, where FCR consistently outperforms other methods both in real or upperbound accuracy (i.e. the probability of correct answer in filtered choices list). We attribute the superiority of FCR to focus on retaining potentially correct options, whereas others aim to directly eliminate incorrect ones. This aligns with the conclusion from PoE-CoT: LLMs are generally underperforms at eliminating incorrect options than selecting correct ones, as errors tend to propagate through the process (Tables 6 and 7).

Table 7. Accuracy (%) on unsolved subsets with different choices list.

Setting	AQ.	CMS.	OB.	Rid.
List1	2.16	0.97	0.57	1.97
List2.1	21.65	47.58	31.03	28.11
List2.2	29.00	62.10	45.98	**49.25**
List3	18.18	29.46	32.76	24.04
List4	26.41	65.01	**58.05**	44.02
List5	**29.39**	**75.52**	48.85	45.70

Bold indicates the best result.

Different reasoning methods. In this section, we compared zero-shot based FCR with some representative few-shot works: ManualCoT (i.e. CoT) [58], Active-Prompt [14], PHP [70] and Auto-CoT [68], as well as some zero-shot methods: Zero-Shot-CoT [27] and Role-Play Prompting [28]. Considering the diverse datasets they used, we select $\mathbb{D}_{low}$ from two widely employed datasets and evaluated based on a single sample size. We solely conducted PHP on AQuA,

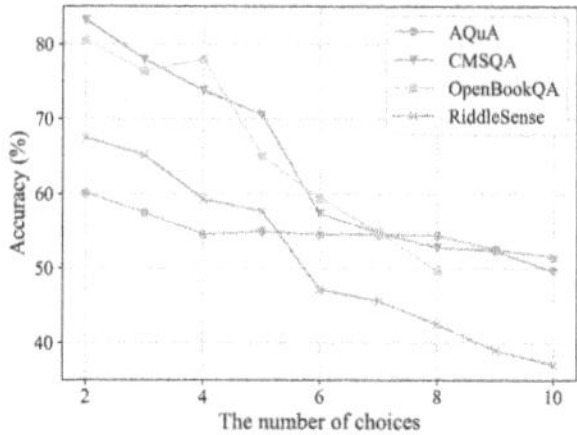

Fig. 5. Impact of different number of choices.

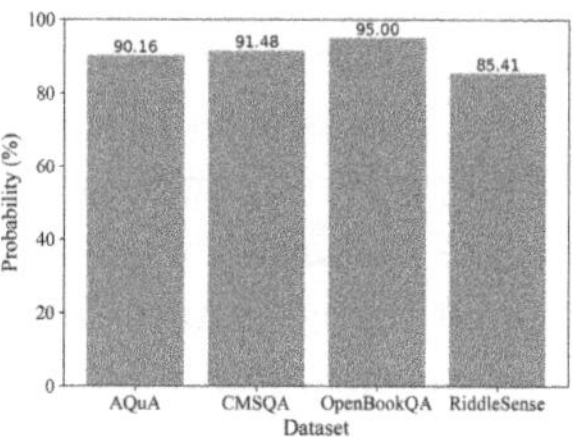

Fig. 6. Probability of containing correct answer.

as it reported results only for arithmetic tasks. As shown in Table 8, FCR achieves the highest accuracy of 49.45% on AQuA, and performs competitively with few-shot methods on CMSQA. A similar trend is shown in Sect. 3.5, where Zero-Shot-CoT approaches or even exceeds Few-Shot-CoT on multiple datasets but still lags on CMSQA. Furthermore, FCR exhibits the highest average accuracy surpassing the sub-optimal zero-shot method by 4.42%, highlighting the strong efficacy without additional human labor.

Study for Irrelevant Choices *Irrelevant information may distract LLM.* [45] investigated the sensitivity of LLM to irrelevant information within questions and proposed to add instruction or exemplars to effectively reduce distractibility. In fact, such irrelevant information is not only limited to the questions,

Table 8. Accuracy (%) with different reasoning methods on $\mathbb{D}_{low}$ in AQuA and CMSQA

Method	AQ.	CMS.	Average
ManualCoT	43.21	56.96	50.09
Active-prompt	42.28	**57.88**	50.08
PHP	44.49	–	–
Zero-Shot-CoT	44.46	45.23	44.85
Role-play prompting	48.20	46.79	47.50
FCR	**49.45**	54.39	**51.92**

Bold indicates the best result.

but also contained in choices list. Therefore, we conducted an analysis on accuracy with different numbers of choices, especially the impact of increasing incorrect options. As in Fig. 5, the accuracy exhibits a noticeable decline with more incorrect options, where we extended choices list by randomly combining wrong answers. To delve deeper, we focused on subsets of problems remaining unsolved by SC [57] with 5 sample size. Then we conducted inference with various choices list as shown in Table 7: (1) presenting the full choices list as List1; (2) combining the correct option with randomly sampled 2 or 1 incorrect ones as List2.1 or List2.2 respectively; (3) using the correct option and deduplicated results from previous inferences as List3; (4) selecting the correct option and choices not included in earlier results as List4; (5) retaining the correct option and randomly picking one from the rest of List4 as List5. The accuracy for List1 close to 0%, while others can significantly enhance performance. However, the correct answers for the test set are unknown in real-world scenario, which leads us to explore the feasibility of utilizing results from previous inference to filter the choices. And we quantified the probability of the correct answer in filtered choices list, as shown in Fig. 6. An average 90.51% of cases retained the correct answers, indicating that earlier results can effectively narrow down the original choices list.

Table 9. Probability of containing strong distractors

Setting	AQ.	CMS.	OB.	Rid.	Avg.
List2.1	51%	46%	26%	61%	46%
List2.2	22%	23%	12%	29%	21.5%

Table 10. Human evaluation on dividing result

	H-Acc	M-Acc	Proportion
$\mathbb{D}_{other}$	50	44	76%
$\mathbb{D}_{low}$	80	86	26%

Table 11. Accuracy (%) beyond MCQs

	SC	DCR
GSM8K	84.75 (7.00)	**85.00 (0.23)**
Word.	82.28 (7.00)	**83.33 (6.88)**

Bold indicates the best result.

Fewer choices lead to better outcomes. Considering the varying impacts of different options have on LLMs, and drawing inspiration from [45], we posit that incorrect choices previously generated by the model-called as strong distractors-exert a more disruptive effect. As shown in Table 7, there is a significant improvement from List3 to List4, with an average increase of 22.26% across four datasets. Furthermore, retaining two choices (List2.2) consistently surpasses those with three choices (List2.1), which can be primarily attributed to the reduced likelihood of encountering strong distractors, as shown in Table 9. Therefore, developing more effective strategies to identify and eliminate such strongly distracting options will become a crucial direction for our future research.

Human Evaluation for Division As shown in Table 10, we sampled 50 data items for $\mathbb{D}_{low}$ and $\mathbb{D}_{other}$ from CMSQA, then reported the accuracy of human[4] (H-Acc) and LLM (M-Acc), as well as evaluated the proportion of hard questions (Proportion). Specifically, we defined hard questions based on [51] as those with: (1) polysemous or ambiguous words, (2) non-general knowledge requirements, or (3) a high degree of overlap among options. It is observed that the proportion of hard questions is higher in $\mathbb{D}_{low}$, and both human and LLM accuracy is lower.

Application Beyond MCQs In previous experiments, all datasets are comprised by MCQs, where the correct answer is included in the choices list. However, there are also non-MCQ scenarios in the real world. Consequently, we applied DCR to GSM8K [11], a high quality cloze-style dataset of grade school math questions, and the symbolic reasoning task Word Sorting from BIG-bench [48], which aimed at alphabetically sorting the given words list. We initially queried the entire test set 5 times, then constructed choices list based on generated answers, converting the datasets into an MCQ format. Subsequently, we divided data items with a threshold (μ) of 0.6 and applied FCR for deeper conquering. From Table 11, DCR achieves accuracy of 85% with 6.23 sample size for GSM8K and 83.33% with 6.88 sample size for Word Sorting, both superior than SC with sample size as 7, which indicates the efficacy of our strategy for datasets beyond MCQs.

3.5   More Results

Zero-Shot Versus Few-Shot By comparing Zero-Shot-CoT [27] and Few-Shot-COT [58] across AQuA [33], GSM8K [11], SVAMP [41] and CMSQA [50] in Table 12, models' zero-shot capabilities are gradually nearing or even surpassing their few-shot counterparts, which is align with the conclusions in recent research [20, 74]. Therefore, our work is entirely free from human intervention and circumvents exemplars construction.

---

[4] Graduate students majoring in computer technology.

Table 12. Comparison between Zero-Shot-CoT and Few-Shot-CoT

Dataset	Zero-Shot-CoT	Few-Shot-CoT
AQuA	54.86 ($\pm$0.67)	53.67 ($\pm$0.67)
GSM8K	79.33 ($\pm$0.34)	79.67 ($\pm$1.18)
SVAMP	78.20 ($\pm$1.82)	81.60 ($\pm$1.34)
CMSQA	69.67 ($\pm$0.77)	77.47 ($\pm$0.96)
Average	70.52	73.10

Different Prompts for FCR Considering the most distinctive feature of FCR is succinct choices list, we conducted a comparison using different prompts, as displayed in Fig. 7. Specifically, "Prompt0" denotes "Let's think step by step.", "Prompt1" is the prompt used in FCR, and "Prompt2" represents "Let's delve deeper into this question to arrive at the best answer.". Across various tasks, the accuracy disparity of FCR with different prompts remains below 2%, without a clear dominance from any single one. Therefore, we believe that the key of good performance for FCR is attributed to a briefer choices list, rather than prompt engineering.

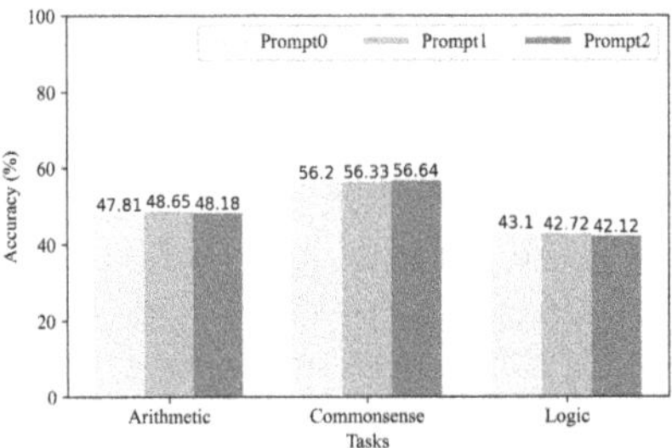

Fig. 7. Accuracy (%) for different prompts across various tasks.

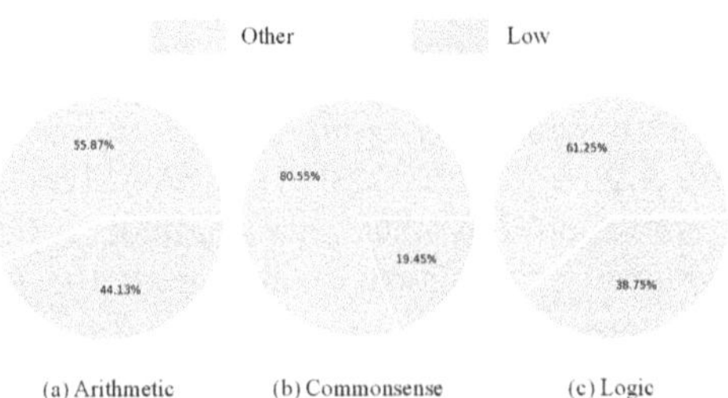

Fig. 8. The average distribution of different subsets across three tasks after the divide stage.

Distribution of Different Subsets Incorporating the dividing results, we conducted a visual statistical analysis to examine the distribution of different confidence subsets among three tasks, as shown in Fig. 8. The proportion of other subsets all exceeds 50% in different tasks and even surpasses 80% in commonsense, which means that we can achieve high accuracy on a substantial portion of data without complex processing. Therefore, based on DCR, we can concentrate more resources on low confidence subsets while effectively avoid redundant process on other ones, which significantly reduce overall expenditure.

Divide:

Q: John farms anemone in what type of facility? **Answer Choices:** (A) michigan (B) swimming pool (C) atlantic ocean (D) nursery (E) gulf of mexico
A1: Let's think step by step. (A) ··· is a state ··· is unlikely ··· farms anemone (B) Anemone are marine ··· not be found in a swimming pool. (C) ··· is a possibility as anemone can be found there ··· (D) ··· a facility where plants are grown, so it is not likely that anemone would be farmed in a nursery. (E) It is likely ··· farms anemone ··· as anemone can be found in ··· Therefore, the most likely answer is (E) Gulf of Mexico. ✗
A2: ··· eliminate (A) and (D) since those are not ocean-related facilities. (C) ··· is a possibility, but we cannot determine ··· (B) ··· is unlikely since anemone is a marine ··· (E) ··· another possibility, as ··· connected to the Atlantic Ocean. ··· answer is (C) Atlantic Ocean or (E) Gulf of Mexico ✗
······

A5: ··· (A) ··· is a state and not a type of facility. (C) and (E) ··· are bodies of water and not facilities. ··· left with (B) and (D) ··· Anemones are typically found in the ocean ··· unlikely ··· in a swimming pool. ··· answer is (D) nursery ✓

Conquer:

Q: John farms anemone in what type of facility? **Answer Choices**: (A) atlantic ocean (B) nursery (C) gulf of mexico
A1: Let's delve deeper into these 3 choices and select the best one. (A) ··· it is unlikely ··· farm anemones directly in the open ocean as ··· difficult to control and manage ··· (B) Anemones can be farmed in specialized facilities called anemone nurseries ··· (C) ··· just like (A), ··· in the open gulf would be challenging due to the lack of control ··· correct answer is (B) nursery. ✓
A2: ··· (A) ··· large body of saltwater, which is unlikely to be a facility ··· (B) ··· Anemone can be grown in a nursery ··· (C) ··· Similar to the Atlantic Ocean, ··· is a natural ecosystem rather than a specific facility··· the most suitable answer is nursery ··· ✓
······

A5: ··· (A) ··· Anemones are typically found in coastal areas or reef environments, rather than open ocean. (B) ··· is a facility where plants or young organisms are grown and nurtured. ··· seems plausible ··· (C) ··· Similar to the Atlantic Ocean, ··· the best answer would be (B) nursery ✓

Fig. 9. Rationales and corresponding standby answer generated in each stage. We use "..." to replace redundant words generated by the LLM for readability.

Case Study We illustrate a question "John farms anemone in what type of facility" with rationales generated in the Divide stage with Zero-Shot-CoT [27], as shown in Fig. 9. LLM effectively eliminates choices (A) and (B). However, it often misses (D) due to focus on the strong association between "nursery" and "plants". Additionally, influenced by the presence of anemone in the Atlantic or Gulf of Mexico, it overlooks key words "farms" and "facility", leading to incorrect select (C) or (E). In the conquer stage, we filter the choices list and guide inference again. LLM can recognize that farming requires a more controlled environment rather than open waters, thereby correctly selecting "nursery". '

4   Related Work

LLMs Reasoning for MCQs. MCQs are prevalent in real world, leading to numerous related datasets, such as MMLU [19], BIG-bench [48], AGIEval [74], CEVAL [21]. Simultaneously, many works have emerged in MCQs community. Reference [43] integrates the question and the choices list to guide the model in selecting the correct option's symbol. Reference [42] reveals that the order of choices can significantly impact the model's performance due to positional bias. Reference [71] shows selection bias, where LLMs prefer options in specific positions. Unlike them, we explore the LLMs' sensitivity to the number of

Table 13. The statistic of datasets.

Dataset	Task type	Eval. Split	#Test (n)	#ChoicesNum ($|\mathbf{C}_i|$)	Infer. Times (t)
AQuA (AQ.)	Arithmetic	Test	254	5	5
Abstract Algebra (Alg.)	Arithmetic	Test	100	4	4
High School Mathematics (Math.)	Arithmetic	Test	270	4	4
CMSQA (CMS.)	Commonsense	Validation	1221	5	5
OpenBookQA (OB.)	Commonsense	Test	500	4	4
ARC Challenge (ARC.)	Commonsense	Test	1165	4	4
RiddleSense (Rid.)	Logic	Validation	1021	5	5
Logical Deduction (Logi.)	Logic	Validation	300	3, 5 or 7	4
Reclor (Rec.)	Logic	Validation	500	4	4
GSM8K	Arithmetic	Test	1319	–	–
Word Sorting (Word.)	Symbolic Reasoning	Validation	252	–	–
SVAMP	Arithmetic	Test	300	–	–

For CMSQA, RiddleSense, Logical Deduction, Reclor and Word Sorting, we select their validation sets as there are no publicly available test sets or labels. GSM8K, Word Sorting and SVAMP are cloze-style dataset without choices list. Particularly, for Logical Deduction, there are 60 questions with $|\mathbf{C}_i|$ as 3, 100 questions as 5, and 140 questions as 7. Therefore, we make a compromise and choose t as 4. Additionally, Word Sorting only includes lists of fewer than 15 words

options and verify that filtering incorrect ones can further improve performance (Table 13).

CoT Prompting in LLMs Reasoning. Recently, CoT prompting methods have greatly enhanced reasoning abilities of LLMs. As the pioneer, Reference [58] generate intermediate reasoning steps by integrating rationales into few-shot examplars. Following it, Reference [5,13,23,25,30,44,57,63,64,75,76] focus on optimizing the thinking process. References [7,8,15,24,62] employ external tools to disentangle computation from LLMs. References [14,46,49,68,77] explore various demonstrations construction. References [12,29,37,65,72] enable models to generate examplars by themselves. References [34,38,59,61,67] introduce the concept of verification. In addition, Reference [45] delves into the distractibility of LLMs by irrelevant context in questions. Reference [70] utilize previously generated answers as hints to progressively guide the model to the correct answer. Reference [28] defines specific roles for the model based on particular task. However, they all process data uniformly, neglecting the problem-solving difficulty. Therefore, we propose DCR, which divides the dataset first and then conquers intricate ones.

5 Conclusion

In this paper, we propose DCR to enhance LLMs for MCQs by dividing dataset based on $\mathcal{CS}$ and subsequently conquering items with low $\mathcal{CS}$. Our evaluation shows that DCR minimizes unnecessary computations for simple problems and substantially improve performance on intricate ones. We also found a positive relation between $\mathcal{CS}$ and accuracy, and fewer choices leading to better results.

Nonetheless, using previously generated results to filter choices fails to effectively eliminate strong distractors and computing $\mathcal{CS}$ through SC is resource-intensive. Therefore, we will develop more efficient strategies for filtering distractions and reducing the computational demand in datasets division in the future.

References

1. Anil, R., Dai, A.M., Firat, O., Johnson, M., Lepikhin, D., Passos, A., Shakeri, S., Taropa, E., Bailey, P., Chen, Z., et al.: Palm 2 technical report. arXiv preprint arXiv:2305.10403 (2023)
2. Bai, J., Bai, S., Chu, Y., Cui, Z., Dang, K., Deng, X., Fan, Y., Ge, W., Han, Y., Huang, F., Hui, B., Ji, L., Li, M., Lin, J., Lin, R., Liu, D., Liu, G., Lu, C., Lu, K., Ma, J., Men, R., Ren, X., Ren, X., Tan, C., Tan, S., Tu, J., Wang, P., Wang, S., Wang, W., Wu, S., Xu, B., Xu, J., Yang, A., Yang, H., Yang, J., Yang, S., Yao, Y., Yu, B., Yuan, H., Yuan, Z., Zhang, J., Zhang, X., Zhang, Y., Zhang, Z., Zhou, C., Zhou, J., Zhou, X., Zhu, T.: Qwen technical report (2023)
3. Balepur, N., Palta, S., Rudinger, R.: It's not easy being wrong: Evaluating process of elimination reasoning in large language models. arXiv preprint arXiv:2311.07532 (2023)
4. Bentley, J.L., Shamos, M.I.: Divide-and-conquer in multidimensional space. In: Proceedings of the eighth annual ACM symposium on theory of computing. pp. 220–230 (1976)
5. Besta, M., Blach, N., Kubicek, A., Gerstenberger, R., Gianinazzi, L., Gajda, J., Lehmann, T., Podstawski, M., Niewiadomski, H., Nyczyk, P., et al.: Graph of thoughts: solving elaborate problems with large language models. arXiv preprint arXiv:2308.09687 (2023)
6. Brown, T., Mann, B., Ryder, N., Subbiah, M., Kaplan, J.D., Dhariwal, P., Neelakantan, A., Shyam, P., Sastry, G., Askell, A., et al.: Language models are few-shot learners. Adv. Neural. Inf. Process. Syst. **33**, 1877–1901 (2020)
7. Chen, W., Ma, X., Wang, X., Cohen, W.W.: Program of thoughts prompting: disentangling computation from reasoning for numerical reasoning tasks. arXiv preprint arXiv:2211.12588 (2022)
8. Chen, Z., Zhou, K., Zhang, B., Gong, Z., Zhao, W.X., Wen, J.R.: Chatcot: Toolaugmented chain-of-thought reasoning on chat-based large language models. arXiv preprint arXiv:2305.14323 (2023)
9. Chowdhery, A., Narang, S., Devlin, J., Bosma, M., Mishra, G., Roberts, A., Barham, P., Chung, H.W., Sutton, C., Gehrmann, S., et al.: Palm: Scaling language modeling with pathways. arXiv preprint arXiv:2204.02311 (2022)
10. Clark, P., Cowhey, I., Etzioni, O., Khot, T., Sabharwal, A., Schoenick, C., Tafjord, O.: Think you have solved question answering? Try arc, the ai2 reasoning challenge. arXiv preprint arXiv:1803.05457 (2018)
11. Cobbe, K., Kosaraju, V., Bavarian, M., Chen, M., Jun, H., Kaiser, L., Plappert, M., Tworek, J., Hilton, J., Nakano, R., et al.: Training verifiers to solve math word problems. arXiv preprint arXiv:2110.14168 (2021)
12. Crispino, N., Montgomery, K., Zeng, F., Song, D., Wang, C.: Agent instructs large language models to be general zero-shot reasoners. arXiv preprint arXiv:2310.03710 (2023)
13. Deb, A., Oza, N., Singla, S., Khandelwal, D., Garg, D., Singla, P.: Fill in the blank: exploring and enhancing llm capabilities for backward reasoning in math word problems. arXiv preprint arXiv:2310.01991 (2023)

14. Diao, S., Wang, P., Lin, Y., Zhang, T.: Active prompting with chain-of-thought for large language models. arXiv preprint arXiv:2302.12246 (2023)
15. Gao, L., Madaan, A., Zhou, S., Alon, U., Liu, P., Yang, Y., Callan, J., Neubig, G.: Pal: Program-aided language models. In: International conference on machine learning, pp. 10764–10799. PMLR (2023)
16. Goldratt, E.M., Cox, J.: The goal: a process of ongoing improvement. Routledge (2016)
17. Guo, D., Yang, D., Zhang, H., Song, J., Zhang, R., Xu, R., Zhu, Q., Ma, S., Wang, P., Bi, X., et al.: Deepseek-r1: incentivizing reasoning capability in llms via reinforcement learning. arXiv preprint arXiv:2501.12948 (2025)
18. Heideman, M., Johnson, D., Burrus, C.: Gauss and the history of the fast Fourier transform. IEEE ASSP Mag. **1**(4), 14–21 (1984)
19. Hendrycks, D., Burns, C., Basart, S., Zou, A., Mazeika, M., Song, D., Steinhardt, J.: Measuring massive multitask language understanding. arXiv preprint arXiv:2009.03300 (2020)
20. Hu, Y., Yang, H., Lin, Z., Zhang, M.: Code prompting: a neural symbolic method for complex reasoning in large language models (2023)
21. Huang, Y., Bai, Y., Zhu, Z., Zhang, J., Zhang, J., Su, T., Liu, J., Lv, C., Zhang, Y., Lei, J., et al.: C-eval: a multi-level multi-discipline Chinese evaluation suite for foundation models. arXiv preprint arXiv:2305.08322 (2023)
22. Jiang, A.Q., Sablayrolles, A., Mensch, A., Bamford, C., Chaplot, D.S., Casas, D.d.l., Bressand, F., Lengyel, G., Lample, G., Saulnier, L., et al.: Mistral 7b. arXiv preprint arXiv:2310.06825 (2023)
23. Jiang, S., Shakeri, Z., Chan, A., Sanjabi, M., Firooz, H., Xia, Y., Akyildiz, B., Sun, Y., Li, J., Wang, Q., et al.: Resprompt: residual connection prompting advances multi-step reasoning in large language models. arXiv preprint arXiv:2310.04743 (2023)
24. Jie, Z., Luong, T.Q., Zhang, X., Jin, X., Li, H.: Design of chain-of-thought in math problem solving. arXiv preprint arXiv:2309.11054 (2023)
25. Jin, Z., Lu, W.: Tab-cot: zero-shot tabular chain of thought. arXiv preprint arXiv:2305.17812 (2023)
26. Knuth, D.E.: Sorting and searching. The art of computer programming **3** (1998)
27. Kojima, T., Gu, S.S., Reid, M., Matsuo, Y., Iwasawa, Y.: Large language models are zero-shot reasoners. Adv. Neural. Inf. Process. Syst. **35**, 22199–22213 (2022)
28. Kong, A., Zhao, S., Chen, H., Li, Q., Qin, Y., Sun, R., Zhou, X.: Better zero-shot reasoning with role-play prompting. arXiv preprint arXiv:2308.07702 (2023)
29. Li, R., Wang, G., Li, J.: Are human-generated demonstrations necessary for in-context learning? arXiv preprint arXiv:2309.14681 (2023)
30. Li, X.L., Shrivastava, V., Li, S., Hashimoto, T., Liang, P.: Benchmarking and improving generator-validator consistency of language models. arXiv preprint arXiv:2310.01846 (2023)
31. Li, Y., Yuan, P., Feng, S., Pan, B., Wang, X., Sun, B., Wang, H., Li, K.: Escape sky-high cost: early-stopping self-consistency for multi-step reasoning. arXiv preprint arXiv:2401.10480 (2024)
32. Lin, B.Y., Wu, Z., Yang, Y., Lee, D.H., Ren, X.: Riddlesense: reasoning about riddle questions featuring linguistic creativity and commonsense knowledge. arXiv preprint arXiv:2101.00376 (2021)
33. Ling, W., Yogatama, D., Dyer, C., Blunsom, P.: Program induction by rationale generation: learning to solve and explain algebraic word problems. arXiv preprint arXiv:1705.04146 (2017)

34. Ling, Z., Fang, Y., Li, X., Huang, Z., Lee, M., Memisevic, R., Su, H.: Deductive verification of chain-of-thought reasoning. arXiv preprint arXiv:2306.03872 (2023)
35. Ma, C., Du, X.: Poe: Process of elimination for multiple choice reasoning. arXiv preprint arXiv:2310.15575 (2023)
36. Mallouk, T.E.: Divide and conquer. Nat. Chem. **5**(5), 362–363 (2013)
37. Mekala, R.R., Razeghi, Y., Singh, S.: Echoprompt: instructing the model to rephrase queries for improved in-context learning. arXiv preprint arXiv:2309.10687 (2023)
38. Miao, N., Teh, Y.W., Rainforth, T.: Selfcheck: Using llms to zero-shot check their own step-by-step reasoning. arXiv preprint arXiv:2308.00436 (2023)
39. Mihaylov, T., Clark, P., Khot, T., Sabharwal, A.: Can a suit of armor conduct electricity? A new dataset for open book question answering. arXiv preprint arXiv:1809.02789 (2018)
40. OpenAI: Gpt-4 technical report. arXiv **abs/2303.08774** (2023)
41. Patel, A., Bhattamishra, S., Goyal, N.: Are NLP models really able to solve simple math word problems? arXiv preprint arXiv:2103.07191 (2021)
42. Pezeshkpour, P., Hruschka, E.: Large language models sensitivity to the order of options in multiple-choice questions. arXiv preprint arXiv:2308.11483 (2023)
43. Robinson, J., Rytting, C.M., Wingate, D.: Leveraging large language models for multiple choice question answering. arXiv preprint arXiv:2210.12353 (2022)
44. Sel, B., Al-Tawaha, A., Khattar, V., Wang, L., Jia, R., Jin, M.: Algorithm of thoughts: enhancing exploration of ideas in large language models. arXiv preprint arXiv:2308.10379 (2023)
45. Shi, F., Chen, X., Misra, K., Scales, N., Dohan, D., Chi, E.H., Schärli, N., Zhou, D.: Large language models can be easily distracted by irrelevant context. In: International conference on machine learning, pp. 31210–31227. PMLR (2023)
46. Shum, K., Diao, S., Zhang, T.: Automatic prompt augmentation and selection with chain-of-thought from labeled data. arXiv preprint arXiv:2302.12822 (2023)
47. Smith, D.R.: The design of divide and conquer algorithms. Sci. Comput. Program. **5**, 37–58 (1985)
48. Srivastava, A., Rastogi, A., Rao, A., Shoeb, A.A.M., Abid, A., Fisch, A., Brown, A.R., Santoro, A., Gupta, A., Garriga-Alonso, A., et al.: Beyond the imitation game: Quantifying and extrapolating the capabilities of language models. arXiv preprint arXiv:2206.04615 (2022)
49. Sun, J., Luo, Y., Gong, Y., Lin, C., Shen, Y., Guo, J., Duan, N.: Enhancing chain-of-thoughts prompting with iterative bootstrapping in large language models. arXiv preprint arXiv:2304.11657 (2023)
50. Talmor, A., Herzig, J., Lourie, N., Berant, J.: Commonsenseqa: a question answering challenge targeting commonsense knowledge. arXiv preprint arXiv:1811.00937 (2018)
51. Tarrant, M., Ware, J., Mohammed, A.M.: An assessment of functioning and non-functioning distractors in multiple-choice questions: a descriptive analysis. BMC Med. Educ. **9**, 1–8 (2009)
52. Team, G., Anil, R., Borgeaud, S., Wu, Y., Alayrac, J.B., Yu, J., Soricut, R., Schalkwyk, J., Dai, A.M., Hauth, A., et al.: Gemini: a family of highly capable multimodal models. arXiv preprint arXiv:2312.11805 (2023)
53. Team, G., Mesnard, T., Hardin, C., Dadashi, R., Bhupatiraju, S., Pathak, S., Sifre, L., Rivière, M., Kale, M.S., Love, J., et al.: Gemma: Open models based on gemini research and technology. arXiv preprint arXiv:2403.08295 (2024)

54. Thoppilan, R., De Freitas, D., Hall, J., Shazeer, N., Kulshreshtha, A., Cheng, H.T., Jin, A., Bos, T., Baker, L., Du, Y., et al.: Lamda: language models for dialog applications. arXiv preprint arXiv:2201.08239 (2022)
55. Touvron, H., Lavril, T., Izacard, G., Martinet, X., Lachaux, M.A., Lacroix, T., Rozière, B., Goyal, N., Hambro, E., Azhar, F., et al.: Llama: open and efficient foundation language models. arXiv preprint arXiv:2302.13971 (2023)
56. Touvron, H., Martin, L., Stone, K., Albert, P., Almahairi, A., Babaei, Y., Bashlykov, N., Batra, S., Bhargava, P., Bhosale, S., et al.: Llama 2: open foundation and fine-tuned chat models. arXiv preprint arXiv:2307.09288 (2023)
57. Wang, X., Wei, J., Schuurmans, D., Le, Q., Chi, E., Narang, S., Chowdhery, A., Zhou, D.: Self-consistency improves chain of thought reasoning in language models. arXiv preprint arXiv:2203.11171 (2022)
58. Wei, J., Wang, X., Schuurmans, D., Bosma, M., Xia, F., Chi, E., Le, Q.V., Zhou, D., et al.: Chain-of-thought prompting elicits reasoning in large language models. Adv. Neural. Inf. Process. Syst. **35**, 24824–24837 (2022)
59. Weng, Y., Zhu, M., Xia, F., Li, B., He, S., Liu, K., Zhao, J.: Large language models are better reasoners with self-verification. CoRR, abs/2212.09561 (2023)
60. Xiong, M., Hu, Z., Lu, X., Li, Y., Fu, J., He, J., Hooi, B.: Can llms express their uncertainty? An empirical evaluation of confidence elicitation in llms (2023)
61. Xue, T., Wang, Z., Wang, Z., Han, C., Yu, P., Ji, H.: Rcot: detecting and rectifying factual inconsistency in reasoning by reversing chain-of-thought. arXiv preprint arXiv:2305.11499 (2023)
62. Yamauchi, R., Sonoda, S., Sannai, A., Kumagai, W.: Lpml: Llm-prompting markup language for mathematical reasoning. arXiv preprint arXiv:2309.13078 (2023)
63. Yan, S., Shen, C., Liu, J., Ye, J.: Concise and organized perception facilitates large language models for deductive reasoning. arXiv preprint arXiv:2310.03309 (2023)
64. Yao, S., Yu, D., Zhao, J., Shafran, I., Griffiths, T.L., Cao, Y., Narasimhan, K.: Tree of thoughts: deliberate problem solving with large language models. arXiv preprint arXiv:2305.10601 (2023)
65. Yasunaga, M., Chen, X., Li, Y., Pasupat, P., Leskovec, J., Liang, P., Chi, E.H., Zhou, D.: Large language models as analogical reasoners. arXiv preprint arXiv:2310.01714 (2023)
66. Yu, W., Jiang, Z., Dong, Y., Feng, J.: Reclor: a reading comprehension dataset requiring logical reasoning. arXiv preprint arXiv:2002.04326 (2020)
67. Zhang, H., Cai, M., Zhang, X., Zhang, C.J., Mao, R., Wu, K.: Self-convinced prompting: few-shot question answering with repeated introspection. arXiv preprint arXiv:2310.05035 (2023)
68. Zhang, Z., Zhang, A., Li, M., Smola, A.: Automatic chain of thought prompting in large language models. arXiv preprint arXiv:2210.03493 (2022)
69. Zhao, F., Lu, C., Wang, Y., Xie, Z., Liu, Z., Qian, H., Huang, J., Shi, F., Meng, Z., Guo, H., et al.: Redone: revealing domain-specific llm post-training in social networking services. arXiv preprint arXiv:2507.10605 (2025)
70. Zheng, C., Liu, Z., Xie, E., Li, Z., Li, Y.: Progressive-hint prompting improves reasoning in large language models. arXiv preprint arXiv:2304.09797 (2023)
71. Zheng, C., Zhou, H., Meng, F., Zhou, J., Huang, M.: On large language models' selection bias in multi-choice questions. arXiv preprint arXiv:2309.03882 (2023)
72. Zheng, H.S., Mishra, S., Chen, X., Cheng, H.T., Chi, E.H., Le, Q.V., Zhou, D.: Take a step back: evoking reasoning via abstraction in large language models. arXiv preprint arXiv:2310.06117 (2023)

73. Zheng, L., Chiang, W.L., Sheng, Y., Zhuang, S., Wu, Z., Zhuang, Y., Lin, Z., Li, Z., Li, D., Xing, E., et al.: Judging llm-as-a-judge with mt-bench and chatbot arena. arXiv preprint arXiv:2306.05685 (2023)
74. Zhong, W., Cui, R., Guo, Y., Liang, Y., Lu, S., Wang, Y., Saied, A., Chen, W., Duan, N.: Agieval: a human-centric benchmark for evaluating foundation models. arXiv preprint arXiv:2304.06364 (2023)
75. Zhou, D., Schärli, N., Hou, L., Wei, J., Scales, N., Wang, X., Schuurmans, D., Cui, C., Bousquet, O., Le, Q., et al.: Least-to-most prompting enables complex reasoning in large language models. arXiv preprint arXiv:2205.10625 (2022)
76. Zhu, Z., Xue, Y., Chen, X., Zhou, D., Tang, J., Schuurmans, D., Dai, H.: Large language models can learn rules. arXiv preprint arXiv:2310.07064 (2023)
77. Zou, A., Zhang, Z., Zhao, H., Tang, X.: Meta-cot: generalizable chain-of-thought prompting in mixed-task scenarios with large language models. arXiv preprint arXiv:2310.06692 (2023)

Energy-Efficient Equality Test with Public Key Encryption and Flexible Authorisation for Sustainable Cloud Computing

Xiaoshuai Zhang[1(✉)], Zhaoqing Wang[1], Zhen Yan[1], Qingdi Han[1], Xi-jun Lin[1], Zhao Huang[3], Guangyuan Zhang[4], Yuhan Gao[2,5], Zhiwen Zheng[2], Haipeng Qu[1], and Jin Liu[2]

[1] Faculty of Information Science and Engineering, Ocean University of China, Qingdao, China
x.zhang@ouc.edu.cn, wzq6465@stu.ouc.edu.cn , hqd@stu.ouc.edu.cn,
linxj77@ouc.edu.cn, quhaipeng@ouc.edu.cn
[2] Hangzhou Dianzi University, Hangzhou, China
zhiwen.zheng@hdu.edu.cn, jinliu@hdu.edu.cn
[3] School of Natural and Computing Sciences, University of Aberdeen, Aberdeen, United Kingdom
zhao.huang@abdn.ac.uk
[4] School of Earth System Science, Tianjin University, Tianjin, China
guangyuanzhang@tju.edu.cn
[5] Lishui Institute of Hangzhou Dianzi University, Lishui, China
yuhangao@hdu.edu.cn

Abstract. Public key encryption with equality test (PKEET) is useful in cloud computing to determine whether two ciphertexts encrypted using different public keys contain the same content part in order to filter or query the encrypted content. However, this is open to an attack by non-authorised clouds performing tests on candidate content parts to reveal it answers the query. To prevent this, PKEET with flexible authorisation (PKEET-FA) has been proposed. However, when PKEET-FA is deployed on low-resource devices in a more sustainable cloud context, such as Internet of Things (IoT) networks, its higher computational cost incurs a higher energy cost due to its complex Bilinear Pairings operations (BP) which are more time-consuming and energy-consuming than point multiplication operations. In this paper, we present a new energy-efficient PKEET-FA scheme called EPKEET-FA. Unlike PKEET-FA and other similar schemes, EPKEET-FA does not use BP operations but instead uses point multiplication operations on elliptic curves. Hence,

Xiaoshuai Zhang and Zhaoqing Wang contributed to this work equally.
Xiaoshuai Zhang and Yuhan Gao: This research was supported in part by the Excellent Young Scientists Fund Program (Overseas) of Shandon Provicne, China (Grant No. 2025HWYQ-033) and the "Leading Goose" R&D Program of Zhejiang Province, China (Grant No. 2023C01218).

it is better suited for sustainable cloud computing use. EPKEET-FA also supports flexible authorisation with a superior energy efficiency that other PKEET-related schemes cannot achieve. A series of experiments are conducted to validate the implementation of EPKEET-FA against similar schemes as baselines. The results show that the energy efficiency of EPKEET-FA is significantly better on the conventional client computer and the low-resource IoT device, as typical end devices of cloud computing.

Keywords: Equality test · Searchable encryption · Sustainable cloud computing

1   Introduction

Cloud computing enables companies and organisations to reduce the cost of ownership and operation of data storage and processing through accessing pooled remote computing resources on demand. A crucial concern is how to control energy consumption without sacrificing too much computing performance [1]. The major goal of sustainable cloud computing is to maximise the energy efficiency in computation, storage and transmission compared to conventional cloud computing [2]. Some surveys have also indicated that the energy cost of clusters in cloud computing could account for more than half of the total energy cost of all clouds [1]. Furthermore, increased energy consumption has also been linked to increased carbon emissions due to the preponderance of carbon-based energy sources. However, there are only few studies considering energy-efficient algorithms for cloud computing to improve sustainability [3]. Whilst the energy-efficiency and computation efficiency of cloud servers dominate, the energy efficiency of a greater wealth of low-resource front-end access devices that are connected to the back-end cloud servers as part of an Internet of Things (IoT) [4], acting as data conduits is also a concern in order to maximise their operational uptime [5].

Data security is a fundamental system requirement for cloud computing [6,7]. Therefore, numerous security schemes based largely upon public key cryptography are supported such as authentication, key exchange (handshakes) and data aggregation [8,9]. Public key encryption with equality test (PKEET) is a security scheme used in cloud computing commonly, which can be applied to examine if two encrypted ciphertexts contain the identical plaintext without exposing the plaintexts. Thus, its main benefit is to keep the document content confidential, e.g., from the cloud server provider while supporting limited checks on the content, i.e., for key words. It supports a search functionality on the server side without decrypting the data to maintain data confidentiality. This is more generally called searchable encryption. A secondary benefit is that the computation cost of decrypting the whole document into plain text to do the test is avoided. The notion of PKEET was firstly presented by Yang et al. [10]. PKEET has a wide range of applications, for example, enabling encrypted documents to be managed on cloud servers without giving decryption key access to the cloud server provider, filtering and routing encrypted emails based upon content, allowing checks to me made on a work-flow of encrypted documents, e.g., to allow queries about a hospital patient's condition and treatment without revealing the full patient history to the inquirer. However, there are two main limitations of PKEET. Firstly, PKEET has no consideration for privacy protection of the test itself, which can be executed without the authorisation from the data owners. Secondly, the energy efficiency of PKEET is low because it is built on Bilinear Pairings [11].

1.1 Related Work

PKEET is a common operation to check sensitive words in cloud computing but it lacks authorisation to issue proper permissions to the cloud server to perform the equality test. To implement the authorisation to protect user privacy, several notions of PKEET with authorisation [12–15] have been proposed. However, these notions all apply time-consuming Bilinear Parings as the public key encryption foundation. The schemes presented by Tang [13–15] are only One-Way against a Chosen-Ciphertext Attack (OW-CCA) for a random oracle, which is a weak security assumption.

In order to generalise the previous notions about authorisation in PKEET, Ma et al. proposed PKEET to also support flexible authorisation (PKEET-FA) [16]. This improves data privacy protection via defining four levels of authorisation granularity: Type-1 user level authorisation, Type-2 ciphertext level authorisation, Type-3 user-specific ciphertext level authorisation and Type-4 ciphertext-to-user (or user-to-ciphertext) level authorisation (see Sect. 2. A for more details).

There are also some other notions related to PKEET. One is called deterministic encryption (DE) proposed by Bellare et al. [17]. DE can be transformed to a specific kind of equality test via encrypting the plaintexts with the same public key. However, in the PKEET model [10], the plaintexts should be encrypted by different users' public keys. Another notion is called public key encryption with keyword search (PEKS) proposed by Boneh et al. [18]. PEKS is a method for searching encrypted keywords in ciphertexts without retrieving plaintexts via trapdoors, where a trapdoor is special information that enables a trapdoor function to be easy to compute in one direction, yet difficult to compute in the inverse direction, without knowing the trapdoor itself.

1.2 Contributions

Bilinear Pairings is selected as the public key encryption method in most of the existing PKEET schemes due to its flexible exponentiation. However, it has a higher energy consumption compared with other public key encryption methods [2]. Note that on average, the time and energy cost of the pairing operation is about five times that of a point multiplication operation on an elliptic curve. There are two recent optimised PKEET schemes without Bilinear Parings that were proposed by Lee et al. [12] and Tang [13]. However, compared with PKEET-FA, the flexibility of the authorisation in these schemes is limited since the scheme in [13] does not support any authorisation. Meanwhile, the scheme in [12] can only support a user-level authorisation (Type-1). Therefore, an optimised PKEET-FA scheme without Bilinear Pairings could be more efficient and cost less energy when applied in cloud computing.

Based upon the above motivations, we propose the EPKEET-FA scheme, which avoids the use of Bilinear Pairings, to improve the energy efficiency for low-resource devices and sustainable clouds. The main methods used in our EPKEET-FA scheme are symmetric encryption and elliptic curve cryptology (ECC). The definitions and security options that our scheme can satisfy are the same as PKEET-FA [16]. Compared with the PKEET-FA scheme as a baseline, EPKEET-FA's computational efficiency for the equality test (including *Authorisation* and *Test*) is much improved with a lower energy consumption that is more suitable for use in both low-resource end devices and conventional computers. Compared with other PKEET schemes [10,13–15], our proposed scheme has the advantage of being significantly more computationally and energy efficient, coupled with its support for authorisation flexibility to protect data access.

1.3 Organisation

The rest of this paper is organised as follows. The definitions of four levels of authorisation granularity in PKEET-FA [16] and the Computational Elliptic Curve Diffie-Hellman (C-ECDH) problem are given in Sect. 5.2. Then, our scheme model, and the definitions and the security options from [16] are introduced in Sect. 5.3. After that, we illustrate our EPKEET-FA scheme in Sect. 4 and prove that the proposed new scheme can satisfy its given security options in Sect. 5. In Sect. 6, the computational efficiency and energy consumption comparison is offered, and the results of the computational efficiency validation the energy efficiency experiments are demonstrated, which is followed by the final section to conclude our work.

2 Preliminaries

2.1 Computational Elliptic Curve Diffie-Hellman (C-ECDH) Problem

The Computational Elliptic Curve Diffie-Hellman (C-ECDH) Problem is defined as follows: Let $E_p(a,b)$ be a secure cryptographic elliptic curve with a base point G. For any point $P \in E$ and $x,y \in_R \mathbb{Z}_p^*$, any probabilistic polynomial-time algorithm $\mathcal{A}$ computes xyP with its advantage:

$$Adv_{\mathcal{A},E_p(a,b)}^{C-ECDH} = Pr[w = xyP | x,y \in_R \mathbb{Z}_p^*, w = \mathcal{A}(P,xP,yP)].$$

The C-ECDH assumption can hold if for any probabilistic polynomial-time algorithm $\mathcal{A}$, its advantage $Adv_{\mathcal{A},E_p(a,b)}^{C-ECDH}$ is negligible.

3   Model and Definition

In this section, we first depict our system model and then recall the definitions and security options presented in the PKEET-FA scheme [16] because our new scheme is proposed under these definitions and security options.

3.1   Scheme Model

There are four entities as shown in Fig. 1: a cloud server, two users, for example, Alice and Bob, and a trusted third party (TTP) in a EPKEET-FA system. The TTP is used to initialise the system and generate the public parameters for users and the cloud server. The ciphertext C (resp. C') encrypted from message M (resp. M') with Alice's (resp. Bob's) public key can be outsourced to the cloud server. Alice and Bob can authorise the cloud server to test the equality of M and M' without decrypting C and C'. In this model, two users can encrypt plaintext and authorise the test from both conventional computers and low-resource devices.

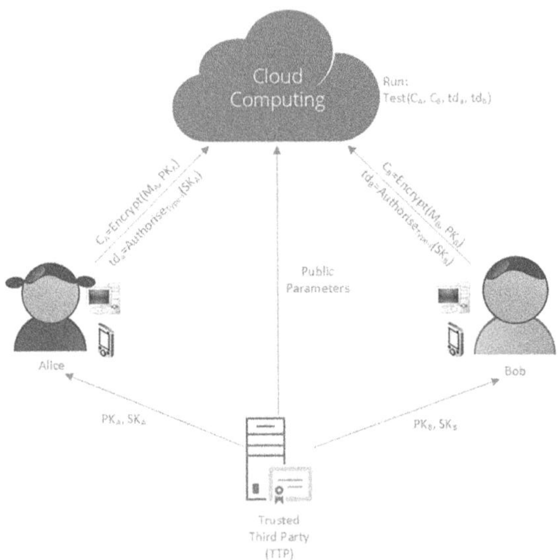

Fig. 1. The system model of EPKEET-FA including the trusted thrid party (TTP), two users and a cloud server

3.2   Scheme Definition

Definition 1 (PKEET-FA) A PKEET-FA scheme consists of the following algorithms:

- *Setup*(λ): takes the security parameter λ to initialize the public parameter pp;

- $KeyGenerator(pp)$: utilizes the public parameter pp to generate a public and private key pair (pk, sk);
- $Encrypt(pp, M, pk)$: uses the public parameter pp, a message M and the user's public key pk to compute the ciphertext C;
- $Decrypt(pp, C, sk)$: uses the public parameter pp, a ciphertext C and the user's private key sk to retrieve the original message M (or an error symbol $\perp$ if the decryption fails).

We assume that the receiver U_i's (resp. U_j's) public and private key pair is (pk, sk) (resp. (pk', sk')), and the corresponding ciphertext is C (resp. C'). For Type-π ($\pi = 1, 2, 3, 4$) authorisation, the algorithm $Auth_\pi(\pi = 1, 2, 3, 4)$ is defined to output a trapdoor to test the equality of C and C'. Then, the algorithm $Test_\pi(\pi = 1, 2, 3, 4)$ is defined to check if C and C' contain the same message or not. There are four types of authorisation as follows.

• *Type-1 Authorisation:*

$Auth_1(sk)$: This algorithm can generate a trapdoor td_1 for U_i via using U_i's private key sk.

$Test_1(C, td_1, C', td_1')$: This algorithm uses ciphertext C, trapdoor td_1, ciphertext C' and trapdoor td_1' to output 1 if C and C' contain the same message or 0 otherwise.

• *Type-2 Authorisation:*

$Auth_2(sk, C)$: This algorithm can generate a trapdoor td_2 for U_i via using U_i's private key sk and ciphertext C.

$Test_2(C, td_2, C', td_2')$: This algorithm uses ciphertext C, trapdoor td_2, ciphertext C' and trapdoor td_2' to output 1 if C and C' contain the same message or 0 otherwise.

• *Type-3 Authorisation:*

$Auth_3(sk, C, C')$: This algorithm can generate a trapdoor td_3 for U_i via using U_i's private key sk, ciphertext C and C'.

$Test_3(C, td_3, C', td_3')$: This algorithm uses ciphertext C, trapdoor td_3, ciphertext C' and trapdoor td_3' to output 1 if C and C' contain the same message or 0 otherwise.

• *Type-4 Authorisation:*

$Auth_4(sk, C)$: This algorithm can generate a trapdoor $td_4 = Auth_2(sk, C)$ for (U_i, C) via using U_i's private key sk and ciphertext C.

$Auth_4'(sk')$: This algorithm can generate a trapdoor $td_4' = Auth_1(sk')$ for U_j via using U_j's private key sk'.

$Test_4(C, td_4, C', td_4')$: This algorithm uses ciphertext C, trapdoor td_4, ciphertext C' and trapdoor td_4' to output 1 if C and C' contain the same message or 0 otherwise.

4   Proposed EPKEET-FA Scheme

In this section, our new scheme EPKEET-FA is proposed firstly and then its correctness and security are proved in the next two parts.

4.1   The Proposed Scheme—EPKEET-FA

Setup(λ) This algorithm outputs public parameters pp in the following steps.

1. Pick a cryptographic secure elliptic curve group $\mathbb{G}$ with a base point G on the curve, and the order of $\mathbb{G}$ is p.

2. Select two secure cryptographic hash functions: $H_1 : \{0,1\}^* \to \{0,1\}^\lambda$, $H_2 : \mathbb{G} \to \{0,1\}^{\lambda+l}$ and $H_3 : \mathbb{G} \to \{0,1\}^\lambda$, where l represents the maximum bit length of all elements in $\mathbb{Z}_p^*$.

3. Select a symmetric encryption algorithm denoted by the symbol SE for the following description. Note that $SE_{key}(M)$ means encrypting the message M with the key key and $SE'_{key}(C)$ means decrypting the ciphertext C with the key key.

4. Output $pp = (\mathbb{G}, p, G, H_1, H_2, SE)$.

KeyGenerate(pp) This algorithm picks $\alpha, \beta \in_R \mathbb{Z}_p^*$ randomly and outputs the user's key pair:

$$(pk, sk) = ((A = \alpha G, B = \beta G), (\alpha, \beta)).$$

Encrypt(pp,M,pk) When the message $M \in \{0,1\}^\lambda$ is given, this algorithm could output the encrypted ciphertext $C = (C_1, C_2, C_3, C_4)$ via following steps:

1. Compute $H_M = H_1(M)$.

2. Use SE to encrypt message M with the key H_M then get the ciphertext $SE_{H_M}(M)$.

3. Pick two random numbers $r1, r2 \in_R \mathbb{Z}_p^*$ then compute

$$C_1 = r_1 G,$$
$$C_2 = r_2 G,$$
$$C_3 = (r_1, H_M) \oplus H_2(r_1 A),$$
$$C_4 = SE_{H_M}(M) \oplus H_1(r_2 B, C_1, C_2, C_3).$$

Decrypt(pp,C,sk) Based upon a given ciphertext $C = (C_1, C_2, C_3, C_4)$, this algorithm executes the following steps to retrieve the plaintext M:

1. Recover r_1 and H_M via computing $C_3 \oplus H_2(\alpha C_1)$.

2. Recover $SE_{H_M}(M)$ via computing $C_4 \oplus H_1(\beta C_2, C_1, C_2, C_3)$.

3. Decrypt $SE_{H_M}(M)$ with the key H_M, $M = SE'_{H_M}(SE_{H_M}(M))$.

4. If $H_1(M) = H_M$ holds, this algorithm outputs M; or, it outputs $\perp$.

In the next part, the process of the four types of authorisation mentioned in Definition 1 will be illustrated.

Alice (whose public and private key pair is (pk, sk)) and Bob (whose public and private key pair is (pk', sk')) are two users in the system. $C = (C_1, C_2, C_3, C_4)$ (resp. $C' = (C'_1, C'_2, C'_3, C'_4)$) is the ciphertext of Alice (resp. Bob). Correspondingly, r_1 and r_2 (resp. r'_1 and r'_2) are the random numbers used to generate the ciphertext C (resp. C').

- *Type-1 Authorisation:*
  $Auth_1(sk)$: This algorithm outputs a trapdoor $td_1 = \beta$.
  $Test_1(C, td_1, C', td'_1)$: This algorithm computes

$$C_4 \oplus H_1(td_1 C_2, C_1, C_2, C_3) = SE_{H_M}(M)$$
$$C_4' \oplus H_1(td_1' C_2', C_1', C_2', C_3') = SE_{H_{M'}}(M')$$

If $SE_{H_M}(M) = SE_{H_{M'}}(M')$ holds, it returns 1, or otherwise 0.

- *Type-2 Authorisation:*

$Auth_2(sk, C)$: This algorithm outputs a trapdoor $td_2 = H_1(\beta C_2, C_1, C_2, C_3)$.

$Test_2(C, td_2, C', td_2')$: This algorithm computes
$$C_4 \oplus td_2 = SE_{H_M}(M)$$
$$C_4' \oplus td_2' = SE_{H_{M'}}(M')$$

If $SE_{H_M}(M) = SE_{H_{M'}}(M')$ holds, it returns 1, or otherwise 0.

- *Type-3 Authorisation:*

$Auth_3(sk, C, C')$: Firstly, this algorithm uses the same steps in *Decrypt* to recover r_1 from C_3. After that, it computes $H_3(r_1 C_1')$ and finally outputs a trapdoor $td_3 = H_3(r_1 C_1') \oplus H_1(\beta C_2, C_1, C_2, C_3)$.

$Test_3(C, td_3, C', td_3')$: This algorithm computes
$$C_4 \oplus td_3 = SE_{H_M}(M) \oplus H_3(r_1 C_1')$$
$$C_4' \oplus td_3' = SE_{H_{M'}}(M') \oplus H_3(r_1' C_1)$$

If $C_4 \oplus td_3 = C_4' \oplus td_3'$ holds, it returns 1, or otherwise 0.

- *Type-4 Authorisation:*

$Auth_4(sk, C)$: This algorithm outputs a trapdoor $td_4 = Auth_2(sk, C) = H_1(\beta C_2, C_1, C_2, C_3)$.

$Auth_4'(sk')$: This algorithm outputs a trapdoor $td_4' = Auth_1'(sk') = \beta'$.

$Test_4(C, td_4, C', td_4')$: This algorithm computes
$$C_4 \oplus td_4 = SE_{H_M}(M)$$
$$C_4' \oplus H_1(td_4' C_2', C_1', C_2', C_3') = SE_{H_{M'}}(M')$$

If $SE_{H_M}(M) = SE_{H_{M'}}(M')$ holds, it returns 1, or otherwise 0.

4.2   Correctness

The following facts hold for any given message M (resp. M'): if $M = M'$, $H_1(M) = H_1(M')$ holds. Furthermore, $SE_{H_M}(M) = SE_{H_{M'}}(M')$ holds as well. Therefore, for any given public and private key pairs (pk, sk) (resp. (pk', sk')) and $C = Encrypt(M, pk)$ (resp. $C' = Encrypt(M', pk')$), the following four types of authorisation hold.

- Type-1 Authorisation: Through the given $td_1 = \beta$ and $td_1' = \beta'$, we can compute

$$C_4 \oplus H_1(td_1 C_2, C_1, C_2, C_3) = SE_{H_M}(M)$$

$$C_4' \oplus H_1(td_1' C_2', C_1', C_2', C_3') = SE_{H_{M'}}(M')$$

  From the above anaylsis, we can state that $SE_{H_M}(M) = SE_{H_{M'}}(M')$ if $M = M'$.

- Type-2 Authorisation: Through the given $td_2 = H_1(\beta C_2, C_1, C_2, C_3)$ and $td_2' = H_1(\beta' C_2', C_1', C_2', C_3')$, we can compute
$$C_4 \oplus td_2 = SE_{H_M}(M)$$

$$C'_4 \oplus td'_2 = SE_{H_{M'}}(M')$$

From the above analysis, we can state that $SE_{H_M}(M) = SE_{H_{M'}}(M')$ if $M = M'$.

- Type-3 Authorisation: The algorithm first computes $H_3(r_1 C'_1)$ and $H_3(r'_1 C_1)$. After that, through the given trapdoors $td_3 = H_3(r_1 C'_1) \oplus H_1(\beta C_2, C_1, C_2, C_3)$ and $td'_3 = H_3(r'_1 C_1) \oplus H_1(\beta' C'_2, C'_1, C'_2, C'_3)$, we can compute

$$C_4 \oplus td_3 = SE_{H_M}(M) \oplus H_3(r_1 C'_1)$$
$$C'_4 \oplus td'_3 = SE_{H_{M'}}(M') \oplus H_3(r'_1 C_1)$$

We notice that $H_3(r_1 C'_1) = H_3(r'_1 C_1)$ holds naturally ($= H_3(r_1 r'_1 G)$). Thus, $C_4 \oplus td_3 = C'_4 \oplus td'_3$ holds if the condition $SE_{H_M}(M) = SE_{H_{M'}}(M')$ is established. This means that $H_M = H_{M'}$ and $M = M'$ should be satisfied. Based on the above analysis, we can state that $C_4 \oplus td_3 = C'_4 \oplus td'_3$ if $M = M'$.

- Type-4 Authorisation: Through the given $td_4 = H_1(\beta C_2, C_1, C_2, C_3)$ and $td'_4 = \beta'$, we can compute

$$C_4 \oplus td_4 = SE_{H_M}(M)$$
$$C'_4 \oplus td'_4 = SE_{H_{M'}}(M')$$

From the above analysis, we can state that $SE_{H_M}(M) = SE_{H_{M'}}(M')$ if $M = M'$.

Note that if $M \neq M'$, $Pr[H_M = H_{M'}]$ is negligible. Even if the hash collision is taken into consideration, symmetric encryption still works since using the symmetric encryption algorithm to encrypt different plaintexts with the same key can always generate different ciphertexts. Thus, $Pr[SE_{H_M}(M) = SE_{H_{M'}}(M')]$ is negligible if $M \neq M'$.

Based upon the analysis above, the following statements hold. For Type-π Authorisation ($\pi = 1, 2, 3, 4$), if $Test_\pi(C, td_1, C', td'_1) = 1$ holds, it means that $SE_{H_M}(M) = SE_{H_{M'}}(M')$ (i.e. $M = M'$). Otherwise, $Pr[Test_\pi(C, td_1, C', td'_1) = 1]$ is negligible if $M \neq M'$.

5   Experimental Validation

In this section, we validate that our proposed EPKEET-FA scheme is more computationally efficient (in terms of the computation time taken) against other state-of-the-art schemes used as baselines: the original PKEET scheme [10], PKEET-FA scheme [16] (major baseline), and other PKEET schemes [12–15]. First, this is done through an analysis of the types of cryptographic operation needed (Sect. 5.1). Second, when the different schemes are implemented and repeatedly executed, we show that there is a clear advantage in terms of the reduced time taken as a metric for the computational efficiency for EPKEET-FA compared to the baseline schemes (Sect. 5.2). Third, we validate that the computational efficiency, in terms of increased time efficiency, actually leads to a significant increase in energy efficiency for EPKEET-FA when compared to the baseline schemes (Sect. 5.3).

According to our system model in Sect. 3.1, we set a conventional computer that can work as a user or node in clouds and a low-resource device for a user to use in the validation. All the results of the conventional computer are implemented on a laptop platform with an Intel i5-4200H processor running at 3.30GHz. The low-resource device used in our experiments is a typical low-resource IoT sensor hub, Raspberry Pi 2. Note that all the implemented schemes are compared under an equivalent cryptographic security level.

For the efficiency implementation in Sect. 5.2, four algorithms (*Encrypt, Decrypt, Authorisation,* and *Test*) for the above PKEET-related schemes are implemented on the conventional computer and on a type of low-resource device. In the energy consumption experiments, the above four algorithms are implemented on a conventional computer. Only two of the algorithms *Encrypt* and *Authorisation* are implemented on the low-resource device based upon our system model since the low-resource device is only used to send encrypted content and authorise tests.

5.1   Theoretic Computation Efficiency Comparison

The major cryptographic operations compared for an efficiency analysis are as follows.

- Mul: represents a point multiplication operation on elliptic curve.
- Exp: represents a modular exponentiation operation.
- Pairing: represents a Bilinear Pairings operation.

Firstly, Table 1 shows a comparison of different cryptographic operations used in the encryption and decryption of seven schemes mentioned above in terms of the number and types of the cryptographic operations. In this table, Enc and Dec represent *Encrypt* algorithm and *Decrypt* algorithm respectively.

Table 1. Quantity of cryptographic operations in *Encrypt* and *Decrypt*

	Enc	Dec
EPKEET-FA	4Mul	2Mul
PKEET-FA [16]	6Exp	5Exp
PKEET [10]	3Exp	3Exp
SG-PKEET [12]	4Exp	3Exp
AoN-PKEET [13]	5Exp	2Exp
FGA-PKEET [14]	4Exp	2Exp
FG-PKEET [15]	4Exp	2Exp

Secondly, the quantity comparison of different cryptographic operations used in the authorisation and equality test is illustrated in the following Table 2. Aut and Test represent *Authorisation* algorithm and *Test* algorithm (equality test), respectively. Note that the proposed schemes in [10, 12–15] cannot support the

Type-2, 3, 4 authorisations and equality tests so they are not listed in the rows of Type-2, 3, 4 comparison. In this table, "not supported" means the scheme cannot support the corresponding algorithms. "0" means the scheme can support the corresponding algorithms without the mentioned three major cryptographic operations (Mul, Exp and Pairing).

Table 2. Quantity of cryptographic operations in *Authorisation* and *test*

		Aut	Test
Type-1	EPKEET-FA	0	2Mul
	PKEET-FA [16]	0	2Pairing+2Exp
	PKEET [10]	Not supported	2Pairing
	SG-PKEET [12]	0	2Exp
	AoN-PKEET [13]	0	2Exp
	FGA-PKEET [14]	3Exp	4Pairing
	FG-PKEET [15]	3Exp	4Pairing
Type-2	EPKEET-FA	2Mul	0
	PKEET-FA [16]	2Exp	2Pairing
Type-3	EPKEET-FA	6Mul	0
	PKEET-FA [16]	2Pairing+2Exp	2Pairing
Type-4	EPKEET-FA	1Mul	1Mul
	PKEET-FA [16]	1Exp	2Pairing+1Exp

5.2 Computational (Time) Efficiency Implementation

We implement the following model based upon MIRACL (Multiprecision Integer and Rational Arithmetic C/C++ Library), which supports standard symmetric-key and asymmetric-key cryptographic algorithms. It can provide all the necessary elliptic curve and Bilinear Pairings primitives to implement cryptographic operations such as modular exponentiation, point multiplication and pairing. The picked pairing curve is *Cocks-Pinch curve* and the elliptic curve used is *secp160r1*.

The first results depicted in Figs. 2 and 3 are the time consumption comparison of the seven schemes' *Encrypt* and *Decrypt* algorithms (defined in Table 1) on the conventional computer and the low-resource device. It is clear that for the encryption (*Encrypt*) and decryption (*Decrypt*) algorithms, other schemes consume much more time to satisfy the equivalent cryptographic security level as compared with our scheme. Especially on the conventional computer, the *Encrypt* algorithm in our scheme only consumes about 34.4% of the time cost of the baseline encrypting algorithm in PKEET-FA, and the time cost of the *Decrypt* algorithm in our scheme drops by 80% when compared with the time cost of the baseline decrypting algorithm in PKEET-FA. Furthermore, for the low-resource device, compared with the time consumption of the baseline encrypting and decrypting algorithms in PKEET-FA, the time cost of the *Encrypt* and *Decrypt* algorithms in our scheme is around $\frac{1}{5}$ and $\frac{1}{8}$ respectively. Therefore, for the encryption and decryption algorithms, the time efficiency of our EPKEET-FA is higher than other schemes' time efficiency when compared.

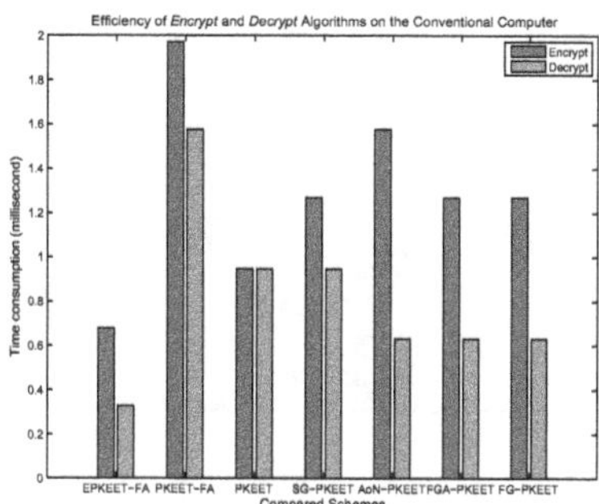

Fig. 2. Time consumption comparison of *Encrypt* and *Decrypt* algorithms on a conventional computer

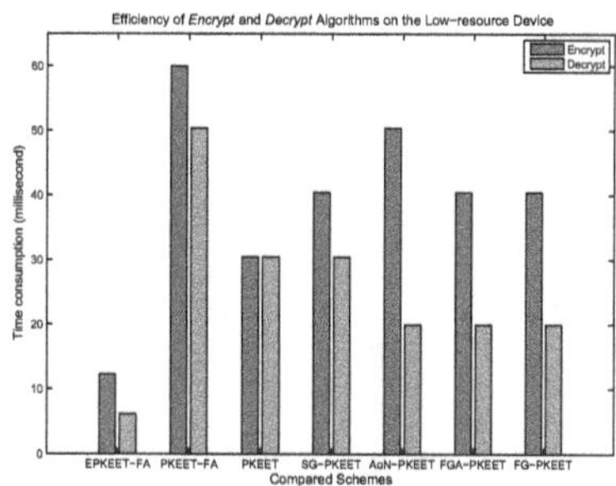

Fig. 3. Time consumption comparison of *Encrypt* and *Decrypt* algorithms on a low-resource device

Next, the second results demonstrated in Figs. 4 and 5 are the time consumption comparison of the seven schemes' *Authorisation* and *Test* (equality test) algorithms in Table 2 on the conventional computer and the low-resource device. Although in Type-1 authorisation, the time cost of our *Authorisation* algorithm is very similar to the time cost of PKEET-FA's *Authorisation* algorithm. For the other three types of authorisation (Type-2, Type-3 and Type-4), the time cost of our *Authorisation* algorithm is about $\frac{1}{4}$ of the time cost of PKEET-FA's *Authorisation* algorithm on average. For the *Test* algorithm, on both the conventional computer and the low-resource device, the time consumption of our

Type-1 and Type-4 schemes is around $\frac{9}{10}$ less than the time consumption of the PKEET-FA's schemes. Moreover, for the Type-2 and Type-3 authorisation, the time consumption of our *Test* algorithms is negligible when compared with the time consumption of PKEET-FA's *Test* algorithms.

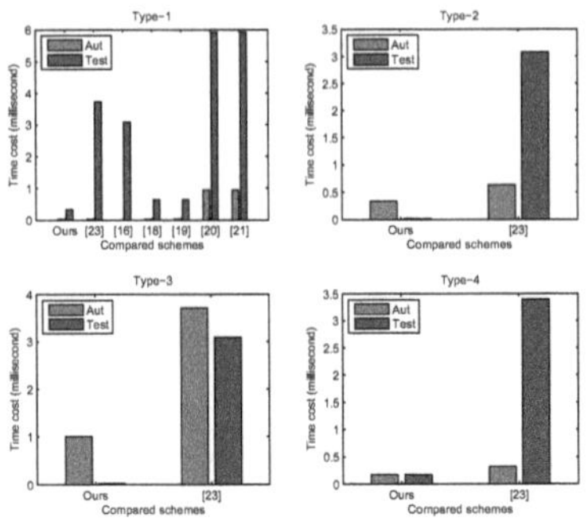

Fig. 4. Time consumption comparison of *Authorisation* (Aut) and *Test* (Test) algorithms on a conventional computer

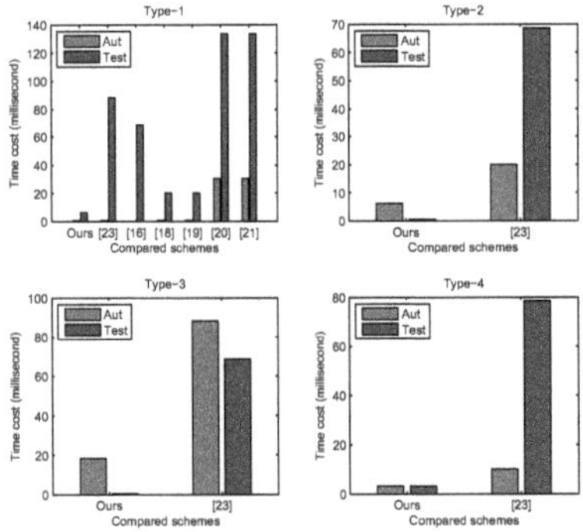

Fig. 5. Time consumption comparison of *Authorisation* (Aut) and *Test* (Test) algorithms on a low-resource device

Note that the proposed schemes in [10, 12–15] cannot support the Type-2, 3, 4 authorisation and equality test. Thus, they are not shown in the sub-figures Type-2, Type-3 and Type-4 of Figs. 4 and 5. Because the PKEET scheme [10] cannot support the *Authorisation* algorithm in Type-1 authorisation, the time cost of PKEET's *Authorisation* algorithms shown in Figs. 4 and 5 is zero.

5.3 Energy Cost Experiments and Comparison

In this section, we compare and analyse the energy consumption of different operations and algorithms used in EPKEET-FA and other baseline schemes based upon some existing work.

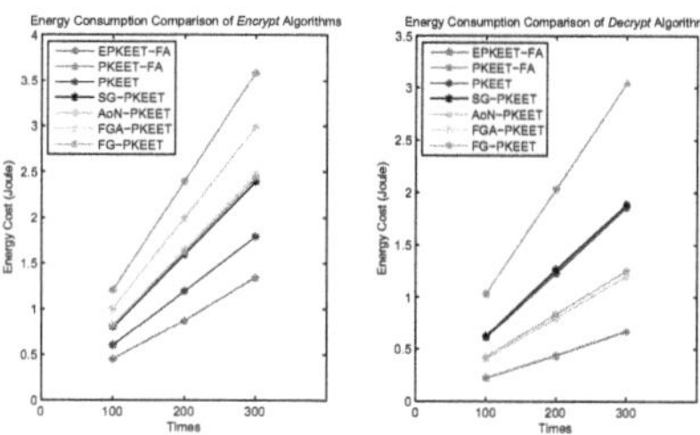

Fig. 6. Energy cost comparison of *Encrypt* and *Decrypt* algorithms on a conventional computer

Energy Cost Experiments There are two parts to the experiments in this section. First, we evaluate the processor's energy cost of four algorithms (*Encrypt, Decrypt, Authorisation* and *Test*) in our proposed EPKEET-FA scheme and other PKEET-related schemes [10,12–16] on a conventional computer. The software we use to measure the energy consumption of the processor is the Intel Power Gadget API. We first measure the baseline energy consumption of the processor E_{base}, then each algorithm is run 100, 200 and 300 times to obtain the accumulated energy cost E_{acc}, respectively. Finally, the energy cost of the processor to execute the algorithm can be obtained by calculating $E_{acc} - E_{base}$. Note that for each algorithm, we repeat the above steps 10 times to acquire the averaged values. The results of this experiment are illustrated in the following figures: Figs. 6, 7 and 8.

In terms of the *Encrypt* and *Decrypt* algorithms in Fig. 6, the energy cost of our scheme is the lowest. Moreover, the energy cost of our scheme is only about $\frac{1}{4}$ of the energy cost of the baseline scheme PKEET-FA.

For the Type-1 *Authorisation* algorithm in Fig. 7, the energy cost of all the schemes is relatively low (around 0.1J), except for the FGA-PKEET and FG-PKEET schemes. But compared with the energy consumption of the PKEET-FA scheme, our scheme's energy cost is apparently lower for the other three types (Type-2, Type-3 and Type-4) of *Authorisation* algorithms in Fig. 7. And the energy cost is reduced by about $\frac{1}{2}$ for our scheme on average. Note that the energy cost of PKEET's *Authorisation* algorithm (Type-1) is not shown in Fig. 7 as the PKEET scheme [10] cannot support the *Authorisation* algorithm in Type-1 authorisation.

In Fig. 8, we can see that the energy cost of our scheme is the lowest overall. Despite our scheme's unnoticeable advantage in the energy cost of Type-1 *Test*

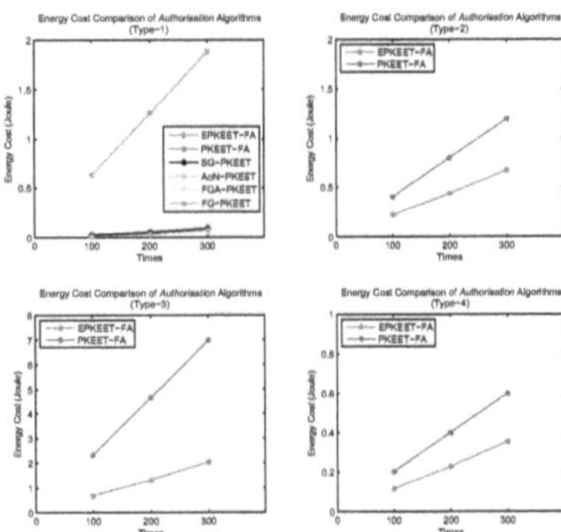

Fig. 7. Energy cost comparison of *Authorisation* algorithms on a conventional computer

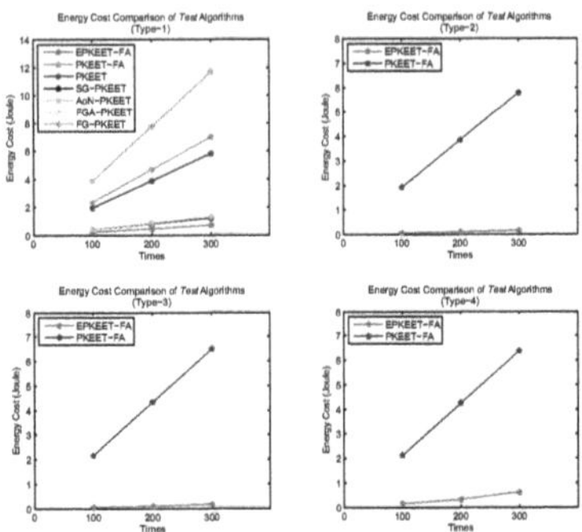

Fig. 8. Energy cost comparison of *Test* algorithms on a conventional computer

algorithm, obviously, the energy cost of our scheme is quite low when compared with the energy cost of PKEET-FA scheme for the other three types of *Test* algorithms. We also notice that the energy cost of the PKEET-FA scheme for its *Test* algorithms increases rapidly with increasing running times but that EPKEET-FA's energy cost is still very low and rises slowly.

Second, based upon our scheme model, we evaluate the platform's energy consumption of two algorithms (*Encrypt* and *Authorisation*) in our EPKEET-FA scheme and other PKEET-related schemes [10, 12–16] on an exemplar low-resource device. Note, for low-resource devices, as they are relatively less mature, there are, in turn, less mature management and monitoring software utilities available. Therefore, we use a current/voltage meter to measure the average baseline power $\bar{P}_{base}$ and the average running power $\bar{P}_{run}$. Then, the average power of running algorithms on the low-resource device $\bar{P}$ can be calculated by $\bar{P} = \bar{P}_{run} - \bar{P}_{base}$. Finally, the average energy cost can be acquired by calculating $\bar{E} = \bar{P}t$, where t is the time cost of the algorithms.

Note that the numbers of repeat times for the execution of the algorithms is the same as that used for a conventional computer. Again, the experiments are repeated 10 times to gain the average results. The results of this experiment are shown in Figs. 9 and 10. Since the PKEET scheme [10] cannot support the *Authorisation* algorithm in Type-1 authorisation, the energy cost of PKEET's *Authorisation* algorithm (Type-1) is not shown in Fig. 10.

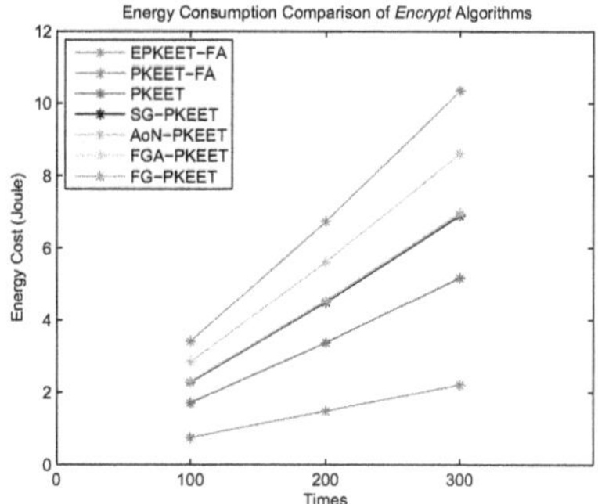

Fig. 9. Energy cost comparison of *Encrypt* algorithms on a low-resource device

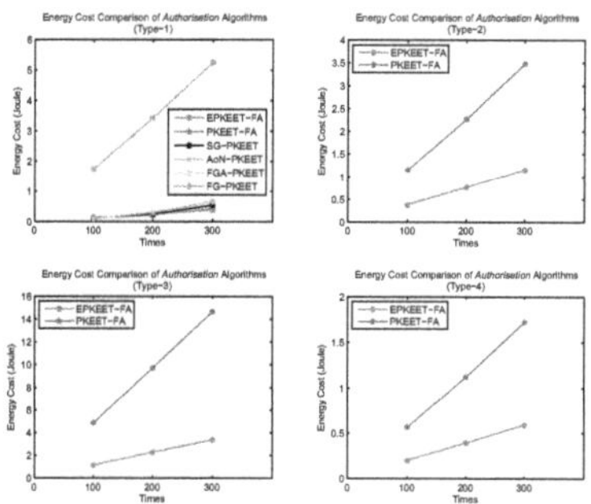

Fig. 10. Energy cost comparison of *Authorisation* algorithms on a low-resource device

From Figs. 9 and 10, we can conclude that the experimental results on the low-resource device are consistent with the earlier energy efficiency results presented for the conventional computer, that is: a) the energy cost of the *Encrypt* algorithm in our EPKEEET-FA scheme is lowest; b) for the Type-2, Type-3 and Type-4 *Authorisation* algorithms, the energy cost of our scheme is quite lower than the baseline scheme's (PKEET-FA) energy cost; c) on average, the energy consumption for these three types of *Authorisation* algorithms is decreased by around $\frac{2}{3}$ in our scheme. Furthermore, compared with the discrepancy of the energy cost's growth rates (Type-2, Type-3 and Type-4 *Authorisation* algorithms) between EPKEET-FA and PKEET-FA in Fig. 7, this discrepancy is more significant for the low-resource device used. This means that the energy cost's growth rate of our scheme is much lower than the rate of PKEET-FA scheme on the low-resource device.

Note that the energy efficiency of the core PKEET-FA operations is reduced on low resource devices such as a Raspberry Pi 2 when compared to a conventional client computer such as a laptop. This we postulate is because the complexity of such cryptographic operations is better optimised in hardware, e.g., the CPU, in a conventional computer.

In summary, compared with the first PKEET-FA scheme [16], our scheme is much more efficient in computation and low energy, especially in terms of the equality test. Furthermore, compared with the original PKEET scheme [10] and other PKEET schemes [12–15], our scheme can offer higher computation efficiency and lower energy cost with more flexible authorisation granularity based upon the results of our validation.

6   Conclusion

In this paper, we propose a EPKEET-FA scheme towards sustainable cloud computing. This scheme follows the security definition and options presented in the PKEET-FA scheme and obviates the need for complicated Bilinear Pairings operations. Compared with PKEET-FA as a baseline scheme, our scheme is more computationally efficient and consumes less energy. Furthermore, our scheme supports authorisation flexibility, higher computational efficiency in terms of the equality test and a lower energy consumption, when compared with other PKEET-related schemes. For cloud computing, applying our PKEET-FA scheme could significantly reduce the computing and energy resource needed to enable cloud computing security, where millions of equality test operations may be executed every day. Therefore, the use of our EPKEET-FA scheme can promote, improved, real-world sustainable and secure cloud computing.

References

1. Baliga, J., Ayre, R.W., Hinton, K., Tucker, R.S.: Green cloud computing: Balancing energy in processing, storage, and transport. Proc. IEEE **99**(1), 149–167 (2011)
2. Mittal, S.: A survey of techniques for improving energy efficiency in embedded computing systems. Int. J. Comput. Aided Eng. Technol. **6**(4), 440–459 (2014)
3. Li, K.: Energy-efficient task scheduling on multiple heterogeneous computers: algorithms, analysis, and performance evaluation. IEEE Trans. Sustain. Comput. **1**(1), 7–19 (2016)
4. Huang, X., Zhang, T., Huang, J., Guo, Y., Huang, G., Yang, H., Zheng, Z., Zhao, L., Jiang, S., Liu, J., Gui, G., Zhang, X.: Ligu-lvm: Linguistic-guided generative large vision model for IOMT clinical ocular disease screening via morphology dissection. IEEE Internet Things J. **12**(10), 13194–13207 (2025)
5. Oshin, T.O., Poslad, S., Zhang, Z.: Energy-efficient real-time human mobility state classification using smartphones. IEEE Trans. Comput. **64**(6), 1680–1693 (2015)
6. Zhao, X., Qu, H., Xu, J., Li, X., Lv, W., Wang, G.G.: A systematic review of fuzzing. Soft. Comput. **28**(6), 5493–5522 (2024)

7. Xu, H., Sun, Y., Zhang, X., Liu, E.: When web 3.0 meets reality: a hyperdimensional fractal polytope p2p ecosystem. IEEE Network **39**(1), 157–164 (2025)
8. Han, Q., Zhang, X., Lu, S., Zhao, X., Yan, Z.: An SGX-based online voting protocol with maximum voter privacy. J. Syst. Architect. **151**, 103144 (2024)
9. Zhang, X., Liu, C., Chai, K.K., Poslad, S.: A privacy-preserving consensus mechanism for an electric vehicle charging scheme. J. Netw. Comput. Appl. **174**, 102908 (2021)
10. Yang, G., Tan, C.H., Huang, Q., Wong, D.S.: Probabilistic public key encryption with equality test. In: Cryptographers' Track at the RSA Conference, pp. 119–131. Springer (2010)
11. Szczechowiak, P., Oliveira, L.B., Scott, M., Collier, M., Dahab, R.: Nanoecc: testing the limits of elliptic curve cryptography in sensor networks. In: Wireless sensor networks, pp. 305–320. Springer (2008)
12. Lee, H.T., Ling, S., Seo, J.H., Wang, H.: Semi-generic construction of public key encryption and identity-based encryption with equality test. Inf. Sci. **373**, 419–440 (2016)
13. Tang, Q.: Public key encryption supporting plaintext equality test and user-specified authorization. Secur. Commun. Netw. **5**(12), 1351–1362 (2012)
14. Tang, Q.: Public key encryption schemes supporting equality test with authorisation of different granularity. Int. J. Appl. Cryptography **2**(4), 304–321 (2012)
15. Tang, Q.: Towards public key encryption scheme supporting equality test with fine-grained authorization. In: Australasian Conference on Information Security and Privacy, pp. 389–406. Springer (2011)
16. Ma, S., Huang, Q., Zhang, M., Yang, B.: Efficient public key encryption with equality test supporting flexible authorization. IEEE Trans. Inf. Forensics Secur. **10**(3), 458–470 (2015)
17. Bellare, M., Boldyreva, A., O'Neill, A.: Deterministic and efficiently searchable encryption. In: Annual International Cryptology Conference, pp. 535–552. Springer (2007)
18. Boneh, D., Di Crescenzo, G., Ostrovsky, R., Persiano, G.: Public key encryption with keyword search. In: International Conference on the Theory and Applications of Cryptographic Techniques, pp. 506–522. Springer (2004)

Localization, Positioning and Tracking Techniques

Enhanced DV-Hop Localization Algorithm for WSNs with Topological Holes

Hanxiang Tu[1,2], Yibing Li[1,2(✉)], Siyu Liu[1,2], and Fang Ye[1,2]

[1] College of Information and Communication Engineering, Harbin Engineering University, Harbin, China
tuhanxiang@126.com, anjing64122@163.com, yefang@hrbeu.edu.cn
[2] The Key Laboratory of Advanced Marine Communication and Information Technology, Harbin, China
liyibing@hrbeu.edu.cn

Abstract. Accurate node localization is crucial for applications such as environmental monitoring and target tracking in wireless sensor networks (WSNs). Distance Vector-Hop (DV-Hop) is a classical range-free localization algorithm widely used due to its hardware-free implementation. However, its performance degrades significantly in the presence of topological holes, where path distortion leads to inaccurate hop count estimation. To address this challenge, this paper proposes IZOA-DV-Hop, an enhanced localization method that integrates the Improved Zebra Optimization Algorithm (IZOA). First, a dual communication radius mechanism is introduced to refine hop count estimation and mitigate distance overestimation in dense regions. Then, a bent-path eliminating method with adaptive angle thresholds based on anchor node density is employed to eliminate intermediate anchor nodes on overly curved paths, effectively reducing distortion in average hop distance estimation caused by topological holes. Finally, IZOA is employed to globally optimize the coordinates of unknown nodes. Simulation results demonstrate that, under network topologies containing O-shaped topological holes, the proposed method achieves significantly higher localization accuracy, reducing average localization error by 30%, 10%, 8% and 6% compared to DV-Hop, WBOA-DV-Hop, IWOA-DV-Hop and TGWO-DV-Hop respectively. Showing good accuracy.

Keywords: Wireless sensor networks · DV-Hop · Topological hole · IZOA

1 Introduction

Wireless Sensor Networks (WSNs), composed of distributed sensor nodes that wirelessly collect, process, and transmit data, are widely applied in domains such

C. Xu et al. (Eds.): MobiMedia 2025, LNICST 670, pp. 133–143, 2026.
https://doi.org/10.1007/978-3-032-16823-8_10

as environmental monitoring, precision agriculture, disaster response, intelligent transportation, and military reconnaissance [1]. Accurate node localization in WSNs is essential for ensuring data integrity and maintaining overall network performance [2]. Developing low-cost and high-precision localization algorithms has thus become a key research direction in WSNs.

WSN localization algorithms are broadly categorized into range-based and range-free methods [3]. Range-based approaches rely on physical parameters such as Received Signal Strength Indicator (RSSI), Time of Arrival (ToA), or Angle of Arrival (AoA), offering high accuracy but at the expense of additional hardware and energy consumption. In contrast, range-free methods estimate positions based on connectivity or hop count information, making them more cost-effective and suitable for large-scale deployments. The Distance Vector-Hop (DV-Hop) algorithm is a widely used range-free method due to its simplicity, hardware independence, and scalability.

Recent studies have enhanced DV-Hop localization accuracy. Sharma et al. [4] used TLBO to improve anchor node placement and coverage, but the method is sensitive to initial anchor positions. Chen et al. [5] proposed a connectivity-weighted DV-Hop with artificial bee colony optimization to refine hop distance estimates, though it's limited by local topology. Zhao et al. [6] introduced CMWN-DV-Hop, using region partitioning and WRLS for better accuracy, but it's computationally intensive. Cao et al. [7] developed OANS DV-Hop with particle swarm optimization to select anchor subsets, reducing errors but with high computational costs. Rehman et al. [8] used LSTM to correct multi-hop errors, but it requires large datasets, limiting use in resource-constrained networks.

In summary, while existing improvements to DV-Hop mainly focus on anchor selection, hop correction, and heuristic optimization, their performance and robustness in networks with topological holes remain limited. To address this issue, this paper proposes a DV-Hop enhancement tailored for such scenarios. The main contributions are as follows: (1) An adaptive angle path elimination mechanism is proposed, which filters redundant curved paths based on the proportion of anchor nodes, reducing the impact of topological holes on hop distance estimation. (2) The Improved Zebra Optimization Algorithm (IZOA) is employed to globally optimize unknown node coordinates during the coordinate inversion stage, enhancing robustness and accuracy in non-uniform topologies. (3) Extensive simulations in networks with O-shaped holes demonstrate that the proposed method outperforms DV-Hop, WBOA-DV-Hop, IWOA-DV-Hop and TGWO-DV-Hop in terms of localization accuracy.

2   Methodology

To improve the localization accuracy of the DV-Hop algorithm in wireless sensor networks with topological holes, this paper proposes a DV Hop localization method enhanced by the Improved Zebra Optimization Algorithm (IZOA). This section first introduces the principles of the traditional DV-Hop algorithm and the Zebra Optimization Algorithm.

2.1 DV-Hop Localization Algorithm

Algorithm Steps The DV-Hop algorithm was first proposed by Niculescu and Nath in 2003 [9], the traditional DV-Hop localization algorithm consists of the following steps. *Step 1: Determining the Minimum Hop Count.* In wireless sensor network, each anchor node (with known coordinates) floods the network with packets carrying its ID, position and an initial hop count of zero. The nodes record and retain the smallest hop count for each anchor, forward the packet with the count incremented by one, and discard any packets with a higher count. This repeats until every node has its minimum hop counts to all anchors. *Step 2: Estimating Average Hop Distance.* Anchor nodes calculate the actual distance and hop count to other anchor nodes based on their own positions and hop counts, thereby deriving the average hop distance from Eq. (1):

$$\text{HopSize}_i = \frac{\sum_{j \neq i} \sqrt{(x_i - x_j)^2 + (y_i - y_j)^2}}{\sum_{j \neq i} h_{ij}} \tag{1}$$

where (x_i, y_i) and (x_j, y_j) are the coordinates of anchor nodes i and j , h_{ij} is the hop count. *Step 3: Position Estimation.* The unknown node estimates its distance to each anchor node based on the received average hop distance and the hop count to the anchor node from Eq. (2):

$$d = \text{HopSize} \times h \tag{2}$$

where h is the hop count from the unknown node to the anchor node. The unknown node utilizes the estimated distances from at least four non-coplanar anchor nodes to construct a system of equations in three-dimensional space for calculating the distances to each anchor node as shown in Eq. ((3):

$$\begin{cases} (x - x_1)^2 + (y - y_1)^2 = d_1^2 \\ (x - x_2)^2 + (y - y_2)^2 = d_2^2 \\ \vdots \\ (x - x_n)^2 + (y - y_n)^2 = d_n^2 \end{cases} \tag{3}$$

The coordinates of the unknown node are then determined by solving the system using the least squares method.

The general flow chart of DV-Hop is described in Fig. 1.

Error Analysis In DV-Hop, the localization error arises chiefly from the quantization of hop count and the bias of the average distance. Discrete hop counts fail to reflect true geometric distances, especially in uneven or complex topologies, while average hop-size estimates between anchors, derived from nonlinear paths, tend to be overestimated. These errors are then amplified by the least-squares solver. Furthermore, in sparse regions, unknown nodes may lack sufficient anchor links, causing localization failures or large deviations.

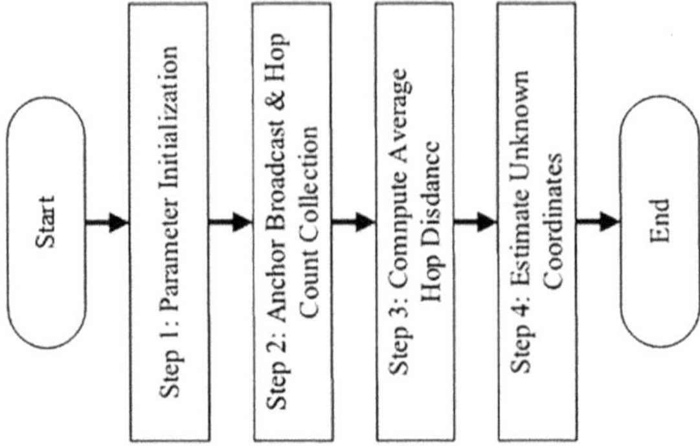

Fig. 1. The flowchart of DV-Hop algorithm.

2.2 Zebra Optimization Algorithm

The Zebra Optimization Algorithm (ZOA), proposed by Trojovská et al. in 2022 [10], is an adaptive metaheuristic inspired by the foraging and predator avoidance behaviors of zebras. It dynamically adjusts search patterns, showing strong convergence and robustness in nonlinear, constrained optimization problems. Its low parameter dependency makes it well-suited for resource-constrained wireless sensor networks, rendering ZOA a promising choice for optimizing the DV-Hop localization algorithm.

The steps of ZOA are shown below. First, the Zebra Optimization Algorithm initializes a population of candidate solutions using a uniform random strategy within the defined bounds:

$$x_{i,j} = lb_j + r \cdot (ub_j - lb_j), \tag{4}$$

where $x_{i,j}$ is the j-th dimension of the i-th zebra, lb_j and ub_j are the lower and upper bounds, and $r \in (0,1)$ is a random number. In the foraging stage, individuals move toward the best-performing zebra according to the following formula:

$$x_{i,j}^{\text{new}} = x_{i,j} + r \cdot (PZ_j - I \cdot x_{i,j}), \tag{5}$$

where PZ_j is the leader's position and I controls the convergence speed. During the defense stage, different movement strategies are triggered based on the probability P, escape or grouping behavior is applied depending on the perceived predator threat, the position update formula is shown below:

$$x_{i,j}^{\text{new}} = \begin{cases} S_1 \cdot x_{i,j} + R(2r - 1)\left(1 - \frac{t}{T}\right) x_{i,j}, & \text{if } P \leq 0.5 \\ S_2 \cdot x_{i,j} + r \cdot (AZ_j - I \cdot x_{i,j}), & \text{otherwise,} \end{cases} \tag{6}$$

where t is the current iteration, T is the maximum iteration, and AZ_j is the attacked zebra's position. The fitness of new positions is evaluated, and individuals are updated accordingly. After each update, the best solution across all iterations is retained.

3   The Proposed Algorithm IZOA-DV-Hop

Under ideal conditions, estimating the coordinates of unknown nodes constitutes a convex optimization problem. However, in practical DV-Hop implementations, errors in distance estimation, topological holes, and multipath effects may introduce multiple local minima into the objective function, reducing localization accuracy. The Zebra Optimization Algorithm (ZOA), known for its balanced search capabilities and low parameter dependency, shows potential in such scenarios but still risks getting trapped in local optima. To address this limitation, this paper introduces improvements to enhance the performance of ZOA in node localization.

3.1   Dual Communication Radius Method

In the traditional DV-Hop, all neighbors within the communication radius are assigned a hop count of 1, regardless of their actual distance, leading to significant quantization errors in uneven topologies. The dual communication radius method reduces this error by using a large radius R_1 and a small radius $R_2 = k \cdot R_1$ $(0 < k < 1)$: during hop counting, if $R_2 < d < R_1$, the hop increment is k; if $R_2 < d < R_1$, it is 1. Figure 2 illustrates this scheme.

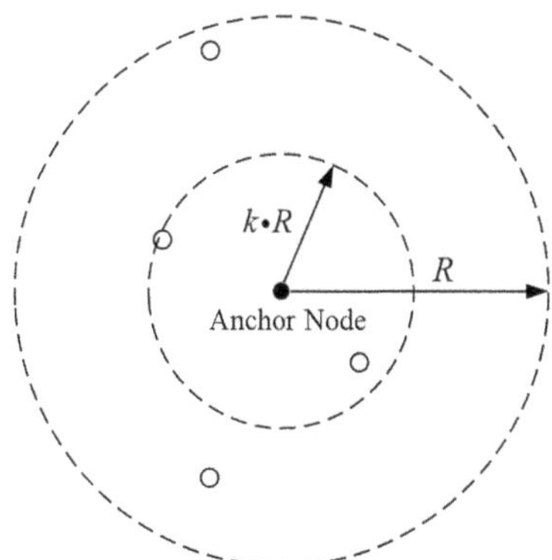

Fig. 2. Diagram of the dual communication radius method

3.2   A Method for Eliminating Bent Paths based on an Adaptive Angle Threshold

In wireless sensor networks with topological holes, communication paths are often forced to detour, exacerbating the non-linear relationship between the shortest path and physical distance, thereby degrading the localization accuracy of the DV-Hop algorithm. To mitigate this problem, [11] proposed an angle-based intermediate anchor node removal method. Specifically, given a shortest path between anchor nodes i and j that passes through an intermediate anchor node k, let a_{ij} , a_{ik}, and a_{jk} denote the Euclidean distances between the corresponding node pairs. Based on the law of cosines, the angle $\angle ikj$ can be computed as shown in Eq. (7):

$$\angle ikj = \arccos\left(\frac{a_{ik}^2 - a_{kj}^2 - a_{ij}^2}{-2 \times a_{kj} \times a_{ij}}\right) \tag{7}$$

If the calculated angle $\angle ikj$ is less than $90°$ or greater than $270°$, the path is considered excessively bent, and the intermediate anchor node k is removed from the adjacency lists of nodes i and j, to reduce the distortion in the estimation of the average hop distance caused by the curvature of the path.

However, the effectiveness of this fixed-angle threshold method is highly dependent on the proportion of anchor nodes in the network. When the anchor node ratio is low, excessive removal of intermediate nodes may reduce connectivity among anchors and even lead to unreachable node pairs, thereby degrading the reliability of hop distance estimation. Conversely, when the anchor node ratio is high, a fixed threshold may fail to eliminate all significantly curved paths, limiting the improvement potential.

To address these limitations, this paper introduces an adaptive angle threshold strategy based on the anchor node ratio, which dynamically adjusts the definition of intermediate paths. The thresholds are given by the formula below:

$$\theta_{\text{lower}} = \min\left(120,\ \max\left(60,\ 90 + 150 \times \left(\frac{N_b}{N} - 0.3\right)\right)\right) \tag{8}$$

$$\theta_{\text{upper}} = \min\left(300,\ \max\left(240,\ 270 - 150 \times \left(\frac{N_b}{N} - 0.3\right)\right)\right) \tag{9}$$

where N_b denotes the number of anchor nodes and N is the total number of nodes. This method allows the removal range to respond adaptively to anchor density, additionally, under extreme anchor node ratio conditions, upper and lower bounds are imposed on the angle threshold to ensure the stability and adaptability of the algorithm, improving thereby the flexibility and robustness of path correction under different topological conditions.

3.3   Improved Zebra Optimization Algorithm

When using the zebra optimization algorithm to calculate node coordinates, there are drawbacks such as slow convergence speed, a tendency to get trapped in local optima, and weak global search capability. This paper introduces multiple strategies to improve the Zebra Optimization Algorithm.

Logistic Chaotic Map Initialization. The optimization performance of the ZOA algorithm is highly sensitive to the quality of its initial population. Traditional random initialization often leads to redundant or clustered individuals, which reduces population diversity and may hinder global search capability. To address this issue, a logistic chaotic map is employed for population initialization, ensuring a more uniform and comprehensive coverage of the solution space. The logistic map is defined in Eq. (10):

$$x_{n+1} = \mu \cdot x_n \cdot (1 - x_n) \tag{10}$$

where $x_n \in [0, 1]$ represents the value of the chaotic sequence, with the initial value typically chosen randomly. $\mu \in [0, 4]$ is the control parameter, usually set to 4 to achieve a fully chaotic state.

Local Perturbation Strategy. In the ZOA foraging phase, individuals tend to converge on the global best (leading zebra), which reduces diversity and risks entrapment in local optima. To counteract this, we introduce a small-probability local perturbation via a dynamic step-size factor, as shown in Eq. (11):

$$\omega = 0.1 \, (ub_j - lb_j) \, \exp\!\left(-30 \, \tfrac{t}{T}\right) \tag{11}$$

The position update formula thus becomes Eq. (12).

$$x_{t+1} = \begin{cases} x_t + a\,(PZ - I\,x_t), & r > 0.01, \\ \omega\,(x_t + a\,(PZ - I\,x_t)), & \text{otherwise,} \end{cases} \tag{12}$$

where $r \in (0, 1)$ decides whether to apply the perturbation.

Opposition-Based Learning Strategy To further enhance the convergence speed and solution accuracy of the Zebra Optimization Algorithm, in this paper, an inverse learning strategy based on dynamic refraction is introduced, and the dynamic refractive index η and the inverse solution solving equation x_{opposite} are shown as follows:

$$\eta = 1.2 - 0.4 \cdot \frac{t}{T} \tag{13}$$

$$x_{\text{opposite}} = x_{\text{new}} - \eta \cdot (x_{\text{new}} - x_{\text{best}}) \tag{14}$$

We then evaluate the fitness of both x_{new} and x_{opp}, retaining the one with the lower fitness for the next iteration.

4   Simulation and Analysis

To evaluate the localization performance of the proposed algorithm under different types of topological holes, three representative network models are designed as simulation scenarios: the C-shaped hole network, the O-shaped hole network, and the square hole network. These models aim to assess the adaptability and robustness of the algorithm across various hole configurations. The corresponding network topology illustrations are shown in Fig. 3.

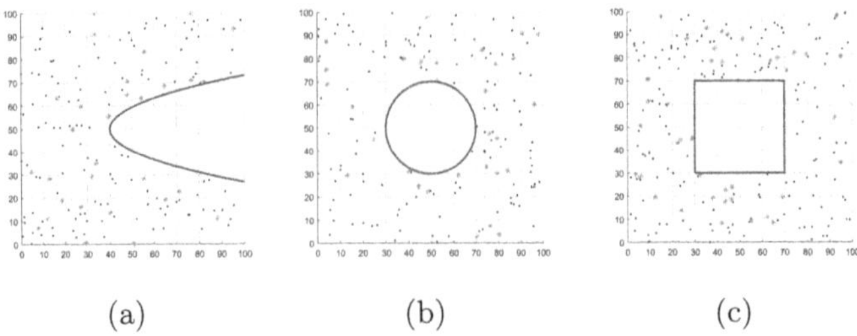

Fig. 3. Topology diagrams of three typical network models with topological holes: **a** C-shaped hole, **b** O-shaped hole, and **c** square hole

4.1 Parameter Settings

To evaluate localization performance, we conducted MATLAB 2022b simulations comparing IZOA-DV-Hop against DV-Hop, WBOA-DV-Hop [12], IWOA-DV-Hop [13] and TGWO-DV-Hop [14] by varying the anchor-node ratio, total node count, and communication radius. Simulation parameters are listed in Table 1.

Table 1. Simulation parameter settings

Parameters	Value
Experiment area	100m×100m
Number of trials	100
Maximum number of iterations	50
Logistic chaotic mapping parameters	4

The formula for calculating the normalized average localization error (ALE/R) of the network is given by Eq. (15):

$$E_{\mathrm{err}} E_{\mathrm{avg}} = \frac{1}{N} \sum_{i=1}^{n} \frac{\sqrt{(x_i - x_i')^2 + (y_i - y_i')^2}}{R} \tag{15}$$

Where (x_i, y_i) and (x_i', y_i') represent the actual and estimated coordinates of the unknown node i, R is the communication radius of the anchor nodes, and N is the total number of unknown nodes.

4.2 Effect of Anchor Node Number on ALE/R

Figure 4 illustrates the impact of the number of anchor nodes on ALE/R under three network topologies, where the total number of nodes is 100 and the communication radius is 30m. The results show that the proposed algorithm effectively reduces localization errors in the presence of topological holes. Moreover, as the number of anchor nodes increases, the normalized average localization error (ALE/R) consistently decreases across all algorithms. Taking the C-shaped hole topology as an example, when the number of anchor nodes is 30, the proposed algorithm reduces ALE/R by 30%, 10%, 7% and 4% respectively, compared to DV-Hop, IWOA-DV-Hop, WBOA-DV-Hop and TGWO-DV-Hop. As the anchor nodes increase in larger intervals, the communication paths between the nodes become redundant, at this point the number of anchor nodes has less effect on the localization accuracy.

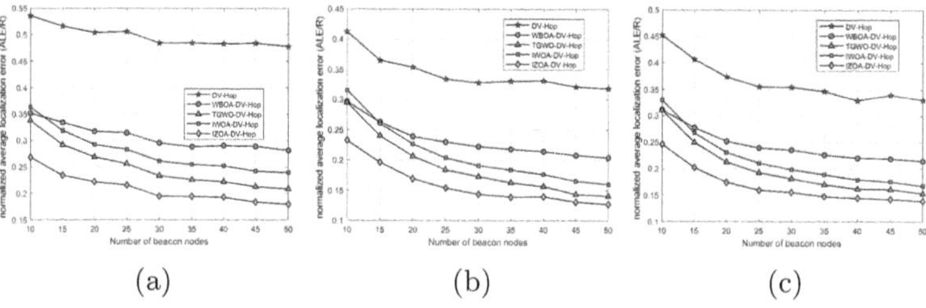

(a)   (b)   (c)

Fig. 4. Effect of anchor node number on normalized average localization error across three network topologies: **a** C-shaped hole, **b** O-shaped hole, and **c** square hole

4.3   Effect of Communication Radius on ALE/R

Figure 5 illustrates the impact of the communication radius on ALE/R under three network topologies, where the total number of nodes is 100 and the number of anchor node is 45. The results show that as the communication radius increases, the ALE/R decreases for all algorithms in the presence of topological holes. In particular, in C-shaped hole network model, when the communication radius is 30, the proposed IZOA-DV-Hop algorithm reduces ALE/R by 29%, 10%, 8% and 3%, respectively, compared to DV-Hop, IWOA-DV-Hop, WBOA-DV-Hop and TGWO-DV-Hop. This is due to the fact that the network becomes more connected as the communication radius increases. When the communication range exceeds 40 meters, using single-hop distance as the minimum measurement unit leads to insufficient resolution in hop-count estimation, consequently increasing the normalized average localization error. The introduction of the dual-communication-range method can effectively mitigate this issue.

4.4   Effect of Total Number of Nodes on ALE/R

Figure 6 illustrates the impact of the total number of nodes on ALE/R under three network topologies, with a communication radius of 30m and 30% anchor nodes. The error decreases steadily as the higher node density improves connectivity and reduces isolated nodes. When the total number of nodes is 200, the proposed IZOA-DV-Hop algorithm reduces the ALE/R by 20%, 8%, 4% and

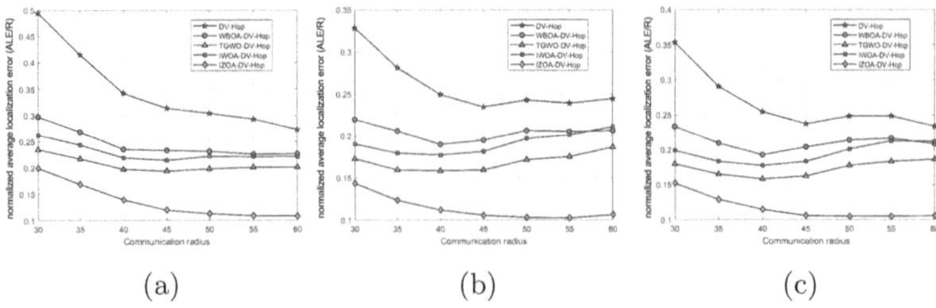

(a)   (b)   (c)

Fig. 5. Effect of communication radius on normalized average localization error across three network topologies: **a** C-shaped hole, **b** O-shaped hole, and **c** square hole

3% in C-shaped hole network model. The normalized average localization error exhibits a steady declining trend with increasing node density.

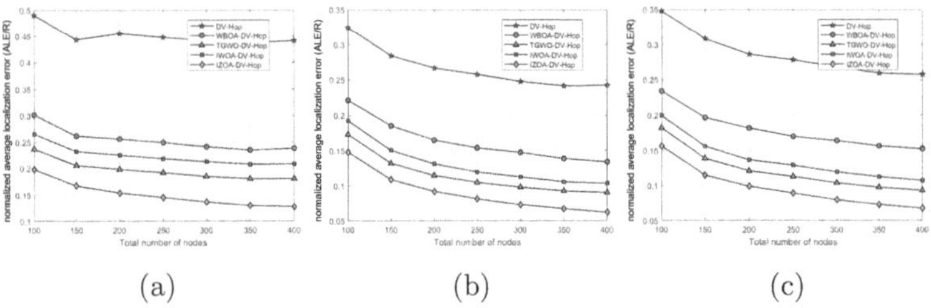

(a)   (b)   (c)

Fig. 6. Effect of total number of nodes on normalized average localization error across three network topologies: **a** C-shaped hole, **b** O-shaped hole, and **c** square hole

5   Conclusion

This paper proposes IZOA-DV-Hop, an enhanced DV-Hop localization algorithm with three key improvements: (1) a dual communication radius mechanism to refine hop-count estimation and reduce distance overestimation in dense areas; (2) a bent-path elimination strategy based on an adaptive angle threshold, which effectively mitigates the impact of topological holes on average hop distance computation; and (3) an improved Zebra Optimization Algorithm (IZOA) with dynamic step-size control and opposition-based learning for robust global optimization. Simulation results conducted in MATLAB 2022b across three typical topological hole models, C-shaped, O-shaped, and square-shaped networks, demonstrate that IZOA-DV-Hop consistently achieves lower the normalized average localization error compared to DV-Hop, WBOA-DV-Hop, IWOA-DV-Hop and TGWO-DV-Hop under varying anchor ratios, node densities, and communication radii. Future work will focus on enhancing algorithmic efficiency and extending its applicability to dynamic and large-scale sensor networks.

References

1. Ren, R., Zhang, L., Han, G.: Static node deployment optimization in wireless sensor networks based on fractional-order chameleon swarm algorithm. Chin. J. Ship Res. (2025)
2. Zhao, W., Jiang, Y., Liu, D.: A high precision positioning algorithm for wireless sensor network nodes. J. Harbin Eng. Univ. **30**(04), 466–471 (2009)
3. Sneha, V., Nagarajan, M.: Localization in wireless sensor networks: a review. Cybern. Inform. Technol. **20**(4), 3–26 (2020)
4. Sharma, G., Kumar, A.: Improved dv-hop localization algorithm using teaching learning based optimization for wireless sensor networks. Telecommun. Syst. **67**(2), 163–178 (2018)
5. Chen, T., Sun, L.: A connectivity weighting dv_hop localization algorithm using modified artificial bee colony optimization. J. Sens. **2019**(1), 1464513 (2019)
6. Zhao, Q., Xu, Z., Yang, L.: An improvement of dv-hop localization algorithm based on cyclotomic method in wireless sensor networks. Appl. Sci. **13**(6), 3597 (2023)
7. Cao, Y., Xu, J.: Dv-hop-based localization algorithm using optimum anchor nodes subsets for wireless sensor network. Ad Hoc Netw. **139**, 103035 (2023)
8. Rehman, A., Mahmood, T., Alahmadi, T.J., Almasoud, A.S., Saba, T.: Energy efficient and robust node localization in WSNS using LSTM optimized dv hop framework to mitigate multihop localization errors. Sci. Rep. **15**(1), 1–23 (2025)
9. Niculescu, D., Nath, B.: Dv based positioning in ad hoc networks. Telecommun. Syst. **22**(1), 267–280 (2003)
10. Trojovská, E., Dehghani, M., Trojovský, P.: Zebra optimization algorithm: a new bio-inspired optimization algorithm for solving optimization algorithm. IEEE Access **10**, 49445–49473 (2022)
11. Bhat, S.J., Venkata, S.K.: An improved DVHOP localization algorithm using a novel angle based node reduction and optimization technique. Discover Appl. Sci. **6**(8), 437 (2024)
12. Peng, D., Zhang, T., Li, S., Yang, Y.: 3d-dv-hop node localization algorithm based on WBOA. Transducer Microsyst. Technol. **43**(03), 139–143 (2024)
13. Wang, L., Liu, J., Qi, J., He, J.: Dv-hop location algorithm based on ranging modification and improved whale optimization. Instrument Tech. Sens. (02):116–121+126 (2022)
14. Feng, X., Li, Y., Sun, Y., Zhong, L.: Improved dv-hop algorithm combining chaotic map and gray wolf algorithm. In: 2022 IEEE 6th Advanced Information Technology, Electronic and Automation Control Conference (IAEAC), pp. 55–61. IEEE (2022)

MixFP:A Transformer-Based Method for UAV Cross-View Geolocation

Xuefei Ma, Yu Yang, Zilong Yang, and Haifeng Zhu[✉]

College of Information and Communication Engineering, Harbin Engineering University, Harbin, China
{maxuefei,yy1394108524,zhuhaifeng}@hrbeu.edu.cn, 2689539178@qq.com

Abstract. The location of unmanned aerial vehicles (UAVs) in GPS-denied environments remains a central challenge in cross-view geolocation tasks, primarily due to large domain discrepancies between aerial and ground-level imagery and the presence of visually similar but semantically distinct scenes. Inspired by multimodal machine learning, we propose a single-stream pyramid transformer network called MixFP. The proposed architecture initially employs convolutional layers to enhance low-level feature representation, followed by a cross-attention mechanism that enables effective interaction and refinement of features across modalities while suppressing irrelevant noise. To further augment the discriminative capacity of the model, we integrate FcaNet to process low-resolution feature maps at multiple stages of the backbone, and employ a feature pyramid network (FPN) to facilitate the fusion of multi-scale representations. Additionally, we incorporate DySample into the pyramid structure to enhance sampling flexibility and boost overall performance. Experimental results on the UL14 benchmark dataset demonstrate the superiority of MixFP, yielding an improvement in the RDS metric from 76.25 to 81.82. Furthermore, MixFP exhibits significant gains in meter-level accuracy (MA), with 3m accuracy increasing by 30.43%, 5m accuracy improving by 18.84%, and 10m accuracy rising by 9.9%.

Keywords: Geo-localization · Deep learning · Transformer · UAV

1 Introduction

Unmanned Aerial Vehicles (UAVs) have emerged as pivotal technological platforms across diverse application domains, owing to their superior maneuverability, flexible deployment, and robust adaptability to dynamic and complex operational environments. As a type of mobile robotic system, localization is fundamental to ensuring stable operation.UAVs primarily rely on the Global Navigation Satellite System (GNSS) [1] for precise positioning. However, in real-world scenarios, GNSS signals are often unreliable due to blockage, environmental interference, or intentional jamming, leading to significant localization errors or signal loss. This poses a major challenge for UAV operation in GNSS-denied

© ICST Institute for Computer Sciences, Social Informatics and Telecommunications Engineering 2026
Published by Springer Nature Switzerland AG 2026. All Rights Reserved
C. Xu et al. (Eds.): MobiMedia 2025, LNICST 670, pp. 144–160, 2026.
https://doi.org/10.1007/978-3-032-16823-8_11

environments, a common issue in both military and civilian contexts. In such conditions, vision-based localization–relying solely on onboard cameras–emerges as a promising alternative. Traditional methods, such as feature point matching, have been widely applied in image stitching and simultaneous localization and mapping (SLAM) [2,3] due to their robustness to scale, rotation, and noise. However, these approaches depend on handcrafted descriptors such as SIFT [4] and SURF [5], which often struggle with large viewpoint and quality variations. Recently, deep learning has enabled the extraction of richer and more robust features, offering more reliable solutions for image matching and localization tasks.

To address the challenge of UAV localization and navigation in GPS-denied environments, two mainstream strategies have emerged within the field of deep learning: one is based on image retrieval methods [6–9], and the other relies on Finding Point Image (FPI) approaches built upon the UL14 dataset [10–13]. The image retrieval-based approach localizes Unmanned Aerial Vehicles (UAVs) by comparing the query image with a database of geotagged reference images (gallery images), identifying the most visually similar matches to infer location. While image retrieval methods have achieved promising results, they still suffer from several limitations: (1) These methods require the construction of a high-resolution image database covering the target area in advance. For large-scale environments, this necessitates the storage of a vast number of image tiles, leading to significant memory demands. Moreover, the features of each tile must be pre-extracted and stored, which incurs high computational cost. If the database is updated, feature extraction must be performed again for the entire dataset. (2) The performance of image retrieval methods heavily depends on the robustness of the feature representations. If the features fail to capture critical visual details, the matching results may be unreliable. Handcrafted features often underperform in complex environments, while deep learning-based features, though more expressive, rely on large-scale annotated datasets for training, which is costly and may lack sufficient generalization ability.

In response to the limitations of retrieval-based localization, Ref. [10] proposed a novel end-to-end visual localization framework, Finding Point with Image (FPI). Unlike traditional methods, FPI directly localizes UAV images within large-scale satellite imagery without requiring a pre-constructed feature database. Inspired by the SiamFC single-object tracking framework, FPI treats the UAV image as the query and the satellite image as the search region, generating a heatmap to indicate the predicted UAV location. Compared to image retrieval methods, FPI avoids the need for extensive pre-processing and storage, enabling real-time and high-precision localization. The dual-stream network used for feature extraction independently encodes UAV and satellite images, but the lack of interaction between them during feature extraction can lead to redundant information and reduced localization accuracy.

To address the above challenges, we propose a novel one-stream network called MixFP designed for UAV self-localization by integrating heterogeneous features. As illustrated in Fig. 1, we compare the processes of image-based point localization using single-stream and two-stream architectures. The proposed network focuses on optimizing the structural design to facilitate early-stage feature integration. Leveraging the architectural advantages of a single-stream model, our method incorporates Transformer-based dynamic attention mechanisms to enhance interaction between heterogeneous features from UAV and satellite images, thereby improving localization accuracy in GPS-denied environments.Our main contributions are summarized as follows:

(1) We introduce MixFP, a new single-stream visual localization framework tailored for UAV navigation in GPS-denied environments. The architecture integrates a convolutional backbone with hybrid attention mechanisms to serve as the core for hierarchical feature extraction and fusion. This unified design facilitates early-stage joint feature representation and relational modeling, thereby enhancing the localization accuracy.
(2) We incorporate FcaNet [14] into the feature fusion module and further design a pyramid-based feature fusion module using a Dysample [15] mechanism. This enables the model to effectively preserve discriminative features on multiple scales, thereby enhancing its overall performance.
(3) Our proposed method achieves state-of-the-art performance on the UL14 dataset. When evaluated using the RDS metric, our model's performance improves from 76.25 to 81.82. Under the MA evaluation metric, the 3 m localization accuracy improves from 22.81% to 29.75%, 5 m accuracy from 44.31% to 52.66%, and 10 m accuracy from 72.32% to 79.48%.

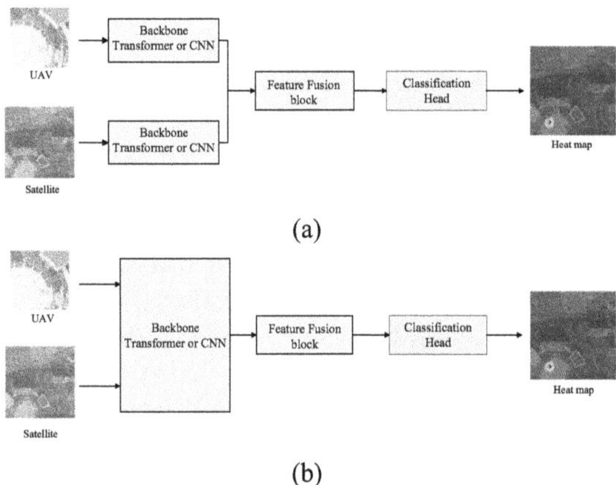

Fig. 1. Comparison between two-stream and single-stream network architectures. (a) Conventional two-stream architecture; (b) single-stream architecture

2   Related Work

2.1   Cross-View Geo-Localization

Cross-view geolocation aims to infer the geographic position of a query image by learning correspondences between images acquired from significantly different viewpoints, such as those captured by satellites and UAVs, or from aerial and ground-level perspectives. Early approaches relied primarily on hand-crafted features to extract keypoints and descriptors from images (e.g., SIFT, SURF), followed by feature matching across views. However, these traditional methods exhibit notable limitations when dealing with significant viewpoint variations, illumination changes, and occlusions in complex environments.

With the advancement of neural networks, new approaches to cross-view geolocalization have emerged. In 2015, Workman et al. [16] used convolutional neural networks (CNNs) to estimate the geographic location of a ground-level query image by matching it with georeferenced aerial images. Lin et al. [17] introduced Where-CNN the same year, creating joint feature representations between street view and bird's-eye images for improved matching. In 2019, Shi et al. [18] proposed a dynamic similarity network utilizing polar transformation and dual-stream CNNs, enhancing accuracy in cross-view localization. Wang et al. [19] introduced LPN in 2021, employing a loop partitioning strategy and attention weighting to focus on fine-grained features near the image's periphery. In 2022, Zeng et al. [20] presented the PLCD framework, which integrates data from ground, UAV and satellite views. Using cross-view representation learning and information diffusion, the framework effectively improves cross-view localization performance. Recently, Dai et al. [21] introduced FSRA, a transformer-based method addressing positional shifts and scale uncertainty, demonstrating strong performance on the University-1652 dataset.

Image retrieval-based methods have developed rapidly in recent years. However, their performance is significantly affected by environmental variations, and the retrieval process in large-scale image databases is often time-consuming, making it difficult to meet real-time localization requirements. To address this, Dai et al. constructed the UL14 dataset, which shifted the traditional paradigm of retrieval-based localization. Instead of retrieving similar images, their approach identifies the location of the UAV by selecting the point with the highest response on a reference map as the predicted position. Nevertheless, existing Finding Point with Image (FPI) methods still suffer from limited localization accuracy.

2.2   Vision Transformer

Transformer [22] is a deep learning architecture based on the self-attention mechanism, initially proposed by Vaswani et al. in the seminal work "Attention is All You Need" in 2017. Originally designed for natural language processing (NLP) tasks [23,24], Transformer models have rapidly extended to other domains, including computer vision, due to their powerful modeling capabilities. In 2020,

Google introduced the Vision Transformer (ViT) [25], which differs from convolutional neural networks (CNN) [26–28] by dividing images into patches and applying self-attention to capture global contextual information. ViT demonstrated remarkable success and inspired a series of subsequent works.Subsequently, extensive research has been conducted to further improve Vision Transformers. Representative developments include the Swin Transformer [29], which introduces a hierarchical design with shifted windows; the Pyramid Vision Transformer (PVT) [30], which incorporates a pyramid structure to enhance multi-scale feature learning; and hybrid architectures such as Convolutional Vision Transformer (CVT) [31] and ConVMAE [32], which integrate convolutional operations into Transformer pipelines. Despite their architectural differences, these models all rely on attention mechanisms and have collectively advanced the performance and scalability of vision Transformer models.

Recent advancements in visual object tracking have significantly improved performance through Transformer-based backbones. These methods enhance tracking accuracy and robustness by utilizing self-attention, spatio-temporal modeling, and feature integration. TransTrack [33] employs multi-channel self-attention to model video sequences, effectively capturing object-background relationships and boosting precision. SwinTrack [34] uses a hierarchical window-based attention mechanism to extract multi-scale features, facilitating cross-window information exchange and capturing both local and global context. MixFormer [35] introduces a Transformer-based single-stream framework with a Mixed Attention Module (MAM), enabling joint feature extraction and interaction. These approaches excel at modeling temporal dependencies, object relationships, and discriminative features, achieving notable improvements in tracking accuracy, robustness, and generalization.

3   Method

In this section, we provide a detailed description of our end-to-end framework and the architectural design of the network. We first present the overall structure of the proposed method and explain how the model performs feature extraction and information interaction between UAV perspective images and satellite imagery. We then describe how the output features from the backbone network are enhanced using the FcaNet module to suppress irrelevant information and emphasize discriminative features. Subsequently, we integrate the Dysample mechanism with a feature pyramid structure to perform multi-scale feature fusion. Finally, the predicted response map is projected back onto the satellite image to generate a heatmap, where the point with the highest response value indicates the predicted location of the UAV.

3.1   Overall Architecture of MIXFP

Our objective is to localize the center position of a UAV image within a given satellite image. As illustrated in Fig. 2,the backbone of our framework is based on

MixViT (ConvMAE) and consists of three main stages. The first two stages use convolutional layers to extract features from UAV and satellite images separately, while the third stage introduces a Mixed Attention Module (MAM), as illustrated in Fig. 3, to perform joint feature extraction and interaction. The MAM is a flexible attention mechanism that unifies the processes of feature extraction and information integration between the target template and the search region. Specifically, the module incorporates both self-attention to extract internal features and cross-attention to facilitate interaction between the UAV and satellite features. Through this dual-attention design, the model effectively aligns heterogeneous representations and enhances semantic consistency across views. The backbone outputs multi-scale satellite features across three stages, which are fused in a pyramid structure to enhance localization. Finally, a heatmap is generated by projecting the prediction onto the satellite image, where the peak response indicates the predicted UAV location.

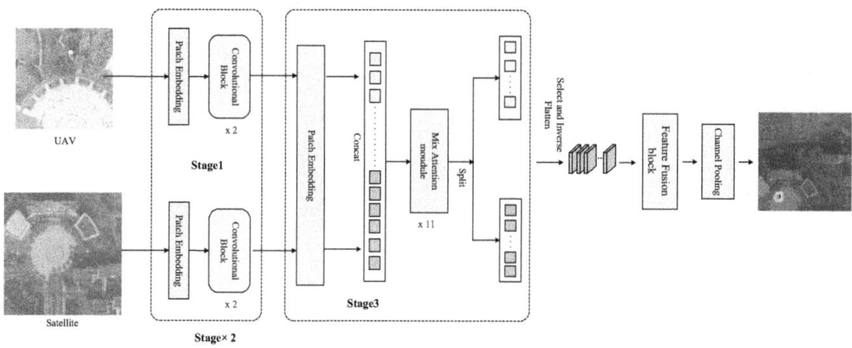

Fig. 2. Overall architecture of MIXFP. The backbone consists of three stages with feature dimensions of 256, 384, and 768.

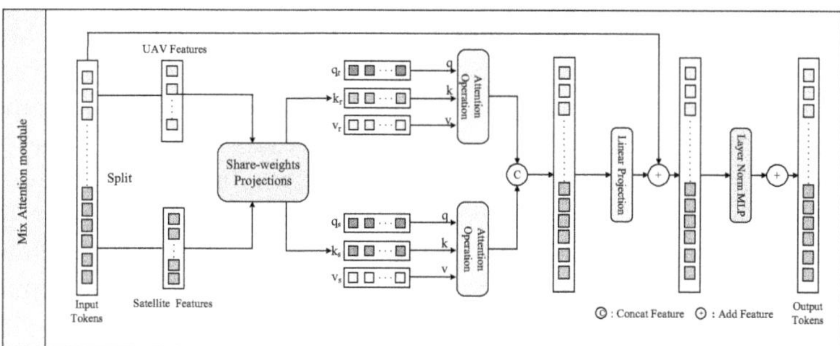

Fig. 3. The Mix Attention module serves as the key component for joint feature extraction and relational modeling.

3.2   Feature Fusion Network

Feature Pyramid Structure : Following the backbone processing, interaction between UAV and satellite features is established. However, point-based localization is a fine-grained task, where different scales of imagery contain varying levels of semantic information. To enhance localization performance, we incorporate a feature pyramid structure, as illustrated in Fig. 4. Specifically, three scales of UAV and satellite features are extracted from the three stages of the backbone. These features are fused using a top-down pathway with lateral connections, enabling effective integration across resolutions. This design mitigates semantic inconsistencies caused by resolution gaps and reduces localization bias from mismatched feature semantics.

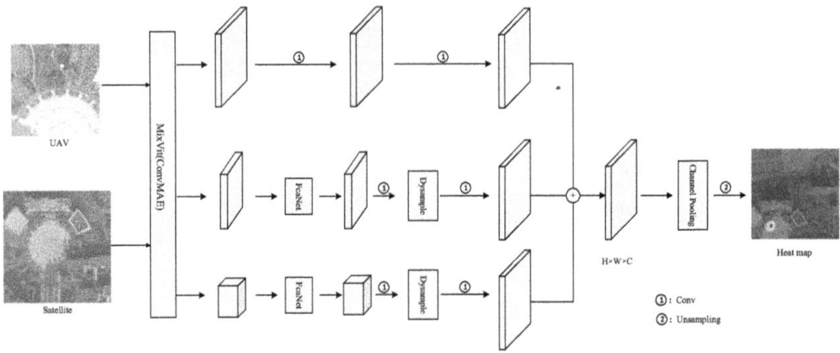

Fig. 4. The satellite feature maps extracted from multiple stages of the backbone MixViT (ConvMAE) are fused and progressively upsampled to produce the final prediction map.

Dynamic Upsampling: DySample [15] is an ultra-lightweight and efficient dynamic upsampling method specifically designed for dense prediction tasks such as semantic segmentation, object detection, and instance segmentation. Compared to traditional upsampling techniques (e.g., bilinear interpolation or transposed convolution), DySample significantly improves performance through a dynamic sampling mechanism. Instead of relying on the complexity of traditional dynamic convolutions, DySample performs upsampling via point sampling. It first interpolates the input feature map into a continuous space using bilinear interpolation, then generates content-aware sampling points. These points are adjusted through offsets predicted by a linear layer, allowing the network to capture sharper edges and finer details. Considering the similarity between point-based localization and semantic segmentation–both requiring pixel-wise classification–we replace the conventional sampling in the feature pyramid structure with DySample. This substitution enables more accurate localization by better capturing edge information and spatial details.

FcaNet: The Frequency Channel Attention Network (FcaNet) [14] is a neural network module based on frequency-domain channel attention. It enhances the representational capacity of convolutional neural networks by introducing a multispectral attention mechanism. The core idea is to analyze feature maps in the frequency domain using the Discrete Cosine Transform (DCT), select important frequency components, and generate channel attention weights to improve model performance. As illustrated in Fig. 5, FcaNet extracts key frequency information based on predefined frequency indices, and then uses fully connected layers and a Sigmoid function to produce attention weights. These weights are applied to the input feature map to highlight informative features and suppress irrelevant ones, enabling the network to better capture image details and texture patterns.

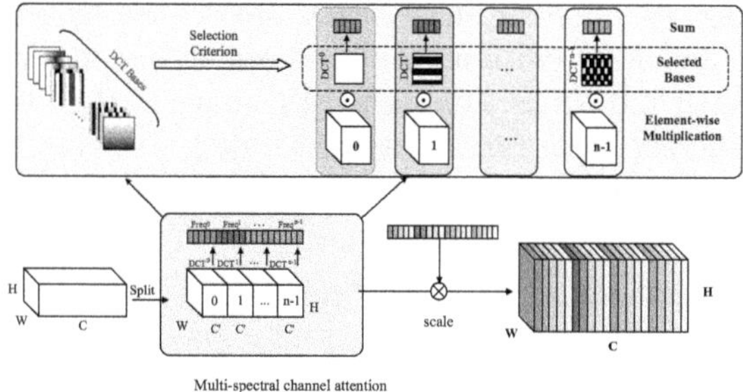

Fig. 5. Schematic of FcaNet

In our framework, we apply FcaNet to enhance the low-scale feature maps from the first two stages of the backbone network. This enhances edge-related features in low-resolution representations, facilitating more effective multi-scale feature fusion in subsequent stages.

4   Experiment

4.1   Implementation Details

In this study, the proposed model is trained on the UL14 dataset, with the backbone initialized using the publicly available pre-trained ConvMAE-B model. To accommodate the model input requirements, satellite images and UAV images are resized to $384 \times 384 \times 3$ and $128 \times 128 \times 3$, respectively. All experiments are conducted on a single NVIDIA GTX 1080Ti GPU. The AdamW [36] optimizer is employed for training, and a cosine annealing learning rate scheduler is adopted, where the minimum learning rate is set to one-hundredth of the initial learning rate to ensure a more stable convergence process.

4.2   Dataset and Evaluation Metrics

(1) **Dataset**: We use the publicly available UL14 dataset in our experiments. As shown in Table 1, UL14 consists of UAV images and their corresponding satellite images. The training set includes 6768 UAV-satellite image pairs collected from 10 universities, while the test set contains 2331 UAV-satellite image pairs from 4 different universities at varying scales. UAV images are sampled at three different flight altitudes (80 m, 90 m, and 100 m), making UL14 a densely sampled dataset. All UAV images are center-cropped and resized to 128 × 128 × 3. Based on the geolocation metadata embedded in UAV images, the corresponding regions in satellite images can be easily retrieved and cropped using different strategies to form matched pairs. The test images are collected from universities that do not overlap with those in the training set. Satellite image scales are defined by setting pixel values between 700 and 1800 (with a ground sampling distance of 0.294 m/pixel) in increments of 100 pixels. For each UAV image in the test set, 12 satellite images at different scale ratios were generated, allowing the evaluation of the model's robustness under multi-scale conditions.

Table 1. Statistics of the UL14 dataset.

Dataset	UAV-view	Satellite-view	Universities
Train	6768	6768	10
Test	2331	27,972	4

(2) **Evaluation Metrics**: To ensure fair comparisons, we adopt the same evaluation metrics as previous works, namely RDS and MA. The MA metric is defined as shown in Eq. 1. It measures the geolocation accuracy in meters by computing the geographical distance between the predicted and ground-truth coordinates. For example, the 5-m accuracy indicates the percentage of test samples whose predicted locations deviate from the ground truth by less than 5 m.

$$MA_{<Km} = \frac{\sum_{i=1}^{N} \mathbb{1}_{SD<Km}}{N} \tag{1}$$

$$\mathbb{1}_{SD<Km} = \begin{cases} 1, & SD < Km \\ 0, & SD \geq Km \end{cases} \tag{2}$$

In the equation, SD denotes the actual spatial distance measured in meters, and K is a tunable threshold. MA represents the proportion of samples whose localization error falls within K meters. The computation of SD is defined in Eq. 3.

$$SD = \sqrt{(\Delta x)^2 + (\Delta y)^2} \tag{3}$$

In the equation, Δx represents the localization error in meters along the longitudinal direction between the predicted position and the ground truth, while Δ y represents the corresponding error in the latitudinal direction.

The RDS is defined in Eq. 4, where dx and dy denote the pixel-wise distances between the predicted and actual positions in the horizontal and vertical directions, respectively. Specifically, dx is the pixel difference along the x-axis, and dy is that along the y-axis. Variables w and h represent the width and height of the satellite image in pixels. The coefficient k is a scaling factor set to 10 in this work. A smaller pixel distance between the predicted and actual positions leads to an RDS score closer to 1, indicating higher accuracy, whereas larger distances yield scores closer to 0.

$$\mathrm{RDS} = e^{-k \times \sqrt{\frac{1}{2}\left(\left(\frac{dx}{w}\right)^2 + \left(\frac{dy}{h}\right)^2\right)}} \tag{4}$$

RDS emphasizes the pixel-level distance between the predicted location and the ground-truth position on the satellite image. Specifically, it evaluates how close the predicted location is to the actual target in terms of pixel displacement, with smaller distances yielding higher scores. In contrast, MA provides a direct measurement of the true spatial distance between the predicted and actual positions.

4.3 Main Results

We compare our method with previous approaches on the UL14 dataset, as shown in Table 2 and Fig. 6. When evaluated using the RDS metric, MixFP demonstrates superior performance over existing methods. Compared to the current state-of-the-art OS-FPI, our model achieves a 5.57% improvement in the RDS score. Additionally, it exhibits significant improvements in localization accuracy at 3 m, 5 m, 10 m, and 20 m thresholds, with gains of approximately 7% (22.81% → 29.75%), 8% (44.31% → 52.66%), 7% (72.32% → 79.48%), and 6% (82.52% → 88.74%), respectively.

Table 2. Comparison of MixFP and other methods on the public UL14 dataset.

Model	Parameters	Inference time	RDS	3 m	5 m	10 m	20 m
MixFP	85.18	2.1×	81.82	29.75	52.66	79.48	88.74
DRL	20.68	3.8×	75.88	13.15	29.83	62.58	83.75
OS-FPI	14.28	1.12×	76.25	22.81	44.31	72.32	82.52
WAMF-FPI	48.94	1.69×	65.33	12.49	26.99	52.62	69.73
FPI	44.48	1×	57.22	–	18.63	38.36	57.67

We further evaluated the performance of each model under different spatial thresholds. Figure 7 illustrates the localization accuracy within 3 m, 5 m, 10 m,

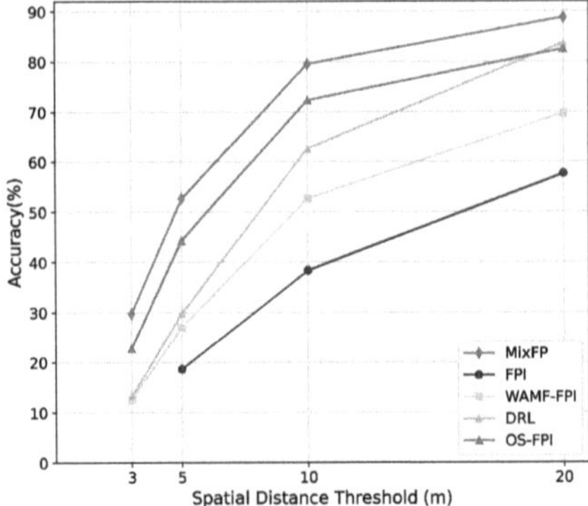

Fig. 6. Evaluation of model performance based on the MA metric

and 20 m ranges. The original FPI model is represented by the the blue curve, WAMF-FPI by the orange curve, DRL by the purple curve, OS-FPI by the green curve, and the proposed MixFP model by the red curve. As shown in the figure, the proposed MixFP achieves substantial improvements in accuracy compared to other methods across all evaluated distance thresholds.

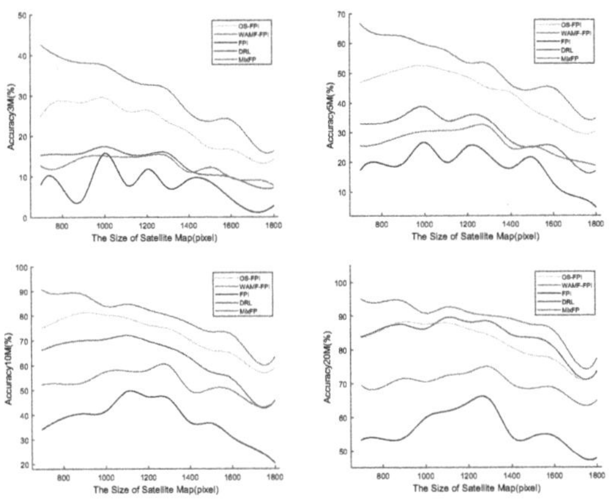

Fig. 7. Performance comparison of different models at different scales.

5   Ablation Experiment

5.1   The Effect of Using the Dysample Feature Pyramid

Shallow feature maps retain high spatial resolution and contain rich spatial detail, while deep feature maps, though lower in resolution, encapsulate more abstract and semantically meaningful information. Directly using low-resolution deep features as the final output may lead to significant spatial information loss, resulting in deviations in UAV localization. To address this issue, we incorporate a feature pyramid structure to enable multi-scale feature fusion and integrate the DySample module to perform point-based upsampling. This method involves bilinearly interpolating the feature maps into continuous space, generating content-aware sampling points, and then adjusting their positions through offsets predicted by a linear layer, effectively preserving edges and fine details, thereby improving localization accuracy.

To ensure fairness, all other parameters were kept consistent in the experiment. Both models used Fcanet after the backbone network. The comparison focuses solely on the performance changes of the model when using conventional upsampling and DySample in the pyramid structure, as shown in Fig. 8. It was observed that the pyramid multi-scale feature fusion module using DySample point sampling significantly outperforms the pyramid feature fusion module using traditional upsampling. The model's performance improved by 4.29% in 3-meter-level positioning accuracy (from 25.46 to 29.75) and by 4.21% in 5-meter-level accuracy (from 48.41 to 52.66). Additionally, the model achieved a 1.2-point improvement in RDS metrics. Figure 10 visualizes the prediction results in the form of a heatmap. From the figure, it can be seen that DySample effectively improves the model's positioning performance on the UL14 dataset.

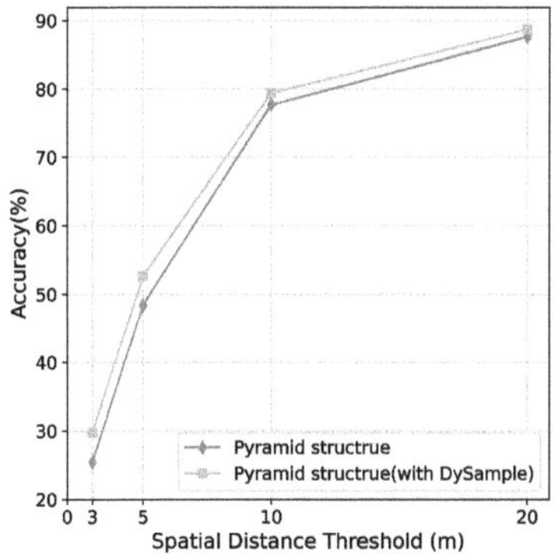

Fig. 8. The impact of DySample in the pyramid structure on MA accuracy

5.2 The Effect of Using FcaNet

FcaNet improves traditional Global Average Pooling (GAP) by introducing the Discrete Cosine Transform (DCT), generating frequency-domain channel attention weights for multi-scale feature maps. This enables better focus on useful information from low-resolution features when merged with high-resolution ones, enhancing feature expressiveness. By filtering mid-high frequency components,

FcaNet captures edges and details in low-resolution maps. The fused features, processed through the Feature Pyramid Network (FPN), significantly improve feature integration. As shown in Fig. 9, this leads to improved meter-level accuracy and a 1-point increase in RDS. Figure 10 shows the heatmap of the fused feature map results. From the figure, it can be seen that FcaNet effectively improves the model's positioning performance on the UL14 dataset.

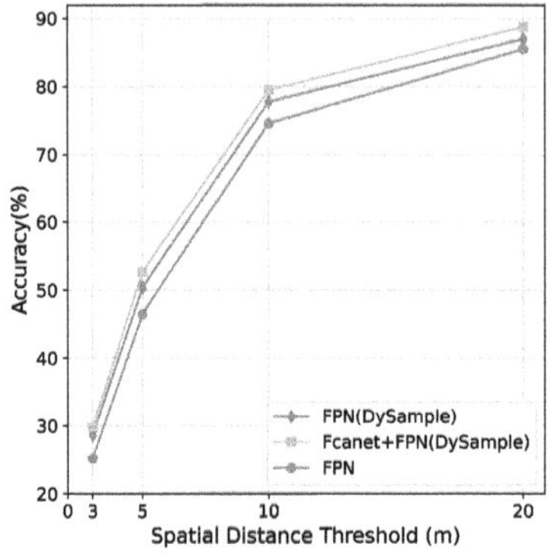

Fig. 9. Change in MA accuracy after the application of FcaNet to low-resolution images in feature fusion

6   Discussion

Through comparative experiments, our model achieves a notable improvement in localization accuracy.In our proposed model, we input the feature maps output by the Transformer model into FcaNet to enhance performance. The Transformer model effectively performs global modeling through its attention mechanism, while FcaNet improves the model's ability to focus on and model locally important features. Experimental results show that applying FcaNet to low-resolution feature maps in the three stages significantly facilitates effective feature fusion between high- and low-resolution images in the feature pyramid, yielding satisfactory results. To further improve model performance, we introduced a feature pyramid structure based on DySample. By extracting feature maps at three different scales from the backbone network, we capture features at various scales of the image. DySample performs point sampling to upsample the input feature maps into continuous space using bilinear interpolation, then generates content-aware sampling points. These points are adjusted through offsets predicted by a linear layer, capturing clearer edges and finer details. These improvements contribute to a significant performance boost in UAV positioning tasks.

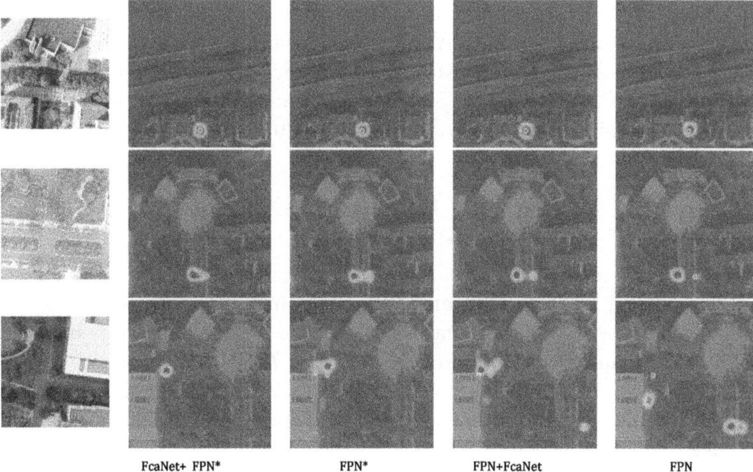

Fig. 10. The predicted heatmaps for UAV images are generated by models with different modules. The discrepancy between the predicted location and the ground-truth is indicated by red text. The label FPN* denotes that the corresponding FPN is equipped with DySample.

7 Conclusions

In a GPS-denied environment, autonomous localization plays a crucial role in UAV development by significantly enhancing safety. Studying the application of remote sensing imagery in UAV visual self-localization is of great importance. Experimental results on the UL14 dataset show that we propose a single-stream network model for UAV cross-view localization, utilizing cross-view matching between remote sensing satellite images and UAV-captured vertical view images in GPS-denied environments. Our model leverages the characteristics of the feature pyramid structure and introduces DySample for point-sampling upsampling to better fuse image information across different scales. Additionally, FcaNet is introduced to facilitate effective feature fusion between high-resolution and low-resolution images in the feature pyramid.

However, we acknowledge that there is still room for further improvement in the model's localization performance and lightweight design. Future work can explore more flexible receptive field designs and address visual issues caused by sensor viewpoint differences, further enhancing the model's performance and applicability. Moreover, we will consider the practical application of the algorithm and design more efficient models to reduce inference time. In increasingly complex environments, we believe our method will contribute to geographic localization in GPS-denied scenarios.

Acknowledgements. This work was supported by the project program of Science and Technology on Micro-system Laboratory(NO.6142804230106),Fundamental Research Funds for the Central Universities(3072024XX0804),National Key R&D Program of China(2022YFE0136800),Open Fund of Key Laboratory of Marine Environmental Survey Technology and Application, Ministry of Natural Resources, P.R. China(MESTA-2022-A006),Harbin Manufacturing Science and Technology Innovation Talent Project(2023CXRCCG010), Special Topic on Laboratory Stable Support for National Defense Basic Research Program(JCKYS2023604SSJS009).

References

1. Alsalam, B.H.Y., Morton, K., Campbell, D., Gonzalez, F.: Autonomous UAV with vision based on-board decision making for remote sensing and precision agriculture. In: 2017 IEEE Aerospace Conference, pp. 1–12. IEEE (2017)
2. Gupta, A., Fernando, X.: Simultaneous localization and mapping (slam) and data fusion in unmanned aerial vehicles: recent advances and challenges. Drones **6**(4), 85 (2022)
3. Zhou, L., Huang, G., Mao, Y., Wang, S., Kaess, M.: Edplvo: efficient direct point-line visual odometry. In: 2022 International Conference on Robotics and Automation (ICRA), pp. 7559–7565. IEEE (2022)
4. Lowe, D.G.: Distinctive image features from scale-invariant keypoints. Int. J. Comput. Vision **60**, 91–110 (2004)
5. Bay, H., Ess, A., Tuytelaars, T., Van Gool, L.: Speeded-up robust features (surf). Comput. Vis. Image Underst. **110**(3), 346–359 (2008)
6. Zheng, Z., Wei, Y., Yang, Y.: University-1652: a multi-view multi-source benchmark for drone-based geo-localization. In: Proceedings of the 28th ACM International Conference on Multimedia, pp. 1395–1403 (2020)
7. Cai, S., Guo, Y., Khan, S., Hu, J., Wen, G.: Ground-to-aerial image geo-localization with a hard exemplar reweighting triplet loss. In: Proceedings of the IEEE/CVF International Conference on Computer Vision, pp. 8391–8400 (2019)
8. Zhu, Y., Sun, B., Lu, X., Jia, S.: Geographic semantic network for cross-view image geo-localization. IEEE Trans. Geosci. Remote Sens. **60**, 1–15 (2021)
9. Tian, X., Shao, J., Ouyang, D., Shen, H.T.: UAV-satellite view synthesis for cross-view geo-localization. IEEE Trans. Circuits Syst. Video Technol. **32**(7), 4804–4815 (2021)
10. Dai, M., Chen, J., Lu, Y., Hao, W., Zheng, E.: Finding point with image: an end-to-end benchmark for vision-based UAV localization. CoRR (2022)
11. Wang, G., Chen, J., Dai, M., Zheng, E.: WAMF-FPI: a weight-adaptive multi-feature fusion network for UAV localization. Remote Sens. **15**(4), 910 (2023)
12. Chen, J., Zheng, E., Dai, M., Chen, Y., Lu, Y.: Os-fpi: A coarse-to-fine one-stream network for uav geo-localization. IEEE J. Selected Top. Appl. Earth Observ. Remote Sens. (2024)
13. Dai, M., Zheng, E., Chen, J., Qi, L., Feng, Z., Yang, W.: Drone referring localization: an efficient heterogeneous spatial feature interaction method for uav self-localization. arXiv preprint arXiv:2208.06561 (2022)
14. Qin, Z., Zhang, P., Wu, F., Li, X.: Fcanet: frequency channel attention networks. In: Proceedings of the IEEE/CVF International Conference on Computer Vision, pp. 783–792 (2021)
15. Liu, W., Lu, H., Fu, H., Cao, Z.: Learning to upsample by learning to sample. In: Proceedings of the IEEE/CVF International Conference on Computer Vision, pp. 6027–6037 (2023)

16. Workman, S., Souvenir, R., Jacobs, N.: Wide-area image geolocalization with aerial reference imagery. In: Proceedings of the IEEE International Conference on Computer Vision, pp. 3961–3969 (2015)
17. Lin, T.Y., Cui, Y., Belongie, S., Hays, J.: Learning deep representations for ground-to-aerial geolocalization. In: Proceedings of the IEEE Conference on Computer Vision and Pattern Recognition, pp. 5007–5015 (2015)
18. Shi, Y., Liu, L., Yu, X., Li, H.: Spatial-aware feature aggregation for image based cross-view geo-localization. Adv. Neural Inform. Process. Syst. **32** (2019)
19. Wang, T., Zheng, Z., Yan, C., Zhang, J., Sun, Y., Zheng, B., Yang, Y.: Each part matters: local patterns facilitate cross-view geo-localization. IEEE Trans. Circuits Syst. Video Technol. **32**(2), 867–879 (2021)
20. Zeng, Z., Wang, Z., Yang, F., Satoh, S.: Geo-localization via ground-to-satellite cross-view image retrieval. IEEE Trans. Multimed. **25**, 2176–2188 (2022)
21. Dai, M., Hu, J., Zhuang, J., Zheng, E.: A transformer-based feature segmentation and region alignment method for UAV-view geo-localization. IEEE Trans. Circuits Syst. Video Technol. **32**(7), 4376–4389 (2021)
22. Vaswani, A., Shazeer, N., Parmar, N., Uszkoreit, J., Jones, L., Gomez, A.N., Kaiser, Ł., Polosukhin, I.: Attention is all you need. Adv. Neural Inform. Process. Syst. **30** (2017)
23. Devlin, J., Chang, M.W., Lee, K., Toutanova, K.: Bert: pre-training of deep bidirectional transformers for language understanding. In: Proceedings of the 2019 Conference of the North American Chapter of the Association for Computational Linguistics: Human Language Technologies, vol. 1 (long and short papers), pp. 4171–4186 (2019)
24. Lan, Z., Chen, M., Goodman, S., Gimpel, K., Sharma, P., Soricut, R.: Albert: a lite bert for self-supervised learning of language representations. arXiv preprint arXiv:1909.11942 (2019)
25. Dosovitskiy, A., Beyer, L., Kolesnikov, A., Weissenborn, D., Zhai, X., Unterthiner, T., Dehghani, M., Minderer, M., Heigold, G., Gelly, S., et al.: An image is worth 16x16 words: transformers for image recognition at scale. arXiv preprint arXiv:2010.11929 (2020)
26. LeCun, Y., Bottou, L., Bengio, Y., Haffner, P.: Gradient-based learning applied to document recognition. Proc. IEEE **86**(11), 2278–2324 (1998)
27. Szegedy, C., Liu, W., Jia, Y., Sermanet, P., Reed, S., Anguelov, D., Erhan, D., Vanhoucke, V., Rabinovich, A.: Going deeper with convolutions. In: Proceedings of the IEEE Conference on Computer Vision and Pattern Recognition, pp. 1–9 (2015)
28. Krizhevsky, A., Sutskever, I., Hinton, G.E.: Imagenet classification with deep convolutional neural networks. Commun. ACM **60**(6), 84–90 (2017)
29. Liu, Z., Lin, Y., Cao, Y., Hu, H., Wei, Y., Zhang, Z., Lin, S., Guo, B.: Swin transformer: hierarchical vision transformer using shifted windows. In: Proceedings of the IEEE/CVF International Conference on Computer Vision.,pp. 10012–10022 (2021)
30. Wang, W., Xie, E., Li, X., Fan, D.P., Song, K., Liang, D., Lu, T., Luo, P., Shao, L.: Pyramid vision transformer: a versatile backbone for dense prediction without convolutions. In: Proceedings of the IEEE/CVF International Conference on Computer Vision, pp. 568–578 (2021)
31. Wu, H., Xiao, B., Codella, N., Liu, M., Dai, X., Yuan, L., Zhang, L.: Cvt: introducing convolutions to vision transformers. In: Proceedings of the IEEE/CVF International Conference on Computer Vision, pp. 22–31 (2021)

32. Gao, P., Ma, T., Li, H., Lin, Z., Dai, J., Qiao, Y.: Convmae: masked convolution meets masked autoencoders. arXiv preprint arXiv:2205.03892 (2022)
33. Sun, P., Cao, J., Jiang, Y., Zhang, R., Xie, E., Yuan, Z., Wang, C., Luo, P.: Transtrack: multiple object tracking with transformer. arXiv preprint arXiv:2012.15460 (2020)
34. Lin, L., Fan, H., Zhang, Z., Xu, Y., Ling, H.: Swintrack: a simple and strong baseline for transformer tracking. Adv. Neural. Inf. Process. Syst. **35**, 16743–16754 (2022)
35. Cui, Y., Jiang, C., Wang, L., Wu, G.: Mixformer: end-to-end tracking with iterative mixed attention. In: Proceedings of the IEEE/CVF Conference on Computer Vision and Pattern Recognition, pp. 13608–13618 (2022)
36. Loshchilov, I., Hutter, F.: Decoupled weight decay regularization. arXiv preprint arXiv:1711.05101 (2017)

Maritime Target Recognition Based on Tensor Alignment Domain Adaptation

Qianrui Guo[1], Xiang Li[2(✉)], and Zhengwei Xu[2]

[1] Institute of Remote Sensing Satellite, China Academy of Space Technology, Beijing 100094, China
guoqianrui1005@163.com
[2] College of Computer and Information Engineering, Henan Normal University, Xinxiang, China
2408283060@stu.htu.edu.cn

Abstract. Maritime vessel type recognition holds significant application value in fields such as maritime safety monitoring, environmental protection, and maritime traffic management. However, due to the complexity and variability of the marine environment, traditional single-modal image recognition methods face numerous challenges in practical applications. This paper proposes a multi-modal fusion network based on tensor alignment and domain adaptation. By combining visible light and infrared image data, the method fully leverages the complementary nature of different modalities, thereby enhancing the model's performance in complex maritime environments. Additionally, adversarial training and tensor alignment techniques are introduced to effectively reduce the disparity between source and target domain features, improving cross-domain adaptation capability. Experiments conducted on a self-collected maritime vessel dataset demonstrate that the proposed method outperforms existing multi-modal fusion methods across multiple evaluation metrics, including accuracy, precision, recall, and F1 score, validating the effectiveness of our approach for maritime vessel type recognition.

Keywords: Maritime target identification · Domain adaptation · Multimodal

1 Introduction

Maritime target recognition is a crucial component of maritime situational awareness and plays a significant role in maritime traffic. Therefore, maritime authorities need to strengthen the supervision and enforcement of maritime traffic to ensure the safety of ship navigation through precise identification and positioning of passing vessels [1–3]. However, traditional recognition methods based on single sensors (such as AIS or radar) have significant limitations under harsh sea conditions: radar is prone to interference from sea clutter, leading to

C. Xu et al. (Eds.): MobiMedia 2025, LNICST 670, pp. 161–173, 2026.
https://doi.org/10.1007/978-3-032-16823-8_12

an increased false alarm rate; optical imaging is limited by cloud cover, fog, and low illumination at night; and AIS data is susceptible to human tampering [4–6]. The complementary characteristics and spatiotemporal asynchrony of these multi-source heterogeneous data create a contradiction, making the construction of a robust target recognition system a key technological bottleneck in the field of maritime regulation.

In this context, multi-modal transfer learning technology demonstrates unique application value. By constructing a cross-modal feature alignment network, it effectively integrates multi-dimensional sensory data, such as visible light, infrared, SAR radar, and AIS, overcoming the physical limitations of single sensors. At the same time, the transfer learning mechanism allows for the adaptive transfer of knowledge models from labeled maritime areas to new monitoring regions, significantly alleviating the difficulties of maritime sample collection and the high cost of labeling. The multi-modal deep transfer framework proposed in this study innovatively introduces cross-domain attention mechanisms and adversarial domain adaptation strategies [7–9], achieving precise ship target recognition and anomaly behavior detection under complex sea conditions. The application of this technology will greatly enhance maritime regulatory authorities' ability to respond to "ghost ship" identification, illegal fishing monitoring, and collision warnings, providing theoretical support and technical assurance for the development of an all-weather, global maritime traffic management system.

Visible light and infrared detection play a crucial role in maritime target recognition [10]. However, there are still many technical challenges in maritime target recognition, such as complex marine environments, uneven backgrounds, and the interference caused by sea surface movement and wind [11,12]. Since acquiring a large amount of labeled maritime target recognition data is both expensive and time-consuming, and data is scarce, we address this issue by using unsupervised domain adaptation (UDA), where the target domain has no labeled samples [13]. Using this technique, there is no need to prepare a custom training dataset, yet the task can still be performed effectively and efficiently.

When applying domain adaptation to multi-modal scenarios, there are two key challenges: (1) how to align the source and target domains and reduce the domain discrepancies [14]; (2) how to align multi-modal data and leverage multi-modal information. Most existing works first perform multi-modal alignment and then apply domain adaptation. Zhou et al. [15] proposed a multi-modal network based on multi-task learning and domain adaptation (MDMN), Xu et al. [16] introduced a multi-modal domain adaptation method that jointly learns feature embeddings from both source and target domains, Zhang et al. [17] proposed the BDANN model, which combines BERT and VGG-19 models for domain adaptation and multi-modal feature fusion, and Munro et al. [18] introduced multi-modal self-supervised adversarial domain adaptation (MM-SADA).

Therefore, in this paper, we design the TALNet model, which unifies multi-modal alignment and domain alignment into a single stage [19]. Figure 1 illustrates the conceptual framework of our model. Our approach has the following advantages: (1) The modality and domain are correlated and interact with each other, thus capturing the rich complementary information between the domain and modality; (2) Multi-modal alignment and domain adaptation are unified in one stage, allowing our model to simultaneously perform domain adaptation while leveraging multi-modal information.

Our contributions are as follows:

(1) Based on the tensor alignment module, we use Tucker decomposition to factorize high-dimensional tensors into low-dimensional tensors, and combine maximum mean discrepancy (MMD) and symmetric KL divergence to experimentally align both modality and domain.
(2) Domain alignment is achieved through the tensor alignment module, combined with adversarial training methods to enhance domain adaptation. During training, label smoothing loss and focal loss are introduced to address the challenges posed by class imbalance. The classification loss and domain adversarial loss weights are dynamically adjusted according to the sample characteristics, effectively improving the model's transferability and generalization performance.
(3) The dynamic domain classifier, which integrates a gradient reversal layer, adjusts the adversarial training intensity. This allows the model to dynamically adjust the domain discrepancies between the source and target domains, thereby enhancing the model's generalization ability.

2 Method

2.1 Overall Framework

We propose a multi-modal domain adaptation network framework that addresses the distribution discrepancy between the source and target domains through tensor alignment with maximum mean discrepancy loss, adversarial training, cross-modal attention mechanisms, and multi-task learning methods.

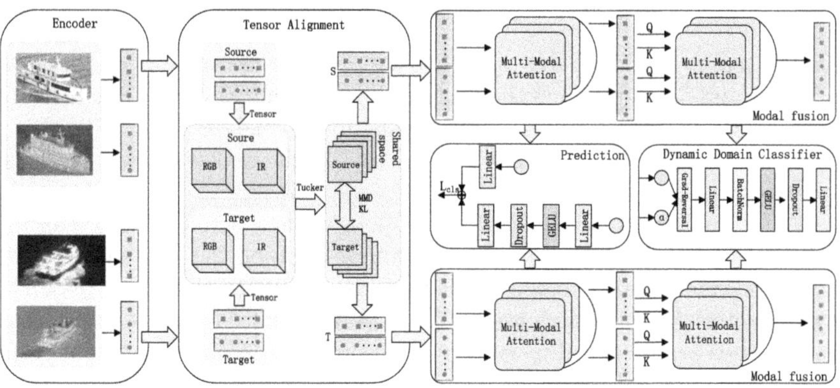

Fig. 1. Network architecture diagram.

The proposed bi-modal domain adaptation network addresses the distribution discrepancy between the source and target domains through feature extraction, alignment, and fusion of visible light and infrared images. The network first uses ResNet50 to extract features from both visible light and infrared images. Then, the features are represented as tensors, and Tucker decomposition is applied to reduce the dimensionality of the high-dimensional tensors, mapping them into a shared space for domain and modality alignment, thereby reducing the differences between domains and modalities. Next, a cross-modal attention mechanism fuses information from the two modalities, further enhancing the model's expressive power. On this basis, the network uses label classifiers and domain classifiers for task classification and domain adaptation, optimizing classification accuracy and domain adaptability through a multi-task loss function. This framework improves the model's performance in cross-domain tasks by effectively aligning the visible light and infrared features of the source and target domains, particularly in visual and infrared image classification tasks under different weather conditions, significantly enhancing the accuracy and generalization ability of the target domain.

2.2 Alignment Based on Tensors

We propose a tensor-based alignment module, which effectively achieves domain and modality alignment by decomposing high-dimensional tensors into low-dimensional tensors and mapping them into a shared space, while simultaneously reducing domain and modality discrepancies.

First, we perform L2 normalization on the input features of visible light and infrared images to ensure that the norm of each feature vector is 1. After feature normalization, we reconstruct the 2D features of visible light and infrared images into 3D tensors. Each image has a feature dimension of $64 \times 64 \times 512$, which is considered as the height, width, and channels of the image. In this process, we reshape the input features into 3D tensors with spatial dimensions and channel dimensions. The reconstruction process is as follows:

$$T = \mathrm{Reshape}(B, 64, 64, 512) \tag{1}$$

where B represents the batch size, 6464 represents the spatial dimensions of the image, and 512 represents the feature channel dimension. The reconstructed tensor follows the standard image processing format, i.e.,$[B, C, H, W]$, C is the number of channels, and H and W are the height and width of the image, respectively.

To effectively reduce the feature dimensions while retaining the core information of the image, we perform Tucker decomposition on the 3D tensors of both visible light and infrared images. Tucker decomposition reduces the dimensionality by factorizing high-dimensional tensors into multiple factor matrices and their core tensor. Specifically, Tucker decomposition decomposes the 3D tensor T into:

$$T \approx G \times U_1 \times U_2 \times U_3 \tag{2}$$

where G is the core tensor, and U_1, U_2, U_3 are the factor matrices along each dimension. After decomposition, the reconstructed tensor can be approximated with a lower rank representation, reducing the feature dimensions while retaining the core features of the original information.

Subsequently, these low-dimensional tensors are mapped to a shared space using kernel functions. To further reduce modality and domain discrepancies, we perform modality alignment by calculating the Maximum Mean Discrepancy (MMD) loss between different modalities within the same domain, and domain alignment by calculating the Kullback-Leibler (KL) divergence. The formula for computing MMD loss is as follows:

$$MMD(U_r, U_I) = \left\| \frac{1}{B} \sum_{i=1}^{B} \phi(U_{r_i}) - \frac{1}{B} \sum_{i=1}^{B} \phi(U_{I_i}) \right\|^2 \tag{3}$$

where $U_r' \in \mathbb{R}^{B \times D}$ is the low-dimensional tensor for visible light, $U_I' \in \mathbb{R}^{B \times D}$ is the low-dimensional tensor for infrared, and $\phi(\cdot)$ is the tensor mapping for kernel function mapping. By minimizing the MMD loss, the model can further align data from different modalities in the shared space, enabling more effective cross-modal learning. The formula for calculating KL divergence is as follows:

$$D_{KL}(P_s \parallel P_t) = \sum_{i=1}^{B} P_s(z_{s_i}) \log \frac{P_s(z_{s_i})}{P_t(z_{s_i})} \tag{4}$$

$$D_{KL}(P_t \parallel P_s) = \sum_{i=1}^{B} P_t(z_{t_i}) \log \frac{P_t(z_{t_i})}{P_s(z_{t_i})} \tag{5}$$

To calculate the symmetrical KL divergence, we use the following formula:

$$KL = D_{KL}(P_s \parallel P_t) + D_{KL}(P_t \parallel P_s) \tag{6}$$

By minimizing the symmetric KL divergence, the model can adjust the feature distributions of the source and target domains, making them more consistent in the shared space, thereby achieving domain alignment. During training, the MMD loss and KL loss are weighted and combined into the total loss:

$$L_{Tal} = \alpha_{MMD} \times MMD + \alpha_{KL} \times KL \tag{7}$$

This weighting strategy helps balance the influence of the two loss functions during the training process, enabling the model to effectively perform domain adaptation throughout the training.

2.3   Modal Fusion

We introduce a cross-modal attention mechanism to fuse visible light and infrared features, thereby enhancing the performance of multi-modal learning tasks. This mechanism enables information transfer and enhancement between different modalities through the combination of self-attention and cross-modal attention.

The core of the cross-modal attention module lies in the combination of multi-head self-attention and cross-modal attention mechanisms. At the initialization of the model, an independent self-attention module is defined for each modality. Specifically, during initialization, three main attention layers are defined: visible light self-attention, infrared self-attention, and cross-modal attention.

First, visible light self-attention is applied to the visible light image features. When the input passes through the self-attention mechanism, the input visible light features are first dimensionally expanded to meet the input requirements of the multi-head attention module. Then, the model performs self-attention operations on these features:

$$vis\_attn = MultiheadAttention(V, V, V) \tag{8}$$

where V represents the visible light features. After the self-attention operation, the model is able to model the internal correlations of the features and learn the long-range dependencies between the features.

Next, infrared self-attention is applied to the infrared image features. Similar to the visible light modality, the features of the infrared image undergo a similar process. After the input features are expanded, the self-attention operation is performed:

$$ir\_attn = MultiheadAttention(V, V, V) \tag{9}$$

Finally, cross-modal attention is used for the interaction between visible light and infrared features, enhancing the information flow between the two modalities. In cross-modal attention, the model first interacts the visible light features, which have undergone self-attention, with the infrared features. Specifically, the visible light features are used as the query (Q), and the infrared features are used as the key (K) and value (V) for attention calculation:

$$cross\_vis = MultiheadAttention(vis\_attn, ir\_attn, ir\_attn) \tag{10}$$

Similarly, cross-modal infrared attention is performed using infrared features as the query, interacting with the visible light features. This cross-modal attention operation helps exchange information between the visible light modality and the infrared modality. Finally, we sum the cross-modal visible light attention and cross-modal infrared attention, generating a feature representation that contains complementary information from both the visible light and infrared modalities.

2.4 Dynamic Domain Classifier

We propose a dynamic domain classifier, which aims to achieve domain adaptation through adversarial training. The domain classifier consists of a gradient reversal layer, fully connected layers, and batch normalization layers. The dynamic domain classifier takes input features, processes them through the gradient reversal layer, and then passes them to the fully connected layers.

The gradient reversal layer is key to adversarial training. Its role is to "reverse" the gradients during the training process, causing the feature extraction module to no longer distinguish between the source domain and the target domain. Instead, it learns features that have strong domain adaptation capabilities. During forward propagation, the gradient reversal layer does not modify the input data; it simply passes the data to downstream network modules. During backpropagation, the gradient reversal layer reverses the gradients calculated by the domain classifier and multiplies them by a coefficient α. This forces the feature extractor to learn features that are ineffective for the domain classifier, meaning the features of the source domain and target domain are as similar as possible.

During training, α typically increases gradually as the training progresses. In the early stages, the gradient reversal layer has a minimal impact on the gradients, mainly helping the model learn the feature extraction task. As training progresses, the value of α increases, thus enhancing the impact of the gradient reversal layer on the gradients. This encourages the feature extractor to learn features that make it more difficult to distinguish between the source domain and the target domain, thereby strengthening cross-domain adaptation capabilities.

We use cross-entropy loss to calculate the domain classification loss. By minimizing the cross-entropy loss, the features of the source domain and target domain become difficult to distinguish in the shared space. The calculation formula for the cross-entropy loss is as follows:

$$L_{\text{domain}} = -(y_s \log(p_s) + y_t \log(p_t)) \tag{11}$$

where y_s and y_t are the true labels of the source domain and target domain, respectively; p_s and p_t are the model's predicted labels for the source domain and target domain.

2.5   Loss Function

In practical scenarios, many datasets suffer from class imbalance. During the data collection process, due to changes in weather, some types of ships have no corresponding data, leading to class imbalance [20]. The class imbalance issue causes the model to become biased towards the more frequent classes. To address this problem, we introduce label smoothing loss and focal loss.

The purpose of label smoothing loss is to prevent the model from making overly confident predictions for specific classes during training, thereby improving the model's generalization ability. We use label smoothing loss to implement the model's classification loss. Label smoothing loss is an improvement on the standard cross-entropy loss:

$$L_{\text{cls}} = -(1 - \epsilon) \cdot \sum_{c=1}^{C} p_c \log q_c - \epsilon \cdot \sum_{c=1}^{C} \frac{1}{c} \tag{12}$$

where p_c is the true label, q_c is the model's predicted label, and ϵ is the label smoothing coefficient, set to 0.1.

Focal loss increases the attention on hard-to-classify samples by introducing a modulation factor, thereby enhancing the model's learning ability on minority class samples. The calculation formula for focal loss is as follows:

$$L_{\mathrm{FL}} = -\alpha_t(1 - p_t)^\gamma \log(p_t) \tag{13}$$

where α_t is the balancing factor used to adjust the weight of different classes, and γ is the focusing factor, usually set to 2, to increase the focus on hard-to-classify samples. We sum the cross-entropy loss and focal loss to obtain the total loss for the dynamic domain classifier:

$$L_{\mathrm{dis}} = L_{\mathrm{domain}} + L_{\mathrm{FL}} \tag{14}$$

Our total loss is:

$$L = \lambda_{\mathrm{cls}} \cdot L_{\mathrm{cls}} + \lambda_{\mathrm{dis}} \cdot L_{\mathrm{dis}} + \lambda_{\mathrm{tal}} \cdot L_{\mathrm{tal}} \tag{15}$$

where $\lambda_{\mathrm{cls}}, \lambda_{\mathrm{dis}}, \lambda_{\mathrm{tal}}$ are the weights for the classification loss, domain loss, and alignment loss, respectively.

3   Experiment

3.1   Data Set

The dataset used in this study is a multimodal ship recognition dataset that we collected at the First Seaside Bathing Beach in Yantai, Shandong, China. This dataset includes images of 14 different types and modalities of ships, with multiple visible light and infrared images for each ship type. In addition, the dataset covers various weather scenarios, including sunny, cloudy, rainy, foggy, and backlit conditions.

3.2   Experimental Environment

This study was conducted on a Windows 10 operating system using the PyTorch 2.6.0 framework, with CUDA 12.6 for accelerated computation. The AdamW optimizer was used, along with various learning rates and training-related parameters. The initial learning rates were as follows: 1e-5 for the visible light feature extractor, 5e-5 for the infrared feature extractor, 5e-4 for the tensor alignment module, 3e-4 for the feature fusion module, 1e-3 for the label classifier, and 2e-3 for the domain classifier, with a weight decay of 1e-4. Both the visible light and infrared feature extractors used ResNet50 as the network architecture.For learning rate scheduling, the experiment used a Warmup learning rate scheduler (pre-warmed via LambdaLR, with the warmup phase lasting for 10 training epochs), ReduceLROnPlateau (which automatically reduces the learning rate when validation metrics stop improving to mitigate overfitting), and CosineAn-nealingLR (which adjusts the learning rate using cosine annealing). The global learning rate was set to 8e-5, with the adversarial training parameter α set to 0.5. The weight for the MMD loss, α_{MMD}, was set to 0.8, and the weight for the KL divergence loss, α_{KL}, was set to 0.2. The alignment loss, λ_{tal}, was initialized at 0.1 and gradually increased throughout the training, reaching a maximum value of 0.4. The domain loss, λ_{dis}, was initialized at 0.3 and gradually decreased over time, with a minimum value of 0.06. The classification loss, λ_{cls}, was determined by the weights of the alignment loss and domain loss, with their total sum being 1.2.The batch size was set to 32, the total number of training epochs was 200, and early stopping was implemented to prevent overfitting.

3.3   Comparative Test

First, to validate the effectiveness of the transfer learning component in our proposed method, this paper compares the experimental results of our method with an experiment where no transfer learning was applied. The performance is evaluated using accuracy, precision, recall, and F1-score as the evaluation metrics.

Table 1. Comparative experiments of the migration part

Task	Weather	Acc	Precision	Recall	F1
Target	Night	63.33	24.61	31.11	27.48
	Backlight	72.22	63.36	57.22	60.13
	Foggy	64.35	49.45	47.00	48.20
	Rainy	38.46	39.13	28.33	32.87
Source → Target	Night	0.22	1.19	0.19	0.33
	Backlight	12.50	10.95	14.75	12.57
	Foggy	6.96	25.00	6.66	10.52
	Rainy	1.04	4.17	1.19	1.85
TALNet	Night	**87.50**	**86.66**	**87.50**	**86.65**
	Backlight	**83.33**	**91.87**	**83.33**	**84.60**
	Foggy	**81.74**	**84.67**	**81.74**	**81.59**
	Rainy	**80.77**	**89.74**	**80.77**	**80.90**

The experimental results are shown in Table 1. The first part presents the results of training the model directly on each weather scenario; the second part shows the results of testing a model trained on sunny weather data across other weather scenarios; and the third part presents the experimental results of our proposed method. Compared with the results from the first and second parts, our proposed method shows significant improvement. This demonstrates that the transfer learning component in our method effectively extracts valuable information from the domain, thereby enhancing the model's generalization ability and improving its performance across different scenarios.

Additionally, to verify the effectiveness of our proposed method in ship target recognition tasks, we compared it with several existing multimodal fusion methods and domain adaptation methods. The dataset used is our collected dataset, with sunny weather data as the source domain and overcast weather data as the target domain.

Table 2. Comparative experiments of the methods

Methods	Acc	Precision	Recall	F1
MMTM	81.82	81.15	85.90	83.46
CAFer	80.73	80.15	84.34	82.19
ADDA	83.95	79.16	85.75	82.32
DAN	83.83	85.21	79.30	82.15
TALNet	**87.50**	**86.66**	**87.50**	**86.65**

The experimental results are shown in Table 2. Our proposed method achieves the best performance across four metrics: accuracy, precision, recall, and F1-score. This indicates that the model effectively combines information from different domains and successfully integrates multimodal data, resulting in significant performance improvements.

From the experimental results, it can be seen that our proposed method, through tensor alignment and domain-adaptive transfer learning strategies, outperforms existing multimodal fusion methods and domain adaptation methods on all evaluation metrics.

3.4   Ablation Experiment

To analyze the impact of tensor alignment and custom loss functions, we conducted several ablation experiments. By comparing the results under different configurations, we can clearly assess the contribution of each module. The experimental results show that the full model (including tensor alignment and loss functions addressing class imbalance) achieved an accuracy of 87.50%. However, when tensor alignment was removed, the accuracy dropped to 75.00%, a decrease of 12.50%. When the loss functions addressing class imbalance were removed, the accuracy decreased to 81.67%, a drop of 5.83%.

The results are shown in Table 3, where we validated the role of tensor alignment and class imbalance loss functions in improving the model's accuracy and robustness. Tensor alignment, by representing features as tensors and promoting modality and domain alignment in a shared space, enhanced the model's robustness and facilitated modality fusion. The loss functions addressing class imbalance further strengthened the model's robustness. In summary, the results of the ablation experiments prove the significant role of tensor alignment and the loss functions that address class imbalance.

Table 3. Module comparison experiments

Module	Acc	Precision	Recall	F1
w/o Tensor	75.00	75.89	75.00	72.08
w/o L_{FL}	85.00	85.14	85.00	83.43
TALNet	**87.50**	**86.66**	**87.50**	**86.65**

4 Summary

This paper presents a multi-modal fusion network based on tensor alignment and domain adaptation, aiming to improve the accuracy and robustness of maritime vessel type recognition. By combining visible light and infrared image data, our method leverages the complementarity between different modalities, enhancing the model's performance in complex maritime environments. In particular, by introducing adversarial training and tensor alignment techniques, the method effectively aligns the feature distributions between the source and target domains, further improving the model's cross-domain adaptability. In the maritime vessel recognition task, the domain classifier and cross-modal attention mechanism help the model handle features from different modalities, thereby improving its robustness. Experiments conducted on a self-collected maritime vessel dataset show that the proposed method outperforms existing multi-modal fusion methods in multiple evaluation metrics such as accuracy, precision, recall, and F1 score. Especially in feature alignment and modality information fusion between the source and target domains, the model demonstrates significant advantages, validating the effectiveness of the proposed method in maritime vessel type recognition.

References

1. Lin, Y., Zhao, H., Ma, X., Ya, T., Wang, M.: Adversarial attacks in modulation recognition with convolutional neural networks. IEEE Trans. Reliab. **70**(1), 389–401 (2020)
2. Ya, T., Lin, Y., Hou, C., Mao, S.: Complex-valued networks for automatic modulation classification. IEEE Trans. Veh. Technol. **69**(9), 10085–10089 (2020)

3. Ya, T.U., Yun, L.I.N., Haoran, Z.H.A., Yu, W.A.N.G., Guan, G.U.I., Shiwen, M.A.O., et al.: Large-scale real-world radio signal recognition with deep learning. Chin. J. Aeronaut. **35**(9), 35–48 (2022)

4. Lin, Y., Ya, T., Dou, Z.: An improved neural network pruning technology for automatic modulation classification in edge devices. IEEE Trans. Veh. Technol. **69**(5), 5703–5706 (2020)

5. Lin, Y., Ya, T., Dou, Z., Chen, L., Mao, S.: Contour stella image and deep learning for signal recognition in the physical layer. IEEE Trans. Cogn. Commun. Netw. **7**(1), 34–46 (2020)

6. Lin, Y., Wang, M., Zhou, X., Ding, G., Mao, S.: Dynamic spectrum interaction of UAV flight formation communication with priority: a deep reinforcement learning approach. IEEE Trans. Cogn. Commun. Netw. **6**(3), 892–903 (2020)

7. Zhengwei, X., Han, G., Chen, C., Liu, L., Wang, Z.: A novel clustering based on consensus knowledge for cross-domain fault diagnoses. IEEE Trans. Instrum. Meas. **72**, 1–10 (2023)

8. Chen, L., Wu, H., Cui, X., Guo, Z., Jia, Z.: Convolution neural network SAR image target recognition based on transfer learning. Chin. Space Sci. Technol. **38**, 45–51 (2018)

9. Changmao, W., Xia, Y., Zhengwei, X., Liu, L., Tang, X., Chen, Q., Fanjiang, X.: Mathematical modelling for high precision ray tracing in optical design. Appl. Math. Model. **128**, 103–122 (2024)

10. Liu, L., Han, G., Zhengwei, X., Shu, L., Martinez-Garcia, M., Peng, B.: Predictive boundary tracking based on motion behavior learning for continuous objects in industrial wireless sensor networks. IEEE Trans. Mob. Comput. **21**(9), 3239–3249 (2021)

11. Liu, L., Zhao, T., Chan, S., Wu, C.: Continuous object tracking via joint global-local binary tree topological transformation in underwater acoustic sensor networks. IEEE Trans. Mob. Comput. **23**(12), 11091–11104 (2024)

12. Liu, L., Han, G., Zhengwei, X., Jiang, J., Shu, L., Martinez-Garcia, M.: Boundary tracking of continuous objects based on binary tree structured SVM for industrial wireless sensor networks. IEEE Trans. Mob. Comput. **21**(3), 849–861 (2020)

13. Liu, L., Han, G., He, Y., Jiang, J.: Fault-tolerant event region detection on trajectory pattern extraction for industrial wireless sensor networks. IEEE Trans. Industr. Inf. **16**(3), 2072–2080 (2019)

14. Han, G., Zhang, Y., Xu, Z., Wang, W.: A novel partial domain adaptation method for cross-domain specific emitter identification. IEEE Trans. Cogn. Commun. Netw. **11**(5), 3232–3244 (2025)

15. Zhou, H., Ma, T., Rong, H., Qian, Y., Tian, Y., Al-Nabhan, N.: MDMN: multi-task and domain adaptation based multi-modal network for early rumor detection. Expert Syst. Appl. **195**, 116517 (2022)

16. Xu, Y., Chen, L., Cheng, Z., Duan, L., Luo, J.: Open-ended visual question answering by multi-modal domain adaptation (2019). arXiv preprint arXiv:1911.04058

17. Zhang, T., Wang, D., Chen, H., Zeng, Z., Guo, W., Miao, C., Cui, L.: BDANN: Bert-based domain adaptation neural network for multi-modal fake news detection. In: 2020 International Joint Conference on Neural Networks (IJCNN), pp. 1–8. IEEE (2020)

18. Munro, J., Damen, D.: Multi-modal domain adaptation for fine-grained action recognition. In: Proceedings of the IEEE/CVF Conference on Computer Vision and Pattern Recognition, pp. 122–132 (2020)

19. Liu, Y., Qiao, L., Lu, C., Yin. D., Lin, C., Peng, H., Ren, B.: OSAN: a one-stage alignment network to unify multimodal alignment and unsupervised domain adaptation. In: Proceedings of the IEEE/CVF Conference on Computer Vision and Pattern Recognition, pp. 3551–3560 (2023)
20. Liu, W., Luo, Z., Cai, Y., Yu, Y., Ke, Y., Junior, J.M., Gonçalves, W.N., Li, J.: Adversarial unsupervised domain adaptation for 3d semantic segmentation with multi-modal learning. ISPRS J. Photogramm. Remote. Sens. **176**, 211–221 (2021)

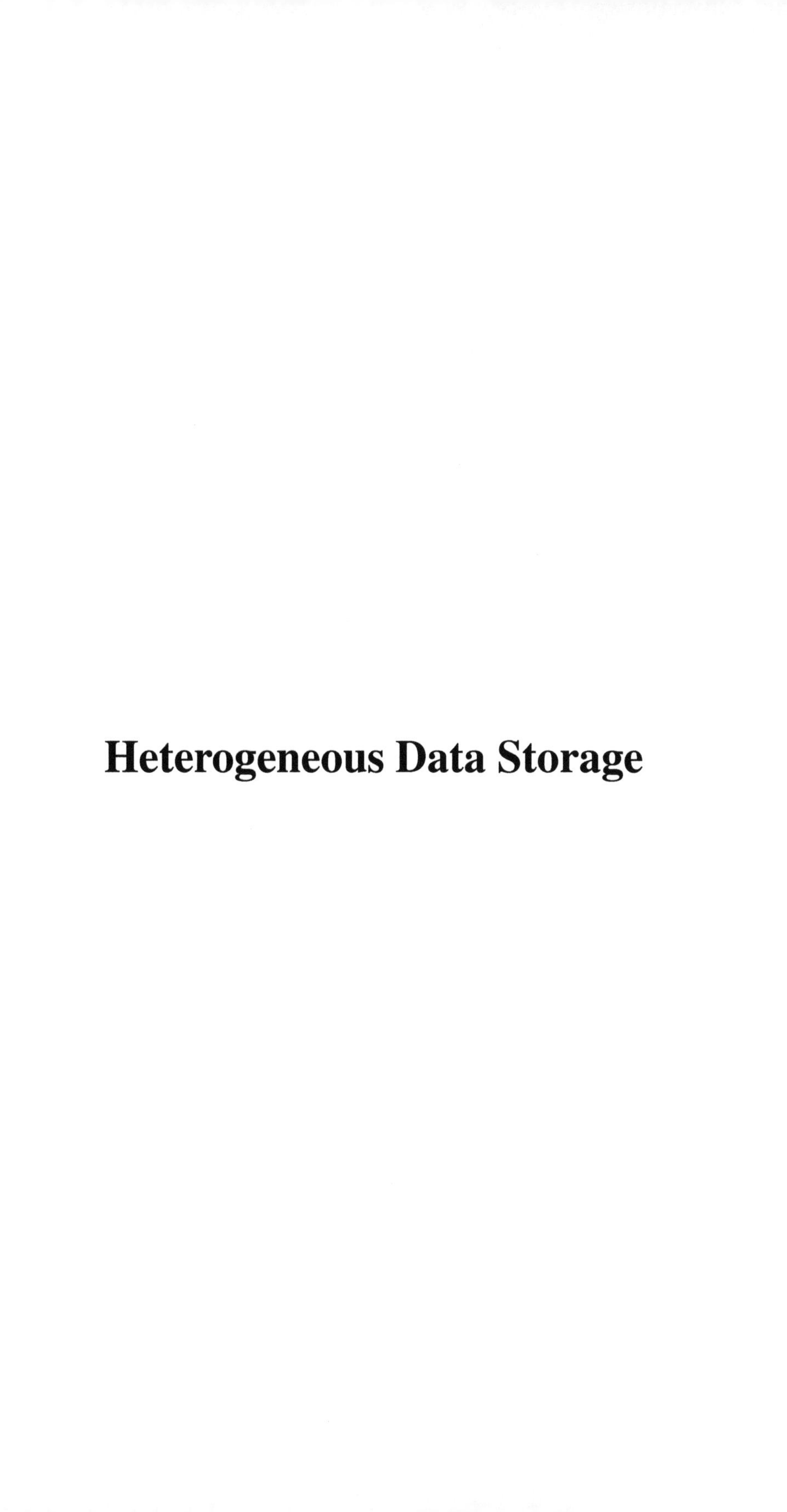

Heterogeneous Data Storage

MDM: Advancing Multi-domain Distribution Matching for Automatic Modulation Recognition Dataset Synthesis

Dongwei Xu[1,2]($\boxtimes$), Jiajun Chen[1,2], Yao Lu[1,2], Tianhao Xia[1,2], Zhuangzhi Chen[1,2], Wei Wang[3], Qi Xuan[1,2], and Yun Lin[4]

[1] Institute of Cyberspace Security, College of Information Engineering, Zhejiang University of Technology, Hangzhou, China
`dongweixu@zjut.edu.cn`
[2] Binjiang Institute of Artificial Intelligence, Zhejiang University of Technology, Hangzhou, China
[3] Science and Technology on Communication Information Security Control Laboratory, Jiaxing, China
[4] College of Information and Communication Engineering, Harbin Engineering University, Harbin, China

Abstract. Recently, deep learning technology has been successfully introduced into Automatic Modulation Recognition (AMR) tasks. However, the success of deep learning is all attributed to the training on large-scale datasets. Such a large amount of data brings huge pressure on storage and model training. To solve this problem, some researchers put forward the method of data distillation, which aims to compress large training data into smaller synthetic datasets to maintain its performance. While numerous data distillation techniques have been developed within the realm of image processing, the unique characteristics of signals set them apart. Signals exhibit distinct features across various domains, necessitating specialized approaches for their analysis and processing. To this end, a novel dataset distillation method—Multi-domain Distribution Matching (MDM) is proposed. MDM employs the Discrete Fourier Transform (DFT) to translate time-domain signals into the frequency domain, and then uses a model to compute distribution matching losses between the synthetic and real datasets, considering both time and frequency domains. Ultimately, two losses are integrated to update the synthetic dataset. We conduct extensive experiments on three AMR datasets. Experimental results show that, compared with baseline methods, our method achieves better performance under the same compression ratio. Further experiments show that our synthetic datasets can generalize well on other unseen models.

Keywords: Automatic modulation recognition · Dataset distillation · Discrete Fourier transform · Distribution matching

C. Xu et al. (Eds.): MobiMedia 2025, LNICST 670, pp. 177–189, 2026.
https://doi.org/10.1007/978-3-032-16823-8_13

1 Introduction

In recent years, deep learning techniques have been gradually introduced into AMR tasks [4,6,10,12,19,24] and have achieved great success. The success of deep learning is due to training on large datasets, but such a large amount of data poses a huge challenge for storage and transmission, and brings a significant amount of time and computing resource overhead for model training. In order to solve this problem, some researchers have proposed a promising direction named dataset distillation (DD), which aims to use limited data to train the model in a more efficient way, thereby reducing the training cost and improving the model performance.

DD was firstly proposed by Wang et al. [22] in 2018, which viewed model parameters as a function about the synthetic dataset and updated the synthetic dataset by minimizing the training loss of the original training data with respect to the synthetic data. Subsequently, Zhao et al. [26] proposed a method named Dataset Condensation (DC). This method updated the synthetic dataset by matching the gradient between the real training set and the synthetic dataset.

Zhao et al. [27] proposed a method based on Distributed Matching (DM), which used a model to extract high-dimensional features of the synthetic dataset and the original training set, and updated the synthetic dataset by matching the distance between the two high-dimensional features.

However, the existing dataset synthesis methods mainly focus on the image domain. Compared with image data, electromagnetic signals have significant differences in data structure and feature dimensions: Images exist as two-dimensional matrix-like spatial signals, with attributes such as length and width, and are functions about space, possessing spatial domain characteristics; while electromagnetic signals are essentially one-dimensional time series, with attributes such as amplitude and phase, and are functions of time, possessing characteristics of different signal domains such as time domain and frequency domain. This difference makes it limited to transfer the dataset synthesis methods from the image domain to the electromagnetic signal domain. Therefore, it is necessary to consider the characteristics of electromagnetic signals and design dataset synthesis methods for the signal domain.

To this end, this paper combines the time domain and frequency domain of the signal to achieve the complementary gain of the information in the two domains.

The time domain signal is first mapped to the frequency domain using the DFT [7], and the DM loss between the real training set and the synthetic dataset is then computed in both time and frequency domains. The two losses are combined as the final objective function. By minimizing the objective function, the optimal synthetic dataset is achieved. Experiments are conducted on three modulated signal datasets: RML2016.10a-high, RML2016.10a [13] and Sig2019-12-high [4]. Additionally, cross-architecture generalization experiments are carried out on the AlexNet [8] and VGG16 [20] models. Random selection, Forgetting [21], DC [26] and DM [27] are taken as baseline methods. Experiments show that compared with baseline methods, MDM performs better under the simliar conditions. At the same time, the synthetic dataset learned by MDM has certain generalization performance. The main contributions of this work are as follows:

- An innovative dataset distillation technique called MDM is introduced. Specifically, MDM transforms the time domain signal into the frequency domain using DFT and integrates the characteristics of both time and frequency domains to distill the data.
- The performance of MDM is evaluated on three signal datasets, and it is compared with Random Select, Forgetting, DC, and DM methods. Experiments demonstrate that MDM achieves optimal classification accuracy in most cases.
- Cross-architecture generalization experiments are conducted on multiple models, and the experimental results indicate that the synthetic dataset learned by MDM can generalize well on previously unseen model architectures.

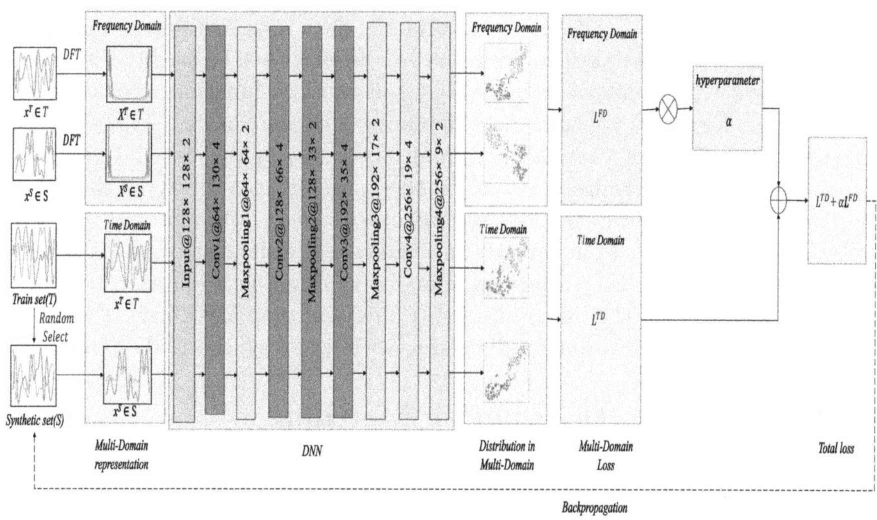

Fig. 1. The framework of Multi-domain Distribution Matching.

2   Related Work

Automatic Modulation Recognition. In recent years, deep learning technology has been gradually introduced into the Automatic Modulation Recognition (AMR) task. Chen et al. [4] proposed a new deep learning framework to improve the recognition accuracy of modulated signals. Lin et al. [19] proposed a time-frequency attention mechanism for automatic modulation recognition based on

Convolutional Neural Networks (CNN). Hou et al. [6] proposed an improved spatio-temporal multi-channel network based on the existing MCLDNN algorithm. Ryu et al. [17] propose a new Automatic modulation recognition (AMR) technique called Joint Equalization and Modulation Classification Based on Constellation Networks (EMC2-Net). Unlike previous work that treated constellation points as images, the proposed EMC2-Net uses a set of 2D constellation points directly to perform modulation recognition. Ansari et al. [2] studied Multi-Layer Perceptron (MLP), Radial Basis Function (RBF), Adaptive Network-based Fuzzy Inference System (ANFIS), Decision Tree (DT), and Naive Bayes model(NB) algorithm to realize and compare digital modulation recognition.

Coreset Selection. Coreset Selection aimed to select a certain proportion of data based on specific measures. Most of these methods incrementally selected important data points based on heuristic selection criteria. For example, Sener et al. [18] selected data points that approach the cluster centers. Aljundi et al. [1] tried to maximize the diversity of samples in the gradient space. Toneva et al. [21] found that samples had different forgetting characteristics, and samples that were easily forgotten contained a large amount of information.

Dataset Distillation. In 2021, Zhao et al. [25] proposed Differentiable Siamese Augmentation (DSA), which brought data augmentation technique to DC and achieved better performance. Li et al. [9] proposed to modify the Dataset Condensation with contrast signals (DCC) of the loss function so that the DC method can effectively capture the differences between classes. George et al. [3] proposed a method of matching training tracks to synthesize datasets. This method involves pretraining a model on the training set and saving the parameters from each round as the expert trajectory. Then, a model with the same architecture is trained from scratch on the synthetic dataset, with its parameters saved as the student trajectory. Finally, the synthetic dataset is updated accordingly. Lu et al. [11] introduced two plug-and-play loss terms, CLoM and CCloM, which provide stable guidance for optimizing synthetic datasets.

3   Multi-domain Distribution Matching

3.1   Dataset Condensation Problem

A large-scale training dataset and a small synthetic dataset can be expressed as follow:

$$T = \{(x_1^T, y_1^T), \ldots, (x_{|T|}^T, y_{|T|}^T)\} \tag{1}$$

$$x^T = [I^T(n), Q^T(n)], n = 0, 1, \ldots, N - 1 \tag{2}$$

$$S = \{(x_1^S, y_1^S), \ldots, (x_{|S|}^S, y_{|S|}^S)\} \tag{3}$$

$$x^S = [I^S(n), Q^S(n)], n = 0, 1, \ldots, N - 1 \tag{4}$$

where $|T|$ indicates that the training dataset T contains $|T|$ signals and labels; x^T represents the signal in the training dataset; each signal x^T is represented by an I channel and a Q channel; each channel has N sampling points; $|S|$ indicates that the synthetic dataset S contains $|S|$ signals and labels; x^S denotes the signal of the synthetic dataset, and $|T| \gg |S|$.

Algorithm 1 Multi-domain Distribution Matching

Input: Training set T, randomly initialized set of synthetic samples S, deep neural network ψ_θ parameterized with θ, probability distribution over parameters P_θ, training iterations K, learning rate η, tunable hyperparameter α.
Output: S.

1: **for** $k = 0$ to $K - 1$ **do**
2:     Sample $\theta \sim P_\theta$
3:     Compute $L^{TD} = E_{\theta \sim P_\theta} \parallel \frac{1}{|T|} \sum_{j=1}^{|T|} \psi_\theta(x_j^T) - \frac{1}{|S|} \sum_{m=1}^{|S|} \psi_\theta(x_m^S) \parallel^2$
4:     Perform DFT on x_j^T and x_m^S:
5:     $X_j^T = DFT(x_j^T)$, $X_m^S = DFT(x_m^S)$
6:     Compute $L^{FD} = E_{\theta \sim P_\theta} \parallel \frac{1}{|T|} \sum_{j=1}^{|T|} \psi_\theta(X_j^T) - \frac{1}{|S|} \sum_{m=1}^{|S|} \psi_\theta(X_m^S) \parallel^2$
7:     Combine two losses $L = L^{TD} + \alpha L^{FD}$
8:     Update $S \leftarrow S - \eta \nabla_S L$
9: **end for**

3.2   Distribution Matching in Time Domain

First, a neural network model ψ_θ is randomly initialized, which is used to obtain low-dimensional embeddings of real signal x^T and synthetic signal x^S. Then the maximum mean discrepancy (MMD) [5] is used to estimate the distance between the real data distribution and the synthetic data distribution. Finally, this distance is taken as a loss function in the time domain, which can be expressed as:

$$L^{TD} = E_{\theta \sim P_\theta} \parallel \frac{1}{|T|} \sum_{j=1}^{|T|} \psi_\theta(x_j^T) - \frac{1}{|S|} \sum_{m=1}^{|S|} \psi_\theta(x_m^S) \parallel^2 \tag{5}$$

where P_θ represents the distribution of network parameters, $\theta \sim P_\theta$ represents θ satisfies the P_θ distribution; TD indicates Time Domain.

3.3   Discrete Fourier Transform

DFT is a basic method in signal analysis that transforms a discrete time series signal from the time domain to the frequency domain.

In order to align with the time domain signal, DFT is performed on $I^T(n)$ and $Q^T(n)$ of signal x^T in the training dataset, and they are then spliced together. The frequency domain signals of the two channels are also obtained, which can be expressed as follows:

$$I^T(k) = | \sum_{n=0}^{N-1} I^T(n)e^{-j2\pi kn/N} |, k = 0, 1, ..., N - 1 \tag{6}$$

$$Q^T(k) = | \sum_{n=0}^{N-1} Q^T(n)e^{-j2\pi kn/N} | \tag{7}$$

$$X^T = [I^T(k), Q^T(k)] \tag{8}$$

where X^T represents the frequency domain representation of each signal in the training dataset; each signal X^T has two channels: $I^T(k)$ and $Q^T(k)$; each channel has N sampling points (the input of the DFT is N discrete points and the output of the DFT is N discrete points). The same operation is performed on the synthetic dataset, which can be expressed as:

$$X^S = [I^S(k), Q^S(k)] \tag{9}$$

where X^S denotes the frequency domain representation of each signal in the synthetic dataset; $I^S(k)$ is the output of $I^S(n)$ after DFT, and $Q^S(k)$ is the output of $Q^S(n)$ after DFT.

3.4   Distribution Matching in Fequency Domain

Then, the low-dimensional embeddings of real signal X^T and synthetic signal X^S from the frequency domain are obtained by using ψ_θ. MMD is used to estimate the distance between the real data distribution and the synthetic data distribution in the frequency domain. The distance is used as a loss function in the frequency domain, which can be expressed as:

$$L^{FD} = E_{\theta \sim P_\theta} \left\| \frac{1}{|T|} \sum_{j=1}^{|T|} \psi_\theta(X_j^T) - \frac{1}{|S|} \sum_{m=1}^{|S|} \psi_\theta(X_m^S) \right\|^2 \tag{10}$$

where FD means Frequency Domain. The framework of MDM is shown in the Fig. 1.

3.5   Combination of Time Domain and Frequency Domain

Inspired by [16], we believe that combining the time and frequency domain information of the signal is better than using only a single signal domain information.

Therefore, we combine the distribution matching loss in the time domain and frequency domain as the total loss:

$$L = L^{TD} + \alpha L^{FD} \tag{11}$$

where α is a tunable hyeprparameter. The value of α in the experiment depends on the dataset. The overall pipeline is summarized in Algorithm 1.

3.6   Update of the Synthetic Dataset

Finally, we update the synthetic dataset through K iterations of the Stochastic Gradient Descent (SGD) method until the objective function converges, thereby obtaining the optimal synthetic dataset, which can be expressed as:

$$S \leftarrow S - \eta \nabla_S L \tag{12}$$

Here, η represents the learning rate, and $\nabla_S L$ represents the gradient of the objective function with respect to the synthetic dataset.

4   Experiments

4.1   Dataset

To evaluate the effectiveness of our method, we conducted experiments on three
signal modulation classification datasets RML2016.10a, RML2016.10a-high, and
Sig2019-12-high.

RML2016.10a uses GNU radio to synthesize electromagnetic signals containing I and Q channels. There are a total of 11 modulation signal categories
in the dataset, QPSK, 8PSK, BPSK, BFSK, 16QAM, 64QAM, CPFSK, PAM4,
AM-SSB, WB-FM and AM-DSB, the first 8 types are digital modulation types,
and the last 3 types are analog modulation types. The dataset uses an electromagnetic signal with a signal-to-noise ratio (SNR) range from -20db to 18dB
and a signal length of 128. We divide the dataset into a training set and a test
set with a ratio of 4:1.

RML2016.10a-high is the part of RML2016.10a dataset with SNRs ranging
from 10 dB to 18 dB. We also divide the dataset into the training set and the
test set with a ratio of 4:1.

Sig2019-12-high is a subset of Sig2019-12, which is a self-generated dataset
by Chen et al. [4]. Sig2019-12 contains 12 modulation types, namely OPSK,
8PSK, BPSK, 4PAM, 8PAM, OQPSK, 16QAM, 32QAM, 64QAM, 2FSK, 4FSK
and 8FSK. The signal-to-noise ratio of the dataset ranges from $-20\,$db to $30\,$db
[12], we select signals above $10\,$dB, comprising a training set of 120,000 signal
samples and a test set with 60,000 signal samples.

4.2   Model Architecture

In our experiments, an AlexNet model is used to learn synthetic dataset. For the
evaluation phase, 5 AlexNet models are randomly initialized and trained from
scratch using the synthesized dataset that has been generated. Their average
test accuracy and standard deviation are then recorded.

Conduct cross-architecture generalization experiments are further conducted.
A synthetic dataset is first trained on one model architecture, and this dataset
is then employed to train models across various other architectures. The
architectures used in the cross-architecture generalization experiments include
AlexNet [8], 1D-ResNet [15], 2D-CNN [14], VGG16 [20], and MCLDNN [23].

4.3   Implementation Details

At the beginning, some training samples from each class in the training set are
randomly selected as the initial synthetic samples. Then, the synthetic dataset is
updated. The epochs for updating the synthetic dataset is 20,000. The optimizer
for updating the synthetic dataset is SGD. The learning rate is related to the
dataset and the number of synthetic samples for each class (Signals Per Class,
SPC). Specifically, for RML2016.10a-high dataset, the optimal learning rate is
10^{-5} when SPC $= 10$, and the optimal learning rate is 10^{-4} when SPC $= 50$

and 100. For RML2016.10a dataset, the optimal learning rate is 10^{-8} when SPC = 10, when SPC = 50 and 100, the optimal learning rate is 10^{-7}. For Sig2019-12-high dataset, the optimal learning rate is 10^{-6} when SPC = 10, when SPC = 50, the optimal learning rate is 10^{-5}, and when SPC = 100, the optimal learning rate is 10^{-4}. The total epochs of iterations is 20,000.

4.4   Results and Analysis

Our method is compared with several baseline methods: Random Selection, Forgetting, DC, and DM. These baselines are briefly summarized as follows:

- Random Selection: This algorithm randomly selects a certain number of training samples from each class of training samples as synthetic samples.
- Forgetting: This method counts how many times a training sample is learned and then forgotten during network training. The samples that are less forgetful can be dropped.
- DC: This method synthesizes a small but informative dataset by matching the loss gradients with respect to the training and synthetic datasets.
- DM: This method aims to minimize the MMD between the synthetic dataset and the real dataset.

Table 1. Testing accuracy (%) comparing to coreset selection and training set synthesis methods.

	RML2016.10a-high			RML2016.10a			Sig2019-12-high		
SPC	10	50	100	10	50	100	10	50	100
Ratio(%)	0.25	1.25	2.5	0.0625	0.3125	0.625	0.1	0.5	1
Random	55.8±1.0	71.8±1.2	75.8±0.8	25.3±2.0	33.8±2.1	38.9±2.2	25.6±1.0	42.5±0.7	53.5±1.4
Forgetting	55.5±0.8	75.0±0.6	**78.6±0.4**	22.9±0.7	33.0±0.6	35.8±1.3	26.7±1.6	43.0±0.5	54.9±1.7
DC	57.5±1.2	71.4±0.2	74.1±0.2	25.3±0.5	33.9±0.7	37.2±0.9	25.7±1.0	37.7±2.2	50.8±1.1
DM	61.3±0.8	74.8±0.2	76.6±1.0	28.9±0.7	38.6±0.6	42.8±0.4	29.1±1.2	47.5±0.6	56.2±0.7
MDM	**62.5±1.4**	**76.0±0.4**	78.1±0.2	**30.1±0.6**	**41.9±0.8**	**43.8±0.7**	**31.0±1.3**	**48.4±1.1**	**57.0±0.8**
Whole dataset	88.02±0.2			56.4±0.2			96.5±0.2		

Comparison to coreset selection methods. Our method is first compared with the coreset selection baselines. As shown in Table 1, only when the dataset is RML2016.10a-high, SPC=100, Forgetting method has better results than MDM. In other cases, MDM is superior to Random Selection method and Forgetting method. This indicates that MDM generally surpasses coreset selection methods in most cases.

Comparison to DC and DM. As can be seen from Table 1, MDM is superior to the DC and DM in all cases. In most cases, our method is more than 1% better than DM. These results illustrate that MDM, by incorporating frequency domain insights, capitalizes on the synergistic relationship between the time and frequency domains. This approach yields superior outcomes compared to DM and DC, which relies solely on time-domain signal information.

4.5 Cross-Architecture Generalization

Cross-architecture generalization experiments are also conducted. Specifically, for the RML2016.10a-high dataset, 50 condensed signals per class are synthesized using two distinct models: AlexNet and VGG16. These synthesized signals are then evaluated across multiple architectures, including AlexNet, 1D-ResNet, 2D-CNN, VGG16, and MCLDNN. In Table 2, the synthetic dataset is learned with one architecture (C) and then evaluated on another architecture (T) by training a model from scratch and testing on real testing data. The experimental results show that the synthetic dataset trained on AlexNet and VGG16 performs best on AlexNet, with strong performance on VGG16 as well. It also achieves promising results on 1D-ResNet, 2D-CNN, and MCLDNN, indicating strong cross-model generalization.

Table 2. Cross-architecture performance (%) with condensed 50 signal/class on RML2016.10a-high.

C\T	AlexNet	2D-CNN	VGG16	1D-ResNet	MCLDNN
AlexNet	74.7±1.0	59.7±0.6	71.2±2.2	52.2±2.2	51.7±3.5
VGG16	73.3±1.2	57.9±1.0	70.2±1.2	50.2±6.6	46.6±2.6

4.6 Ablation Study

Herein, we study the influence of weight coefficient α on the performance of synthetic datasets. Table 3 shows the relationship between the performance of synthetic datasets and weight coefficient α on RML2016.10a-high dataset. The experimental results show that for RML2016.10a-high dataset, the optimal weight coefficient α is 0.5 when SPC=10, the optimal weight coefficient α is 0.5 when SPC=50, and the value of α has little effect on the result, and α is 0.4 when SPC=100.

Table 3. Comparison of performance for different values of α on RML2016.10a-high.

SPC	α	0.1	0.2	0.3	0.4	0.5	0.6	0.7	0.8	0.9
10	Acc(%)	60.5±0.7	62.0±1.0	60.1±0.7	61.2±1.6	**63.1±1.4**	59.1±1.0	62.8±1.1	60.3±1.1	61.4±0.8
50	Acc(%)	75.6±0.3	75.2±0.7	75.1±0.7	75.2±0.8	**76.0±0.4**	75.5±0.3	74.1±0.7	75.3±0.2	75.4±0.4
100	Acc(%)	77.9±0.4	77.2±0.7	77.1±1.1	**78.1±0.2**	77.8±0.5	77.4±0.6	77.8±0.5	77.4±0.3	76.3±1.2

Figure 2 further presents the performance analysis of different α values under the RML2016.10a-high dataset. It can be seen from the figure that when SPC is 10, the highest accuracy rate is 63.1% ($\alpha = 0.5$), and the lowest is 58.1%

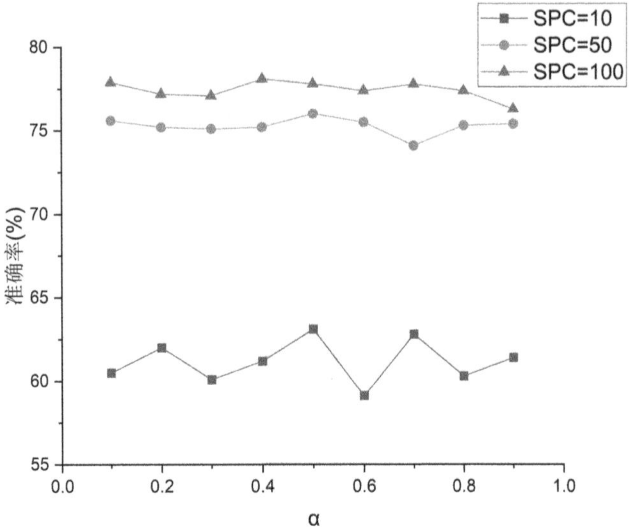

Fig. 2. Performance analysis of different α values on RML2016.10a-high dataset.

($\alpha = 1.0$). When α increases from 0.1 to 0.5, the accuracy rate first rises, then drops, and then rises again, reaching the highest point at $\alpha = 0.5$. This indicates that within this range, the performance of the synthetic dataset is best when $\alpha = 0.5$. When α continues to increase to 0.9, the accuracy rate fluctuates greatly, suggesting that the performance of the synthetic dataset is highly sensitive to changes in α when SPC $= 10$. When SPC is 50, the highest accuracy rate is 76.0% ($\alpha = 0.5$). In the case of SPC $= 50$, when α increases from 0.1 to 0.9, the accuracy rate fluctuates less, indicating that the performance of the synthetic dataset is less sensitive to changes in $\alpha = 0.5$ when SPC $= 50$. When SPC is 100, the highest accuracy rate is 78.1% ($\alpha = 0.4$). Similar to the case of SPC $= 50$, the accuracy rate fluctuates less at different α values, suggesting that the performance of the synthetic dataset is less sensitive to changes in α when SPC $= 100$.

4.7   Visualization

This paper also visualizes the data of the RML2016.10a-high dataset and the synthetic dataset. Figure 3 shows the waveform diagrams of each modulation category in the RML2016.10a-high dataset, and Fig. 4 presents the time-domain waveform diagrams of each modulation type in the synthetic dataset. By comparing the two figures, it can be observed that the waveform shapes of the AM-DSB modulation types in the two datasets are very similar, and other types also have a certain degree of similarity. This proves that the signals in the synthetic dataset well match the characteristics of the signals in the training set.

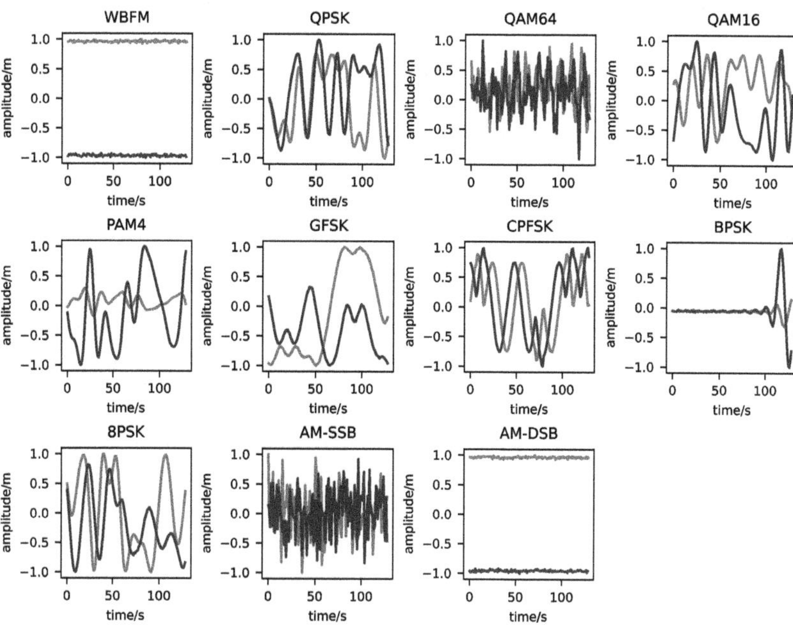

Fig. 3. Waveform diagrams of signals of different modulation categories in the RML2016.10a-high dataset.

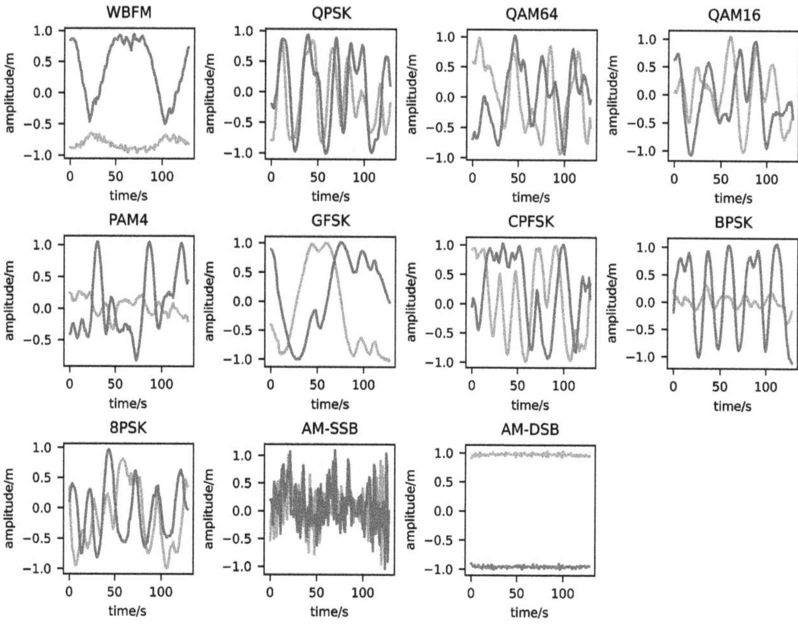

Fig. 4. Waveform diagrams of signals of different modulation categories in the synthetic dataset.

5   Conclusion

In this paper, we propose a novel dataset distillation method named MDM. MDM maps the time domain signal to the frequency domain by DFT, and combines the time domain and frequency domain characteristics of the signal to distill the data, which makes up the gap of the dataset distillation method in the task of signal modulation recognition. Experiments reveal that the proposed method outperforms existing baselines and can generalize well on other unseen models.

Acknowledgments and Disclosure of Funding. This work was partially supported by the Key R&D Program of Zhejiang under Grant 2022C01018, by the National Natural Science Foundation of China under Grant U21B2001, 62301492 and 61973273, by the China Postdoctoral Science Foundation under Grant Number 2024M762912 and by the Postdoctoral Science Preferential Funding of Zhejiang Province of China under Grant ZJ2024060.

References

1. Aljundi, R., Lin, M., Goujaud, B., Bengio, Y.: Gradient based sample selection for online continual learning. Adv. Neural Inform. Process. Syst. **32** (2019)
2. Ansari, S., Alnajjar, K.A., Saad, M., Abdallah, S., El-Moursy, A.A.: Automatic digital modulation recognition based on genetic-algorithm-optimized machine learning models. IEEE Access **10**, 50265–50277 (2022)
3. Cazenavette, G., Wang, T., Torralba, A., Efros, A.A., Zhu, J.Y.: Dataset distillation by matching training trajectories. In: Proceedings of the IEEE/CVF Conference on Computer Vision and Pattern Recognition, pp. 4750–4759 (2022)
4. Chen, Z., Cui, H., Xiang, J., Qiu, K., Huang, L., Zheng, S., Chen, S., Xuan, Q., Yang, X.: Signet: a novel deep learning framework for radio signal classification. IEEE Trans. Cogn. Commun. Netw. **8**(2), 529–541 (2021)
5. Gretton, A., Borgwardt, K.M., Rasch, M.J., Schölkopf, B., Smola, A.: A kernel two-sample test. J. Mach. Learn. Res. **13**(1), 723–773 (2012)
6. Hou, S., Fan, Y., Han, B., Li, Y., Fang, S.: Signal modulation recognition algorithm based on improved spatiotemporal multi-channel network. Electronics **12**(2), 422 (2023)
7. Jenkins, W.K.: Fourier series, fourier transforms and the dft. In: Mathematics for Circuits and Filters, pp. 83–111. CRC Press (2022)
8. Krizhevsky, A., Sutskever, I., Hinton, G.E.: Imagenet classification with deep convolutional neural networks. Adv. Neural Inform. Process. Syst. **25** (2012)
9. Lee, S., Chun, S., Jung, S., Yun, S., Yoon, S.: Dataset condensation with contrastive signals. In: International Conference on Machine Learning, pp. 12352–12364. PMLR (2022)
10. Lin, Y., Tu, Y., Dou, Z.: An improved neural network pruning technology for automatic modulation classification in edge devices. IEEE Trans. Veh. Technol. **69**(5), 5703–5706 (2020)
11. Lu, Y., Chen, X., Zhang, Y., Gu, J., Zhang, T., Zhang, Y., Yang, X., Xuan, Q., Wang, K., You, Y.: Can pre-trained models assist in dataset distillation? arXiv preprint arXiv:2310.03295 (2023)

12. Lu, Y., Zhu, Y., Li, Y., Xu, D., Lin, Y., Xuan, Q., Yang, X.: A generic layer pruning method for signal modulation recognition deep learning models. arXiv preprint arXiv:2406.07929 (2024)
13. O'shea, T.J., West, N.: Radio machine learning dataset generation with GNU radio. In: Proceedings of the GNU Radio Conference, vol. 1 (2016)
14. O'Shea, T.J., Corgan, J., Clancy, T.C.: Convolutional radio modulation recognition networks. In: Engineering Applications of Neural Networks: 17th International Conference, EANN 2016, Aberdeen, UK, September 2–5, 2016, Proceedings 17, pp. 213–226. Springer (2016)
15. O'Shea, T.J., Roy, T., Clancy, T.C.: Over-the-air deep learning based radio signal classification. IEEE J. Selected Top. Signal Process. **12**(1), 168–179 (2018)
16. Qi, P., Zhou, X., Zheng, S., Li, Z.: Automatic modulation classification based on deep residual networks with multimodal information. IEEE Trans. Cogn. Commun. Netw. **7**(1), 21–33 (2020)
17. Ryu, H., Choi, J.: Emc 2-net: Joint equalization and modulation classification based on constellation network. In: ICASSP 2023-2023 IEEE International Conference on Acoustics, Speech and Signal Processing (ICASSP), pp. 1–5. IEEE (2023)
18. Sener, O., Savarese, S.: Active learning for convolutional neural networks: a core-set approach. arXiv preprint arXiv:1708.00489 (2017)
19. Shangao, L., Yuan, Z., Yi, G.: Learning of time-frequency attention mechanism for automatic modulation recognition. IEEE Wirel. Commun. Lett. **11**(4), 707–711 (2022)
20. Simonyan, K., Zisserman, A.: Very deep convolutional networks for large-scale image recognition. arXiv preprint arXiv:1409.1556 (2014)
21. Toneva, M., Sordoni, A., Combes, R.T.d., Trischler, A., Bengio, Y., Gordon, G.J.: An empirical study of example forgetting during deep neural network learning. arXiv preprint arXiv:1812.05159 (2018)
22. Wang, T., Zhu, J.Y., Torralba, A., Efros, A.A.: Dataset distillation. arXiv preprint arXiv:1811.10959 (2018)
23. Xu, J., Luo, C., Parr, G., Luo, Y.: A spatiotemporal multi-channel learning framework for automatic modulation recognition. IEEE Wirel. Commun. Lett. **9**(10), 1629–1632 (2020)
24. Zhang, X., Zhao, H., Zhu, H., Adebisi, B., Gui, G., Gacanin, H., Adachi, F.: Nasamr: neural architecture search-based automatic modulation recognition for integrated sensing and communication systems. IEEE Trans. Cogn. Commun. Netw. **8**(3), 1374–1386 (2022)
25. Zhao, B., Bilen, H.: Dataset condensation with differentiable Siamese augmentation. In: International Conference on Machine Learning, pp. 12674–12685. PMLR (2021)
26. Zhao, B., Mopuri, K.R., Bilen, H.: Dataset condensation with gradient matching. arXiv preprint arXiv:2006.05929 (2020)
27. Zhao, B., Bilen, H.: Dataset condensation with distribution matching. In: Proceedings of the IEEE/CVF Winter Conference on Applications of Computer Vision, pp. 6514–6523 (2023)

Multimedia-Based Signal Processing

Spatio-Temporal Aware Cross-Modal Retrieval

Yubo Wang, Shihao Wang, Xufeng Gu, and Yun Lin[(✉)]

Harbin Engineering University, Harbin, Heilongjiang 150001, China
{wangyubo1,guxufeng,linyun}@hrbeu.edu.cn, wangshihao1657@163.com

Abstract. This paper addresses the challenges of spatiotemporal heterogeneity and cross-modal semantic gaps in maritime ship data by proposing a spatiotemporal-aware joint hashing method for radiation signal-image association retrieval. A dual-stream network is designed to extract temporal signal features (via a multi-layer convolutional architecture with dynamic time-frequency capture) and spatial image features (using a DenseNet-based feature pyramid with adaptive pooling and cross-modal fusion). A Spatio-Temporal Perception Module (STPM) enhances feature representation through heterogeneous encoding and cross-attention mechanisms. The joint hashing framework innovatively integrates: 1) a bipolar quantization function generating compact binary codes preserving cross-modal correlations, and 2) a multi-level similarity fusion strategy dynamically weighting signal-image hash matrices and their fused representation. The hybrid loss combines contrastive, quantization, and similarity preservation objectives with staged optimization. Evaluated on a 16-class multimodal dataset (visible images and radiation signals) from Yantai Port, China, the method achieves 97.6% mAP@50, outperforming baselines by 13.1%. This work provides an effective solution for cross-modal retrieval in marine heterogeneous data environments.

Keywords: Cross-modal association retrieval · Hash similarity fusion · Spatio-Temporal Perception.

1 Introduction

With the advancement of maritime monitoring systems, multi-source data fusion is replacing single-modal perception [1–3]. Surveillance cameras, radars, and AIS provide complementary ship data (visual appearance, motion trajectories, and positions), forming multimodal maritime databases. However, current research primarily focuses on single-modal approaches like image-based vessel re-identification [4–6], which face challenges in complex sea conditions: optical sensors suffer from environmental interference (fog, low light), while radiated signals (radar/AIS) lack fine-grained visual details despite all-weather capability.

C. Xu et al. (Eds.): MobiMedia 2025, LNICST 670, pp. 193–208, 2026.
https://doi.org/10.1007/978-3-032-16823-8_14

Cross-modal fusion methods [7,8] have emerged but rely on handcrafted features and rigid spatio-temporal alignment, failing to adapt to nonlinear signal-image associations in dynamic marine environments. Cross-modal retrieval offers an alternative solution, yet traditional correlation analysis methods struggle with complex spatio-temporal features. While deep hashing improves efficiency [9, 10], existing methods overlook the unique spatio-temporal coupling: signals encode temporal motion evolution while images contain spatial structures, causing feature space heterogeneity.

To address this, we propose a Spatio-Temporal Perceptual Hashing (STPH) framework for signal-image cross-modal retrieval. STPH integrates spatio-temporal perception and joint hash coding through: (1) A multi-stream network capturing temporal signal patterns and spatial image features via deformable convolutions and hybrid attention; (2) A bipolar quantization module generating compact hash codes (128 bits) with cross-modal consistency; (3) A multi-level similarity fusion strategy adaptively weighting modalities. Core contributions include:

1. **Spatio-temporal cross-attention mechanism (STCA)**: Solves cross-modal isomorphism through progressive feature alignment and course learning, achieving 97.6% mAP@50 under complex sea states.
2. **Lightweight hash architecture**: Combines bipolar quantization with cross-modal contrastive and similarity-preserving losses, optimized via gating networks.

2   Proposed Method

This section first outlines the key notation employed throughout this paper. Subsequently, it provides a detailed account of our research work, covering the definition of notation and research problems, an overview of the framework, the objective function, and the corresponding optimization approach.

2.1   Symbol System and Problem Formulation

We employ $\mathcal{X} = \{a_i, b_i\}_{i=1}^{n}$ to denote the collection of n instance pairs within each mini-batch. In detail, $a_i \in \mathbb{R}^{d_a}$ corresponds to the i-th original visual instance (i.e., image), whereas $b_i \in \mathbb{R}^{d_b}$ refers to the i-th signal instance—where d_a and d_b stand for the feature dimensions of the visual data and signal data, respectively. For any randomly sampled training mini-batch $\mathcal{X} = \{a_i, b_i\}_{i=1}^{n}$, $G_{\text{vis}} \in \mathbb{R}^{n \times d_g}$ and $H_{\text{sig}} \in \mathbb{R}^{n \times d_h}$ represent the feature embeddings derived from the modality-specific feature encoders (dedicated to visual and signal data, respectively). Here, d_g and d_h denote the dimensions of the visual feature vectors and signal feature vectors, in that order.

With the derived features G_{vis} and H_{sig} at hand, we utilize the modality-specific autoencoders $g_a(G_{\text{vis}}, \phi_a)$ and $h_b(H_{\text{sig}}, \phi_b)$ to learn a common hash coding space. Let $C_{\text{V,S}} \in \{-1, +1\}^{n \times k}$ denote the hash codes generated by the visual-specific or signal-specific autoencoders, where ϕ_a and ϕ_b are the learnable parameters of the visual autoencoder network and signal autoencoder network, respectively. Moreover, the cosine similarity function is represented by $\cos(\cdot,\cdot)$, while $\mathrm{sign}(\cdot)$ stands for the sign function—both of which are specifically formulated in the following manner:

$$\cos(u_p, v_q) = \frac{u_p^T v_q}{\parallel u_p \parallel_2 \parallel v_q \parallel_2} \tag{1}$$

$$\mathrm{sign}(z) = \begin{cases} +1, & z > 0 \\ -1, & z \leq 0 \end{cases} \tag{2}$$

2.2 Framework Overview

Depicted in Fig. 1, the architecture presented in this study encompasses four core modules, namely the deep-level feature refinement module, spatio-temporal awareness module, hash coding module, and similarity fusion module.

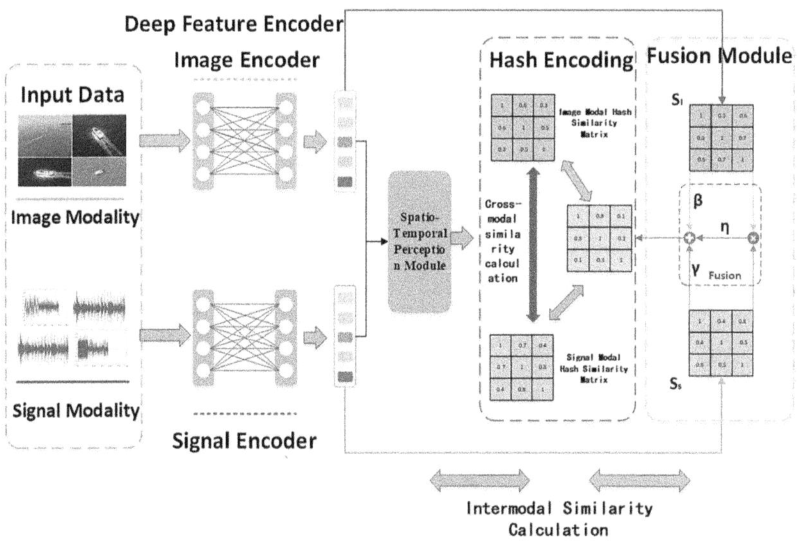

Fig. 1. Spatio-temporal aware cross-modal retrieval framework.

This core module employs a dual-branch architecture to extract high-order semantic features from images and radiation signals, enabling cross-modal semantic alignment. Unlike unimodal hashing methods that process heterogeneous data independently, our approach captures intrinsic cross-domain consistency through joint optimization.

Image Branch: Utilizes transfer learning with ImageNet-pretrained DenseNet-161. The 121-layer densely connected network constructs feature pyramids through four dense blocks (each containing multiple convolution layers) to mitigate gradient vanishing and enhance multi-scale feature reuse. For input $V \in \mathbb{R}^{224 \times 224 \times 3}$, the encoder outputs feature maps $F_v^{\text{feat}} \in \mathbb{R}^{7 \times 7 \times 2208}$. During fine-tuning, parameters of the first three dense blocks are frozen to preserve generic representations, while the fourth dense block and projection layers are updated. **Features are compressed to 2208-dimensional vectors by global average pooling, then projected to a low-dimensional latent space of dimension d via a learnable matrix $W_p \in \mathbb{R}^{2208 \times d}$ (where $d = 128$ is the target latent space dimension), yielding a compact image representation $f_v \in \mathbb{R}^{128}$:**

$$f_v = W_p^{\top} \left(\frac{1}{7^2} \sum_{i=1}^{7} \sum_{j=1}^{7} F_v^{\text{feat}}(i, j, :) \right) \tag{3}$$

Signal Branch: Processes time-frequency signals $S \in \mathbb{R}^{2 \times L}$ through a hierarchical four-stage 1D convolutional architecture. Each stage contains:

- **Convolutional layer** with kernel sizes decreasing across stages (Stage 1: 64, Stage 2: 32, Stage 3: 16, Stage 4: 8) to capture multi-scale temporal patterns
- **Batch norm** with a momentum parameter of 0.1 and an epsilon value of 1e-5 is adopted for stabilizing activation dynamics
- **ReLU activation** for non-linear transformation
- **Max-pooling** with kernel size 2 and stride 2 for dimensionality reduction

This design progressively expands the receptive field from local to global scales, extracting hierarchical abstract features for time-frequency pattern recognition. Output features are flattened and projected to 128-dimensional space matching the image branch.

Spatio-Temporal Perception Module This section details the Spatio-Temporal Perception Feature Enhancement Module (STPM), which is located after the dual-branch encoder and specializes in solving the nonlinear anisotropy of the signal-image two-modality in the dual domain of time and space. The module consists of three synergistic subunits: signal temporal dynamics enhancement, image spatial semantic enhancement and cross-modal spatio-temporal cross-coupling. The overall mapping relation can be formalized as:

$$\mathcal{S}_{\text{enh}} : \left(F_{\text{sig}}, F_{\text{img}} \right) \rightarrow \left(F_{\text{sig}}^*, F_{\text{img}}^* \right) \tag{4}$$

where F_{sig} and F_{img} are the features output from the deep feature extraction module, and F_{sig}^* and F_{img}^* are the enhanced higher-order representations.

Signal Timing Dynamic Enhancement [16–18]: Non-smooth radiated source signals have sharp mutations in the time-frequency plane such as pulse fronts, frequency shortcuts, etc., and fixed-sampling convolution is unable to fully capture such localized heterogeneous patterns. Let the standard convolutional kernel sense domain be $\mathcal{R} = \{p_k\}_{k=1}^{|\mathcal{R}|} \subset \mathbb{Z}^2$, and we learn the offset ∇p_k at each center point p_0:

$$\Delta p_k = \mathrm{Softmax}\left(\mathbf{W}_p * [\nabla_t F_{\mathrm{sig}}, \mathcal{E}(F_{\mathrm{sig}})]\right)_k \tag{5}$$

$$\mathcal{E}(F_{\mathrm{sig}}) = -\sum_{tf} F_{\mathrm{sig}}(t, f) \log F_{\mathrm{sig}}(t, f) \tag{6}$$

where $\nabla_t F_{sig}$ is the time gradient which represents the rate of change of the signal's frequency content with respect to time. It is crucial for capturing the dynamics of the signal, particularly in scenarios where sharp mutations occur, such as pulse fronts and frequency shortcuts. And $\mathcal{E}$ is the time-frequency energy entropy.

The enhanced convolution output is the following.

$$F'_{\mathrm{sig}}(p_0) = \sum_k w_k F_{\mathrm{sig}}\left(p_0 + p_k + \Delta p_k\right) \tag{7}$$

The physical meaning can be viewed as an adaptive expansion of sampling points in high-entropy regions to focus on transient energy clusters.

Deformable convolution is responsible for "finding the right points", but how to allocate attention among these points still requires more fine-grained modeling. We split this work into two paths:

1. Local time-domain sliding-window attention mimics the physiological process of "transient integration" in the auditory system by allowing only the current ω frames to interact with the frames before and after it, preventing distant noise from entering the field of view. The weights are calculated as follows:

$$\alpha_{ij}^{(t)} = \frac{\exp\left(Q_i^\top K_j\right)}{\sum_{|i-k| \leq w} \exp\left(Q_i^\top K_k\right)} \tag{8}$$

$$Q, K = F'_{\mathrm{sig}} \mathbf{W}_Q, F'_{\mathrm{sig}} \mathbf{W}_K \tag{9}$$

2. Consider each frequency slot as a graph node by frequency domain graph convolution, and filter the cross-frequency coupling relationship by spectral convolution. Let $\tilde{L} = \tilde{D}^{-1/2} \tilde{A} \tilde{D}^{-1/2}$ be a symmetric normalized Laplacian with self-loop, then:

$$\mathbf{Z} = \sigma(\tilde{L} F'_{\mathrm{sig}} \mathbf{W}_g) \tag{10}$$

The "harmonic correlation" can be propagated in the Laplace eigenspace.

At time step t, the feature embeddings derived from the two branches are fused via a gating mechanism, with the corresponding gating formula specified as follows:

$$\gamma_t = \sigma\left(\mathbf{w}_\gamma^\top [B(t), h_{t-1}]\right), \tag{11}$$

$$F^*_{\text{sig}}(t, :, :) = \gamma_t \mathbf{Z}_t + (1 - \gamma_t) \sum_j \alpha_{ij}^{(t)} V_j \tag{12}$$

Image Spatial Semantics Enhancement: Ship imagery exhibits multi-scale semantics: high-resolution details (e.g., masts), meso-scale hull contours, and global layouts. To overcome conventional FPNs' limitations in cross-level modeling, we introduce: 1) Pyramid-apex channel-space co-attention for joint channel-region prioritization; 2) Spatial transformers with relative encoding capturing long-range geometry; 3) Recursive residual feedback injecting high-level semantics into low-level features for detail-semantic equilibrium.

The module performs two steps: first evaluates "which channel is the most important", and then determines "which regions of the image are the most eye-catching". The first step is to use the "Compression $\rightarrow$ Two Layer Perceptron $\rightarrow$ Sigmoid" process, which is given by the formula:

$$A_c = \sigma \left(\mathbf{W}_2 \delta \left(\mathbf{W}_1 \text{GAP} \left(F_{\text{img}} \right) \right) \right) \tag{13}$$

where GAP first compresses the spatial information into channel vectors and then lets $\delta(\cdot)$(ReLU) and Sigmoid learn the nonlinear mapping.

Subsequently, the "edge/texture" high response is extracted using maximum pooling, then spliced with the original features, convolved with 1×1 to compress the channels, and finally sigmoided to obtain the domain:

$$A_s = \sigma \left(\text{Conv}_{1 \times 1} \left[F_{\text{img}}; \text{GMP} \left(F_{\text{img}} \right) \right] \right) \tag{14}$$

The two weights are reweighted after doing the *Hadamard* product to get the detail-semantic concurrent $\tilde{F}_{img} = A_c \odot A_s \odot F_{img}$.

Relative position encoding is then introduced because it can do "dynamic meshing" in the global context, and is particularly good at capturing rigid body transformation invariance. In order to allow the Transformer to perceive position information without forcing it to memorize absolute coordinates, we use additive relative encoding:

$$P_{\text{rel}}(i, j, m, n) = \text{PE}(i - m) + \text{PE}(j - n),$$
$$\text{PE}(k) = [\sin(\omega_k), \cos(\omega_k)]_{k=0}^{K-1}, \quad \omega_k = 2^k \pi \tag{15}$$

This design preserves the positional differences and captures both long and short period laws using Fourier bases. Transformer outputs the F^*_{img} after three layers of stacking.

Cross-modal spatio-temporal interaction: To bridge the inherent heterogeneity between temporal signal evolution and spatial image distributions, we propose a Spatial-Temporal Cross-Attention (STCA) mechanism. STCA projects both modalities onto a unified spatio-temporal manifold, establishing implicit geometric correspondences through joint feature alignment.

Specifically, let the signal branch output features as $\mathbf{S} \in {}^{L \times F}$, where L denotes the time step and F denotes the frequency dimension; and the spatial feature representations generated by the image network branch are denoted as $\mathbf{S} \in \mathbb{R}^{\alpha \times \beta \times \gamma}$—where α and β correspond to the height and width of the feature map, respectively, and γ denotes the channel count. To achieve uniform processing, the signal features are first reshaped into $\tilde{\mathbf{S}} \in {}^{L \times G \times D}$ by a nonlinear mapping function $\phi(\cdot)$, where G denotes the pseudo spatial grid size, and D is the feature dimension after mapping. The mapping keeps the time dimension unchanged, while the frequency dimension F is projected to the pseudo-space dimension G to establish an implicit correspondence between the time-frequency domain of the signal and the image space, formalized as:

$$\tilde{\mathbf{S}} = \phi(\mathbf{S}) : \mathbb{R}^{L \times F} \to \mathbb{R}^{L \times G \times D} \tag{16}$$

Subsequently, a multi-scale relative position coding function $\Psi(\cdot)$ is introduced for signal and image features, which employs a combination of sine and cosine functions, inspired by the theory of Fourier series expansions, to capture spatio-temporal motion patterns at different scales:

$$\Psi(p) = \left[\sin\left(\frac{p}{10000^{2i/D}} \right), \cos\left(\frac{p}{10000^{2i/D}} \right) \right]_{i=0}^{D/2-1} \tag{17}$$

where p denotes the spatial or temporal location index and D is the coding dimension. This coding method can capture both low-frequency macroscopic motion trends and characterize high-frequency microscopic jitter, which enhances the model's capacity to capture spatio-temporal characteristics.

The spatio-temporal cross-attention mechanism fuses the information complementarity of signal and image modalities in a gated form. Let the query matrix obtained after signal feature mapping be $\mathbf{Q}_S$, the key-value matrix after image feature mapping be $\mathbf{K}_I$, $\mathbf{K}_V$, and the attention weights are computed by dot product and then soft-maximized:

$$\mathbf{A} = \mathrm{softmax}\left(\frac{\mathbf{Q}_S \mathbf{K}_I^\top}{\sqrt{d_k}} \right) \tag{18}$$

where d_k is the key vector dimension to ensure stable values. The image features are weighted and summed using this weight matrix to obtain the cross-modal attention output:

$$\mathbf{O} = \mathbf{A}\mathbf{V}_I \tag{19}$$

In order to dynamically balance the contributions of the two modalities, gating coefficients α are introduced, whose generation process is performed by learning the amount of mutual information between the signal features and the image features:

$$\alpha = \sigma\left(\mathbf{W}_\alpha [\mathbf{S}; \mathbf{I}] + b_\alpha \right) \tag{20}$$

where σ represents Sigmoid activation, $[\cdot; \cdot]$ represents feature splicing, and $\mathbf{W}_\alpha$, b_α are learnable parameters. When the signal features contain rich discriminative time-frequency modes (e.g., unique modulation signals), α approaches 1, prioritizing the retention of signal information; conversely, when the image features provide critical spatial structure, α is automatically reduced to avoid information flooding, reflecting the dynamic adaptability of cross-modal feature fusion. The final spatio-temporal cross-feature expression is:

$$\mathbf{F}_{ST} = \alpha \cdot \tilde{\mathbf{S}} + (1 - \alpha) \cdot \mathbf{O} \tag{21}$$

Through the above design, the spatio-temporal perception module effectively bridges the differences between the signal time-frequency domain and the image spatial domain, utilizes the unified spatio-temporal manifold and the adaptive dynamic gating mechanism, realizes the in-depth fusion and synergistic enhancement of the two modalities, significantly strengthens the discriminative power and robustness of the cross-modal features, and provides rich and complementary higher-order spatio-temporal characterization for the subsequent hash coding.

Hash Encoding Module Building on the spatio-temporal module's cross-modal alignment and fusion, the hash coding module maps convert high-dimension feature representations into compact binary vectors with the preservation of spatio-temporal correlations. Traditional sign-based hashing suffers from non-differentiability and quantization error accumulation, limiting code discriminability. To address this, we propose a bipolar quantization architecture with multilevel similarity fusion for efficient differentiable hashing.

Aiming at the heterogeneity of the signal and image modalities in the feature space, the hash coding module adopts a dual-stream self-encoder structure to map the modal specificity of the two modal features respectively. Let the signal features output from the spatio-temporal perception module be $\mathbf{F}_S$ and the image features be $\mathbf{F}_I$, which are mapped to the common subspace by the orthogonally constrained projection matrices $\mathbf{W}_S \in {}^{d \times k}$ and $\mathbf{W}_I \in {}^{d \times k}$:

$$\begin{aligned} \mathbf{H}_S &= \mathbf{F}_S \mathbf{W}_S, \\ \mathbf{H}_I &= \mathbf{F}_I \mathbf{W}_I \end{aligned} \tag{22}$$

The projection matrix satisfies the orthogonality constraint $\mathbf{W}_S^\top \mathbf{W}_S = \mathbf{I}, \mathbf{W}_I^\top \mathbf{W}_I = \mathbf{I}$, which ensures that the mapping directions of different modes maintain the angle invariance on the unit hypersphere, thus maintaining the geometric consistency between modes.

To solve the gradient vanishing problem in the traditional binarization process, the asymptotic hyperbolic tangent smoothing function (tanh) is designed:

$$\mathbf{B} = \tanh(\beta(t)\mathbf{H}) \tag{23}$$

where the temperature coefficient $\beta(t)$ grows linearly with the number of training rounds, so that the output gradually approaches the discrete boundary from the initial continuous interval [-1,1], realizing a smooth transition and promoting gradient flow.

To reduce the quantization error, distributional alignment loss based on Wasserstein distance is proposed:

$$\mathcal{L}_{\text{quant}} = \sum_{m \in \{v,s\}} \left[\left\| B_m - \text{sign}(h_m) \right\|_2^2 \right] +$$
$$\lambda_{\text{orthe}} \left(\left\| W_v^T W_v - I \right\|_F + \left\| W_s^T W_s - I \right\|_F \right) \tag{24}$$

The first of these constrains the distributional consistency of the continuous hash code h_m with the binary code B_m via the Wasserstein distance, and the second enforces the orthogonality of the projection matrices W_v and W_s to avoid intermodal feature distortions.

The cross-modal contrast loss uses a modified symmetric InfoNCE loss:

$$\mathcal{L}_{\text{cont}} = -\frac{1}{2\,m} \sum_{i=1}^{m} \left[\log \frac{e^{B_v^{(i)} \cdot B_s^{(i)}/\tau}}{\sum_{j=1}^{m} e^{B_v^{(i)} \cdot B_s^{(j)}/\tau}} + \log \frac{e^{B_s^{(i)} \cdot B_v^{(i)}/\tau}}{\sum_{j=1}^{m} e^{B_s^{(i)} \cdot B_v^{(j)}/\tau}} \right] \tag{25}$$

where $s_{ij} = \cos(B_v^{(i)}, B_s^{(j)})$ is the cosine similarity and the temperature coefficient $\tau = 0.07$ controls the intensity of difficult sample mining. This loss function forces positive sample pairs $(B_v^{(i)}, B_s^{(i)})$ to be tightly aligned in the embedding space while pushing away negative sample pairs through two-way contrast learning.

Similarity Fusion Module In order to effectively integrate the temporal and spatial correlation properties of the signal and image modalities, this section constructs a three-level similarity matrix based on hash codes:

Intra-modal similarity: the autocorrelation matrix between the signal and image instances is computed with the following formula:

$$S_s^{\text{intra}} = \text{TopK}\left(\frac{B_s B_s^T}{\|B_s\|_F}, k = 50 \right) \tag{26}$$

$$S_v^{\text{intra}} = \text{TopK}\left(\frac{B_v B_v^T}{\|B_v\|_F}, k = 50 \right) \tag{27}$$

where the TopK() operation retains the first 50 maximum similarities in each row, effectively suppressing noisy associations.

Cross-modal similarity: construct a two-way interaction matrix with the following formula:

$$S_{\text{cross}} = \lambda \cdot \text{Mask}\left(\frac{B_s B_r^T}{\|B_s\|_F} \right) + (1 - \lambda) \cdot \text{Mask}\left(\frac{B_v B_s^T}{\|B_v\|_F} \right) \tag{28}$$

where $\text{Mask}(\cdot)$ is filtered using Gaussian thresholding $\sigma = 0.6$, generated by a gated network:

$$\lambda = \sigma\left(W_g \left[\text{GAP}\left(f_v^{st}\right) \oplus \text{GMP}\left(f_s^{st}\right) \right] + b_g \right) \tag{29}$$

where the inputs to the gating network are Global Average Pooling (GAP) of the image features and Global Maximum Pooling (GMP) of the signal features, and the fusion weights are output through the Sigmoid function.

Next, the semantic retention similarity matrix is proposed:

$$S_A = \alpha \cdot S_s^{\text{intra}} + \beta \cdot S_v^{\text{intra}} + \gamma \cdot S_{\text{cross}} \tag{30}$$

The weight parameters are dynamically generated via learnable vectors:

$$[\delta, \epsilon, \zeta] = \text{Softmax}\left(W_\theta \left[\text{LSTM}(\bar{g}_a) \oplus \text{GRU}(\bar{g}_b)\right]\right) \tag{31}$$

where $\bar{g}_a$ and $\bar{g}_b$ are the feature mean vectors of the image and signal, respectively, which are spliced after LSTM (image) and GRU (signal) timing modeling.

2.3 Objective Function and Optimization

Constructing multi-granularity similarity constraints based on the semantic retention similarity matrix S_A generated by the dynamic fusion module. The weight coefficients ζ and ξ are hyperparameters that control the relative importance of each term in the loss function. These values are empirically chosen and tuned through a grid search validation process to optimize model performance. Specifically, ζ adjusts the contribution of the similarity constraint $L(S_A\|YY^T)$, while ξ controls the regularization term involving $B^T LB$.

$$\mathcal{L}_{\text{sim}} = \left\|S_A - YY^T\right\|_F^2 + \zeta \text{KL}(S_A \| YY^T) + \xi \text{Tr}(B^T LB) \tag{32}$$

The total loss function is the weighted sum of the above four losses:

$$\mathcal{J}_{\text{overall}} = \gamma_1 \mathcal{J}_{\text{align}} + \gamma_2 \mathcal{J}_{\text{quant}} + \gamma_3 \mathcal{J}_{\text{sim}} \tag{33}$$

Optimizing weighting parameters using a phased course learning strategy:

1. **Cross-modal feature alignment stage (initial 20 epochs):** $\gamma_1 = 1.0, \gamma_2 = 0.5, \gamma_3 = 0.3$, with a focus on cross-modal representation learning;
2. **Binary hash coding stage (epochs 2150):** $\gamma_1 = 0.8, \gamma_2 = 1.2, \gamma_3 = 0.6$, aiming to strengthen the quantization constraints;
3. **Integrated fine-tuning stage (from epoch 51 onwards):** $\gamma_1 = 0.5, \gamma_2 = 1.5, \gamma_3 = 1.0$, achieving a balance between prediction accuracy and model robustness.

The optimization process uses the *AdamW*-algorithm with an initial learning rate of 3e-4 and a decay of 30% every 10 rounds.

3   Experiments

Datasets The dataset adopted in this study is a cross-modal ship dataset collected via shore-based field operations at Yantai Port in Shandong Province, which contains two modalities: visible images and radiated source signals. The dataset covers 16 types of individual ships, and more than 3,000 images and 1,600 radiated source signals have been collected. Among them, the visible light images were captured by a DJI drone equipped with a visible light sensing camera, while the radiation source signals were collected by the SM200C device. After the acquisition, the AIS message information was used to assist in realizing the correlation of the multimodal data, and a complete dataset was constructed. The dataset covers diverse marine environments such as cloud, rain, fog, backlight and low visibility conditions, and also contains a variety of challenging attributes including intra-plane rotational transformation, extra-plane rotational deformation, scale perturbation, and subtle intraclass differences (Fig. 2).

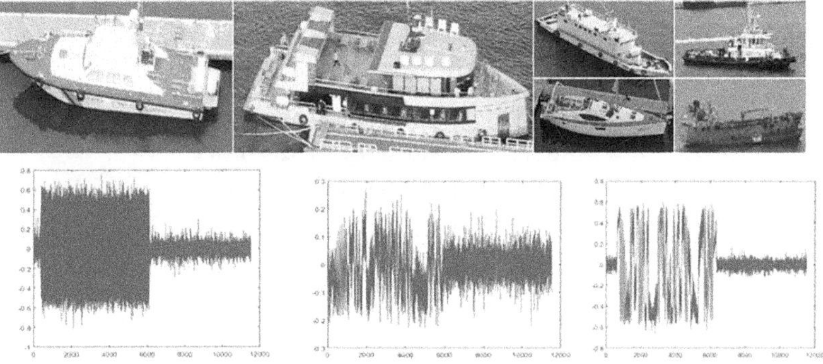

Fig. 2. Example of a multimodal ship dataset.

Baseline Methodologies and Assessment Indicators To impartially validate the efficacy of the proposed framework, we adopt several representative cross-modal hashing approaches as comparative baselines in our experimental evaluations, encompassing DADCH [11], ASSH [12], DLSDH [13], HX_MAN [14], and LEBD [15]. These baseline methods are indicative of the cutting-edge advances in recent years, with all of them leveraging deep learning architectures to construct their respective model frameworks. For most of these comparative approaches, the source code and corresponding experimental data are publicly available in their original publications.

For our experimental evaluations, we adopt a broadly used retrieval evaluation criterion, mean average precision (mAP), which serves to assess the retrieval performance of the proposed method relative to other competing techniques. In detail, mAP is formally defined as below:

$$mAP = \frac{1}{M_q} \sum_{i=1}^{M_q} \frac{1}{M_s} \sum_{s=1}^{M_s} p_s \cdot \zeta(s) \tag{34}$$

Here, M_q represents the cardinality of the query set, M_t denotes the count of genuine neighbors for the query sample, M_s stands for the size of the retrieved set, and p_s indicates the precision value of the s-th retrieved sample. Additionally, when $\zeta(s) = 1$, it signifies that the s-th retrieved sample has consistent semantic labels with the query instance; otherwise, $\zeta(s) = 0$.

For the experimental setup, ReLU activation functions are adopted for all network layers. As for the optimizer, we employ mini-batch SGD with a learning rate of 0.001, an L2 regularization coefficient of 6e-5, and a momentum of 0.8. Regarding the experimental environment, and deployed on NVIDIA RTX4060Ti GPUs.

Table 1. Comparison results of mAP@50 for cross-modal retrieval tasks

Task	Method	Hash code length			
		16	32	64	128
I→S	DADCH	0.731	0.792	0.823	0.845
	ASSH	0.845	0.866	0.920	0.933
	DLSDH	0.863	0.877	0.895	0.903
	HX_MAN	0.812	0.835	0.847	0.852
	LEBD	0.810	0.842	0.878	0.929
	Ours	**0.923**	**0.945**	**0.953**	**0.976**
S→I	DADCH	0.719	0.780	0.842	0.879
	ASSH	0.822	0.840	0.877	0.916
	DLSDH	0.832	0.852	0.865	0.899
	HX_MAN	0.841	0.853	0.872	0.913
	LEBD	0.811	0.832	0.882	0.919
	Ours	**0.919**	**0.921**	**0.943**	**0.958**

Empirical Findings and Analysis with Discussion mAP Performance Evaluation: Table 1 presents the mAP@50 performance of the proposed framework in comparison with competing approaches for the cross-modal image-radiation source signal retrieval task, covering four hash code lengths (16-bit, 32-bit, 64-bit, and 128-bit). To further corroborate the efficacy of the presented approach, we conduct performance comparisons between our method and state-of-the-art cross-modal hashing retrieval techniques on the real-world mining dataset under varying hash code lengths, with the corresponding mAP@100 results summarized in Table 2. Specifically, mAP@50 refers to the mean average precision of retrieving the top 50 most similar samples, while mAP@100 denotes the mean average precision of the top 100 similar samples sorted by hash distance. Based on the quantitative results presented in Tables 1 and 2, the following key conclusions are derived:

1. The approach we developed surpasses all comparative cross-modal hashing methods on the target dataset, demonstrating strong retrieval capability in the image-to-radiation source signal cross-modal retrieval task. Of note, even with concise binary hash codes, it maintains impressive precision—validating its ability to learn discriminative, high-quality binary hash representations under compact code lengths.
2. When compared with cutting-edge cross-modal hashing methods from the past two years, our proposed method attains optimal performance across all tested hash code lengths. More precisely, it delivers performance improvements of 4.3%–13.1% and 4.3%–13.0% for the image-to-radiation source signal retrieval task, while achieving notable gains of 3.9%–7.9% and 4.0%–8.3% for the radiation source signal-to-image retrieval task, respectively.
3. Most reference cross-modal hashing methods exhibit better performance with longer hash codes but suffer a sharp efficacy decline when using shorter ones. As shown in Tables 1 and 2, our developed method remains competitive and secures superior results even under short hash code setups. In detail, when the hash code length is reduced to 16-bit, the mAP values of comparative baseline approaches plummet, while the 16-bit mAP of our method is on par with the results of other methods using 64128-bit codes—effectively confirming the high efficiency and effectiveness of our proposed approach.

Ablation Study To quantitatively analyze the individual contributions of the core modules within the proposed fusion framework the Spatio-Temporal Perceptual Hashing (STPH) framework, we conducted a rigorous ablation study using the Yantai Port vessel dataset. The evaluation metric used is mAP@50 for the cross-modal retrieval task. Table 3 presents the key comparative data regarding, four variant models were constructed by progressively removing key modules for comparison: Baseline (which includes only the basic feature extraction network and shared hashing layer) as the reference model; Ours-L_{STPM} (which removes the Local Spatio-Temporal Perception Module); Ours-L_{Cross} (which removes the cross-modal similarity computation module); Ours-L_{Inter} (which removes the intra-modal similarity computation module); and the full Ours model.

The experimental results clearly highlight the irreplaceability of each module. Firstly, removing the Local Spatio-Temporal Perception Module (LSTPM) caused a significant performance degradation. Compared to the complete model's mAP@50 of 97.6%, Ours-L_{STPM} only achieved 61.0%, a drop of 36.6%. This demonstrates the critical role of LSTPM in preserving the spatio-temporal semantic integrity of the original vessel data, achieved through the collaborative mechanism of signal time-frequency enhancement and image adaptive pooling.

Table 2. Comparison results of mAP@100 for cross-modal retrieval tasks

Task	Method	Hash code length			
		16	32	64	128
I→S	DADCH	0.715	0.772	0.813	0.831
	ASSH	0.830	0.852	0.905	0.918
	DLSDH	0.850	0.862	0.880	0.888
	HX_MAN	0.798	0.820	0.832	0.838
	LEBD	0.795	0.828	0.863	0.914
	Ours	0.908	0.930	0.938	0.961
S→I	DADCH	0.705	0.765	0.827	0.864
	ASSH	0.808	0.825	0.837	0.901
	DLSDH	0.818	0.837	0.850	0.884
	HX_MAN	0.826	0.838	0.857	0.898
	LEBD	0.812	0.820	0.870	0.907
	Ours	0.908	0.910	0.932	0.947

Table 3. Results of ablation experiments

Task	Method	Result	Task	Method	Result
I→S	Ours-L_{STPM}	0.610	S→I	Ours-L_{STPM}	0.592
I→S	Ours-L_{Inter}	0.697	S→I	Ours-L_{Inter}	0.644
I→S	Ours-L_{Cross}	0.784	S→I	Ours-L_{Cross}	0.775
I→S	Ours	0.976	S→I	Ours	0.958

Notably, the independent contribution of the cross-modal similarity computation module was fully validated: when the cross-modal similarity computation module was removed (Ours-L_{Cross}), the performance dropped drastically to 69.7%, a decrease of 29.6% from the complete model. Similarly, the absence of the intra-modal similarity learning module (Ours-L_{Inter}) also caused a notable loss in performance (Ours-L_{Inter}: 78.4%, a 12.9% decrease), emphasizing the fundamental importance of intra-modal similarity constraints in maintaining hashing discriminability. Ultimately, the complete framework with 97.6% mAP@50 significantly outperforms all variants, empirically demonstrating the practical validity of the synergistic optimization mechanism the fusion framework presented in this study.

4   Conclusion

This study proposes a novel deep learning framework for cross-modal ship data retrieval between electromagnetic radiation signals and optical images, effectively addressing spatio-temporal heterogeneity. Integrating a dual-stream spatio-temporal cross-attention network enables synergistic learning of dynamic time-frequency signal patterns and spatial image features. A bipolar quantization function and multi-level similarity fusion strategy ensure compact hash codes preserving cross-modal correlations. Validation on a 16-class maritime dataset demonstrates superior performance (97.6%).

The primary theoretical contribution is a unified spatio-temporal mapping paradigm bridging electromagnetic and visual modalities, offering robust real-time multi-source maritime monitoring under challenging conditions. However, practical challenges like signal loss, image blur, and harsh weather may impact performance. Future work will focus on mitigating signal degradation and enhancing image clarity via multi-sensor fusion and noise-resistant models.

The framework's extensibility to radar-infrared and other multi-modal marine sensing systems enhances applicability. Future research will prioritize lightweight architecture optimization and open-set retrieval for unidentified vessel recognition. This work lays the foundation for next-generation intelligent maritime perception systems with enhanced cross-modal interoperability and environmental resilience.

References

1. Yan, C., Gong, B., Wei, Y., Gao, Y.: Deep multi-view enhancement hashing for image retrieval. IEEE Trans. Pattern Anal. Mach. Intell. **43**(4), 1445–1451 (2020)
2. Gong, Q.K., Wang, L.D., Lai, H.J., et al.: Vit2hash: unsupervised information preserving hashing. arXiv preprint (2022). arXiv:2201.05541
3. Dubey, S.R., Singh, S.K., Chu, W.T.: Vision transformer hashing for image retrieval. In: Proceedings of the 2022 IEEE International Conference on Multimedia and Expo (ICME), pp. 1–6. IEEE, Taipei (2022)
4. Ghahremani, A., Kong, Y., Bondarev, E., et al.: Towards parameter-optimized vessel re-identification based on iornet. In: Computational Science–ICCS 2019, Lecture Notes in Computer Science, vol. 11540, pp. 125–136. Springer, Faro (2019)
5. Qiao, D., Liu, G., Dong, F., et al.: Marine vessel re-identification: a large-scale dataset and global-and-local fusion-based discriminative feature learning. IEEE Access **8**, 27744–27756 (2020)
6. Xian Y., Xian J., Lu, L., et al.: FGSR: a fine-grained ship retrieval dataset and method in smart cities. Wirel. Commun. Mob. Comput. (2022). Article ID 3859267
7. Lu, Y., Ma, H., Smart, E., et al.: Fusion of camera-based vessel detection and ais for maritime surveillance. In: Proceedings of the 26th International Conference on Automation and Computing, pp. 1–6. IEEE (2021)
8. Qu, J., Guo, Y., Lu, Y., et al.: Intelligent maritime surveillance framework driven by fusion of camera-based vessel detection and ais data. In: Proceedings of the 2022 IEEE 25th International Conference on Intelligent Transportation Systems, pp. 2280–2285, IEEE (2022)
9. Jiang Q.Y., Li, W.J.: Deep cross-modal hashing. In: Proceedings of the IEEE Conference on Computer Vision and Pattern Recognition (CVPR), pp. 3232–3240, IEEE (2017)

10. Cao, Y., Long, M., Wang, J., et al.: Correlation autoencoder hashing for supervised cross-modal search. In: Proceedings of the 2016 ACM International Conference on Multimedia Retrieval, pp. 197–204, ACM (2016)
11. Wang, X.Y., Wang, Z.Q., Xiong, W.: Deep asymmetric discrete cross-modal hashing method. J. Comput. Appl. **42**(8), 2461–2470 (2022). (in Chinese)
12. Wang, H., Ge, H.: Cross-modal hash retrieval based on attention mechanism and semantic similarity. Comput. Mod. **8**, 44–53 (2023). (in Chinese)
13. Wu, Y.: Research on cross-modal supervised discrete hashing method based on dictionary learning. Master's thesis, Shandong University (2020). (in Chinese)
14. Wu, J.X., Lu, Q., Li, W.X.: Cross-modal hashing network based on multi-modal attention mechanism. Comput. Eng. Appl. **58**(20), 229–239 (2022). (in Chinese)
15. Wang, Y.X., Tian, J.R., Chen, Z.D., et al.: Label-enhanced discrete cross-modal hashing method. J. Softw. **34**(7), 3438–3450 (2023). (in Chinese)
16. Sun, L., Xue, R., Lin, Y.: Specific emitter identification technology based on multi-domain signal feature knowledge graph. In: Proceedings of the 18th National Conference on Radio Wave Propagation, Harbin Engineering University (2023). (in Chinese)
17. Yue, W., Qi, L., Li, S.: Parallel multi-model fusion spectrum prediction based on multi-channel feature extraction. In: Proceedings of the MobiMedia 2023: Mobile Multimedia Communications (2023)
18. Zhao, B., Wang, S., Xu, C., et al.: Modal invariant joint representation learning for missing multimodal ship image classification. In: Proceedings of the 6th International Conference on Robotics, Intelligent Control and Artificial Intelligence (RICAI), pp. 1340–1343 (2024)

DeepSeekVision: Dual-Stream Compressed Architecture for Marine Object Identification with Visual Feature Distillation

Yongqi Li, Zhengwei Xu[✉], Peiji Huang, Jianliang He, and Shuman Huang

College of Computer and Information Engineering, Henan Normal University,
Xinxiang, China
2408283059@stu.htu.edu.cn

Abstract. Existing vision-based maritime target recognition methods suffer significant performance degradation under conditions of low-resolution cameras or occlusion. The navigational data in AIS signals can provide supplementary information to alleviate this issue. However, constructing a robust maritime target recognition model using multimodal sensor data remains a challenge due to the differences between modalities. This paper proposes a dual-stream heterogeneous collaborative learning method based on DeepSeek, which guides maritime target recognition by extracting information from visual sensors. It also improves model robustness by utilizing feature distillation to reduce the impact of noise. To achieve model lightweighting, knowledge from DeepSeek is transferred to a student network, significantly reducing the model's parameter size and computational complexity while maintaining performance. The F1 score and accuracy on a self-constructed maritime multimodal dataset demonstrate the superior performance of the DeepSeaNet method compared to existing state-of-the-art maritime target recognition methods.

Keywords: Maritime target recognition · Multimodal · Feature distillation · Lightweighting · Transfer learning

1 Introduction

In recent years, the monitoring of offshore operational areas has attracted significant attention. As a critical safeguard for the safety and efficiency of offshore operations, establishing a comprehensive monitoring system is of paramount importance. This system encompasses both dynamic monitoring of offshore targets and ecological environmental monitoring, with the aim of real-time tracking of the operational status of offshore targets, preventing potential accidents, and protecting the marine ecological environment. Traditional monitoring methods primarily rely on simple instrumentation and neural networks. However, these approaches face numerous limitations in complex offshore environments, such

C. Xu et al. (Eds.): MobiMedia 2025, LNICST 670, pp. 209–220, 2026.
https://doi.org/10.1007/978-3-032-16823-8_15

as low efficiency, poor real-time performance, and significant susceptibility to weather conditions and sea states. Therefore, it has become an urgent priority to enhance the automation and intelligence of offshore target monitoring through the use of advanced technological means.

Offshore target recognition technology is primarily divided into two categories: acoustic vision and optical vision. Acoustic vision has advantages in long-distance target recognition; however, due to acoustic blind zones and multipath effects, it has limitations in short-distance target recognition. While optical vision can provide rich image information, it is often compromised by environmental disturbances at sea (such as low light and noise), resulting in poor image quality. In recent years, the integration of artificial intelligence and deep learning technologies for offshore target detection using optical vision has gradually become a research hotspot. However, relying solely on either optical or acoustic vision may affect the accuracy of target recognition. As a result, researchers have begun exploring methods that combine visible light images with AIS source signals to achieve more accurate and reliable target recognition. This approach takes full advantage of the intuitive nature of visible light images and the penetrability of AIS source signals. By fusing multi-source data, it can effectively enhance target recognition performance in complex marine environments, providing new technological avenues for applications such as offshore target recognition.

Maritime target recognition methods can be divided into two categories: those based on manually designed features and those based on deep learning features. Traditional manually designed feature methods typically rely on handcrafted feature extraction, which requires designing specific features tailored to particular application scenarios. These methods lack generality and perform poorly in terms of robustness in complex environments. With the development of deep learning technologies, deep learning-based maritime target recognition methods have been widely studied and have demonstrated superior performance in practical applications. Especially under complex environmental conditions, deep learning methods can automatically learn features from images and videos, significantly improving recognition accuracy and system robustness. Lu et al. [1] designed a framework that integrates visual detection and AIS data, using the YOLOv5 model for vessel detection, and combining distance and azimuth angle estimation with AIS data for correlation. Huang et al. [2] proposed a maritime multi-target tracking technology based on an improved Single Shot Multibox Detector (SSD) and DeepSORT algorithm. Chen et al. [3] introduced a ship tracking method that combines video and Automatic Identification System (AIS) reports, using a Kalman filter to enable continuous localization and tracking of specific vessels in video surveillance. Liu et al. [4] designed an intelligent edge-driven, efficient multi-source data fusion method, using the lightweight YOLOX-s network for real-time ship detection. Wu et al. [5] proposed an information fusion algorithm based on AIS and video data, using a Kalman filter to merge AIS and video data.Although these methods use current vessel features, such as position, azimuth, and motion, to match AIS and visual targets, they neglect the importance of historical information, which limits recognition accuracy.

However, the complexity of the marine environment often leads to various issues in the collected images, such as noise, blue-green color distortion, low contrast, and blurring, which directly impact recognition accuracy. To effectively address these challenges, this paper innovatively applies a feature distillation method, training a student network to learn the powerful feature extraction capabilities of a multi-modal large model. This significantly enhances the feature extraction process and provides strong support for improving target recognition accuracy. Based on this background, this paper proposes a novel offshore target recognition method for complex marine environments, combining feature learning with a dual-stream heterogeneous collaborative learning network. The main contributions are as follows:

1. Feature distillation technology is introduced for cross-modal knowledge transfer. Through the DeepSeek-VL module and the feature distillation mechanism, we achieve precise alignment and knowledge transfer of global and local visual features, ensuring efficient information transmission and optimized feature representation.
2. A dual-stream heterogeneous collaborative learning framework is proposed, which integrates multimodal data from visual images and ship IQ signals. By fully exploiting the complementarity between different modalities, the framework effectively enhances the accuracy and robustness of ship target recognition.
3. We have constructed a multimodal dataset that integrates noise-enhanced images of maritime targets with corresponding AIS signals. This dataset provides a high-quality multimodal resource for maritime target detection and recognition tasks.

Experimental results show that our algorithm outperforms traditional methods in both accuracy and recall, demonstrating its effectiveness. The proposed method has strong scalability and can be further optimized for real-time performance in the future, promoting the intelligent development of offshore target monitoring.

2   Methodolgy

2.1   DeepSeaNet Framework

We propose a multimodal heterogeneous collaborative architecture that achieves holographic perception and intelligent recognition of ship targets under complex maritime conditions by constructing a spatiotemporal feature decoupling and collaborative optimization mechanism for visual and radio frequency signals.

As shown in Fig. 1, this framework adopts a hierarchical intelligent processing paradigm. In the visual perception layer, a multi-scale spatiotemporal collaborative feature extraction network is designed [6]. The global semantic encoder, using Transformer, effectively aggregates the overall feature patterns

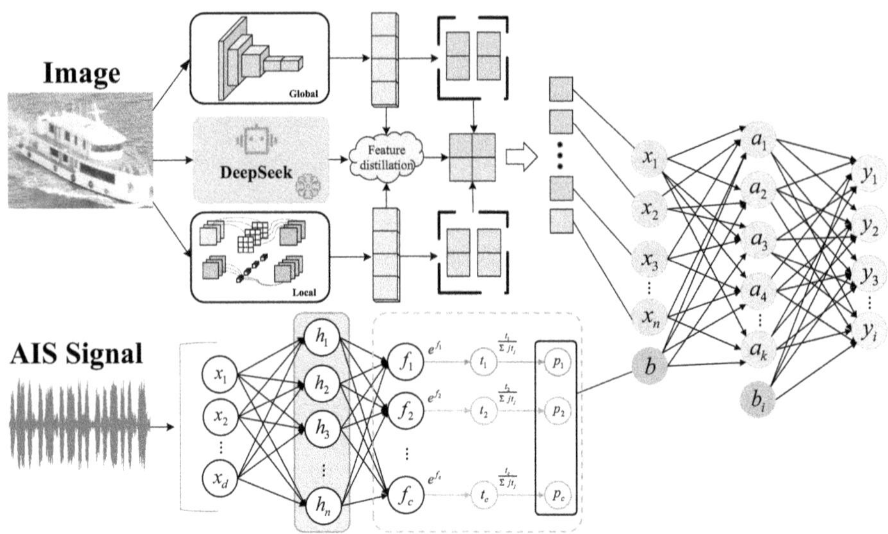

Fig. 1. DeepSeaNet network.

of vessels, capturing macroscopic vessel behavior patterns. Meanwhile, the local detail encoder, based on Convolutional Neural Networks (CNN) [7], dynamically extracts local detail features of the vessel, precisely characterizing the micro-level movement trajectory of the ship [8]. In the radio frequency analysis layer, a time-frequency dual-stream deep network is employed. Through the collaborative effect of adaptive wavelet basis functions and three-dimensional residual convolutions, the time-varying Doppler-azimuth joint feature tensor of the ship's IQ signal is extracted [9]. Finally, we design a quantized feature aggregation engine based on differential manifold theory. By introducing a dynamic tensor entanglement mechanism in non-commutative geometric space, the multimodal features are fused in a hyperplane, enabling maritime situational awareness.

2.2 Heterogeneous Feature Extraction

For signal data, we use the pre-trained ResNet-18 model for feature extraction, which effectively captures high-level semantic information from the signals, providing precise feature representations for subsequent tasks, thereby improving the recognition performance of the entire multimodal learning framework.

For image features, we first design a local feature extractor based on deformable convolution, aiming to capture local detail features of the image. This extractor consists of multiple layers of convolutional operations, where we use 3×3 convolution kernels for the convolution layers [10]. By adjusting the stride and padding parameters, we control the spatial dimensions of the feature maps. The formula is:

$$F_{loc} = W_{\mathrm{conv}} * X + b_{\mathrm{conv}} \tag{1}$$

In this context, W_{conv} represents the convolution kernel weights, X denotes the input image, b_{conv} is the bias, and the operation $*$ signifies the convolution operation. Then, after each convolutional layer, batch normalization is applied to accelerate convergence and improve training stability. The calculation formula is as follows:

$$\hat{F}_{\text{loc}} = \frac{F_{\text{local}} - \mu_B}{\sqrt{\sigma_B^2 + \epsilon}} \cdot \gamma + \beta \tag{2}$$

Where μ_B and σ_B^2 the mean and variance of the mini-batch, γ and β are the learnable parameters, and ϵ is a small constant added for numerical stability. Finally, the ReLU activation function is applied to introduce non-linear transformation, as follows:

$$F_{local} = \max(0, \hat{F}_{\text{loc}}) \tag{3}$$

By progressively extracting local features from low-level to high-level through multiple convolutional layers, it provides crucial local information support for ship recognition.

Next, to capture the global dependencies in the image, we design a Transformer-based global feature extractor. This extractor utilizes a window attention mechanism and a shifted window strategy to extract global contextual features while maintaining computational efficiency.We first divide the input image into fixed-size patches and flatten them into a one-dimensional vector sequence X_p. Then, we use a Transformer encoder [7], which consists of multiple layers of encoders, each including multi-head self-attention and a feedforward neural network [11]. After that, we design a window attention mechanism that calculates attention within local windows, reducing computational complexity. Next, the attention value matrix V is multiplied to obtain F_{glocal}, and the calculation formula for F_{glocal} is as follows:

$$F_{glocal} = \text{softmax}\left(\frac{QK^T}{\sqrt{d_k}}\right) \cdot V \tag{4}$$

Where Q, K, and V represent the query matrix, key matrix, and value matrix, respectively, and d_k is the dimension of the key.

Next, we design a feature fusion module that employs a gating mechanism to achieve feature aggregation. First, the features are compressed by using a 1×1 convolution to reduce the number of channels across different feature levels:

$$F'_{\text{layer}} = W_{1 \times 1} \cdot F_{\text{layer}} + b_{1 \times 1} \tag{5}$$

Next, the features are concatenated by joining the compressed features along the channel dimension, forming a multi-scale feature map:

$$F_{\text{fused}} = \text{Concat}(F'_{\text{local}}, F'_{\text{global}}, F'_{\text{distill}}) \tag{6}$$

Finally, residual connections are introduced to ensure the effective transfer of information:

$$F_{\text{out}} = F_{\text{fused}} + F_{\text{input}} \tag{7}$$

The above approach effectively integrates both local and global features, providing comprehensive global and local information for maritime target recognition.

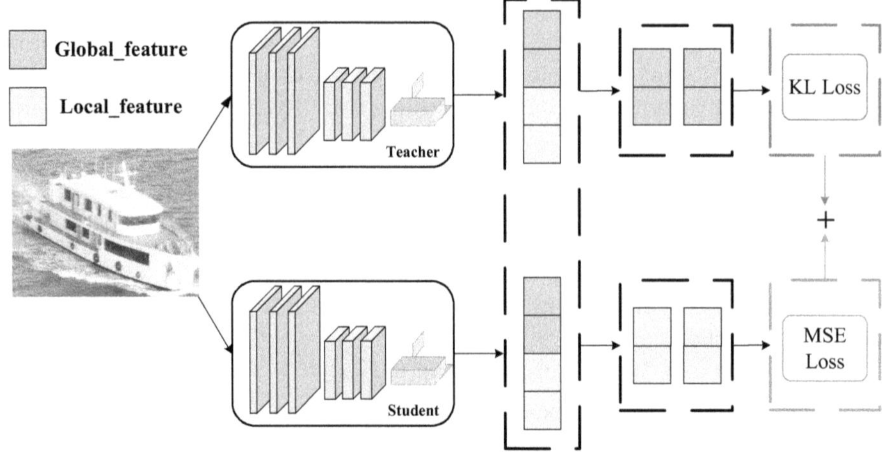

Fig. 2. Feature distillation net.

2.3　Feature Distillation

To enhance the image feature representation capabilities, we introduce the feature distillation module. This module uses a frozen pre-trained $DeepSeek - VL$ model to extract visual features and enhances the backbone network through distillation techniques.

As shown in Fig. 2, we use $DeepSeek - VL$ as the teacher model to process the input image and generate high-resolution features F_{high} and low-resolution features F_{low}. Then, the extracted features are aligned with F_{global} and F_{local} through projection layers, where the projection operation is defined as:

$$F'_{\text{high/low}} = W_{\text{proj}} \cdot F_{\text{high/low}} + b_{\text{proj}} \tag{8}$$

Where W_{proj} and b_{proj} represent the projection weights and bias, respectively. After alignment, we design a distillation loss function consisting of the KL divergence and MSE loss to guide the model in learning the feature representations from the pre-trained model. The KL divergence loss is used to measure the difference between the model's output F_{global} and the high-resolution feature F_{high}. The formula for the KL divergence loss is:

$$L_{\text{KL}} = \sum_i F_{high}(i) \log \left(\frac{F_{high}(i)}{F_{global}(i)} \right) \tag{9}$$

The MSE loss is used to compare the Euclidean distance between the model's feature F_{local} and the pre-trained model's feature F_{low}. The formula for the MSE loss is:

$$L_{\text{MSE}} = \frac{1}{N} \sum_{i=1}^{N} \|F_{local}(i) - F_{low}(i)\|_2^2 \tag{10}$$

The total distillation loss is the combination of the KL divergence loss and the MSE loss, which can be expressed as:

$$L_{\text{distill1}} = \alpha L_{\text{KL}} + \beta L_{\text{MSE}} \tag{11}$$

Where α and β are hyperparameters, and the optimization goal is to improve classification performance while closely matching the feature representations of the pre-trained model.Through feature distillation, the model can learn richer visual features, thereby enhancing its ability to recognize maritime targets.

We propose a collaborative attention mechanism, which aims to optimize the fusion of local and global features through the weighted combination of spatial and channel attention. Specifically, the collaborative attention mechanism can be expressed by the following formula:

$$A_{\text{local}} = \sigma(W_{\text{spatial}}(F_{\text{local}})) \cdot F_{\text{local}} \tag{12}$$

$$A_{\text{global}} = \sigma(W_{\text{channel}}(F_{\text{global}})) \cdot F_{\text{global}} \tag{13}$$

Where $W_{spatial}$ and $W_{channel}$ are the learned spatial and channel-level weights, and σ is the Sigmoid activation function. Through this mechanism, we can effectively facilitate the flow of information between different features, ensuring that the joint features of images and signals are more fully utilized within the network. Ultimately, we effectively integrate the image and signal features and perform recognition through a fully connected layer. During the training process, we also compute the weighted sum of cross-entropy loss and feature distillation loss to achieve joint optimization:

$$\mathcal{L}_{\text{total}} = \mathcal{L}_{\text{ce}} + \alpha \cdot \mathcal{L}_{\text{distill}} \tag{14}$$

Where $\mathcal{L}_{\text{ce}}$ is the cross-entropy loss, $\mathcal{L}_{\text{distill}}$ is the feature distillation loss, and α is the weight coefficient.

3 Experiments and Discussion

3.1 Descriptions of the Datasets

The dataset used in this study is a self-collected multimodal ship recognition dataset from Yantai's First Seaside Bathing Beach in Shandong, China. It comprises images of 16 ship types and corresponding IQ signals. Each ship type has multiple images and signal data. Besides, it encompasses diverse maritime conditions like cloudiness, rain, fog, backlighting, and low visibility, along with challenging attributes such as in-plane and out-of-plane rotation, scale variation, thermal crossover, and small intra-class variations. The equipment for image and AIS source signal collection is respectively shown in Figs. 3 and 4.

Fig. 3. Visible light image acquisition equipment.

Fig. 4. AIS source signal acquisition equipment.

3.2 Experimental Environment

The experiment was conducted on an NVIDIA L40S GPU, using the PyTorch framework for model training and evaluation. The training was performed in a single-GPU computing environment. The specific hardware configuration includes an NVIDIA L40S GPU with 45GB of VRAM, enabling efficient processing of image and signal data. The operating system is Ubuntu 20.04, with Python version 3.10. The main dependencies include PyTorch 2.01 and CUDA 12.2.The experiments were conducted using the AdamW optimizer with an initial learning rate of 1e-4 and a weight decay of 1e-4. The batch size was set to 32, and the model was trained for a total of 50 epochs. To mitigate overfitting, a dropout rate of 0.3 was applied. The learning rate schedule employed a warm-up strategy followed by cosine annealing, with the minimum learning rate set to 1e-6. Additionally, an early stopping mechanism was implemented to halt training if validation performance plateaued.

3.3 Compare with Advanced Methods

To validate the effectiveness of the proposed model in the maritime target recognition task, we compared it with several existing multimodal fusion methods. We selected six mainstream methods for comparison, including Concat, Sum, Gate, MMTM, Transformer, and CAFer. These methods were evaluated based on four metrics: accuracy, precision, recall, and F1-score. The experimental results are shown in Table 1 and Fig. 5. Firstly, based on the proposed method, the model achieved the best performance across four metrics: accuracy, precision, recall, and F1-score. Specifically, the accuracy reached 91.7% precision was 92.1% recall was 91.7% and the F1-score was 91.8%This indicates that the model can effectively fuse image and signal data in complex environments, leading to significant performance improvements. From the experimental results, it is evident that our proposed method, through feature distillation and multimodal fusion strategies, surpasses existing multimodal fusion methods across all evaluation metrics. Particularly in terms of precision and recall, the DeepSeaNet method outperforms other approaches, demonstrating the advantage of our method in effectively fusing visual and signal information. The image modality makes a significant contribution to the maritime target recognition task, especially in image recognition, where it provides rich semantic information. Meanwhile, the signal modality also plays a key role in dynamic target detection and depth estimation tasks. In conclusion, the model we proposed, based on feature distillation and multimodal fusion, not only enhances the accuracy of maritime target recognition but also optimizes the model's robustness, enabling it to effectively handle various challenges in complex environments.

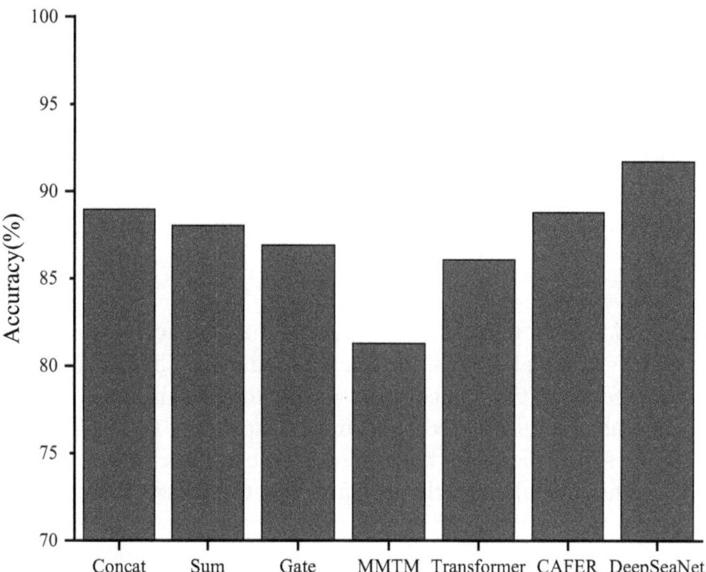

Fig. 5. Comparison result chart with different methods.

3.4   Ablation experiment

To analyze the impact of feature distillation and multimodal fusion on model performance, we conducted several ablation experiments. By comparing the results under different configurations, we can clearly assess the contribution of each module. The experimental results show that the complete model (with

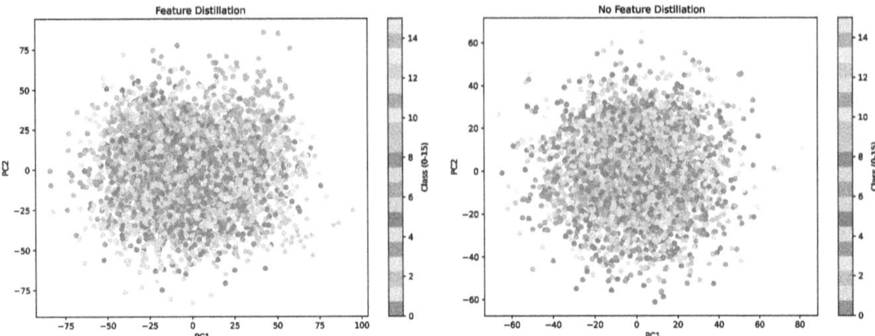

Fig. 6. Comparison of feature extraction effectiveness with and without feature distillation.

Table 1. Experimental results of different methods

Method	Acc (%)	Precision (%)	Recall (%)	F1 (%)
Concat	88.95	89.01	88.95	88.73
Sum	88.04	88.47	87.99	88.12
Gate	86.92	87.64	86.92	86.28
MMTM	81.29	81.54	81.29	80.58
Transformer	86.10	86.50	86.10	85.80
CAFer	88.80	88.90	88.80	88.52
DeepSeaNet	91.70	92.10	91.70	91.80

feature distillation and image-signal bimodal fusion) achieved an accuracy of 90.5%However, when feature distillation was removed, the accuracy dropped to 78.4% a decrease of 12.1% the comparison results are shown in Fig. 6. Further removing the image modality led to a drop in accuracy to 70.9% a decrease of 19.6%When the signal modality was removed, the accuracy decreased to 80.2% a drop of 10.3%These results clearly indicate that the image modality contributes the most to the task, especially in capturing vessel appearance features, while the signal modality plays a crucial complementary role in target detection and tracking in dynamic environments. The ablation experiment results are shown in Table 2. We validated the key role of feature distillation and multimodal fusion in improving the model's robustness and accuracy. Feature distillation significantly enhanced recognition performance through cross-modal knowledge transfer, while the image modality played a dominant role in capturing appearance features. Overall, the ablation results further confirm that the synergistic interaction between the image and signal modalities is crucial for the success of the task.

Table 2. Experimental results under different configurations

Configuration	Acc (%)	Precision (%)	Recall (%)	F1 (%)
w/o Feature distillation	78.4	79.7	78.4	78.1
w/o Image modality	70.9	73.8	70.9	71.2
w/o Signal modality	80.2	81.1	80.2	79.7
Baseline	91.7	92.1	91.7	91.8

4 Conclusion

This paper proposes a feature distillation-based multimodal fusion network, DeepSeaNet, aimed at improving the accuracy and robustness of maritime target recognition. By combining visual images and IQ signal data, the proposed method fully utilizes the complementarity between different modalities, enhancing the performance of maritime target recognition models in complex environments. The introduction of feature distillation further improves the model's robustness, enabling it to better handle issues such as image blurring and occlusion. Experiments conducted on a self-collected multimodal dataset show that DeepSeaNet outperforms existing multimodal fusion methods across multiple evaluation metrics, including accuracy, precision, recall, and F1-score. Particularly in terms of accuracy and robustness, DeepSeaNet demonstrates significant advantages, validating the effectiveness of the feature distillation and multimodal fusion strategies in maritime target recognitionr.

References

1. Lu, Y., Ma, H., Smart, E., Vuksanovic, B., Chiverton, J., Prabhu, S.R., Glaister, M., Dunston, E., Hancock, C.: Fusion of camera-based vessel detection and AIS for maritime surveillance. In: 2021 26th International Conference on Automation and Computing (ICAC), pp. 1–6. IEEE (2021)
2. Huang, Z., Qinyou, H., Mei, Q., Yang, C., Zheng, W.: Identity recognition on waterways: a novel ship information tracking method based on multimodal data. J. Navig. **74**(6), 1336–1352 (2021)
3. Chen, J., Hu, Q., Zhao, R., Guojun, P., Yang, C.: Tracking a vessel by combining video and AIS reports. In: 2008 Second International Conference on Future Generation Communication and Networking, vol. 2, pp. 374–378. IEEE (2008)
4. Liu, R.W., Guo, Y., Nie, J., Hu, Q., Xiong, Z., Yu, H., Guizani, M.: Intelligent edge-enabled efficient multi-source data fusion for autonomous surface vehicles in maritime internet of things. IEEE Trans. Green Commun. Netw. **6**(3), 1574–1587 (2022)
5. Man, W., Zhiyong, L.: The information fusion based on AIS and video data. In: 2016 5th International Conference on Computer Science and Network Technology (ICCSNT), pp. 336–339. IEEE (2016)
6. Ya, T.U., Yun, L.I.N., Haoran, Z.H.A., Yu, W.A.N.G., Guan, G.U.I., Shiwen, M.A.O., et al.: Large-scale real-world radio signal recognition with deep learning. Chin. J. Aeronaut. **35**(9), 35–48 (2022)

7. Lin, Y., Zhao, H., Ma, X., Ya, T., Wang, M.: Adversarial attacks in modulation recognition with convolutional neural networks. IEEE Trans. Reliab. **70**(1), 389–401 (2020)
8. Lin, Y., Ya, T., Dou, Z.: An improved neural network pruning technology for automatic modulation classification in edge devices. IEEE Trans. Veh. Technol. **69**(5), 5703–5706 (2020)
9. Lin, Y., Ya, T., Dou, Z., Chen, L., Mao, S.: Contour stella image and deep learning for signal recognition in the physical layer. IEEE Trans. Cogn. Commun. Netw. **7**(1), 34–46 (2020)
10. Lin, Y., Wang, M., Zhou, X., Ding, G., Mao, S.: Dynamic spectrum interaction of UAV flight formation communication with priority: a deep reinforcement learning approach. IEEE Trans. Cogn. Commun. Netw. **6**(3), 892–903 (2020)
11. Ya, T., Lin, Y., Hou, C., Mao, S.: Complex-valued networks for automatic modulation classification. IEEE Trans. Veh. Technol. **69**(9), 10085–10089 (2020)
12. Bae, J.-H., Yeo, D., Yim, J., Kim, N.-S., Pyo, C.-S., Kim, J.: Densely distilled flow-based knowledge transfer in teacher-student framework for image classification. IEEE Trans. Image Process. **29**, 5698–5710 (2020)
13. Hinton, G., Vinyals, O., Dean, J.: Distilling the Knowledge in a Neural Network. arXiv preprint arXiv:1503.02531 (2015)
14. Luo, Z., Hsieh, J.-T., Jiang, L., Niebles, J.C., Fei-Fei, L.: Graph distillation for action detection with privileged modalities. In: Proceedings of the European Conference on Computer Vision (ECCV), pp. 166–183 (2018)
15. Park, W., Kim, D., Lu, Y., Cho, M.: Relational knowledge distillation. In: Proceedings of the IEEE/CVF Conference on Computer Vision and Pattern Recognition, pp. 3967–3976 (2019)
16. Touvron, H., Cord, M., Douze, M., Massa, F., Sablayrolles, A., Jégou, H: Training data-efficient image transformers & distillation through attention. In: International Conference on Machine Learning, pp. 10347–10357. PMLR (2021)
17. Zhengwei, X., Han, G., Liu, L., Martinez-Garcia, M., Wang, Z.: Multi-energy scheduling of an industrial integrated energy system by reinforcement learning-based differential evolution. IEEE Trans. Green Commun. Netw. **5**(3), 1077–1090 (2021)
18. Zhengwei, X., Han, G., Liu, L., Zhu, H., Peng, J.: A lightweight specific emitter identification model for IIOT devices based on adaptive broad learning. IEEE Trans. Industr. Inf. **19**(5), 7066–7075 (2022)
19. Liu, L., Han, G., Zhengwei, X., Jiang, J., Shu, L., Martinez-Garcia, M.: Boundary tracking of continuous objects based on binary tree structured SVM for industrial wireless sensor networks. IEEE Trans. Mob. Comput. **21**(3), 849–861 (2020)
20. Zhengwei, X., Han, G., Zhu, H., Liu, L., Guizani, M.: Adaptive de algorithm for novel energy control framework based on edge computing in IIOT applications. IEEE Trans. Industr. Inf. **17**(7), 5118–5127 (2020)

Domain Adaptation Method for Lying Posture Recognition Under Category Misalignment

Xu Jiao[1], Zhaoming Li[2], Qiliang Li[1(✉)], Shunan Wu[3], and Jing Bai[4]

[1] College of Engineering, Peking University, Beijing, China
qiliang.li@pku.edu.cn
[2] College of Information and Communication Engineering, Harbin Engineering University, Harbin, China
[3] Peking University Nanchang Innovation Institute, Nanchang, China
[4] Beijing Haidian District Center for Disease Control and Prevention, Beijing, China

Abstract. To address poor generalization in lying-posture recognition for healthcare monitoring—caused by scarce data and category misalignment in real-world deployment—we propose a clustering-based transfer-learning framework. First, we analyze the limitations of conventional transfer strategies, such as fine-tuning and shallow-layer freezing, as well as domain-adaptation techniques, when the source and target domains differ (e.g., mattress thickness of 5 cm and 20 cm). To mitigate accuracy loss due to category misalignment, we introduce Structured Regularized Deep Clustering (SRDC), which enhances cross-domain feature alignment and discrimination. Experiments demonstrate that SRDC achieves a mean accuracy of 84.36%, even when some categories are absent, significantly improving model generalization in semi-supervised cross-domain settings. This approach provides a robust and scalable solution for real-world healthcare applications.

Keywords: Lying posture recognition · Semi-supervised learning · Clustering · Domain adaptation · Category misalignment · SleepMatrix

1 Introduction

Lying posture recognition, a pivotal technology for health monitoring and sleep quality analysis, holds substantial value in medical care and smart home systems [1–3]. Monitoring recumbent postures and their transitions on beds can yield clinically informative data, including assessments of patient mobility and the risk of developing hospital-acquired pressure injuries (HAPIs). However, practical scenarios exhibit significant inter-individual posture variations (e.g., prone postures are rare during actual sleep), leading to pronounced category

This research was funded by the Peking University Nanchang Innovation Institute.

C. Xu et al. (Eds.): MobiMedia 2025, LNICST 670, pp. 221–231, 2026.
https://doi.org/10.1007/978-3-032-16823-8_16

misalignment between the source domain (training data) and the target domain (deployment environment). Specifically, while the source domain must encompass diverse potential postures to ensure generalization, the target domain often suffers from limited categories due to personal habits or environmental constraints. Such misalignment severely undermines conventional transfer learning methods (e.g., domain alignment or maximum classifier discrepancy), where redundant categories distort feature distributions, degrade recognition accuracy and even induce conditional distribution collapse [4] (Fig. 1).

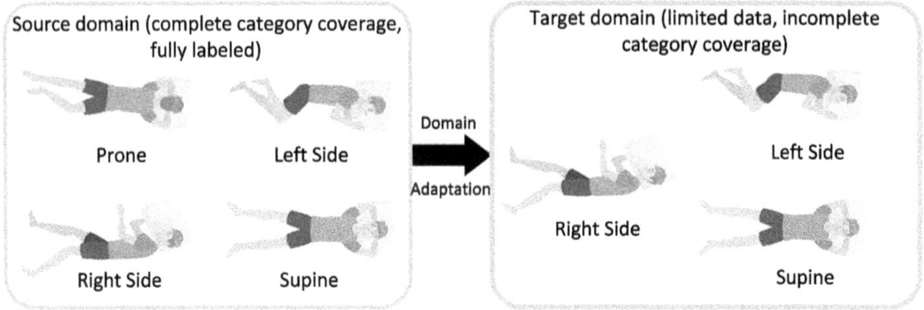

Fig. 1. Adaptation of the recumbency domain under the category mismatch.

Existing research predominantly assumes category alignment between domains, relying on feature alignment or distribution matching [5]. However, in misaligned scenarios, methods like MCD [6] fail to distinguish redundant categories, resulting in chaotic cross-domain feature mapping and performance deterioration. Furthermore, unlabeled target domain data exacerbate instability due to pseudo-label noise. To address these challenges, we propose a dual optimization framework integrating feature space refinement and label information mining.

This paper introduces a Structure-Regularized Deep Clustering (SRDC) [7] method to resolve data scarcity and category misalignment. First, hybrid training is conducted using source domain labels and high-confidence target pseudo labels to initialize cross-domain generalization. Next, dynamic clustering center optimization minimizes KL divergence [8] between category distributions, progressively aligning source and target domains. Concurrently, a soft source sample selection strategy prioritizes source samples resembling target feature distributions, further enhancing generalization. Finally, joint optimization of feature extractors and clustering modules enforces domain-invariant representations, achieving precise category alignment. This paper focuses on classifying lying postures collected by array type sensors under different mattress thicknesses.

The structure is as follows: Sect. 2 introduces dataset collection. Section 3 presents theoretical basis and transfer learning framework of SRDC. Section 4 shows experimental results on recognition accuracy under different network structures and transfer learning algorithms' impact on target domain accuracy. And Sect. 5 summarizes and prospects.

2   Dataset Collection

This research is based on the SleepMatrixnoncontact sleep monitoring system developcd by Beijing MicroVibration DataNet Technology Corporation. Eight pressure pads were placed between the bed frame and the mattress, as shown in Fig. 2. Each pressure pad, spaced 80 cm in length and 14 cm in width, consists of 8 pressure sensors about 10 cm apart. Each pad uses an STM32F103-series microcontroller for 40 Hz sampling, transmitting data via CAN protocol to a computer for processing [9].

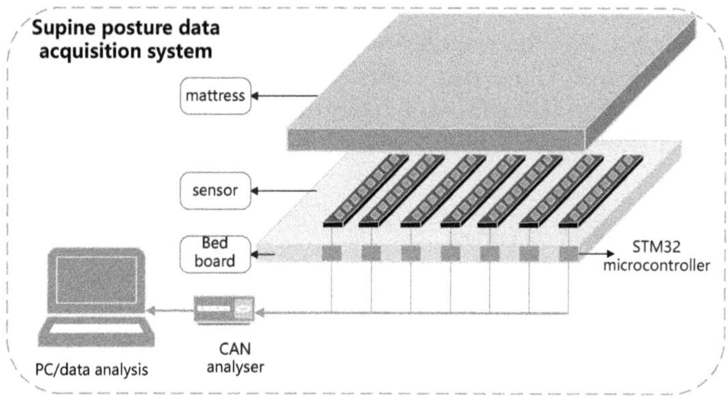

Fig. 2. Adaptation of the recumbency domain under the category mismatch.

During the data collection process, a total of 30 subjects were recruited to collect data on a mattress with a thickness of 5 cm. For each posture, data were collected for 10 sec, resulting in a total of 168 movements. The collected data were further divided into segments of 5 sec each, ultimately forming a dataset of 10,080 entries. Subsequently, this dataset was randomly divided into training and testing sets in a ratio of 6:4. In actual deployment, due to the uncontrollable nature of the target environment, it is often challenging to obtain a large number of training samples that match the deployment environment [10]. Therefore, this paper considered a mattress with a thickness of 20 cm as an unknown deployment environment and additionally recruited 5 subjects for data collection. For each posture, data were collected for 10 sec, resulting in a total of 168 movements. The data were similarly divided into segments of 5 seconds each, ultimately yielding 1680 entries. Among these, approximately 4 entries per category were used as labeled samples to assist in model training, with the remaining data divided into training and testing sets in a ratio of 6:4.

3   Structured Regularized Domain-Adaptive Clustering Method

3.1   System Framework

The model aims to solve domain adaptation between source and target domains, especially enhancing learning performance on the target domain. It combines data from both domains to boost target-domain learning. Based on AlexNet, it uses convolutional layers for feature extraction and fully connected layers for classification, with Dropout and ReLU for better expression, and Xavier initialization for weight adjustment. The domain adaptation system framework is shown in Fig. 3. For data processing, source and target-domain data are handled by custom data loaders. Source-domain data provide labeled information for supervised learning, while target-domain data generate pseudo-labels via clustering for unsupervised learning. To improve target-domain generalization, consistency loss and clustering loss are combined. During training, the model is optimized using cross-entropy loss for classification, along with target-domain clustering and consistency losses. Clustering methods like K-means, Kernel K-means [11] and Spherical K-means [12] effectively partition target-domain features and generate pseudo-labels.

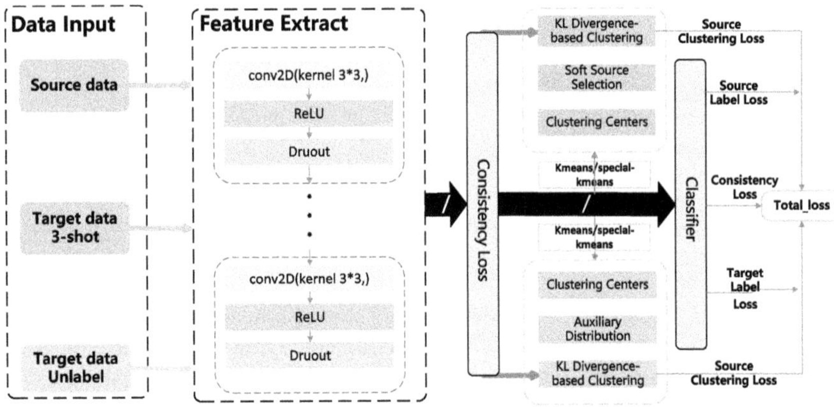

Fig. 3. Framework of the cluster domain adaptation system.

3.2   K-Means Cluster Center Optimization

This paper addresses the issue of insufficient target domain samples and class misalignment in posture recognition tasks within medical monitoring scenarios. It proposes a method based on SRDC to alleviate the overfitting of source domain information inherent in traditional transfer methods. This approach enhances the model's generalization ability and robustness on the target domain, thereby improving the recognition accuracy of cross-domain transfer.

(1.) Cluster Center Optimization: To ensure that the target domain data can be reasonably aligned with the source domain class distribution, this paper first utilizes a deep network to map both source and target domain data into a feature space and initializes cluster centers, with feature vectors represented as $z_i^t = \phi(x_i^t)$. In the training process, to dynamically optimize category division, this paper adopts the following clustering probability allocation formula to gradually adjustthe feature relationship between data samples and cluster centers:

$$p_{i,k} = \frac{\exp\left((1 + \|\mathbf{z}_i - \mu_k\|^2)^{-1}\right)}{\sum_{k'=1}^{K} \exp\left((1 + \|\mathbf{z}_i - \mu_{k'}\|^2)^{-1}\right)} \tag{1}$$

where $p_{i,k}$ denotes the probability that the i-th data sample belongs to the k-th cluster, $\mathbf{z}_i$ is the feature vector of the i-th data sample, and μ_k is the center of the k-th cluster.

(2.) Clustering Alignment: This work aligns target and source-domain category distributions through a novel source-data soft-selection strategy, which reduces the negative impact of category misalignment and stabilizes the learning of domain-invariant features. Experimental results demonstrate that SRDC maintains robustness and generalizability in category-misaligned scenarios while significantly improving recognition accuracy.

Building on the structured similarity assumption, our method further optimizes cluster centers by calculating domain-specific centers during each update and using their means as final adapted cluster centers. This balanced alignment approach prevents the cluster centers from excessively leaning towards either domain or specific categories, ensuring fair representation across both domains:

$$\mu_k^{\text{adapt}} = \frac{1}{2}(\mu_k^s + \mu_k^t) \tag{2}$$

This strategy reduces the feature distribution bias between the source and target domains, ensuring effective clustering of target domain samples even under category misalignment. The clustering process is shown in Fig. 4:

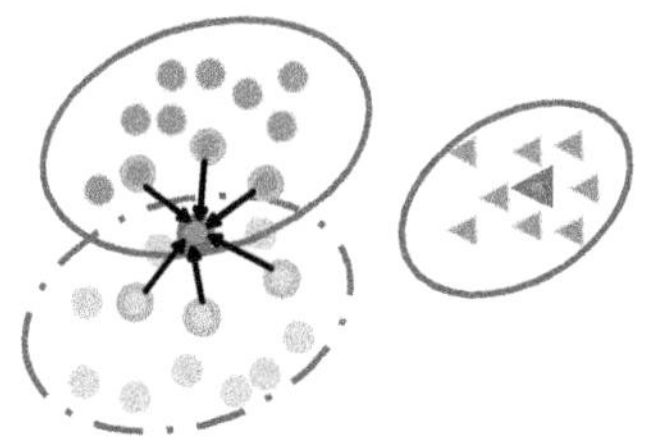

Fig. 4. Mean cluster centers diagram.

3.3   Deep Discriminative Target Clustering

Traditional unsupervised domain adaptation methods usually rely on explicit feature alignment of source domain and target domain. Although this alignment method can improve the transfer effect to a certain extent, it is easy to destroy the inherent discrimination ability of the target data. To solve this problem, SRDC proposes the idea of deep discriminative object clustering. This method uses the feature representation of the target data in the middle layer of the deep neural network to perform discriminative clustering on the target data, and directly reveals the intrinsic category structure of the target data. By clustering the target data in the feature space, SRDC can effectively avoid the structure loss caused by explicit alignment in traditional methods, thereby improving the classification performance of the target data and enhancing the discrimination ability of the target domain data. By minimizing the KL divergence between the predicted label distribution and the auxiliary distribution, combined with feature space clustering, the discriminative structure of the target domain data can be directly revealed. The destruction of the intrinsic discrimination ability of the target by explicit domain alignment is avoided. The objective function of the deep discriminative objective clustering part in the SRDC method consists of two parts: KL divergence and cluster balance constraint. By jointly optimizing these two objectives, SRDC ensures that the target data can achieve discrimination in both feature space and label space, thus enhancing the classification ability of the target data. The specific objective function is formulated as:

$$L_{f \circ \phi_t} = \mathrm{KL}(Q_t \parallel P_t) + \sum_{k=1}^{K} \rho_k^t \log \rho_k^t \tag{3}$$

We then calculate the predicted label distribution of the target data using KL divergence (P_t) and auxiliary label distribution (Q_t) of the target data. By minimizing the KL divergence $\mathrm{KL}(P_t \parallel Q_t)$, the network adjusts the predicted labels to approximate the auxiliary labels, thereby optimizing the target-data classification performance.

$$L(Q \parallel P_k) = \sum_{i} y_i \log \left(\frac{P_k(y_i | x_i)}{Q(y_i | x_i)} \right) \tag{4}$$

where Q_i is the auxiliary label distribution of the target data sample $\mathbf{z}_i^t$, and P_i is the network prediction distribution.

Cluster assignment balance term: The goal of the second part is to ensure that the number of samples in each cluster is as balanced as possible in the clustering process through the cluster assignment balance term ρ_k^i, to avoid the degradation problem that some clusters have too many samples and other clusters have too few samples. The formula is:

$$\rho_k^i = \frac{1}{n_t} \sum_{i=1}^{n_t} q_{i,k}^i \tag{5}$$

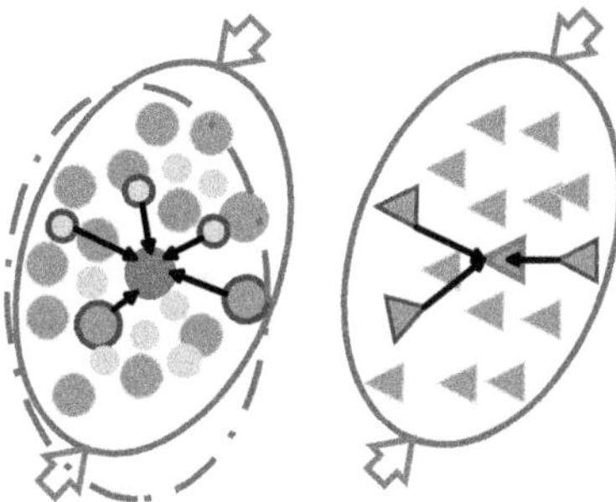

Fig. 5. Soft clustering with KL divergence diagram.

where $q_{i,k}^t$ is the target sample, x_i^t is the probability of belonging to cluster k and n_t is the number of samples in the target domain. The KL divergence-based soft clustering process is shown in Fig. 5.

3.4 Source-Domain Structural Regularization

In semi-supervised domain adaptation tasks, the distribution discrepancy between source and target domains is a key factor contributing to performance degradation in transfer learning. To address this challenge, we propose a ground-truth label-guided structural regularization method. It builds an auxiliary probability distribution using the true labels of source domain data, replacing the source feature based auxiliary distribution used in conventional methods. Specifically, it first creates a class-conditional probability distribution based on the true class labels of source samples, and then integrates this distribution as a regularization term into model training. This ground-truth label-based auxiliary distribution more accurately reflects the data's inherent class structure, achieving structured constraints on the source domain feature space. Compared to traditional methods, this regularization strategy has the following advantages: firstly, it avoids the bias from estimating the auxiliary distribution directly from raw data; secondly, by explicitly leveraging supervised information, it ensures that the regularization process aligns with the classification task's objective; and finally, it effectively retains discriminative structural features related to classification in the data.

$$L^s = -\frac{1}{n_s} \sum_{j=1}^{n_s} \sum_{k=1}^{K} \mathbb{I}[k = y_j^s] \log p_{j,k}^s \tag{6}$$

This method guides the decision boundary of the classifier fusing the source domain labels, causing features of the same category in the target domain to fall into the same region, thereby achieving implicit alignment between the source and the target domains. By constraining the transfer process in the target domain with the supervisory signal from the source domain labels, it ensures that the structural information of the source data can be effectively transferred to the target data, thereby enhancing the discriminative ability of the target data.

3.5   Soft Source Sample Selection

SRDC optimizes the transfer effect of source data on target data through a soft sample selection strategy. This strategy calculates the similarity between source samples and the cluster centers of the target domain and assigns dynamic weights to each source sample. Samples with higher weights make greater contributions to the learning of target data, while those with lower weights contribute less. This mechanism enables the model to focus on source samples that are similar to the feature space of the target data, thereby suppressing the distribution shift between the source and target domains. As a result, it enhances the robustness of cross-domain transfer and improves the classification capability in the target domain.

This paper calculates the weights of the source samples based on the cosine similarity between the source samples and the target cluster centers. The formula for weight calculation is as follows:

$$w_j^s = \frac{1}{2} \left(1 + \frac{\mu_{y_j^s}^t \cdot z_j^s}{\|\mu_{y_j^s}^t\| \|z_j^s\|} \right) \in [0, 1] \tag{7}$$

where $\mu_{y_j^s}^t$ is the clustering center of the target domain, z_j^s is the feature representation of the source sample, $\|.\|$ table demonstration number, which is used to calculate the cosine similarity between the source sample and the target cluster center. By adjusting the weights of the source domain supervision loss, the contribution of source samples to the target data is enhanced.

$$L_{f \circ \phi_s} = -\frac{1}{n_s} \sum_{j=1}^{n_s} w_j^s \sum_{k=1}^{K} I[k = y_j^s] \log p_{j,k}^s \tag{8}$$

where $p_{j,k}^s$ is the prediction probability of the source sample j on class k and w_j^s is the corresponding weight. The process of soft selection of source domain data is shown in Fig. 6.

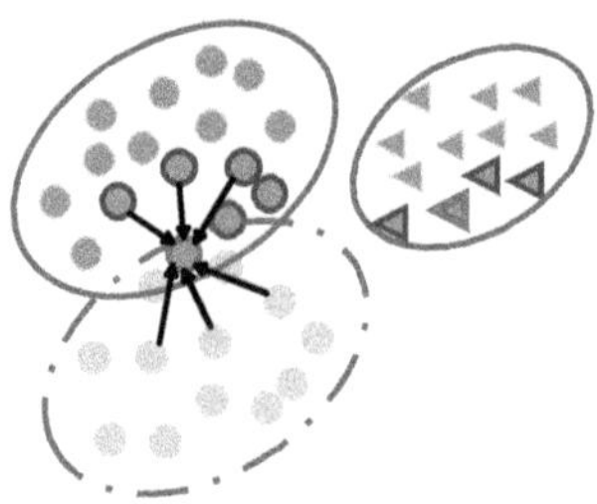

Fig. 6. Soft selection of source domain data diagram.

4 Results and Analysis

Initial data preprocessing involves: A proportion of 0.03 of the target domain samples is used as labeled data to assist model training, and the remaining data are divided into training and testing sets in a 6:4 ratio. In the experiments, the training parameters are set as follows: batch size is 16, the total number of epochs is 200, the initial learning rate (lr) is 0.001 and other parameters include momentum (0.9) and weight decay (1×10^{-4})t, which represents the optimal value derived from multiple independent experimental trials. the K-means clustering parameter K (number of clusters) was set to 12, corresponding to the number of posture categories in our classification system (Table 1).

Table 1. Comparison of structural regularization cluster field adaptation experiments.

Method	Full-Src	Full-tar	NoSupine-tar	NoProne-tar	NoLeft-tar	NoRight-tar	Avg. Mis
MCD	95.25	85.49	77.39	83.76	86.48	80.25	81.97
CDAD [13]	93.42	50.41	56.60	72.17	57.51	56.53	60.70
DEC	97.92	77.10	76.87	80.11	84.12	79.73	80.21
SRDC	98.31	82.72	86.48	81.26	86.27	82.78	84.20
SRDC-S	98.54	82.42	81.13	84.72	89.01	82.57	84.36

From the experimental results, it can be observed that due to the significant difference in mattress thickness between the source and the target domains, the accuracy of all transfer methods on the target domain is lower than that on the source domain. When the source domain data is complete, all methods can achieve a high accuracy rate (over 95%). However, in the presence of distribution shifts or class misalignment in the target domain, there are noticeable differences in the recognition effects of different methods.

Among different transfer learning methods, the performance of CDAD declines most significantly, with an average accuracy of only 60.7% under class misalignment, indicating its weaker adaptability to class missing scenarios. The DEC method performs well on the complete target domain and shows a significant improvement in accuracy under class misalignment, which verifies the effectiveness of the dynamic optimization of cluster centers. When the target domain experiences class missing, the classification recognition ability of MCD is significantly reduced, which is analyzed to be due to the blurring of the model's decision boundary, affecting the performance. This indicates that MCD relies on the matching of the source domain class distribution and struggles to adapt to misaligned target domain classes (Fig. 7).

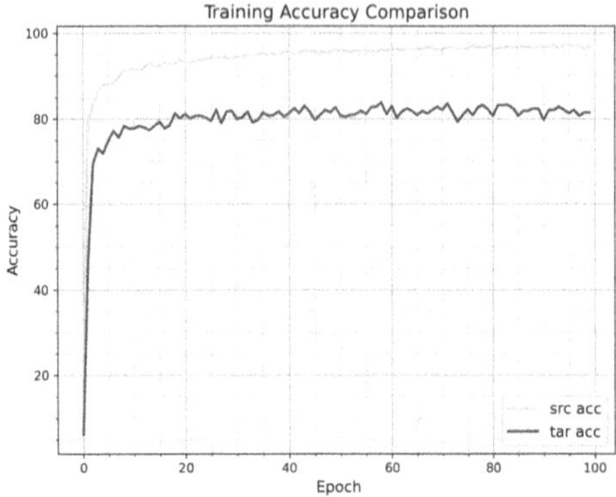

Fig. 7. SRDC-S NoProne accuracy curve.

In contrast, the SRDC method, through clustering optimization and source domain regularization strategies, can more robustly handle class missing issues and performs better on the target domain. This is because SRDC primarily relies on the optimization of cluster centers, enhancing the clustering structure in the feature space, allowing target domain data to effectively align with source domain features even under misaligned classes, while maintaining high recognition accuracy.

Observing the accuracy curve of SRDC-S for lying posture, it is evident that the method's accuracy increases rapidly. After 25 epochs of training, it essentially reaches a high level of accuracy and maintains this level thereafter. This indicates that the method possesses an efficient clustering feature optimization mechanism, which is capable of quickly capturing the inherent class structure of the target domain data and achieving effective model transfer.

5   Conclusion

This paper constructs two datasets of lying posture based on array piezoelectric sensors under two different deployment environments. On this basis, it investigates the problem of lying posture recognition under semi-supervised field category misalignment scenarios and compares methods based on maximizing class differences and clustering through experiments. Ultimately, the clustering-based SRDC-S method demonstrates stronger recognition capabilities under class misalignment. Even when some class samples are missing in the target domain, the average accuracy is as high as 84.36%, while maintaining good recognition performance in the source domain. Although this is model transfer under specific scenarios, it provides valuable reference for subsequent research. In future research, we plan to conduct transfer learning studies under unsupervised conditions of data categories to more comprehensively monitor lying posture states.

References

1. Heydarzadeh, M., Nourani, M., Ostadabbas, S.: In-bed posture classification using deep autoencoders. In: 38th Annual International Conference of the IEEE Engineering in Medicine and Biology Society (EMBC). IEEE **2016**, 3839–3842 (2016)
2. Lindgren, M., Unosson, M., Fredrikson, M., Ek, A.-C.: Immobility–a major risk factor for development of pressure ulcers among adult hospitalized patients: a prospective study. Scand. J. Caring Sci. **18**(1), 57–64 (2004)
3. Xu, X., Lin, F., Wang, A., Song, C., Hu, Y., Xu, W.: On-bed sleep posture recognition based on body-earth mover's distance. In: IEEE Biomedical Circuits and Systems Conference (BioCAS). IEEE **2015**, 1–4 (2015)
4. Wang, M., Lin, Y., Jiang, H., Sun, Y.: Tespda-sei: Tensor embedding substructure preserving domain adaptation for specific emitter identification. Phys. Commun. **57**, 101973 (2023)
5. Fu, X., Peng, Y., Liu, Y., Lin, Y., Gui, G., Gacanin, H., Adachi, F.: Semisupervised specific emitter identification method using metric-adversarial training. IEEE Internet Things J. **10**(12), 10778–10789 (2023)
6. Saito,K., Watanabe, K., Ushiku, Y., Harada, T.: Maximum classifier discrepancy for unsupervised domain adaptation. In: Proceedings of the IEEE conference on computer vision and pattern recognition, pp. 3723–3732 (2018)
7. Tang, H., Chen, K., Jia, K.: Unsupervised domain adaptation via structurally regularized deep clustering. In: Proceedings of the IEEE/CVF Conference on Computer Vision and Pattern Recognition, pp. 8725–8735 (2020)
8. Banerjee, A., Merugu, S., Dhillon, I. S., Ghosh, J.: Clustering with bregman divergences. J. Mach. Learn. Res. **6**, 1705–1749 (2005)
9. Jiao, X., Wang, X., Wang, X., Liu, Z.: Noncontact sleep monitoring system under a mattress. IEEE access **9**, 111203–111213 (2021)
10. Feng, Z., Zha, H., Xu, C., He, Y., Lin, Y.: Fcgcn: Feature correlation graph convolution network for few-shot individual identification. IEEE Trans. Consum. Electron. **70**(1), 2848–2860 (2023)
11. Girolami, M.: Mercer kernel-based clustering in feature space. IEEE Trans. Neural Networks **13**(3), 780–784 (2002)
12. Dhillon, I.S., Modha, D.S.: Concept decompositions for large sparse text data using clustering. Mach. Learn. **42**, 143–175 (2001)
13. Long, M., Cao, Z., Wang, J., Jordan, M. I.: Conditional adversarial domain adaptation. Adv. Neural Inf. Process. Syst. **31** (2018)

Mobile Crowdsensing

Adaptive Signal Modulation Classification During Testing

Zewen Wu, Wenlong Fan, Liang Kou, and Meiyu Wang[✉]

Hangzhou Dianzi University, Hangzhou 310018, Zhejiang, China
{232270037,kouliang,wangmeiyu}@hdu.edu.cn

Abstract. Automatic modulation classification (AMC) is a fundamental task in modern wireless communication systems, crucial for enabling adaptive spectrum management and intelligent signal processing. This paper investigates the performance enhancement of AMC through the integration of ResNet and advanced test-time adaptation (TTA) techniques. We first demonstrate the superiority of ResNet over conventional CNNs on two benchmark datasets, RML2016.10A and RML2018.01A, especially under low SNR conditions. To further improve robustness against distribution shifts in practical deployments, we propose two novel TTA methods: Test-Time Adaptation with Temperature Scaling (TATS) and Test-Time Adaptation with Self-Distillation (TASD). These methods adaptively refine the model predictions during inference by optimizing batch normalization parameters, without requiring labeled target data or structural changes to the pretrained model. Experimental results show that TATS and TASD consistently outperform mainstream TTA approaches, achieving significant accuracy gains across varying SNR levels. Our work highlights the potential of combining deep residual learning with adaptive inference strategies to build more resilient AMC systems suitable for real-world wireless environments.

Keywords: Modulation classification · Deep learning · ResNet · Test-time adaptation

1 Introduction

Automatic modulation classification (AMC) is a crucial technology in modern wireless communication systems. It supports key functions like adaptive spectrum access, interference detection, and intelligent signal processing [1]. With the wide application of cognitive radio, drone communication, and military communication, there is a growing demand for automatic modulation classification methods with high accuracy and robustness [2]. However, current automatic modulation classification technology faces several challenges: Complex and dynamic radio environment. Issues such as multipath fading, hardware non-idealities, and dynamic noise interference often degrade signal quality [3]. In low SNR conditions, these problems pose a serious challenge to system performance:

C. Xu et al. (Eds.): MobiMedia 2025, LNICST 670, pp. 235–247, 2026.
https://doi.org/10.1007/978-3-032-16823-8_17

Limited flexibility of traditional methods: Traditional automatic modulation classification approaches predominantly depend on handcrafted feature extraction and statistical modeling techniques. While these methods have demonstrated effectiveness under controlled or static channel conditions, they inherently lack the flexibility and robustness required to adapt to the dynamic and complex wireless communication environments encountered in real-world applications. The manual design of features is often labor-intensive and prone to suboptimal performance when channel characteristics change, such as varying multipath fading, Doppler shifts, or interference patterns. Consequently, these methods exhibit limited generalization capability, resulting in degraded classification accuracy when applied to unseen or altered channel conditions [4]. Distribution shift problem in deep learning methods: Deep learning-based AMC approaches have achieved substantial advancements by automatically learning hierarchical and discriminative features directly from raw signal data. Nevertheless, a critical challenge impeding their practical deployment lies in the discrepancy—or distribution shift—between training and testing data domains. Typically, deep models are trained on datasets collected under idealized or specific channel conditions that may not adequately represent the diversity and variability encountered in operational environments. When deployed, these models face channel effects, noise levels, hardware imperfections, and device-specific factors that deviate significantly from their training distributions. This domain mismatch often leads to a pronounced decline in model generalization ability and a consequent sharp drop in classification performance. Addressing this distribution shift is essential to ensure that deep AMC models maintain high accuracy and reliability across diverse and time-varying wireless scenarios [5].

To address the challenges above, we propose test-time adaptation (TTA) strategies with improvements in both the source and target domains:

(1) Residual networks, with their skip connections, effectively mitigate the gradient vanishing problem in deep networks. They enhance deep feature extraction and have become a powerful structure in modulation classification. ResNet excels at capturing complex modulation patterns, significantly improving classification accuracy across different SNR levels.

(2) We introduce TTA into ResNet-based modulation classification models to enhance their adaptability and robustness under varying SNR conditions. Specifically, we propose two novel methods: TATS (TTA with Temperature Scaling) and TASD (TTA with Self-Distillation). Notably, these methods do not require modifying the pre-trained model structure. Instead, they optimize BN layer parameters during inference, making them highly practical and deployable.

We systematically evaluate our methods on the RML2016.10A [6] modulation classification benchmark dataset and the RML2018.01A dataset [7]. The results show that across various SNR conditions, especially in low-SNR scenarios, the ResNet model combined with TATS and TASD significantly outperforms traditional TTA methods in classification accuracy and prediction stability. This confirms the effective integration of deep residual learning with TTA strategies, showing great potential for building robust and practical automatic modulation classification systems.

2 Related Work

2.1 Domain Generalization

Domain generalization (DG) aims to enhance model robustness against domain shifts by training on multiple source domains, thereby enabling models to generalize effectively to previously unseen target domains. In AMC, domain shift remains a critical issue, as variations in signal propagation conditions, hardware differences, and environmental noise substantially degrade model performance [8]. Unlike domain adaptation (DA), which assumes access to unlabeled target domain data during training, DG strictly relies on source domain data without prior exposure to the target environment. This fundamental characteristic renders DG particularly suitable for real-world AMC applications where obtaining target domain data is impractical due to security constraints, dynamic spectrum conditions, or operational limitations [9].

Early DG methodologies predominantly focused on feature alignment techniques, including adversarial domain alignment, contrastive learning, and the extraction of domain-invariant features. For example, MixStyle, a plug-and-play module, improves DG by mixing feature statistics at the batch level, thereby synthesizing representations of unseen domains within the feature space. This approach effectively increases feature diversity without requiring additional labeled data or incurring increased model complexity, demonstrating its efficacy across various DG scenarios [10]. Complementary to this, self-supervised learning strategies have been employed to strengthen feature extraction robustness. Self-supervised pretext tasks such as denoising autoencoders, rotation prediction, and solving jigsaw puzzles encourage models to learn more generalizable representations. In medical image segmentation, the Denoising Y-Net (DeY-Net) framework exemplifies this approach by integrating denoising training to extract domain-invariant features, leading to improved cross-domain generalization [11]. Inspired by these advances, self-supervised feature refinement techniques have recently been investigated within AMC to counteract feature degradation caused by environmental variability. Furthermore, transformer-based domain generalization (DG) methods have gained attention due to their global attention mechanisms, which capture long-range dependencies and reduce sensitivity to local domain shifts. Gao et al. [12] applied adversarial domain-generalized transformers to cross-corpus speech emotion recognition, while Sanyal et al. [13] introduced domain-specificity inducing transformers for source-free adaptation. Qiao et al. [8] further demonstrated the effectiveness of transformers in robust multi-modal object recognition. Compared to traditional convolutional neural networks, transformers can better model global context, improving generalization across domains. Recent studies demonstrate that combining convolutional inductive biases with transformer-based feature extractors achieves superior DG performance in signal classification tasks. This hybrid architecture effectively balances local feature robustness and global context awareness, rendering it particularly advantageous in addressing challenges posed by electromagnetic interference and dynamically varying spectral environments [11].

Despite these advancements, DG methods face intrinsic limitations when applied to complex, real-world scenarios. First, the generalization capability of DG models is highly contingent upon the diversity and representativeness of the source domains utilized during training [10]. Insufficient variability in the training data may lead to learned features that poorly generalize to target domains exhibiting significant distributional shifts, causing performance degradation in practical deployments. Second, many DG frameworks depend on sophisticated optimization techniques, such as episodic training and adversarial domain augmentation, which, while effective in enhancing generalization, introduce considerable computational overhead [9].

Additionally, DG approaches typically lack mechanisms for dynamic model adaptation during inference, rendering them less effective in coping with extreme domain shifts such as severe signal attenuation, spectral fluctuations, or hardware-induced distortions [11]. Since these methods are built upon predefined domain-invariant properties learned during training, they may fail to adapt when confronted with unforeseen conditions, resulting in substantial drops in classification accuracy. Consequently, in highly dynamic and unpredictable environments, exclusive reliance on DG may be inadequate for maintaining model stability and adaptability.

2.2 Test-Time Adaptation

AMC, the problem of covariate shift is pervasive and fundamentally challenging. Covariate shift refers to the scenario where the distribution of input features varies between the training and testing phases, while the distribution of the output labels remains consistent [14]. In practical wireless communication systems, this phenomenon frequently arises due to a multitude of factors, including environmental noise fluctuations, varying signal sampling conditions, and hardware-induced inconsistencies [15]. These variations lead to significant discrepancies in the statistical properties of the received signals, which can severely undermine the performance and generalization capability of AMC models trained under ideal or controlled conditions [16].

To effectively mitigate the adverse effects of covariate shift, TTA methods have been proposed as a dynamic solution [17]. Unlike traditional training paradigms that fix model parameters prior to deployment, TTA methods adapt the model during the inference stage by utilizing unlabeled test data. This approach enables the model to dynamically recalibrate and better align with the feature distribution of the current test domain, thereby enhancing both generalization and robustness in real-world operational environments [18].

A foundational TTA technique involves the recalibration of batch normalization (BN) layer statistics [19]. Since BN layers maintain running estimates of feature mean and variance, updating these statistics based on test samples allows the model to adapt to domain-specific distribution shifts. Building on this, the Tent method [20] introduces an adaptive strategy grounded in the principle of minimum entropy. Tent selectively optimizes only the scaling and shifting parameters of BN layers, minimizing the output entropy of the model predictions on test data to encourage confident and consistent classification. This lightweight adaptation effectively improves model robustness without modifying the overall network architecture.

Another prominent TTA approach is pseudo-labeling, which leverages high-confidence predictions as surrogate labels to enable self-supervised fine-tuning of the model on unlabeled test data [21]. By iteratively refining the model with these pseudo-labels, the system can gradually adapt to the specific characteristics of the current domain. The Enhanced Adaptive Tent Algorithm (EATA) [22] further improves upon Tent by integrating a sample selection mechanism to filter reliable test instances and a parameter regularization strategy to balance adaptation speed with model stability. This combination mitigates the risk of error accumulation and preserves the integrity of the model during test-time updates.

These TTA strategies hold particular promise for AMC tasks, where low SNR conditions and channel variability present substantial challenges. The ability to adapt in situ to diverse channel impairments and device heterogeneity is crucial for maintaining high classification accuracy. However, it is important to note that most existing TTA research has been primarily focused on image-based applications, such as object recognition and semantic segmentation. Consequently, the direct application and evaluation of these methods in the domain of automatic modulation classification remain relatively underexplored.

Developing and tailoring efficient TTA techniques specifically for communication signals is therefore of great significance. Such advancements can substantially enhance the robustness and adaptability of modulation classifiers across a wide range of wireless environments and hardware platforms. By enabling models to self-adjust in response to real-time signal variations, TTA methods offer a practical and scalable approach to overcoming the limitations imposed by domain shifts, ultimately contributing to more reliable and intelligent wireless communication systems..

3 Proposed Method

3.1 The Structure of Neural Networks

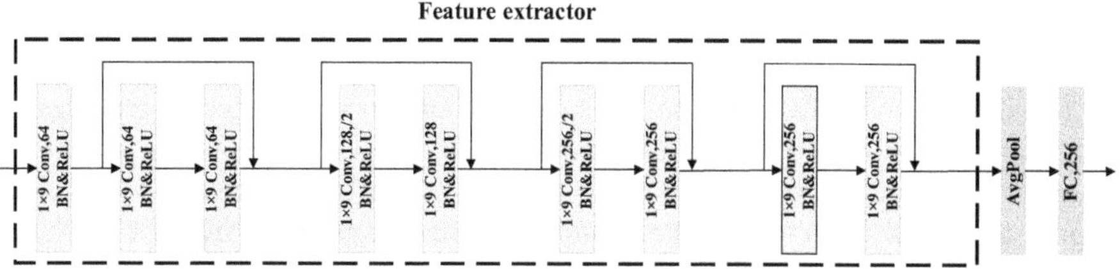

Fig. 1. Structure of the ResNet-based feature extractor. The architecture consists of sequential residual blocks composed of 1D convolutional layers and batch normalization, enabling deep feature learning from raw modulation signals. The final representations are passed through an average pooling layer and a fully connected layer (FC256) to obtain compact and discriminative features for classification and adaptation.

The backbone of our automatic modulation classification model is a tailored ResNet architecture specifically designed for one-dimensional signal inputs. The network consists of a series of convolutional blocks that progressively extract and abstract features from the input signal, while maintaining efficient gradient propagation through residual connections (Fig. 1).

The architecture begins with four sequential convolutional layers, each employing a kernel size of 1×9 to capture temporal dependencies in the input signal. The first three convolutional layers have 64 filters each, and are followed by batch normalization and ReLU activation functions to stabilize training and introduce non-linearity. The fourth convolutional layer increases the number of filters to 128 and applies a stride of 2, effectively performing downsampling to reduce the temporal dimension while enhancing feature richness.

Following this, the network further processes the data through two convolutional layers with 128 and 256 filters respectively, the latter again using a stride of 2 for further downsampling. Subsequently, the network includes three additional convolutional layers with 256 filters each, allowing deeper feature extraction at a higher level of abstraction. Each convolutional layer is consistently followed by batch normalization and ReLU activation to maintain stable and efficient learning.

After the convolutional stages, a global average pooling layer is applied to aggregate temporal features into a fixed-size representation, which is then fed into a fully connected layer with 256 units. This final layer produces the feature embedding used for classification.

This ResNet design leverages the benefits of residual learning by alleviating gradient vanishing issues, enabling the training of deeper networks that effectively capture complex modulation patterns. The combination of strided convolutions for downsampling and batch normalization for feature standardization contributes to robust and discriminative feature learning, which is critical for achieving high accuracy in AMC tasks under varying signal conditions.

3.2 TTA Based on Temperature Scaling and Self-Knowledge Distillation

In this study, we propose an enhanced Test-Time Adaptation (TTA) framework inspired by Tent, with a primary focus on optimizing target domain adaptation through two mechanisms: TATS and TASD. To ensure both stability and efficiency, we update only the affine parameters (γ and β) in the BN layers, which are linear (scaling and shifting) and low-dimensional (channel-wise). The process consists of two steps: normalization and transformation. First, the input x is normalized as $\bar{x} = (x - \mu)/\sigma$, where μ and σ are dynamically estimated from the test batch. Next, the affine transformation produces the output $x' = \gamma\bar{x} + \beta$. Both γ and β are optimized via backpropagation from the respective loss functions of TATS and TASD, enabling effective adaptation to distribution shifts and noise interference without altering the core model weights. Specifically, the optimization follows gradient descent updates as follows:

$$\gamma \leftarrow \gamma - \eta\frac{\partial\mathcal{L}}{\partial\gamma}, \ \beta \leftarrow \beta - \eta\frac{\partial\mathcal{L}}{\partial\beta} \tag{1}$$

Entropy minimization loss is a simple yet effective unsupervised loss that encourages model confidence to facilitate learning from data. The entropy minimization loss can be expressed as:

$$\mathcal{L} = -\frac{1}{N}\sum_{i=1}^{N}\sum_{j=1}^{C} p_{ij}\log(p_{ij}) \tag{2}$$

During the fine-tuning process, high-confidence samples with high-probability predictions typically contribute little to the weight updates, as the gradients derived from them are relatively small. This occurs because such samples often have sharp logit distributions, which are indicative of the model's overconfidence in its predictions. Overconfident predictions can lead to suboptimal learning, as the model becomes less sensitive to further refinements or corrections from these samples (Fig. 2).

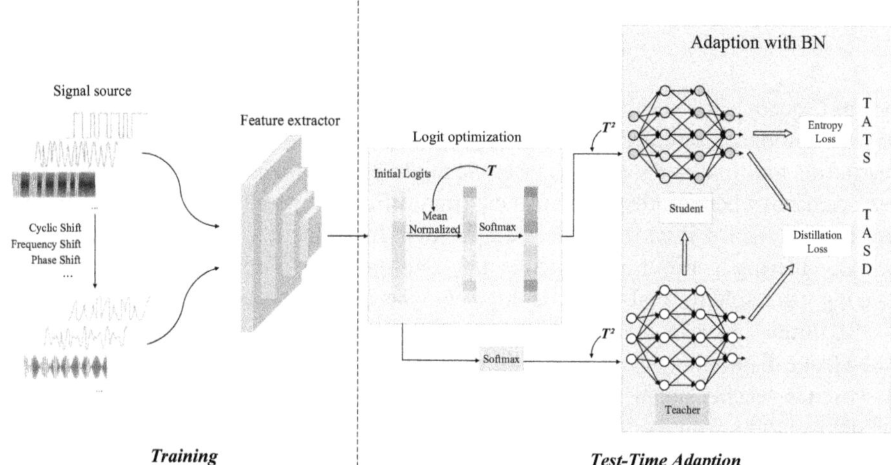

Fig. 2. Overall architecture of the proposed test-time adaptive modulation recognition framework. The ResNet-based feature extractor processes distorted input signals, producing logits that are normalized and used for adaptation. During inference, two strategies are applied: TATS uses temperature scaling with entropy loss to reduce overconfidence, while TASD applies self-distillation to align predictions, both updating only BN parameters for lightweight adaptation.

To address this challenge, we propose the use of temperature scaling, a technique that helps in reducing the sharpness of the logit distributions without altering the overall model predictions. This approach preserves the semantic information embedded in the predictions, ensuring that the model's output remains consistent with the true labels. By softening the logits, temperature scaling allows the model to assign relatively larger losses to high-confidence samples. This adjustment, in turn, facilitates faster learning by encouraging the model to focus more on fine-tuning and improving its understanding of these samples, rather than being locked into already-confident predictions. By making the high-confidence samples more informative and adaptable, temperature scaling helps in mitigating overfitting and enhances the model's ability to generalize [23]. Based on this principle, we introduce the TATS method, which efficiently improves model performance during inference without requiring changes to the core network architecture. Here, we present the TATS method:

$$\hat{z}_{ij} = \frac{z_{ij} - \mu_j}{T \cdot \sigma_j}, T = 2\sigma \tag{3}$$

$$p_{ij} = \frac{\exp(\hat{z}_{ij})}{\sum_{j=1}^{C} \exp(\hat{z}_{ij})} \tag{4}$$

where μ and σ represent the mean and standard deviation of the logits, respectively, and T is the temperature parameter. By applying the Softmax function to the scaled logits, we normalize them to obtain the predicted probabilities for each class. The loss function is defined as follows:

$$\mathcal{L} = -\frac{1}{N} \sum_{i=1}^{N} \sum_{j=1}^{C} p_{ij} \log(p_{ij}) \cdot T^2 \tag{5}$$

where C denotes the number of classes. This approach increases the model's sensitivity to low-confidence samples without changing its predictions. Maintaining the ability to learn from multiple categories enhances the model's generalization, especially in unseen test scenarios where the distribution of data may differ. Temperature scaling, applied only during inference, softens the model's output logits, enabling it to adapt to new categories without altering its pre-trained architecture. This approach is computationally efficient, making it suitable for real-world deployment where resources are limited.

To further improve generalization during test-time adaptation, we incorporate a self-knowledge distillation mechanism. This approach leverages the model's own predictions as a pseudo-teacher signal, facilitating consistency-based learning that aligns the adapted model's outputs with its original predictions. Specifically, by halting the gradient flow through the teacher predictions p_{ij}^{initial}, the loss function encourages the temperature-scaled student predictions to approximate these fixed teacher outputs. This strategy effectively enforces output consistency and stabilizes the adaptation process, preventing drastic deviations from the pretrained model's learned knowledge. The proposed TASD method, along with its corresponding loss function, is formally defined as follows:

$$\mathcal{L} = -\frac{1}{N} \sum_{i=1}^{N} \sum_{j=1}^{C} p_{ij}^{\text{initial}} \log(p_{ij}) \cdot T^2 \tag{6}$$

To prevent overconfidence during adaptation, the model uses its own prior predictions as stabilizing targets. By aligning its outputs with these prior distributions, the model reduces the risk of overfitting to noisy or uncertain test data, thereby maintaining more reliable and consistent predictions. This self-guided approach ensures the model adapts effectively without diverging from its learned knowledge.

4 Experiments

In this section, we conduct a comprehensive evaluation of the proposed methods on two widely-used AMC benchmark datasets: RML2016.10A and RML2018.01A. We first compare the baseline performance of conventional CNN and ResNet without any TTA to highlight the advantage of deeper residual architectures. Subsequently, we analyze the effectiveness of several TTA strategies, including mainstream methods such as BN statistics recalibration, Tent, PL, and EATA, alongside our proposed methods—TATS and TASD. The goal is to demonstrate how TTA techniques enhance the model's robustness and accuracy across varying SNR conditions.

4.1   Baseline Comparison Between CNN and ResNet

Tables 1 and 2 summarize the classification accuracies of CNN and ResNet models without TTA on the RML2016.10A and RML2018.01A datasets, respectively. Across both datasets, ResNet consistently outperforms CNN under all tested SNR levels, confirming the superiority of residual learning in capturing complex modulation features.

On the RML2016.10A dataset (Table 1), ResNet achieves noticeable gains, especially under challenging low-SNR conditions. For instance, at 6 dB SNR, ResNet improves accuracy by approximately 1.85% over CNN (75.036% vs. 73.182%), and at 0 dB, the margin remains evident (32.100% vs. 30.445%). Similarly, on the RML2018.01A dataset (Table 2), ResNet achieves higher accuracy across all SNRs, with a maximum gain of 2.59% at 8 dB (60.780% vs. 58.192%).

These results validate that ResNet's skip connections effectively alleviate gradient vanishing and enable deeper feature extraction, thereby enhancing modulation classification performance under diverse channel conditions.

Table 1. Accuracy (%) Comparison on RML2016.10A between CNN and ResNet.

SNR (dB)	CNN	ResNet
14	76.773	77.755
12	76.691	77.400
10	76.273	76.909
8	75.864	76.400
6	73.182	75.036
4	64.491	65.109
2	44.909	46.010
0	30.445	32.100

Table 2. Accuracy (%) Comparison on RML2018.01A between CNN and ResNet.

SNR (dB)	CNN	ResNet
14	96.702	96.981
12	95.477	95.500
10	86.759	87.156
8	58.192	60.780
6	30.276	31.563
4	12.820	13.024
2	9.117	9.536
0	5.350	5.651

4.2 Comparison of Different Test-Time Adaptation Methods

Tables 3 and 4 report the performance of several mainstream test-time adaptation (TTA) methods applied to the ResNet backbone on the RML2016.10A and RML2018.01A datasets. Compared methods include batch normalization (BN) statistics recalibration, Tent (entropy minimization), pseudo-labeling (PL), EATA (efficient entropy-based adaptation), and our proposed TATS and TASD. These baseline methods represent the dominant paradigms in current TTA research and provide a strong comparative foundation. While more recent TTA strategies exist, our choice of mainstream, well-recognized methods ensures a fair and broadly accepted benchmark.

Despite the apparent simplicity of TATS and TASD, they demonstrate consistently superior or competitive performance across a wide range of SNR conditions. On the RML2016.10A dataset (Table 3), both methods outperform all baselines at most SNR levels. For instance, at 0 dB SNR—a particularly challenging condition—TATS and TASD achieve 62.60% and 62.70% accuracy, respectively, surpassing Tent (61.70%) and BN (61.50%). The performance gain is even more evident at low-to-medium SNRs (2–10 dB), where both methods maintain stable improvements.

On the more challenging RML2018.01A dataset (Table 4), similar trends are observed. At 4 dB SNR, TATS attains 50.47% accuracy, outperforming BN (44.61%) and Tent (48.90%) by a significant margin. TASD also exhibits competitive results under the same conditions. These improvements highlight the robustness of our methods in generalizing across different datasets and distribution shifts.

Table 3. Comparison (%) of TTA methods and mainstream methods on RML2016.10A.

SNR (dB)	BN	Tent	PL	EATA	TATS	TASD
14	77.264	77.636	77.536	77.610	78.010	77.900
12	76.200	76.746	76.773	76.700	77.155	76.927
10	76.073	76.200	76.164	76.118	77.720	77.510
8	76.809	76.710	76.010	76.110	77.127	77.073
6	75.864	75.582	75.255	75.200	76.664	76.727
4	75.710	75.418	75.455	75.373	76.573	76.582
2	70.210	70.800	70.700	70.700	72.164	72.101
0	61.500	61.700	61.410	61.410	62.600	62.701

Table 4. Comparison (%) of TTA methods and mainstream methods on RML2018.01A.

SNR (dB)	BN	Tent	PL	EATA	TATS	TASD
14	96.936	97.126	97.148	97.146	97.200	97.204
12	96.267	96.230	96.254	96.253	96.265	96.266
10	92.281	91.380	91.249	91.244	91.457	91.434

(continued)

Table 4. (*continued*)

SNR (dB)	BN	Tent	PL	EATA	TATS	TASD
8	81.328	80.882	80.227	80.226	81.359	81.417
6	65.210	65.450	64.507	64.558	66.290	66.554
4	44.610	48.901	44.241	46.300	50.473	49.541
2	24.675	25.739	24.500	25.277	27.130	26.413
0	16.015	16.710	16.128	16.012	17.015	16.720

The advantages of TATS and TASD can be attributed to their distinct adaptation mechanisms. TATS employs temperature scaling to reduce logit sharpness, mitigating model overconfidence and enabling better learning from low-confidence samples. TASD introduces a self-distillation framework, which aligns the model's prediction with its own softened output, enhancing consistency without requiring external supervision. Notably, both methods only update BN parameters during inference, ensuring lightweight and efficient adaptation without altering model architecture or requiring labeled target data.

In summary, although TATS and TASD may not appear structurally novel, their effectiveness lies in the practical design and consistent performance across SNR conditions. Their ability to improve test-time robustness and generalization under severe noise validates their value as strong TTA solutions for real-world modulation recognition tasks.

5 Conclusion

In this paper, we conducted a thorough evaluation of automatic modulation classification performance using ResNet and CNN architectures, highlighting the superiority of residual networks in capturing complex signal features across varying SNR conditions. To address the challenge of distribution shifts encountered during deployment, we proposed two novel test-time adaptation methods: TATS and TASD which dynamically optimize the model during inference without modifying the core network parameters. Experimental results on the RML2016.10A and RML2018.01A datasets demonstrated that our methods consistently outperform traditional TTA techniques, particularly under low-SNR scenarios where signal degradation is severe. These improvements confirm the effectiveness of integrating temperature scaling and self-knowledge distillation mechanisms for robust modulation classification. Future work will focus on extending these adaptive strategies to more diverse real-world communication scenarios and exploring their synergy with other deep learning architectures.

References

1. Huynh-The, T., Pham, Q.V., Nguyen, T.V., et al.: Automatic modulation classification: a deep architecture survey. IEEE Access **9**, 142950–142971 (2021)
2. Dong, B., Liu, Y., Gui, G., et al.: A lightweight decentralized-learning-based automatic modulation classification method for resource-constrained edge devices. IEEE Internet Things J. **9**(24), 24708–24720 (2022)

3. De Alwis, C., Kalla, A., Pham, Q.V., et al.: Survey on 6G frontiers: trends, applications, requirements, technologies and future research. IEEE Open J. Commun. Soc. **2**, 836–886 (2021)
4. Swami, A., Sadler, B.M.: Hierarchical digital modulation classification using cumulants. IEEE Trans. Commun. **48**(3), 416–429 (2000)
5. Lin, Y., Zhao, H., Ma, X., et al.: Adversarial attacks in modulation recognition with convolutional neural networks. IEEE Trans. Reliab. **70**(1), 389–401 (2020)
6. O'Shea, T.J., West, N.: Radio machine learning dataset generation with GNU radio. In: Proceedings of the GNU Radio Conference, vol. 1, no. 1 (2016)
7. O'Shea, T.J., Roy, T., Clancy, T.C.: Over-the-air deep learning based radio signal classification. IEEE J. Sel. Top. Signal Process. **12**(1), 168–179 (2018)
8. Qiao, Y., Li, K., Lin, J., et al.: Robust domain generalization for multi-modal object recognition. In: 2024 5th International Conference on Artificial Intelligence and Electromechanical Automation (AIEA), pp. 392–397. IEEE (2024)
9. Zhou, Q., Zhang, K. Y., Yao, T., et al.: Test-time domain generalization for face anti-spoofing. In: Proceedings of the IEEE/CVF Conference on Computer Vision and Pattern Recognition, pp. 175–187 (2024)
10. Fu, J., Zhong, Y., Yang, F.: Adversarial domain generalization with mixstyle. In: 2022 International Conference on Advanced Robotics and Mechatronics (ICARM), pp. 379–385. IEEE (2022)
11. Wen, R., Yuan, H., Ni, D., et al.: From denoising training to test-time adaptation: Enhancing domain generalization for medical image segmentation. In: Proceedings of the IEEE/CVF Winter Conference on Applications of Computer Vision, pp. 464–474 (2024)
12. Gao, Y., Wang, L., Liu, J., Dang, J., Okada, S.: Adversarial domain generalized transformer for cross-corpus speech emotion recognition. IEEE Trans. Affect. Comput. **15**(2), 697–708 (2024)
13. Sanyal, S., Asokan, A.R., Bhambri, S., Kulkarni, A., Kundu, J.N., Babu, R.V.: Domain-specificity inducing transformers for source-free domain adaptation. In: Proceedings of the IEEE/CVF International Conference on Computer Vision (ICCV), pp. 18882–18891 (2023)
14. Hamidi-Rad, S., Jain, S.: Mcformer: a transformer based deep neural network for automatic modulation classification. In: 2021 IEEE Global Communications Conference (GLOBECOM), pp. 1–6 (2021)
15. Hao, X., Feng, Z., Yang, S., Wang, M., Jiao, L.: Automatic modulation classification via meta-learning. IEEE Internet Things J. **10**(14), 12276–12292 (2023)
16. Nie, J., Zhang, Y., He, Z., Chen, S., Gong, S., Zhang, W.: Deep hierarchical network for automatic modulation classification. IEEE Access **7**, 94604–94613 (2019)
17. Awais, M., Iqbal, M.T.B., Bae, S.-H.: Revisiting internal covariate shift for batch normalization. IEEE Trans. Neural Netw. Learn. Syst. **32**(11), 5082–5092 (2020)
18. Nair, N.G., Satpathy, P., Christopher, J., et al.: Covariate shift: a review and analysis on classifiers. In: 2019 Global Conference for Advancement in Technology (GCAT), pp. 1–6. IEEE (2019)
19. Shanmugam, D., Blalock, D., Balakrishnan, G., et al.: Better aggregation in test-time augmentation. In: 2021 IEEE/CVF International Conference on Computer Vision (ICCV), pp. 1194–1203 (2021)
20. Wang, D., Shelhamer, E., Liu, S., et al.: Tent: fully test-time adaptation by entropy minimization. arXiv preprint arXiv:2006.10726 (2020)
21. Lee, D.H.: Pseudo-label: the simple and efficient semi-supervised learning method for deep neural networks. In: Workshop on Challenges in Representation Learning, ICML 3(2), p. 896 (2013)
22. Niu, S., Wu, J., Zhang, Y., et al.: Efficient test-time model adaptation without forgetting. In: International Conference on Machine Learning, pp. 16888–16905. PMLR (2022)

23. Zhang, J., Qi, L., Shi, Y., Gao, Y.: Domainadaptor: a novel approach to test-time adaptation. In: Proceedings of the IEEE/CVF International Conference on Computer Vision, pp. 18971–18981 (2023)

Real-Time Stream Data Mining

A Strong Robust Bearing Fault Diagnosis Method Based on Improved Transformer

Feng Guo[1], Jingchao Li[1(✉)], Jing Zhao[1], Ying Cao[2], and Wenjie Wu[2]

[1] College of Electronic and Information Engineering, Shanghai Dianji University, Shanghai, China
{Jingchao_lijc,Jing_zhaojing}@sdju.edu.cn
[2] China United Gas Turbine Technology, LTD, Shanghai, China
Ying_caoying01@spic.com.cn

Abstract. The complex latent features in bearing fault signals can be automatically extracted and recognized through deep learning. However, numerous interference factors in real-world operating environments, such as different types and strengths of noise, variations in operating conditions, and instability in the quality of training data, can significantly affect fault diagnosis accuracy. To solve this problem, this study proposes a bearing fault diagnosis method that offers enhanced robustness under low SNR in varying working conditions: Firstly, neural networks are used to adaptively embed signals under different working conditions. Secondly, a novel fault diagnosis model, SFFormer, is proposed based on the Transformer architecture, incorporating LSTM units and residual structures to improve the model's ability to capture the temporal relationships of features in sequential data. Finally, the rationality of the model design is verified through ablation experiments, which also enhance the interpretability of the model. This research, based on various operational data from the CWRU public dataset, designs 14 tasks with varying conditions and adds Gaussian white noise, pink noise, and Laplace noise with fluctuations ranging from 10 dB to −5 dB. Experimental results show that the proposed model achieves an accuracy of 98.36% in variable operating condition tasks. The model exhibits strong robustness in all experiments, providing a new solution for the fault diagnosis field.

Keywords: Intelligent fault diagnosis · Noisy environment · Transformer · Variable operating conditions

1 Introduction

Rolling bearings are one of the most critical mechanical components in industrial production. Their health condition not only significantly affects production efficiency but can sometimes even endanger the lives of operators. Due to the harsh working conditions, bearings frequently experience wear or failures during operation, which in turn affects the performance of both the bearings and the equipment. Therefore, continuous monitoring of bearing health is of significant importance.

C. Xu et al. (Eds.): MobiMedia 2025, LNICST 670, pp. 251–262, 2026.
https://doi.org/10.1007/978-3-032-16823-8_18

In the early stages of fault diagnosis, bearing fault detection primarily relied on machine learning algorithms and the expert experience of domain engineers to determine whether the bearing was healthy [1–4]. However, the effectiveness of these methods in practical applications is unstable due to the heavy reliance on expert experience for feature selection. As a result, deep learning algorithms capable of automatically extracting high-quality features have been introduced to the field [5–8]. In recent years, the Transformer model has demonstrated its powerful learning capabilities in various fields. Tang et al. [9] are said to be the first to introduce the Transformer structure into the field of bearing fault diagnosis. They tested it using data from different operating conditions as training and testing sets, achieving recognition accuracy of over 99% in variable operating conditions. This indicates that the learning capability of the multi-head attention mechanism and the Transformer model structure can played a significant role in fault diagnosis. However, their noise resistance experiment showed that this model, originating from the NLP field, does not perform well directly in the fault diagnosis domain, with diagnostic accuracy dropping sharply at 0 db. Once fault features are "smoothed" by noise, the attention mechanism is no longer able to focus effectively. Yao et al. [10] improved the Transformer by adding a soft-threshold module and replacing the normalization layers and attention mechanism. As a result, the Transformer model achieved better noise resistance, with a diagnostic accuracy of 97% under 0 db white and pink noise. Han et al. [11] improved the attention mechanism by using a residual structure and an enhanced MSCNN attention mechanism, enabling the attention mechanism to effectively focus on fault features even in high-noise environments. Xu et al. [12] improved the Transformer structure using CNNs, significantly enhancing the model's ability to extract local features and improving its noise resistance. However, the performance of these methods when operating conditions change still needs to be validated through experiments.

In real-world working environments, the conditions of machinery are often variable. For example, the operating speed and motor load of machinery are mostly not fixed, which leads to deformation of signal features and changes in feature distribution. Even when the bearing's operating environment is extremely harsh, certain sharp noises may coincidentally match the fault features and be incorrectly identified as fault features by the model. These issues pose a severe challenge to the adaptive capability of fault diagnosis algorithms. To address these issues, this study proposes a novel fault diagnosis method and conducts experimental validation in simulated harsh working environments. The main contributions are as follows: Firstly, To address the Transformer model's capability in feature recognition for signal sequences, the study improves it with an LSTM module and necessary structures to better adapt to fault diagnosis tasks, enabling it to more easily learn the dependency relationships between features in fault signal sequences. Secondly, in order to make the Transformer structure perform better in this field, a simple and effective embedding method was adopted to process variable operating condition data. Finally, the model is tested more comprehensively and rigorously by simulating complex working conditions in real-world environments, providing stronger evidence of the advantages of the proposed method. Additionally, ablation experiments are used to explain the rationality and effectiveness of the model design.

2 Method

2.1 Embedding

Let the input signal have a length of L, which is first divided into N segments, each with a segment length of S, so the signal can be represented as

$$X = [x_1, x_2, x_3, ..., x_N] \tag{1}$$

where $x_N \in R^S$. Then, a trainable linear transformation is applied to map each segment into a higher-dimensional D-dimensional vector:

$$X_{k\prime} = [x_1 E, x_2 E, x_3 E, \ldots x_S E] \tag{2}$$

where E denotes the parameter matrix of the linear transformation. At this stage, it cannot be guaranteed that the model can comprehensively extract information from the signal segments; therefore, multiple additional linear transformations are required to learn various information in the fault signal, such as rotational speed, fault type, and noise type. The method employed is still trainable, and thus the final output is:

$$X' = X_{1\prime} + X_{2\prime} + X_{3\prime} + \ldots + X_{k\prime} \tag{3}$$

where k denotes the number of embeddings.

2.2 Transformer

The key to the success of the Transformer model lies in its proposed multi-head attention mechanism (MSA). Prior to this, attention mechanisms were often used in other models to assist in enhancing model performance. In the Transformer, however, attention mechanisms are innovatively used as the core structure. Traditional attention mechanisms tend to focus on a single feature, leading to lower efficiency. In contrast, Transformer uses MSA to focus on multiple features in the input information, learning the neural network through numerous simple matrix operations. This significantly improves the parallel computing efficiency and overall performance of the model. MSA consists of multiple self-attention mechanisms, and each attention head computes an attention score matrix Z:

$$Z = Softmax\left(\frac{Q_m \cdot K_m}{\sqrt{d_k}}\right) \cdot V_m \tag{4}$$

Here, Q, K, and V represent the query matrix, key matrix, and value matrix, respectively. By calculating the dot product of Q and K, the attention map is obtained, which is then divided by $\sqrt{d_k}$ to prevent large dot products that may cause vanishing or exploding gradients. Finally, a fully connected network is used to convert the multiple matrices into the size of the original data slice.

Another important structure in the Transformer is the Feed Forward layer, which employs a two-layer fully connected structure. The function of the attention mechanism is to enrich the global information in the data, allowing the model to focus on feature locations and thereby enhancing its learning capability. The role of the Feed Forward layer is to help the model consolidate a large amount of training data, enabling it to have better "memory" performance (Fig. 1).

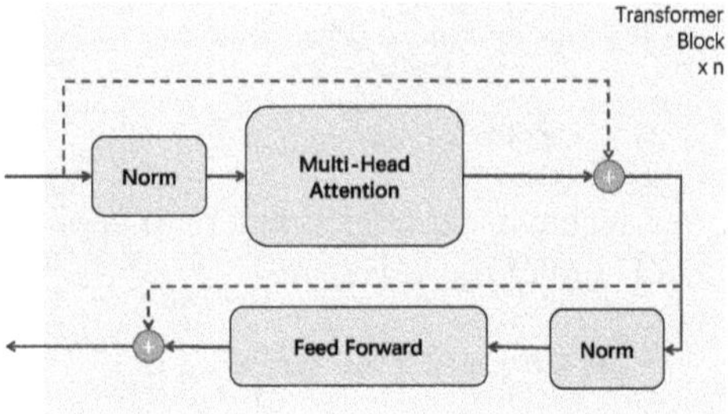

Fig. 1. Transformer structure diagram.

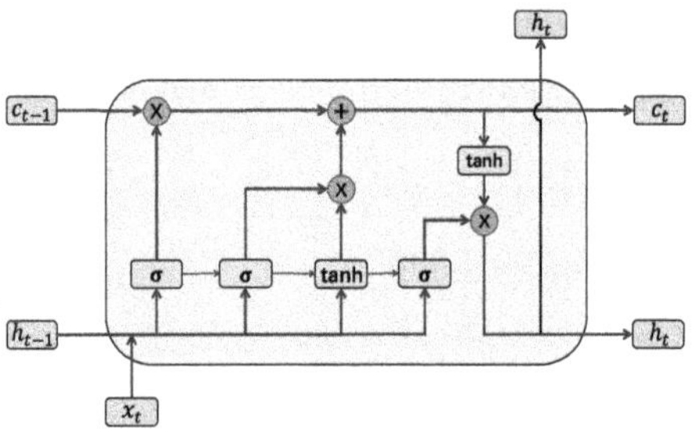

Fig. 2. LSTM structure diagram.

2.3 LSTM

Long Short-Term Memory (LSTM) is an improvement to the traditional Recurrent Neural Network (RNN) and can capture historical information across the entire input data. RNN has several drawbacks, including the potential for vanishing or exploding gradients during backpropagation, which LSTM addresses with its unique neuron structure. Figure 2 shows the internal structure of an LSTM neuron. The main idea of LSTM is to control the information flow along the time axis through several gates to capture information at each time step. The three most important gates are the forget gate, input gate, and output gate. The input gate acts as a filter, deciding which information is worth remembering and updating it to the next state. The forget gate determines which useless information from the previous unit state and new input data should be forgotten or discarded. The output gate determines the information that should be output at the next unit state. As shown in Fig. 3, the output C_{t-1} from the previous step interacts with H_{t-1} and input x_t to calculate a series of intermediate parameters, based on the output from the previous time step and the input from the current time step, in order to adjust its internal state. The specific calculation process is as follows:

$$i_t = \sigma(W_i x_t + V_i h_{t-1} + b_i) \tag{5}$$

$$f_t = \sigma\left(W_f x_t + V_f h_{t-1} + b_f\right) \tag{6}$$

$$o_t = \sigma(W_o x_t + V_o h_{t-1} + b_o) \tag{7}$$

$$c_t = f_t \odot c_{t-1} + i_t \odot \tanh(W_c x_t + V_i h_{t-1} + b_i) \tag{8}$$

$$h_t = o_t \odot \tanh(c_t) \tag{9}$$

Here, x_t and h_t represent the input and output of the neuron, respectively, i_t, f_t, o_t are the activation vectors for the input gate, forget gate, and output gate, and all W and V are trainable parameter matrices, with σ denoting the sigmoid activation function.

2.4 Proposed Method

Based on Transformer and previous excellent neural network designs, this paper proposes a more robust fault diagnosis method. First, the signals are embedding using MLP to minimize the differences between signals caused by factors such as operating conditions, noise, and signal acquisition. Then, the Transformer which can fuse signals from different operating conditions to the same distribution (SFFormer) is used to identify the sequential features of the signals. The key components of SFFormer lie in the multi-head attention mechanism (MSA) and the LSTM module. Finally, a classifier is used to determine the fault type. The specific workflow is shown in Fig. 3.

The Transformer model is primarily designed for discrete sequences. In the NLP field, embedding methods are used to map the input sequences to a reasonable representation space, while also embedding necessary information such as positional information. Directly inputting data into the model often leads to poor performance, so methods such as MLP and CNN are commonly used for preprocessing signals. Considering the effectiveness and efficiency of fault diagnosis, this method chooses MLP to perform dimensionality reduction and expansion on fault signals, adapting to eliminate feature differences between data and the influencing factors contained in the data. The structure of MLP is simple, and its learning ability is more efficient compared to advanced models. And subsequent experiments have shown that MLP can effectively improve diagnostic performance.

MSA enables the model to effectively identify fault features, while the LSTM module helps the model find temporal correlations in the signal, allowing the identified fault features to be contextually validated to eliminate the influence of external factors. If MSA and LSTM models are simply used separately for fault signal recognition through joint learning methods, the capabilities of these two structures cannot be effectively combined. Therefore, it is necessary to introduce some residual structures to organically integrate the LSTM module with Transformer, allowing the fault features recognized by both to undergo repeated cross-validation to improve the final recognition accuracy. Unlike traditional models, the hybrid architecture used in this study performs exceptionally well in capturing sequential patterns and broader sequence-to-sequence dependencies, thanks to the collaborative integration of LSTM memory cells and the attention mechanism. The memory units of LSTM can capture long-term dependencies, while MSA can capture fault information at a particular moment. This collaborative integration further facilitates signal fusion through multi-level computations in the proposed model.

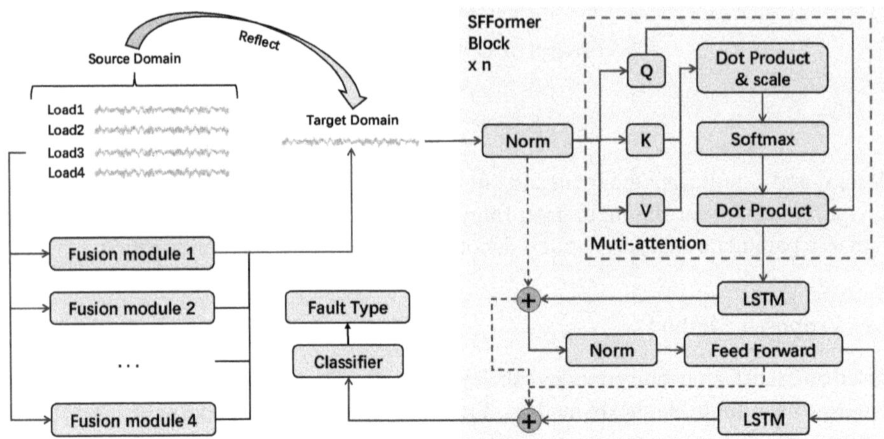

Fig. 3. Framework of proposed method.

3 Performance Validation

3.1 Experience Description

The CWRU dataset is one of the most important datasets in the fault detection field, and many studies use it as a benchmark for bearing fault detection [13]. It collects data under four different load conditions (0HP, 1HP, 2HP, 3HP), with a vibration signal sampling frequency of 48 kHz. Each load condition includes four types of data: normal, ball fault (BO), inner race fault (IR), and outer race fault (OR), with three fault sizes (0.007 inch, 0.014 inch, and 0.021 inch) for each fault type, resulting in a total of ten types of data. A time-series vibration sequence of length 48,000 samples was tested for each fault type. In addition, the data characteristics of the CWRU dataset are idealized, with minimal environmental noise, which helps experimenters add experimental noise as needed.

First, the data is divided into four subsets according to operating conditions, and then the time-series vibration sequences are segmented using a sliding window data augmentation method. In this experiment, the window size is 2048 and the step size is 400, so each fault type yields 4000 data samples, resulting in a total of "4 × 10 × 4000" data samples, where 4000 data samples are divided for each of the 10 fault types under 4 different operating conditions. Then, different numbers of subsets are used as the training set, and the remaining subsets are used as the test set, resulting in 14 variable operating condition tasks as shown in Table 1.

Furthermore, to more comprehensively test the robustness and effectiveness of the model, three additional types of noise were introduced: Gaussian noise, pink noise, and Laplace noise. The difference between these three types of noise lies in their spectral distributions, which enables them to simulate different common environmental noises.

Gaussian is widely used to simulate noise in natural and industrial environments; Pink noise is more suitable for simulating background noise in mechanical systems; Laplace noise often used to represent anomalies such as mutations or mechanical failures and equipment wear.

3.2 Noise Experiment Under Variable Operating Conditions

To ensure the fairness and comparability of the experiments, the model proposed in [14] was used in this experiment, and testing was conducted without changing the model structure. Among the models mentioned in the literature, CNN, ResNet, and BiLSTM are widely used in real-world industrial applications. Considering the practicality and stability of the models, these three most representative models were selected as the baseline comparison models in this experiment. It is worth mentioning that, to match the fault diagnosis task, the structures and parameters of these models in the literature were carefully adjusted. CNN, as a groundbreaking model in deep learning, has greatly advanced fields such as image recognition and signal recognition, and still has significant applications in the current industrial sector. Based on research on convolutional structures, the ResNet model was introduced as a deeper version of CNN, achieving better performance in many time-insensitive tasks. To compare the effectiveness of the proposed model in extracting sequential patterns in signals, the most advanced version of the RNN family, BiLSTM, was also selected for this experiment. Additionally, a native Transformer model was used for comparative testing.

This experiment aims to evaluate the impact of noise on the fault diagnosis model under varying operating conditions, especially the effect of noise level changes on the model's recognition performance. To achieve this, training and testing were conducted for different tasks under varying operating conditions based on the task division in Table 1, with three types of noise added. During the noise addition process, the signal-to-noise ratio (SNR) was adjusted from 10 db to -5 db, with a step size of 5 db. To obtain stable and reliable results, the average test accuracy of 10 experiments was used as the performance metric for the model. The experimental results are shown in Table 2, where each result represents the average value of the variable operating condition tasks shown in Table 1. Furthermore, to further analyze the model's performance across different variable operating condition tasks, the accuracy of each noise task at 0 db was selected and visualized as a radar chart in Fig. 4.

Table 1. Task division for variable operating conditions

Task	Tarin dataset/number	Test dataset/number
A	Load 0 /4000	Load 1,2,3 /12000
B	Load 1 /4000	Load 0,2,3 /12000
C	Load 2 /4000	Load 0,1,3 /12000
D	Load 3 /4000	Load 0,1,2 /12000
E	Load 0,1 /8000	Load 2,3 /8000

(continued)

Table 1. (*continued*)

Task	Tarin dataset/number	Test dataset/number
F	Load 0,2 /8000	Load 1,3 /8000
G	Load 0,3 /8000	Load 1,2 /8000
H	Load 1,2 /8000	Load 0,3 /8000
I	Load 1,3 /8000	Load 0,2 /8000
J	Load 2,3 /8000	Load 0,1 /8000
K	Load 0,1,2 /12000	Load 3 /4000
L	Load 0,1,3 /12000	Load 2 /4000
M	Load 0,2,3 /12000	Load 1 /4000
N	Load 1,2,3 /12000	Load 0 /4000

It can be observed that all models experience fluctuations of no more than 2% between of noise, ResNet exhibits the most drastic fluctuations, with an average 10 db and 0 db, while a sharp decline occurs between 0 db and −5 db. Under the three types accuracy decrease of 6.77%, while the proposed model shows the least fluctuation, with an average accuracy decrease of 3.19%. The proposed model performs the best under all experimental conditions, achieving an accuracy of 99% at 10 db and over 94% at −5 db. CNN, as the most commonly used fault diagnosis model in real-world applications, also performs well, with accuracies of 97% and over 92% in the 10 db and −5 db noise environments, respectively.

The worst performer is BiLSTM, which nearly loses its applicability at − 5 db. BiLSTM is suited for processing long sequence inputs, which makes it more susceptible to being misled by noise. CNN compresses and fits the training data using a 2D convolution module, resulting in higher accuracy. ResNet uses more convolution operations and deeper layers, but its recognition performance is much lower than CNN. This suggests that while convolution operations can greatly reduce noise interference, they are prone to overfitting and the loss of data features during computation, which negatively impacts performance in variable operating conditions and high-noise tasks. Although Transformer and BiLSTM have lower accuracy, their accuracy fluctuations are the smallest between 10 db and 0 db. When the noise intensity increases by a factor of 10, the data distribution becomes further chaotic, and the accuracy decrease does not exceed 0.5%. This indicates that although they are unable to completely distinguish between noise and features, they can steadily learn some latent fault features or feature associations.

Table 2. Classification results of variable operating conditions

Nosie type	Model	Noise strength			
		10 db	5 db	0 db	− 5 db
Gaussian	CNN	97.57	96.34	95.70	92.45
	Resnet	93.97	93.74	92.245	85.24

(*continued*)

Table 2. (*continued*)

Nosie type	Model	Noise strength			
		10 db	5 db	0 db	− 5 db
	BiLSTM	91.47	90.37	90.997	87.24
	Transformer	93.30	93.05	93.187	88.85
	Proposed	99.72	98.72	97.08	94.10
Pink	CNN	97.32	96.48	95.80	92.48
	Resnet	94.36	94.05	92.24	85.53
	BiLSTM	91.74	91.32	90.272	86.50
	Transformer	93.15	93.14	92.95	89.32
	Proposed	98.97	98.26	97.19	94.06
Laplace	CNN	97.19	96.56	95.52	92.11
	Resnet	93.91	93.86	92.48	85.88
	BiLSTM	91.63	91.18	90.83	86.36
	Transformer	93.67	93.31	91.70	90.13
	Proposed	98.85	98.03	97.45	94.00

The radar chart shows that the accuracy fluctuations of ResNet and BiLSTM exceed 10% under all types of noise, with Transformer exhibiting fluctuations as high as 20%. CNN, due to its efficient and simple convolution structure, is able to adaptively learn fault features from training data under different operating conditions. The experimental results show that the configuration of the training data causes the recognition accuracy to fluctuate drastically between 90% and 100%. When experimental conditions such as the test bench and bearing brand remain constant, but factors like the bearing rotational speed change, the distribution of fault vibration data is significantly altered, greatly affecting the model's learning effectiveness. The proposed model achieves more stable performance in various types of tasks, with recognition accuracy exceeding 99% when trained on data from three operating conditions, and accuracy approaching 98% when trained on data from two operating conditions. Experiments show that the proposed model effectively combines the advantages of Transformer and LSTM, eliminating their sensitivity to operating conditions and noise, ultimately achieving the best performance in variable operating conditions with various noise levels.

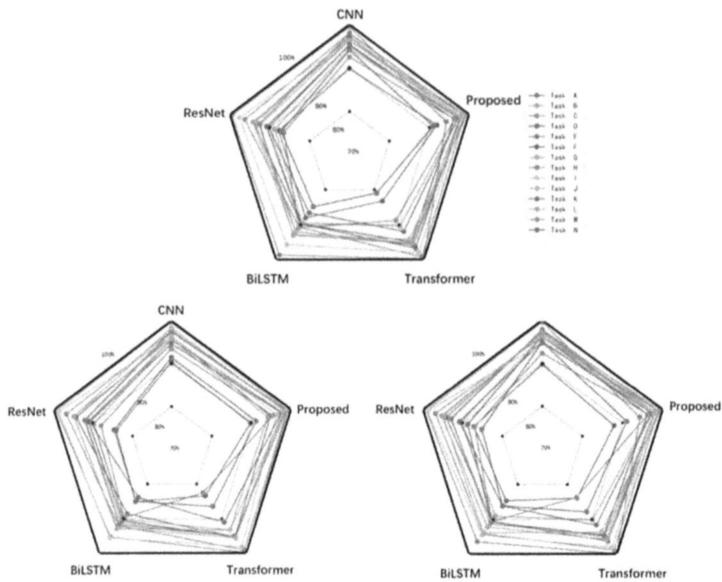

Fig. 4. Experimental results of various variable operating conditions tasks.

4 Ablation Test

To analyze the contribution of each module in the proposed method and discuss its rationale, we attempted to remove the multiple varying working condition signal fusion module (MFM), the LSTM module, and the residual module (RM) from the model to study the impact of different modules on the overall performance. At the same time, the necessity of the residual module (RM) for the LSTM module was discussed.

Gaussian white noise with $SNR = -5$ dB was selected as the experimental condition for diagnostic performance testing of each ablation model, with the results shown in Fig. 5 and Table 3. Clearly, all three modules enhance the model's ability to distinguish fault signal features in noisy environments, and their combination significantly improves the model's robustness. Although the MFM module provides some improvement to each model, its impact is greatest on the ablation model that includes both LSTM and RM, where the recognition accuracy increased by 2.3%, ultimately reaching 99%. When the RM module is removed, the proposed model degenerates into a simple joint learning model connecting LSTM and Transformer. The organic integration of RM, however, improves accuracy by 1.7%.

Table 3. Classification results of SFFormer's ablation models

Structure	Modalities					
MFM	√	*	√	*	√	*
LSTM	√	√	√	√	*	*

(*continued*)

Table 3. (continued)

Structure	Modalities					
RM	√	√	*	*	*	*
Accuracy	99.06	96.75	96.47	95.01	95.14	94.33

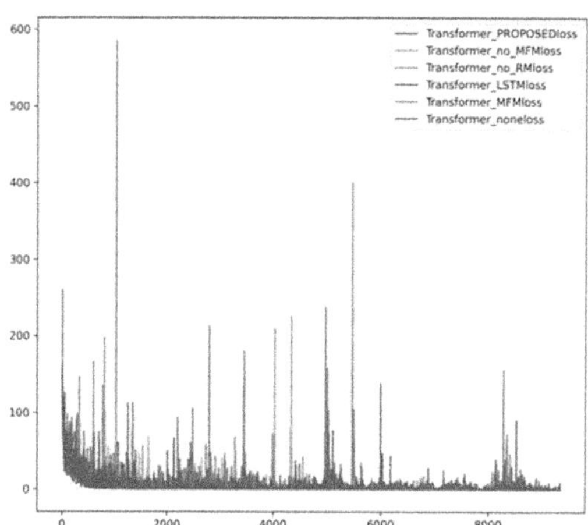

Fig. 5. Loss variation of SFFormer's ablation models during training iterations.

5   Conclusion

This study proposes a more practical and robust bearing fault diagnosis method for real-world fault diagnosis problems. First, by performing adaptive fusion on the signals, a representation mapping from the source domain to the target domain is established for fault state recognition. Secondly, by improving the Transformer structure, the model is better able to identify fault information in the fault signals, and an SFFormer model is proposed to help the model extract forward and backward feature associations in the signal. In tasks with various types of noise under changing operating conditions, the proposed method outperforms other compared deep learning methods in diagnostic accuracy under unknown operating conditions, with robustness. Subsequently, fluctuation noise was introduced into the variable operating condition task for in-depth testing, further validating the effectiveness of the method. Experimental validation suggests the great potential of the MFM module and SFFormer model as foundational components for fault diagnosis.

Acknowledgments. Supported by Shanghai Heavy-duty Gas Turbine United Innovation Program (UIC Program) (GYQJ-2023–1–06), the "Dawn" Program of Shanghai Education Commission (23SG55) and Shanghai Science and Technology Development Funds (No. 23QA140380).

References

1. Cui, B., Weng, Y., Zhang, N.: A feature extraction and machine learning framework for bearing fault diagnosis. Renew. Energy **191**, 987–997 (2022). https://doi.org/10.1016/j.renene.2022.04.061

2. Kumar, H.S., Upadhyaya, G.: Fault diagnosis of rolling element bearing using continuous wavelet transform and K- nearest neighbour. Mater. Today Proc. **92**, 56–60 (2023). https://doi.org/10.1016/j.matpr.2023.03.618

3. Wang, B., Qiu, W., Hu, X., Wang, W.: A rolling bearing fault diagnosis technique based on recurrence quantification analysis and Bayesian optimization SVM. Appl. Soft Comput. **156**, 111506 (2024). https://doi.org/10.1016/j.asoc.2024.111506

4. Hong, L., Chen, Z., Wang, Y., Shahidehpour, M., Wu, M.: A novel SVM-based decision framework considering feature distribution for power transformer fault diagnosis. Energy Rep. **8**, 9392–9401 (2022). https://doi.org/10.1016/j.egyr.2022.07.062

5. Peng, X., Xu, H., Wang, J., Liu, J., He, C.: Ensemble multiple distinct ResNet networks with channel-attention mechanism for multisensor fault diagnosis of hydraulic systems. IEEE Sensors J. **23**(10), 10706–10717 (2023). https://doi.org/10.1109/JSEN.2023.3263924

6. Nacer, S.M., Nadia, B., Abdelghani, R., Mohamed, B.: A novel method for bearing fault diagnosis based on BiLSTM neural networks. Int. J. Adv. Manuf. Technol. **125**(3–4), 1477–1492 (2023). https://doi.org/10.1007/s00170-022-10792-1

7. Chen, X., Zhang, B., Gao, D.: Bearing fault diagnosis base on multi-scale CNN and LSTM model. J. Intell. Manuf. **32**(4), 971–987 (2021). https://doi.org/10.1007/s10845-020-01600-2

8. Zhang, S., Ye, F., Wang, B., Habetler, T.G.: Semi-supervised bearing fault diagnosis and classification using variational autoencoder-based deep generative models. IEEE Sensors J. **21**(5), 6476–6486 (2021). https://doi.org/10.1109/JSEN.2020.3040696

9. Tang, J., Zheng, G., Wei, C., Huang, W., Ding, X.: Signal-transformer: a robust and interpretable method for rotating machinery intelligent fault diagnosis under variable operating conditions. IEEE Trans. Instrum. Meas. **71**, 1–11 (2022). https://doi.org/10.1109/TIM.2022.3169528

10. Yao, D., Zhou, T., Yang, J.: Intelligent framework for bearing fault diagnosis in high-noise environments: a location-focused soft threshold denoising approach. IEEE Sens. J. **24**(7) (2024)

11. Han, S., Sun, S., Zhao, Z., Luan, Z., Niu, P.: Deep residual multiscale convolutional neural network with attention mechanism for bearing fault diagnosis under strong noise environment. IEEE Sensors J. **24**(6), 9073–9081 (2024). https://doi.org/10.1109/JSEN.2023.3345400

12. Xu, Z.: A strong anti-noise and easily deployable bearing fault diagnosis model based on time–frequency dual-channel Transformer (2024)

13. Download a Data File | Case School of Engineering [Online]. Available: https://engineering.case.edu/bearingdatacenter/download-data-file. Accessed: 27 Dec. 2024

14. Zhao, Z., et al.: Deep learning algorithms for rotating machinery intelligent diagnosis: an open source benchmark study. ISA Trans. **107**, 224–255 (2020). https://doi.org/10.1016/j.isatra.2020.08.010

AI for Communication

A Coordinated Mitigation Scheme
for UAVs Under Co-channel Interferences

Junyi Wang[1,2], Haibo Ding[3], and Fang Ye[1,2(✉)]

[1] College of Information and Communication Engineering, Harbin Engineering
University, Harbin, China
`Junyi.Wang@hrbeu.edu.cn`, `Fang.Ye@hrbeu.edu.cn`
[2] Key Laboratory of Advanced Marine Communication and Information Technology,
Ministry of Industry and Information Technology, Harbin, China
[3] Yangzhou Marine Electronic Instrument Institute Project Management Office,
Yangzhou, China
`853644079@qq.com`

Abstract. The scarcity of spectrum resources and the broadcast
nature of wireless channels pose severe challenges to the security of
UAV-assisted communication systems. Traditional physical layer secu-
rity(PLS) schemes rely on artificial noise to enhance security, but the
resulting co-channel interference can degrade the system's secrecy transmission rate. This paper proposes a PLS communication scheme based on
co-channel interference coordination, where co-channel interference arising from spectrum reuse replaces artificial noise to interfere with eavesdroppers while reducing interference to legitimate users. In this scheme,
when the transmitter sends signals to legitimate users, power allocation
and phase configuration are jointly optimized. A convex optimization
model is constructed to achieve interference coordination by aiming at
the phase cancellation of interference at the legitimate users, and under
power constraints, the Lagrange dual method is used to derive the optimal power allocation strategy to maximize the system's secrecy transmission rate. Simulation results show that under both static and dynamic
scenarios, the user SINR exceeds 30 dB and the secrecy capacity C surpasses 10 bit/Hz, ensuring low interference to users while maintaining
communication security.

Keywords: multi-UAV system · physical layer security · co-channel
interference · secrecy transmission rate

1 Introduction

Unmanned Aerial Vehicle (UAV)assisted wireless communication has garnered
significant attention due to its flexibility, rapid deployment capabilities, and
broad coverage potential, making it a key enabler for future wireless networks.
Compared to single-UAV deployments, UAV swarms can deliver more reliable

C. Xu et al. (Eds.): MobiMedia 2025, LNICST 670, pp. 265–276, 2026.
https://doi.org/10.1007/978-3-032-16823-8_19

service and cover larger areas, especially in complex or dynamic environments. With the advancement of 5G and beyond, UAV communications are being increasingly integrated into domains such as agriculture, logistics, and emergency rescue [1,2]. However, the intrinsic broadcast nature of wireless channels makes these systems inherently vulnerable to eavesdropping, raising critical concerns about communication confidentiality [3,4].

To address these issues, recent research efforts have focused on incorporating physical layer security (PLS) techniques into UAV communication systems [5]. Strategies such as joint trajectory and resource allocation [6], robust design against uncertain eavesdropper positions [7], and the use of UAVs as mobile relays [8] have shown potential in enhancing secrecy capacity. However, many of these schemes rely heavily on the injection of artificial noise or full-duplex jamming, which, while effective at degrading the eavesdropper's signal, often introduce significant co-channel interference to legitimate users and suffer from excessive power consumption [9,10].

Moreover, as UAV densities increase and spectrum reuse becomes more prevalent, co-channel interference among UAVs becomes inevitable [11]. Existing studies primarily regard such interference as detrimental and seek to mitigate or avoid it. Yet, these approaches often overlook the dual role that co-channel interference can play–both as a challenge and a potential security-enhancing resource.

This work reconsiders the role of co-channel interference and explores how it can be strategically coordinated and exploited to enhance system-level communication security. Unlike traditional schemes that rely solely on artificial noise or user-specific jamming, this design leverages the inherent interference from spectrum sharing as a substitute for artificial noise. By incorporating phase-controlled auxiliary signals and optimizing power allocation under total power constraints, interference is intentionally suppressed at legitimate receivers while being maintained or even amplified at unknown eavesdropper locations.

Through this approach, the interference becomes dual-purpose: it protects communication confidentiality by confusing potential eavesdroppers, while cooperative interference cancellation ensures that legitimate users experience minimal degradation. Compared to existing PLS methods, the proposed mechanism achieves better power efficiency, does not rely on the knowledge of eavesdropper locations, and exhibits robustness across both static and dynamic UAV deployment scenarios.

2   System Model

Considering the air-to-ground (A2G) communication scenario illustrated in Fig. 1 (a), the system consisted of M single antenna UAVs is deployed as aerial base station to jointly serve N ground users (GUs) via cooperative downlink transmission. Simultaneously, a passive eavesdropper is setted within the communication area and intercepted the legitimate transmissions silently.

All UAV-to-GU communication links are assumed to follow a line-of-sight (LoS) propagation to keep consistent with typical UAV-based communication environments. To improve spectrum efficiency and to conserve bandwidth resources, the UAVs adapt co-channel transmission, i.e., they share the same frequency band while serving different users, which inevitably introduced CCI.

Each UAV_m transmits a signal s_{mm} carrying useful informations to its intended user GU_m. Additionally, to control the interference experienced by other legitimate users, UAV_m also transmits auxiliary signals s_{mn} for other users GU_n $(n \neq m)$. Figure 1(b) shows Useful signal, Interference cancellation signal, Interference, and their sum vectors. By adjusting the transmit power allocated to each signal, UAV_m can regulate the interference imposed on both legitimate users and potential eavesdroppers.

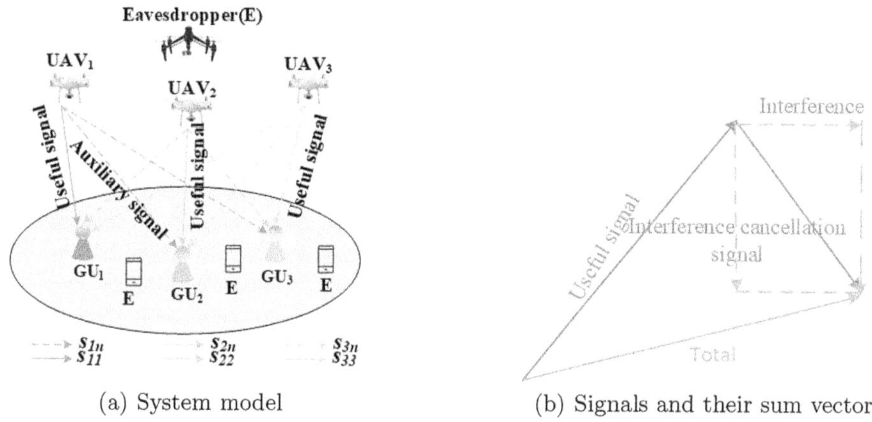

(a) System model   (b) Signals and their sum vector

Fig. 1. Schematic diagram of the A2G communication network.

In this scheme, the received signals of GU_n can be expressed as

$$y_n = + p_{nn}f_{nn}x_n + \sum_{m=1,\,m\neq n}^{M} p_{mn}f_{mn}x_n + \sum_{k=1,\,k\neq n}^{N} p_{nk}f_{nn}x_k \\ + \sum_{m=1,\,m\neq n}^{M} \sum_{k=1,\,k\neq n}^{N} p_{mk}f_{mn}x_k \tag{1}$$

where p_{mn} represents the transmit power allocated by UAV_m to signal s_{mn}, and f_{mn} represents the channel gain between UAV_m and user GU_n. In Eq. 1, each term on the right-hand side is defined as useful singal, auxiliary singal, interference cancelation singal, and interference signal, respectively. The signal-to-interference-plus-noise ratio (SINR) at the legitimate user GU_n is given by

$$SINR_n = \frac{|p_{nn} * f_{nn}|^2}{|I_n|^2 + N_i^2} \tag{2}$$

where N_i^2 denotes background noise and I_n represents the interference received by GU_n.

The total received signal ye_n at the eavesdropper when intercepting GU_n's transmission is

$$ye_n = p_{nn}f_{ne}x_n + \sum_{m=1,m\neq n}^{M} p_{mn}f_{me}x_n + \sum_{k=1,k\neq n}^{N} p_{nk}f_{ne}x_k$$
$$+ \sum_{m=1,m\neq n}^{M}\sum_{k=1,k\neq n}^{N} p_{mk}f_{me}x_k \tag{3}$$

While co-channel interference degrades the communication quality for legitimate users, it also interferes with the eavesdropper. The SINR at the eavesdropper when intercepting signals from GU_n is expressed as

$$SINRe_n = \frac{|p_{nn} * f_{ne}|^2}{|Ie_n|^2 + N_i^2} \tag{4}$$

where, Ie_n is the interference at the eavesdropper. These correspond to the third and fourth terms on the right-hand sides of Eq. 1 and Eq. 3, respectively. As previously defined in Ref [12], the secrecy transmission rate is the difference between the capacity of the legitimate and the eavesdropping links, given by

$$C_n = log_2 \frac{1 + SINR_n}{1 + SINRe_n} \tag{5}$$

Here, we hope to regulate the transmission power of s_{mn} to manipulate interference levels. The goal is to maintain high interference at the eavesdropper while minimizing its impact on legitimate users.

3   Problem Formulation

In Sect. 2, we hope to enhance communication security by adjusting the transmission power of s_{mn}. However, it should be confirmed whether the power allocation can achieve the target, which will be discussed in this section. For ease of analysis, a dual-UAV scenario will be discussed first, and then the conclusion will be extended to a multi-UAV scenario. As depicted in Fig. 2, the UAVs are positioned directly above their respective target users, while the eavesdropper moves along the ground following the indicated direction. Taking the GU_1 as an example, its $|Ie_1|^2$ and $|I_1|^2$ are in the following range of values

$$|p_{12}||f_{11}|^2 - |p_{22}||f_{21}|^2 \leq |I_1|^2 \leq |p_{12}||f_{11}|^2 + |p_{22}||f_{21}|^2$$
$$|p_{12}||f_{1e}|^2 - |p_{22}||f_{2e}|^2 \leq |Ie_1|^2 \leq |p_{12}||f_{1e}|^2 + |p_{22}||f_{2e}|^2 \tag{6}$$

The interference will be minimized if the two signals are out of phase, and maximized if they are in phase. Therefore, to minimize interference at legitimate users under the given power allocation, it is necessary to ensure that the interference signal and the interference cancellation signal are in opposite phases. As for the eavesdroppers, their locations will contribute two situations: (1) $|p_{12}f_{11}| = |p_{22}f_{21}|$; (2) $|p_{12}f_{11}| \neq |p_{22}f_{21}|$.

(1) $|p_{12}f_{11}| = |p_{22}f_{21}|$: the interference is totally canceled for GU_1. The minimum of $|Ie_1|^2$ can be reached to $|p_{12}||f_{1e}|^2$ - $|p_{22}||f_{2e}|^2$ only if the signals are in opposite phase. Interference will be remained unless the locations of eavesdropper and user are in coincident.

(2) $|p_{12}f_{11}| \neq |p_{22}f_{21}|$: it means the interference is partly remained for GU_1, with its partial derivative

$$\frac{\partial|I_1|^2}{\partial|p_{12}|} = \begin{cases} -2|p_{12}||f_{11}|^2, |p_{12}f_{11}| < |p_{22}f_{21}| \\ -2|p_{12}||f_{11}|^2, |p_{12}f_{11}| > |p_{22}f_{21}| \end{cases} \tag{7}$$

A typical piecewise parabolic form can be observed with its schematic diagram shown in Fig. 2. As the eavesdropper moved along the black arrow in Fig. 2(a), the interference caused by UAV_1 gradually become smaller than that caused by UAV_2. While $|p_{12}f_{1e}|^2 > |p_{22}f_{2e}|^2$, we can obtain

$$\frac{\partial|Ie_1|^2_{min}}{\partial|p_{12}|} = 2|p_{12}||f_{11}|^2 \frac{h^2}{h^2 + x_1^2} \tag{8}$$

where h is UAV altitude and x_i refers to the distance between eavesdropper and GU_i. The absolute value of $|Ie_1|^2_{min}$'s slope is much smaller than that of $|I_1|^2$'s. Moreover, while fully cancelling interference at the GU_1, $|Ie_1|^2_{min}$ equals to $|p_{22}f_{21}|^2(\frac{h^2}{h^2+x_1^2} - \frac{h^2}{h^2+x_2^2})$, which is larger than 0 as x_1 should be smaller than x_2 significantly to ensure a larger interference caused by UAV_1 (Position 1). Therefore, the interference relationships between the user and the eavesdropper the interference cancellation can be depicted by Fig. 2(b). Similarly, when $|p_{12}f_{1e}|^2 < |p_{22}f_{2e}|^2$ (Position 2), the same analysis applies, and the relationship was given by Fig. 2(c). It can be observed that the minimum residual interference at the eavesdropper, $|Ie_1|^2_{min}$, is consistently greater than the interference at the legitimate user, $|I_1|^2$. This disparity improves system security by ensuring that the eavesdropper is more affected by interference. Furthermore, at the position 3 where $|p_{12}f_{1e}|^2 = |p_{22}f_{2e}|^2$, achieving antiphase of the signal will be challenging (it can be only satisfied at the position of $GU1$), thus a significant amount of interference will still exist.

On the basis, we extend the scenario to the $M = N > 2$ one. The minimum interferences can be given as

$$|Ie_n|^2_{min} = \sum_{k=1,k\neq n}^{N} (|p_{nk}f_{ne}|^2 - \sum_{m=1,m\neq n}^{M} |p_{mk}f_{me}|^2)$$

$$|I_n|^2_{min} = \sum_{k=1,k\neq n}^{N} (|p_{nk}f_{nn}|^2 - \sum_{m=1,m\neq n}^{M} |p_{mk}f_{mn}|^2) \tag{9}$$

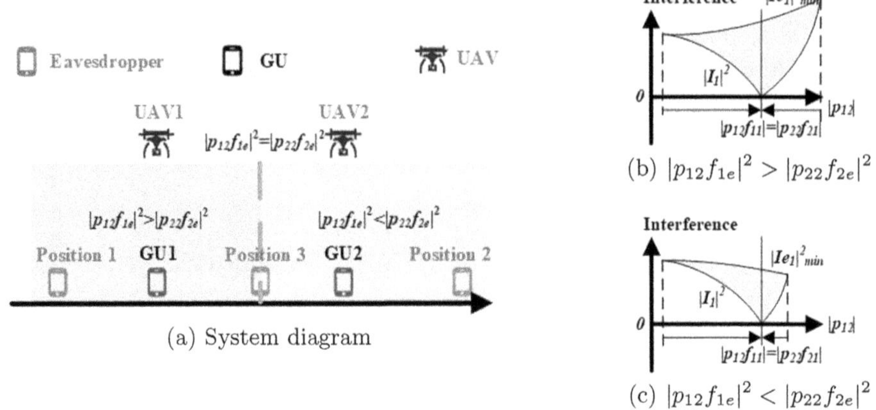

Fig. 2. Schematic diagram of the interference under dual-UAV communication scenario during interference cancellation

Similar with the scenario of dual-UAV comminication, the minimum $|I_n|^2_{min}$ will be achieved if $|p_{nk}f_{nn}|^2$ is close to $\sum_{m=1,m\neq n}^{M}|p_{mk}f_{mn}|^2$. Referring to the analysis under dual-UAV scenario, the minimum of remained interference of the eavesdropper can be expressed as

$$|Ie_n|^2_{min} = \sum_{k=1,k\neq n}^{N} \sum_{m=1,m\neq n}^{M} |p_{mk}f_{me}|^2 |\frac{h^2}{h^2 + x_n^2} - \frac{h^2}{h^2 + x_m^2}| \qquad (10)$$

Regardless of whether the magnitude of the interference signal is greater than, less than, or equal to the magnitude of the cancellation signal, the interference cancellation strategy remained effective in the scenario when $M = N > 2$.

According to Eq. 5 and Fig. 2, it can be concluded that C is primarily determined by the legitimate user's SINR during interference cancellation. Therefore, the optimization problem is to optimize the SINR of legitimate users under the interference cancellation strategy. Considering the power constraints of UAV signal transmission, the objective function can be defined as

$$(P1) \max_{\{p_{ij}\}} \omega_i = \frac{\left| p_{ii}f_{ii} + \sum_{k\in N,k\neq i} p_{ki}f_{ki} \right|^2}{N_i^2 + \sum_{j\in N,j\neq i}\left| p_{ij}f_{ii} + \sum_{k\in N,k\neq i} p_{kj}f_{ki} \right|^2} \qquad (11)$$

$$s.t. \left[|p_{i1}|^2 + |p_{i2}|^2 + \dots + |p_{iN}|^2 \right] \leq P$$

4 Optimization Design of Interference Cancellation

Assuming there is an optimal solution p^* that satisfies the following ideal phase condition:

$$\angle p_{kj} + \angle f_{kk} = -\angle I_{kj}, k = j \tag{12}$$

where $\angle$ represents the phase of each vector. Equation 12 gives the critical condition that phase discrepancy can be eliminated. That is, the interference cancellation signal is expected to remain in reverse phase with the interference signal. The modulus and further optimizations will be analyzed here.

Assuming the optimal solution of Eq. 12 (i.e., p^*_{kj}) exists, the corresponding optimization problem for UAV_1 can be further formulated as

$$(P2) \max_{\{|p_{1k}|\}} \omega_1 = \frac{a|p_{11}|^2|f_{11}|^2}{N_i^2 + \sum_{k \neq i}(|I_{1k}| - |p_{1k}||f_{11}|)^2} \tag{13}$$

$$s.t. \sum_{k \in N} |p_{1k}|^2 \leq P$$

where $I_{ij} = \sum_{k \in N, k \neq i} p_{kj} f_{ki}$, denotes the interference weight associated with the data symbol x_k received. $a \in (0, 2)$ is a random variable that models the perturbation introduced by the auxiliary signal on the magnitude of the useful signal. It can be readily verified that problem (P2) is a convex optimization problem that satisfies the Slater condition. For facility, we introduce a slack variable η_1 to equivalently reformulate (P2) as the following optimization problem

$$\max_{\{|p_{1k}|\}} \eta_1$$

$$s.t. a|p_{11}|^2|f_{11}|^2 \geq \eta_1 \left[N_i^2 + \sum_{k \neq 1}(|I_{1k}| - |p_{1k}||f_{11}|)^2 \right] \tag{14}$$

$$\sum_{k \in N} |p_{1k}|^2 \leq P$$

The Lagrangian of the problem (P2) is given by

$$\mathcal{F}(\eta_1, \eta_2, \eta_3, |p_{1k}|) = \eta_1 + \eta_2 \left[a|p_{11}|^2|f_{11}|^2 - \eta_1 N_i^2 - \eta_1 \sum_{k \neq 1}(|I_{i1}| - |p_{1k}||f_{11}|)^2 \right]$$

$$+ \eta_3 \left[P - \sum_{k \in N} |p_{1k}|^2 \right] \tag{15}$$

here, $\eta_2 > 0$, $\eta_3 > 0$. According to the KKT condition, the partial derivative of the function $\mathcal{F}$ with respect to $|p_{1k}|$, η_1, η_2 and η_3 should be 0, and we will get

$$|\hat{p}^*_{1k}| = \left| \frac{I_{1k}}{f_{11}} \right| \tag{16}$$

Minimizing interference to legitimate users consequently maximizes the SINR of the target user. According to Eq. 5, interference at the eavesdropper persists unless it experiences the same channel gain as the legitimate user–an unlikely scenario in practical deployments. Therefore, even with reduced interference at the legitimate user, an eavesdropper at a different location still suffers from significant interference, ensuring secure communication within the system. Similarly, while $N > 2$, we will get

$$|\hat{p}_{1k}^*| = \left| \frac{\sum\limits_{k \neq 1} I_{1k}}{f_{11}} \right| \tag{17}$$

In other words, the conclusions from $N = 2$ are extended to the case where $N > 2$. Specifically, the transmission and cancellation power allocation strategy for UAV base stations is to minimize interference as much as possible, with the remaining power entirely allocated to transmitting useful signals.

5   Simulated Results and Discussions

To validate effectiveness of the proposed scheme, a static scenario is designed as shown in (Fig. 3(a), where the eavesdropper is positioned at coordinates (50, 50, 0). Three UAVs are deployed, which hover 400 m above their respective target users. The SINR and secrecy transmission rate C are extracted under no, partial, and full interference cancellation conditions for GU_1. In addition, a 100×100 grids of eavesdroppers are placed around the optimal position to analyze how the secrecy rate varies with the eavesdropper's location. Aerial eavesdroppers at 200 m above the ground are also considered for comparison.

Moreover, several typical dynamic scenarios are selected to further validate the proposed scheme:

(i) The relative positions among UAVs remain constant, as do the relative positions among users. The UAVs alter their relative positions to users either by ascending (defined as $MS1$, in Fig. 3(b)) or rotating (defined as $MS2$, in Fig. 3(c)).

(ii) The relative positions among users remain constant while the positions among UAVs change (defined as $MS3$, in Fig. 3(d)).

(iii) The relative positions among UAVs remain constant while the relative positions among users change (defined as $MS4$, in Fig. 3(e)).

In all dynamic scenarios, an eavesdropper is assumed to be located at the coordinate $(0, 0, 0)$ to investigate the dynamic evolution of system-level communication security.

The simulated parameters are listed in Table 1. First, the effectiveness of the interference cancellation strategy is validated. Figure 4 (a) illustrates the SINR variation of the new user as it moves closer to or further from GU_1.

The results indicate that the new user achieves an optimal SINR only when it is exactly co-located with GU_1, where the interference is effectively cancelled.

At all other positions, the SINR is significantly lower as the interference persists. Figure 4(b) and (c) illustrates the variation trends of user SINR and C under no interference cancellation, partial interference cancellation, and complete interference cancellation. As the interference is gradually eliminated, the user's SINR increases significantly and eventually stabilizes above 30 dB. C exhibits a similar trend, eventually stabilizing above 10 bit/Hz, with the final stable value being very close to the theoretical maximum value derived.

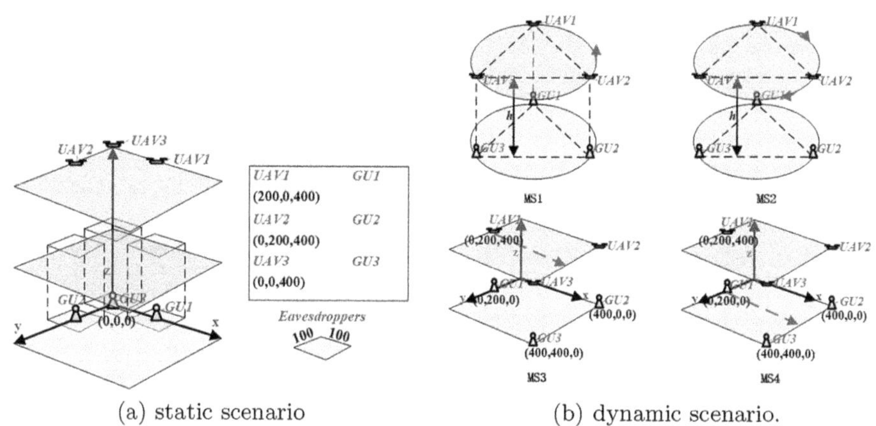

(a) static scenario   (b) dynamic scenario.

Fig. 3. Schematic diagram of the interference under dual-UAV communication scenario during interference cancellation.

Table 1. Simulated parameters.

Parameter	Symbol	Value
Flight altitude of UAVs	h	400 m
Total transmission power of UAV	P	0.1 W
Wavelength	λ	0.01 m
Grain constant	k	1
Environment noise	N_i^2	-174 dBm/Hz
Bandwidth	B	100 MHz

Figure 5(a)-(b) illustrates the variation in the secrecy transmission rate (C) of a user (e.g., user 3) when an eavesdropper is positioned either near or far from the user (specifically, directly above the user). It can be observed that regardless of the eavesdropper's proximity to the user, the overall C remains within a favorable range (approximately 10 bits/s). The user's C significantly decreases only when the eavesdropper's position exactly coincides with that of the user.

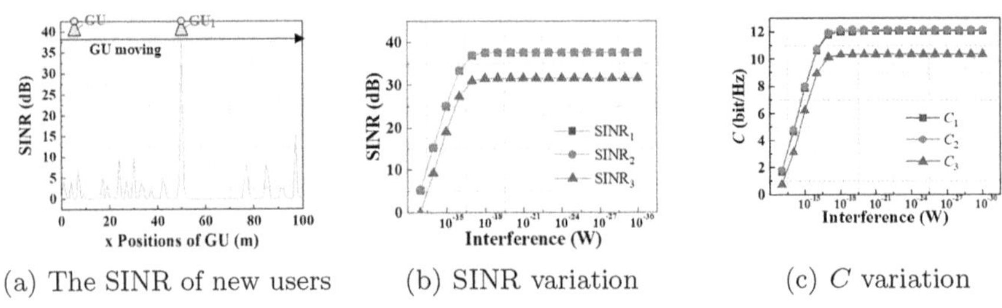

(a) The SINR of new users   (b) SINR variation   (c) C variation

Fig. 4. SINR and C variation during interference cancellation.

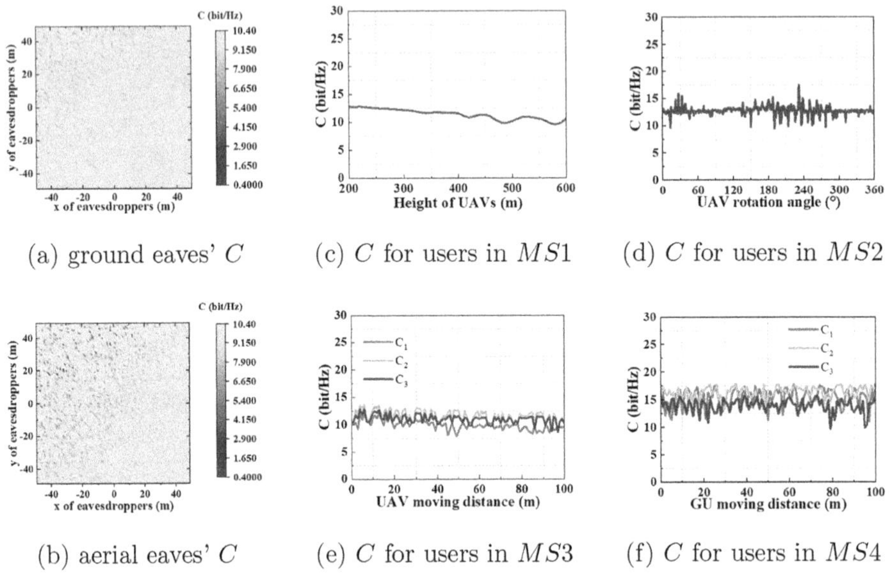

(a) ground eaves' C (c) C for users in $MS1$ (d) C for users in $MS2$

(b) aerial eaves' C (e) C for users in $MS3$ (f) C for users in $MS4$

Fig. 5. Simulated results under different verification scenarios.

However, such a scenario is improbable in practice, as an eavesdropper within a legitimate user's direct line of sight can be easily detected and mitigated.

Once there is a positional difference between the eavesdropper and the user, the eavesdropper continues to experience substantial interference, as evidenced by Fig. 4. This implies that the interference cancellation strategy is also effective in interfering with most eavesdroppers at unknown locations, thereby ensuring the system's secrecy.

Figure 5(c)-(f) illustrates the dynamic evolution of the secure transmission rates in dynamic scenarios. Regardless of the basic scenario, secure transmission rates for each user fluctuate within a range and ultimately stabilize at a level indicative of good communication quality. The scenarios described encompass both typical and special cases of UAVs transmitting useful signals to users. Any practical scenario can be decomposed into the movement patterns of these described scenarios. Thus, the proposed interference cancellation scheme effectively meets the current requirements for communication secrecy between UAVs and target users, achieving a relatively ideal state.

6 Conclusions

In this study, we propose a secure communication scheme based on co-channel interference assisted interference cancellation. The scheme can continuously suppress the interference from the eavesdropper, thereby enhancing the confidentiality of multi-UAV communication system. Simulation results validate the effectiveness of the proposed strategy in eliminating interference at legitimate users, increasing resistance against eavesdroppers, and improving the overall security performance of the system.

References

1. Kim, M., Lee, J.: Outage probability of UAV communications in the presence of interference. In: 2018 IEEE Global Communications Conference (GLOBECOM), pp. 1–6. IEEE, Abu Dhabi, United Arab Emirates (2018)
2. Hou, Y.Q., Tao, H., Gong, J.B., et al.: Cooperative path planning of USV and UAV swarms under multiple constraints. Chin. J. Ship Res. **16**(1), 74–82 (2021). https://doi.org/10.19693/j.issn.1673-3185.02091
3. Khawaja, W., Guvenc, I., Matolak, D.W., et al.: A survey of air-to-ground propagation channel modeling for unmanned aerial vehicles. IEEE Commun. Surv. Tutor. **21**(3), 2361–2391 (2019). https://doi.org/10.1109/COMST.2019.2915069
4. Wang, Y., An, G., Wang, C., et al.: Technology application and development trend of intelligent unmanned system. Chin. J. Ship Res. **17**(5), 9–26 (2022). https://doi.org/10.19693/j.issn.1673-3185.02705
5. Xu, F., Ahmad, S., Naveed, M., et al.: Beyond encryption: exploring the potential of physical layer security in UAV networks. J. King Saud Univ. Comput. Inf. Sci. **35**(8), 101717 (2023). https://doi.org/10.1016/j.jksuci.2023.101717
6. Safa, K., Mustafa, K., Mohamed-Slim, A., et al.: Exploiting tethered and untethered UAVs: a hybrid aerial communication system. Sci. Rep. Sci. Rep. **15**, 15882 (2025). https://doi.org/10.1038/s41598-025-99761-8
7. Li, B., Fei, Z., Zhang, Y., et al.: Secure UAV communication networks over 5G. IEEE Wirel. Commun. **26**(5), 114–120 (2019). https://doi.org/10.1109/MWC.2019.1800458
8. Khuawaja, L.A., Chen, Y., Zhao, N., et al.: A survey of channel modeling for UAV communications. IEEE Commun. Surv. Tutor. **20**(4), 2804–2821 (2018). https://doi.org/10.1109/COMST.2018.2856587
9. Zheng, G., Krikidis, I., Li, J., et al.: Improving physical layer secrecy using full-duplex jamming receivers. IEEE Trans. Signal Process. **61**(20), 4962–4974 (2013). https://doi.org/10.1109/TSP.2013.2269049
10. Zhou, Y., Yeoh, P.L., Chen, H., et al.: Secrecy outage probability and jamming coverage of UAV-enabled friendly jammer. In: The 11th International Conference on Signal Processing and Communication Systems (ICSPCS), pp. 1–6. Surfers Paradise, Australia (2017)

11. Shamsoshoara, A., Khaledi, M., Afghah, F., et al.: Distributed cooperative spectrum sharing in uav networks using multi-agent reinforcement learning. In: 2019 16th IEEE Annual Consumer Communications & Networking Conference (CCNC), pp. 1–6, IEEE, Las Vegas, USA, (2019)
12. Wang, Q., Chen, Z., Mei, W., et al.: Improving physical layer security using UAV-enabled mobile relaying. IEEE Wirel. Commun. Lett. **6**(3), 310–313 (2017). https://doi.org/10.1109/LWC.2017.2680449

Q-LOQ: Quantile-Optimized Loss for Low-bit Quantization

Yanan Liu[1,2], Zheng Dou[1], Boyang Song[1], Sicheng Zhang[1(✉)], and Qiao Tian[3]

[1] College of Information and Communication Engineering, Harbin Engineering University, Harbin 150001, China
{s322087067,2015080325,s322087067,2015080325}@hrbeu.edu.cn
[2] Academy of Electronics and Information Technology, Beijing, China
[3] College of Computer Science and Technology, Harbin Engineering University, Harbin 150001, China

Abstract. Specific Emitter Identification (SEI) distinguishes radiation sources by extracting unique signal features. However, when deploying such models, the large number of parameters often leads to excessive memory usage, hindering practical application. To address this issue, we propose a dynamic adaptive quadratic quantization scaling algorithm, which treats the scaling factor as a trainable parameter and dynamically optimizes quantization boundaries during training. Additionally, we employ a quantile Huber loss function to reduce the sensitivity of quantized weights to quantization errors, enhancing model robustness. A regularization term is also introduced to facilitate optimizer convergence. Experimental results demonstrate that our approach achieves low-bit-width model compression with an accuracy loss of less than 2%, closely matching the performance of the original model. This method significantly reduces memory consumption, compresses model size, and maintains recognition accuracy, enabling efficient inference on resource-constrained devices.

Keywords: SEI · Deep learning · Model quantification · Quantile Huber loss function

1 Introduction

Specific Emitter Identification (SEI) constitutes an essential capability within electronic reconnaissance, facilitating the precise geolocation of signal emitters amidst complex electromagnetic environments [1]. Artificial intelligence architectures - particularly deep neural networks - have demonstrated robust discriminative capacities in signal characterisation, establishing deep learning as a cornerstone technology within contemporary signal processing research [2]. These

This work is supported by the National Natural Science Foundation of China under Grant 62201172.

C. Xu et al. (Eds.): MobiMedia 2025, LNICST 670, pp. 277–287, 2026.
https://doi.org/10.1007/978-3-032-16823-8_20

computational approaches not only enhance feature extraction fidelity and classification accuracy, but have successfully been operationalised for critical tasks including signal modulation categorisation [3]. Current research paradigms for discrete emitter discrimination encompass: exploitation of RF fingerprint artefacts; dimensional reduction through machine learning techniques; integration of attention mechanisms within deep learning architectures; and implementation of decoupled representation learning frameworks to address long-tail identification challenges [4].

The growing complexity of modern neural network architectures poses significant challenges for deploying deep learning solutions on edge devices. These compute-intensive models demand substantial hardware resources, often rendering practical implementation impractical or entirely unfeasible. Thus, there is an urgent need to develop lightweight methods that can reduce model complexity while maintaining acceptable accuracy levels, thereby enabling efficient deployment on resource-constrained platforms [5].

To address this limitations, we propose a novel quantization approach incorporating a quantile threshold loss function. This method effectively maintains the recognition accuracy of the quantized model while achieving the desired computational efficiency.

1. We use quantile to determine the distribution characteristics of the model parameters and utilize the Herberger loss function to achieve optimal error representation for the partitioned intervals, thereby improving the accuracy of quantifying the intervals.
2. We introduce the Huber loss function to optimize the error representation in piecewise intervals. The Huber loss function can precisely capture minor deviations while effectively suppressing the interference of outliers in the optimization process. Through this flexible error handling approach, we are able to achieve optimal quantization effects in different error intervals, thereby significantly improving the accuracy of interval quantization.

The structure of this paper is as follows: The first part introduces the background of SEI. The second part discusses the related work of model quantification. The third part introduces the implementation theory of this method. The fourth part analyzes the experimental results of network quantization. The fifth part gives the conclusion of this paper.

2   Related Works

Model quantization is an efficient model compression technique. It reduces the storage requirements and computational complexity of models by decreasing the number of bits needed to represent neural network weights and activation values [6]. This process not only effectively alleviates the computational burden on hardware devices but also accelerates model inference. As a result, deep learning models become more deployable on resource-constrained edge devices while maintaining their accuracy.

Quantization methods are primarily categorized into two types: Quantization-Aware Training (QAT) and Post-Training Quantization (PTQ) [7]. Quantization-Aware Training integrates quantization parameters during the model training phase [8]. By simulating the effects of quantization, it allows the model to adapt to the quantization-induced errors throughout the training process. Although this approach can better optimize the performance of the quantized model, it requires retraining the entire model, which results in higher training time and computational costs. In contrast, Post-Training Quantization is applied after the model has been trained, using a small set of calibration data to adjust the model for quantization [9]. This method does not require retraining and is thus more efficient and less computationally intensive, although it may sometimes come at the cost of some model accuracy.

Recent progress in model quantization has unveiled diverse strategies to harmonize accuracy and efficiency. By examining how quantization errors in individual layers impact overall model performance, researchers have employed optimization techniques to identify the optimal bit width for each layer [11]. This tailored approach minimizes accuracy loss while reducing computational demands. Other work has modeled parameter quantization as a discrete optimization problem, using the alternating direction multiplier method to derive effective solutions [12]. These studies reveal that post-quantization performance degradation is closely tied to the linear combination of reconstruction errors across layers. Meanwhile, the integration of meta-learning with adaptive quantization training has enabled models to dynamically adjust to different bit widths, significantly enhancing accuracy in adaptive scenarios [13]. In addition, the bit width allocation, quantization map construction, equipment deployment and precision measurement are combined into a cohesive workflow, and a new method of mixed precision quantization is designed. The multi-objective Bayesian optimization generates the Pareto optimal solution [14]. Collectively, these efforts reflect a trend towards more sophisticated and flexible quantization methods, optimizing model performance across diverse deployment environments.

In post-training quantization methods, the quantization task can be decomposed into weight quantization and exploration of optimal quantization distances. Ranking loss can be introduced into the quantization objective to preserve the functionality of attention mechanisms after quantization [15]. Alternatively, inter-layer correlations can be fully exploited to mitigate overfitting through activation regularization, and annealed optimization of discrete variables can be employed, offering new insights for large-scale combinatorial optimization problems involving discrete variables.

Despite some progress in quantization performance, existing methods fall short in addressing quantization error impacts in the context of radiation source individual identification. To bridge this gap, we propose a quantization method based on quantile-optimized loss function error updates to further enhance model performance.

3   Method

3.1   Loss Function for Quantile Optimization

In post training quantization, the initial weights of the model have already been determined and do not need to be trained again. At this time, the balance error only needs to consider the task loss caused by weight disturbance before and after quantization. After Taylor expansion and ignoring higher-order terms, an optimization objective of reconstructing the feature map layer by layer can be obtained. Therefore, the weight optimization objective of the model is designed as a continuous local optimization problem, which is suitable for using loss descent for optimization.

The weights and activation data distributions of different layers in the model vary greatly. Therefore, the Huber loss function, which can adjust the parameters of each layer separately, is used to optimize each layer of data separately. When outlier data has a significant impact, the Huber loss can effectively reduce the loss caused by L2 norm while ensuring the speed of loss reduction. The formula is expressed as follows:

$$L_\delta(y, f(x)) = \begin{cases} \frac{1}{2}(y - f(x))^2, & \text{if } |y - f(x)| \leq \delta \\ \delta|y - f(x)| - \frac{1}{2}\delta^2, & \text{if } |y - f(x)| > \delta \end{cases} \tag{1}$$

where, y represents the true value, $f(x)$ represents the predicted value, and δ is the hyperparameter. When the error is less than δ, the L2 norm is used, which is suitable for fine errors; otherwise, the L1 norm is used to reduce the impact of outliers, achieving a balance in the model's sensitivity to errors by utilizing δ.

The data distribution of quantization errors is mostly concentrated near the zero point, with only a small number of outliers scattered. The concentrated distribution of data causes rounding errors with small error values, while outliers cause truncation errors with large error values. Therefore, in the process of optimizing errors, the main consideration is to use L2 norm optimization for centrally distributed data, while using L1 norm optimization for discrete points.

Quantile is a statistical concept that can intuitively reflect the distribution of data, effectively describing the central tendency and dispersion of data. Quantiles are numerical values located at specific positions in a dataset arranged in order of size, such as median, quartile, etc. This chapter introduces quantiles as a means of determining weight distribution.

Quantiles can subdivide different spaces of data. If the distance between quantiles is narrow, it indicates that the data is more concentrated; otherwise, it is scattered. Therefore, by comparing the quantiles of features, the differences in feature distributions can be compared. Dividing the different convolutional layers in the model into quantiles, in order to effectively distinguish the discrete distribution of parameters, the 90% percentile of the weight error is selected as the criterion for determining the sensitivity of the error distribution.

3.2   Regularization Constraint Optimization

In response to the issue of two types of inclusion errors mentioned in the previous section, when minimizing the loss, we hope to minimize the feature map error before and after quantization while also minimizing the two types of inclusion errors. Therefore, both types of inclusion errors are added to the optimization objective to achieve simultaneous convergence. To ensure the consistency of convergence, the two types of errors are trained step by step. First, the error of the weight inclusion λ is updated, and the loss of the secondary inclusion μ is updated preferentially to convergence, and then the secondary quantization loss is frozen.

Quantization is a process of approximating a discrete number to the nearest integer boundary. The quantization result can be viewed as a binary classification problem, with only two possible outcomes of approximating to the upper or lower bound. However, fixed two outcomes cannot be used to achieve the training process. Therefore, rounding error is adjusted to a trainable variable and treated as a continuous relaxation variable to achieve adaptive quantization.

To enhance its continuity, the inclusion error $r \in [0,1]$ is mapped through the Sigmoid function. To ensure the consistency of the boundaries, the range of r is expanded to $[a,b]$, but during the actual quantization process, the value of r does not change. This transforms the relative position range of the quantization error r into $(0,1)$, overlapping with the Sigmoid function, thus converting the error training convergence problem into a convergence issue with respect to the Sigmoid function.

In order to accelerate the convergence speed of relaxed variables, this section designs a regularization function:

$$H(x) = 1 - x^{\beta} - (1 - x)^{\beta} \tag{2}$$

The regularization term becomes steeper near 0 and 1, which can effectively accelerate the convergence of the target towards 0 or 1, and add annealing parameters to control the constraint strength of the regularization term.

4   Experiment

4.1   Dataset and Experimental Setup

The experimental setup includes 50 types of ADS-B signals, collected using the SM200B wireless signal detection equipment with a bandwidth of 160MHz. The collection process utilizes an omnidirectional antenna operating at a frequency of 1090MHz. There are 25,000 samples for each signal type, with data formatted as IQ sequences of size 2×4800. The Signal-to-Noise Ratio (SNR) ranges from -20dB to 20dB, with an interval of 2dB. The dataset is divided with a ratio of 8:2 for the training set to the test set. Adam optimizer was used, with parameters set to cosine annealing learning rate and an initial value of 4×10^{-5}. The loss function is selected as L2 norm. The weight training round of the model is set to 2000 times, while the activation training round is set to 500 times.

4.2 Comparison of Different Quantification Methods and Rounding Rules

In the experiment, the quantization range is first defined, and experiments are set up to verify the effects of symmetric quantization and asymmetric quantization. Different quantization strategies are added to the quantization types to initialize zeros and scaling factors. During the initialization process, in order to ensure the stability of input and output, 8-bit quantization is set for the first convolutional layer and the last fully connected layer, while 4-bit quantization is performed for the middle layer.

The quantization strategies used in this experiment include global MinMax quantization, dynamic MSE MinMax quantization, and KLD quantization, the result is shown in Fig. 1.

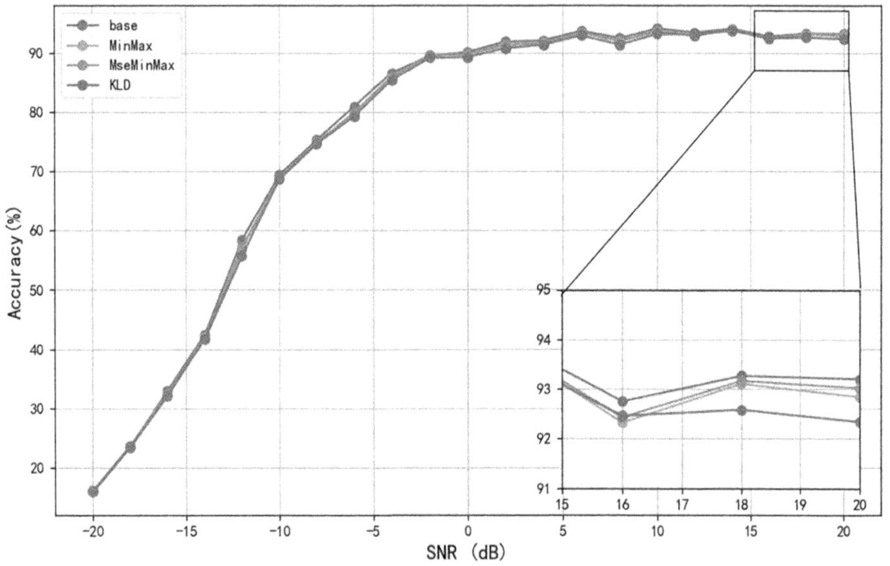

Fig. 1. Comparison of the effects of different initialization strategies.

Roughly speaking, as the signal-to-noise ratio increases, the recognition accuracy under all quantization strategies shows an upward trend and tends to stabilize, approaching or exceeding 90%. However, as the signal-to-noise ratio increases, the performance differences of various quantization strategies gradually narrow, and ultimately under high signal-to-noise ratio conditions (SNR greater than 10dB), the accuracy of all quantization models is extremely similar, maintaining above 90%.

We compared the basic rounding rules of nearest rounding, random rounding, and adaptive rounding, and applied all three rounding rules to the pruned standard model. The optimization effect of adaptive quantization based on traditional rounding method is compared with that of general asymmetric quantization. The comparison results are shown in Fig. 2.

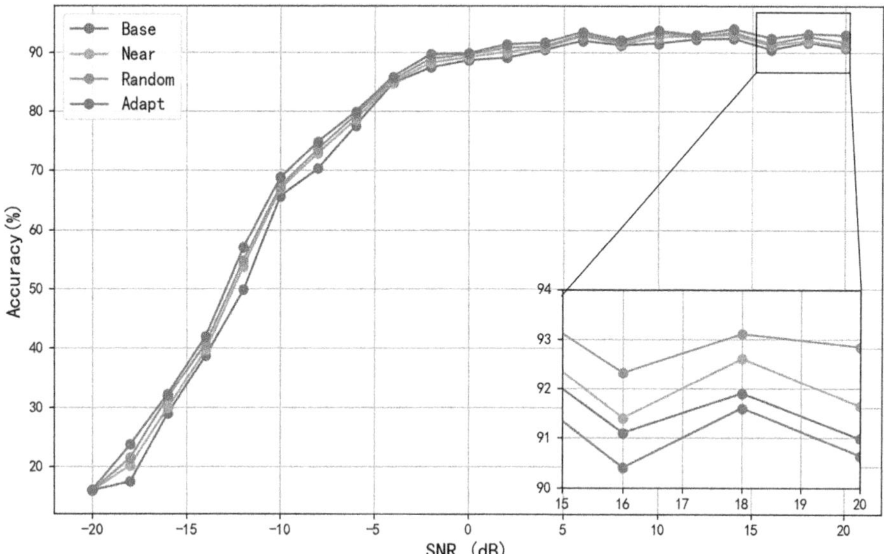

Fig. 2. Performance improvement of adaptive quantization compared to traditional quantization.

It can be observed that the adaptive trainable parameter rounding method has the fastest improvement in recognition accuracy, followed by nearest rounding and basic asymmetric quantization, while random rounding has the slowest improvement speed. Among them, the accuracy of the adaptive trainable parameter rounding method is the highest, close to 93%. In the high signal-to-noise ratio range (15dB to 20dB), the recognition accuracy of the adaptive trainable parameter rounding method fluctuates slightly, but overall it still remains above 92%.

Among various rounding strategies, adaptive rounding quantization based on trainable parameters also showed a maximum improvement of 1.5% in recognition performance compared to recent rounding and random rounding strategies. This indicates that adjusting the target parameters to variables that continuously update as the loss decreases can dynamically adjust all optimization objectives of all models through continuous iteration, which is significantly better than fixed parameter optimization.

4.3   Effect and Error Analysis of Different Loss Functions

The optimization method represents the error in feature map reconstruction during the quantization process through a loss function. The real loss reduction curve is shown in Table 1.

Table 1. Loss values at 2000 rounds

Loss type	Value at 2000 rounds
Total loss	$106.018 \rightarrow 34.152$
Weight Rebuild loss	$0.214 \rightarrow 1.252 \rightarrow 0.761$
Approximation inclusion loss	$95.824 \rightarrow 33.391$
Quadratic inclusion	$9.284 \rightarrow 9.192$

In the process of loss reduction, frozen block training was used to train two trainable parameters. In the first 20% of the training process, only the second-order rounding loss parameter was used to converge the weight reconstruction loss, expanding the impact of the second-order loss on the overall quantization effect. The weight parameters were excessively optimized and deviated from the optimal value of the whole. Therefore, when freezing the quadratic weights and optimizing only the approximate rounding weight parameters, it will result in weight updates and significant expansion of the quadratic loss error.

The performance of the quantized model based on quantile optimization using the Herberger loss function is shown in Fig. 3. At the same time, L1 norm, L2 norm, and Fisher diagonal matrix loss were selected as comparison loss functions to evaluate their effectiveness.

The L2 norm has a stronger effect than the L1 norm, indicating that the model parameters used in this chapter have more concentrated weights and fewer discrete points, but the difference in effect is small. The optimization process of the Fisher matrix depends on the gradient values before and after the model, which are constantly adjusted during training, resulting in an unstable optimization process. The quantile based Herbert loss balances the low sensitivity of the L1 norm and the overfitting effect of the L2 norm, improving the effect by about 1% compared to a single loss function. This verifies the effectiveness and reliability of the optimization angle in this chapter.

Quantify the baseline model using different methods and validate it on the test set. The specific test accuracy results are shown in Table 2. By comparing the recognition accuracy of different quantization methods on the ADS-B dataset under 20dB signal-to-noise ratio conditions, two comparison methods are listed in the table: AdaRound quantization method and BRECQ quantization method. When the original model uses FP32 (32 bit floating-point number) as the standard bit width, the recognition accuracy of the model can reach 93.94%. However, when W4A4 (4-bit weight and 4-bit activation) is used as the quantization bit width, the recognition accuracy of our method is the highest, at

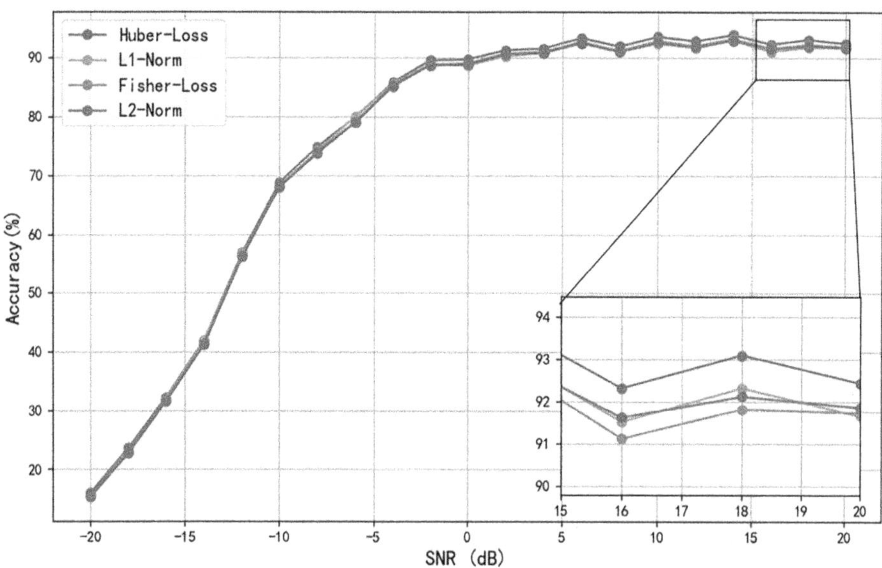

Fig. 3. Comparison of the experimental results of Herbert loss function optimization.

92.84%, which is only about 1% lower than the original model accuracy, but low bit width compression is achieved through quantization. The recognition accuracy of AdaRound method is close to that of BRECQ method at the same bit width, with 92.34% and 92.42% respectively, slightly lower than the accuracy of our method by 0.5% and 0.42%, demonstrating that our method maintains good recognition accuracy while compressing low bit width models.

Table 2. Comparison of recognition accuracy of different quantification methods.

Method	Bit width	Accuracy
Base	FP32	93.94%
AdaRound	W4A4	92.34%
BRECQ	W4A4	92.42%
Ours	W4A4	92.84%

5   Conclusion

To address the deployment challenges of complex neural networks on low-resource devices in SEI, we propose a novel quantization method using a quantile-based threshold loss function. This method characterizes model parameters through quantiles and optimizes interval errors using the Huber loss function, which captures minor deviations while suppressing outliers. This achieves optimal quantization accuracy while maintaining efficiency and acceptable performance. Experimental results show that the optimized algorithm in this paper achieves low bit width model compression with an accuracy loss of no more than 2%, achieving good results compared to traditional methods.

References

1. Ya, T., Yun, L., Haoran, Z., Zhang, J., Yu, W., Guan, G., Shiwen, M.: Large-scale real-world radio signal recognition with deep learning. Chin. J. Aeronaut. **35**(9), 35–48 (2022)
2. Chen, Y., Yu, L., Yao, Y., Zhu, L.: Individual identification technology of communication radiation sources based on deep learning. In: 2020 IEEE 20th International Conference on Communication Technology (ICCT). pp. 1301–1305 (2020)
3. Zhang, S., Yang, Y., Zhou, Z., Sun, Z., Lin, Y.: Dibad: a disentangled information bottleneck adversarial defense method using Hilbert-Schmidt independence criterion for spectrum security. IEEE Trans. Inf. Forensics Secur. (2024)
4. Zha, H., Wang, H., Feng, Z., Xiang, Z., Yan, W., He, Y., Lin, Y.: Lt-sei: Long-tailed specific emitter identification based on decoupled representation learning in low-resource scenarios. IEEE Trans. Intell. Transp. Syst. **25**(1), 929–943 (2024)
5. Lin, Y., Jia, J., Wang, S., Ge, B., Mao, S.: Wireless device identification based on radio frequency fingerprint features. In: ICC 2020-2020 IEEE International Conference on Communications (ICC), pp. 1–6. IEEE (2020)
6. Singh, M., Mohanty, L., Gupta, N., Bansal, Y., Garg, S.: Q-net compressor: adaptive quantization for deep learning on resource-constrained devices. In: 2024 International Conference on Computing, Sciences and Communications (ICCSC), pp. 1–6 (2024)
7. Chen, P.Y., Lin, H.C., Guo, J.I.: Multi-scale dynamic fixed-point quantization and training for deep neural networks. In: 2023 IEEE International Symposium on Circuits and Systems (ISCAS), pp. 1–5 (2023)
8. Wang, C.E., Tai, Y.S., Wu, A.Y.: Fq4dm: Full quantization for diffusion model. In: 2024 IEEE 34th International Workshop on Machine Learning for Signal Processing (MLSP), pp. 1–6 (2024)
9. Ozerov, A., Kleijn, W.B.: Asymptotically optimal model estimation for quantization. IEEE Trans. Commun. **59**(4), 1031–1042 (2011)
10. Chen, Q., Teng, Y., Zhang, H., Jiang, K., Duan, Q., Li, X., Zhao, X., Li, R.: Post-training quantization for longformer with chunkwise quantization granularity and optimized percentile. In: 2022 7th International Conference on Computer and Communication Systems (ICCCS), pp. 27–31 (2022)
11. Zhou, Y., Moosavi-Dezfooli, S.M., Cheung, N.M., Frossard, P.: Adaptive quantization for deep neural network. In: Proceedings of the AAAI Conference on Artificial Intelligence, vol. 32 (2018)
12. Chen, S., Wang, W., Pan, S.J.: Deep neural network quantization via layer-wise optimization using limited training data. In: Proceedings of the AAAI Conference on Artificial Intelligence, vol. 33, pp. 3329–3336 (2019)
13. Youn, J., Song, J., Kim, H.S., Bahk, S.: Bitwidth-adaptive quantization-aware neural network training: a meta-learning approach. In: European Conference on Computer Vision, pp. 208–224. Springer (2022)

14. Miriyala, S.S., Suhas, P., Tiwari, U., Rajendiran, V.N.: Mixed precision neural quantization with multi-objective Bayesian optimization for on-device deployment. In: ICASSP 2024-2024 IEEE International Conference on Acoustics, Speech and Signal Processing (ICASSP), pp. 6260–6264. IEEE (2024)
15. Liu, Z., Wang, Y., Han, K., Zhang, W., Ma, S., Gao, W.: Post-training quantization for vision transformer. Adv. Neural. Inf. Process. Syst. **34**, 28092–28103 (2021)

MAAB: Multi-scale Dynamic Adaptive Attention Mechanisms for Cross-Domain Specific Emitter Identification

Hongyu Zou[1], Meiyu Wang[1,1]($\boxtimes$), Juzhen Wang[1], and Guangzhen Si[2]

[1] Hangzhou Dianzi University, Hangzhou, China
wangmeiyu@hdu.edu.cn
[2] Zhejiang University of Technology, Hangzhou, China

Abstract. Cross-domain specific emitter identification (SEI) is vital for RF systems management but faces challenges from temporal signal variability, hardware state drifts, and cross-domain feature distribution mismatches. We propose a Multi-scale Adaptive Attention Block (MAAB) architecture addressing these issues through coordinated multi-temporal feature learning, combining a Multi-scale Dilated Convolution Module (MDCM) that captures hierarchical patterns via progressive dilation rates and a Dynamic Adaptive Attention Module (DAAM) enabling channel-wise feature recalibration. The MDCM-DAAM synergy facilitates robust cross-scale feature alignment while maintaining hardware fluctuation resilience. Our framework integrates MK-MMD distribution matching with adversarial domain adaptation, creating a dual optimization mechanism that simultaneously minimizes inter-domain discrepancies and enhances discriminative feature transfer. Comprehensive evaluations using real-world WiFi datasets confirm the system's superior performance, demonstrating 12.7% accuracy improvement over conventional methods in cross-scenario tests. The proposed solution achieves 94.2% average identification accuracy across diverse operational conditions, particularly excelling in handling temporal window variations and long-term hardware degradation effects, proving its practical viability for real-world SEI deployment under non-stationary signal environments.

Keywords: Cross-domain · Specific emitter identification · Multi-scale domain adaptation · Domain-adversarial · Attention mechanisms

1 Introduction

With the rapid evolution of wireless communication technologies, the number of smart devices is growing exponentially. Applications such as mobile internet and the Internet of Things (IoT) are continuously expanding, making wireless networks increasingly vital across various industries [1, 2]. However, the openness and broadcast nature of wireless communication also expose systems to significant security threats. Traditional cryptography-based security mechanisms at higher layers are becoming inadequate in

C. Xu et al. (Eds.): MobiMedia 2025, LNICST 670, pp. 288–305, 2026.
https://doi.org/10.1007/978-3-032-16823-8_21

the face of increasingly sophisticated attacks. As a physical-layer security enhancement technique, Specific Emitter Identification enables the unique identification and authentication of wireless transmitters by analyzing the naturally generated Radio Frequency Fingerprints (RFFs) during signal transmission [3]. Since RFFs originate from subtle hardware imperfections, they are inherently difficult to forge or replicate [4], providing intrinsic security to wireless systems without relying on conventional key-based methods. Consequently, SEI has become a key area of focus in physical-layer security research [5].

In recent years, deep learning has achieved remarkable progress in SEI by leveraging its powerful capabilities in automatic feature extraction and representation learning [6], attaining impressive identification performance on benchmark datasets. Nevertheless, under real-world complex conditions, deep learning-based SEI still faces several critical challenges. In practical applications, factors such as time-varying wireless channels, hardware aging, noise interference, and multipath effects cause substantial differences in data distribution between the training and testing data [7, 8]. Additionally, due to high annotation costs and the difficulty of data acquisition, it is often impractical to collect large-scale, high-quality datasets that comprehensively cover all possible environmental variations. This exacerbates the issue of performance degradation in deep models [9].

To tackle the challenge posed by distributional changes in signal samples, Domain Adaptation (DA) techniques have demonstrated their effectiveness. As a key branch of transfer learning, DA addresses the distribution mismatch between source and target domains, enabling knowledge transfer across domains. Existing DA approaches can be categorized into adversarial learning methods and feature alignment/distribution matching techniques. For instance, in adversarial learning, [10] integrated Continuous Wavelet Transform (CWT) and Domain-Adversarial Neural Networks (DANN) to achieve high identification accuracy across communication devices operating on different carrier frequencies. In [11], a multi-layer convolutional feature extractor was used in conjunction with adversarial training to align deep fingerprint features across domains. In terms of feature alignment [12], proposed a prototype-based bidirectional alignment strategy that leverages the relationship between features and their class-wise prototypes to enable class-level transfer, improving inter-class discriminability under global cross-domain feature alignment. Addressing the challenge of modulation variation under limited samples [13], introduced a DA-based SEI approach using Maximum Mean Discrepancy (MMD) to reduce the domain gap. In [14], a feature transformation and alignment network was developed to alleviate performance degradation in cross-domain SEI through explicit feature alignment. Collectively, these methods illustrate how DA strategies, focused on adversarial training and feature distribution alignment, can effectively address cross-domain challenges in SEI.

However, the emitter signals from different classes are not always of fixed scale—variations in signal duration, frequency, or sampling rate often lead to scale inconsistency among signals. As a result, conventional SEI methods struggle to generalize in cross-domain scenarios, particularly under dynamic conditions such as frequency shifts, channel noise, and environmental changes. Therefore, addressing temporal scale inconsistencies and enhancing the robustness and adaptability of SEI models under dynamic environments have become pressing challenges in the field.

To this end, we propose a domain-adaptive SEI method tailored for cross-domain and multi-scale signal identification. The major contributions of this work are as follows:

For multi-scale cross-domain alignment of emitter signals, we propose a Multi-scale Adaptive Attention Block tailored to the hierarchical and multi-scale characteristics of emitter features. The MAAB consists of two components: a Multi-scale Dilated Convolution Module and Dynamic Adaptive Attention Module. The MDCM is designed to capture feature representations of the input signal under different scales. Further, the DAAM computes attention weights across channels based on the MDCM outputs at various scales, balancing the contributions of each scale and enabling effective feature alignment of emitter signals under varying scale conditions.

In terms of implicit domain-invariant feature learning for emitter signals, this paper builds upon the MAAB-based multi-scale cross-domain alignment and further integrates MK-MMD distribution alignment loss with adversarial training loss. First, adversarial training is employed to enhance the model's cross-domain robustness. Second, the MK-MMD loss is used to minimize the feature distribution discrepancy between domains, further reinforcing the domain invariance of the learned feature representations. Ultimately, this approach enables implicit feature sharing and knowledge discovery across domains for emitter signal recognition.

2   Related Work

2.1   Deep Learning Methods for SEI Feature Extraction

As one of the most significant breakthroughs in artificial intelligence, deep learning has made substantial progress in the field of Specific Emitter Identification in recent years. By leveraging optimized network architectures and training strategies, deep learning models benefit from deeper structures, stronger representation capabilities, and faster convergence speeds, making it feasible to process large-scale emitter datasets. In [6], a SEI method based on Convolutional Neural Networks (CNN) was proposed, which directly processes raw I/Q signal data for identification. Compared to traditional RF-based approaches, this method significantly improved recognition accuracy. In [15], the authors introduced a SEI approach that incorporates Complex-Valued Neural Networks (CVCNN) and model compression techniques. By exploring the coupling relationships between the in-phase and quadrature components of complex-valued signals, the method achieved higher recognition accuracy while reducing network complexity. In [16], a multi-head attention-based method was proposed to extract frequency-domain features by applying Fast Fourier Transform (FFT), demonstrating superior performance compared to many existing frequency-domain feature extraction techniques. In [17], a joint Attention-CNN network was designed and validated on real-world datasets. The results indicated that the combined attention-CNN architecture effectively mitigated the impact of limited training samples on model performance.

These methods effectively extract discriminative transmitter features from signals and perform well on fixed benchmarks. However, they often neglect the impact of varying environmental or signal conditions, which can lead to a sharp decline in SEI model accuracy. Therefore, strategies to mitigate these variations and improve SEI system robustness in dynamic environments are essential.

2.2 Domain Adaptation for SEI

Domain Adaptation, as a key branch of transfer learning, aims to address the issue of data distribution discrepancies between the source domain and the target domain. DA techniques seek to transfer knowledge learned from the source domain to the target domain, thereby mitigating the adverse effects of distribution shift and enhancing model performance on cross-domain tasks. Most DA methods utilize dual-branch deep network architectures to represent the source and target domains. The training process of such networks typically involves two types of loss: a classification loss computed using labeled source domain samples, and a domain adaptation loss designed to reduce domain discrepancy. The latter primarily includes domain discrepancy losses and adversarial domain losses.

Domain discrepancy-based methods generally aim to minimize the statistical distance between source and target domains using appropriate metrics. One of the foundational approaches in this category is the DANN [18]. Other commonly used discrepancy metrics include MMD [19], Correlation Alignment (CORAL) [20], and Wasserstein Distance [21].

In the context of Specific Emitter Identification, DA techniques have been shown to improve model robustness across varying frequencies, environments, or hardware conditions. For instance, [22] proposed a Deep Adversarial Domain Adaptation (DADA) network, which integrates deep neural networks with adversarial learning to perform unsupervised transfer learning for RFFs-based SEI. This method effectively addresses the feature discrepancy between source and target domains. Moreover, in addressing the challenge of modulation variation under limited data scenarios, [23] developed an adversarial domain adaptation approach based on Wasserstein distance. This method employs a Wasserstein-guided unsupervised domain adaptation strategy to further enhance identification accuracy and robustness.

While DA-based SEI methods show promise, challenges persist in real-world scenarios, especially with signal scale inconsistencies and multi-frequency transformations. This work explores fine-grained feature extraction and domain alignment strategies to enhance cross-domain SEI performance under these constraints.

3 Proposed Method

3.1 Overall Architecture

The overall architecture of the proposed MAAB is illustrated in Fig. 1. It comprises a multi-scale cross-domain alignment network and a latent domain-invariant learning module. First, the multi-scale alignment network utilizes a carefully designed MDCM to capture hierarchical feature representations from the input signal. The MDCM consists of six parallel convolutional branches, each configured with distinct kernel sizes and dilation rates. This design enables the network to extract multi-granularity features ranging from fine-grained local details to broader global contexts. To further enhance the representational capacity, a DAAM is integrated. This mechanism computes channel-wise attention weights for the outputs of each scale-specific branch, effectively balancing the contributions of features at different temporal scales. Next, the latent domain-invariant learning module takes the multi-scale features as input and improves cross-domain robustness through a dual-constraint mechanism. On one hand, a MK-MMD-based distribution alignment loss is applied to minimize the feature distribution gap between the source and target domains. On the other hand, an adversarial training strategy is employed by incorporating a Gradient Reversal Layer (GRL) to optimize a domain discriminator, which further encourages domain-invariant feature learning. During training, the combination of these two loss functions enhances the domain adaptability of the model, thereby enabling accurate cross-domain identification of specific emitters.

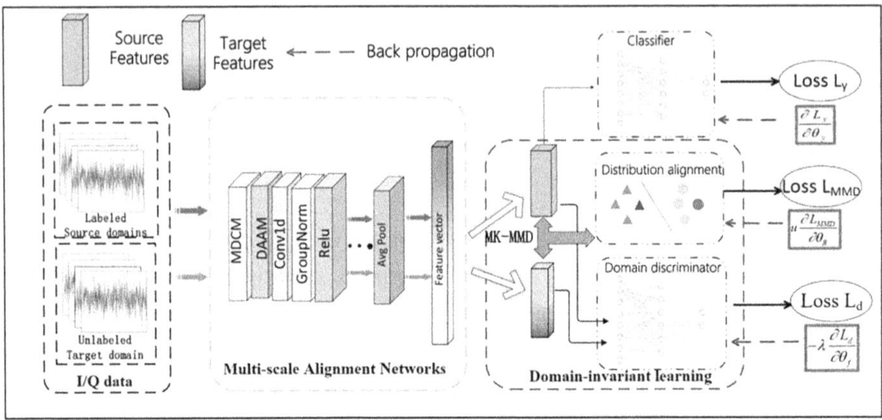

Fig. 1. Overall architecture of MAAB.

3.2 Multi-scale Cross-Domain Alignment for Emitter Signals

(1) Multi-scale Dilated Convolution Module

In conventional convolutional layers, the kernel size is pre-defined and fixed, which determines the spatial receptive field covered by the convolution operation. However, the appropriate region for extracting meaningful features varies across different scenarios. As a result, the ability of a convolutional layer to capture discriminative features is heavily dependent on the selected kernel size. Since the effective temporal patterns may differ under varying conditions, the discriminative capability of convolutional operations is closely linked to the choice of kernel dimensions. To address this limitation, Multi-Scale Convolutional Neural Networks (MSCNN) have been developed, utilizing parallel convolution branches with different kernel sizes to extract features across multiple scales [11]. However, our MDCM differs from conventional multi-scale structures. Instead of relying solely on varying kernel sizes, The MDCM module leverages dilated convolutions with variable dilation rates to obtain multi-scale representations. By inserting zeros between the weights of a convolution kernel, dilated convolutions effectively enlarge the receptive field without increasing the number of parameters. Through adjusting the dilation rate, the network can extract features at different temporal resolutions, enabling a broader and more flexible perception of signal patterns than standard convolution.

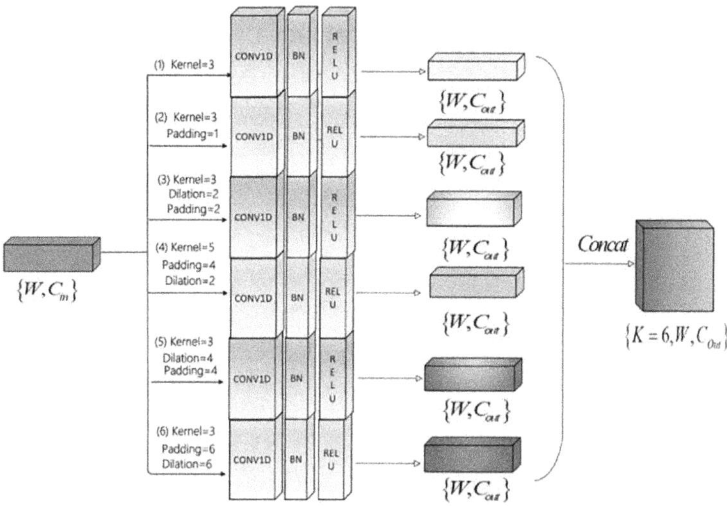

Fig. 2. The structure of MDCM

The detailed structure is illustrated in Fig. 2. We design a multi-scale parallel dilated convolution module, which consists of six structurally similar yet functionally complementary convolutional branches. By configuring the convolutional parameters differently across branches, the module achieves multi-granularity feature extraction. Specifically, each branch follows a unified architectural pattern of Conv1d, Batch Normalization (BN), and ReLU activation, while the core convolution operations are tailored with distinct kernel sizes and dilation rates to target different temporal resolutions.

(2) Dynamic Adaptive Attention Module

The module models the channel relationships in the multi-scale feature maps and assigns weights accordingly. This is achieved by applying different scale-based feature compression methods, such as global average pooling, global max pooling, and regional adaptive pooling in parallel, extracting channel-wise statistical information from multiple dimensions. The features from each branch are then concatenated and passed through a shared fully connected network, which models the complex inter-channel dependencies through nonlinear transformations. Finally, a Sigmoid function is used to generate the multi-scale fused channel attention weights, dynamically enhancing discriminative features while suppressing redundant information. This process improves the model's ability to adapt to and represent features at different scales. The specific operations are illustrated Fig. 3.

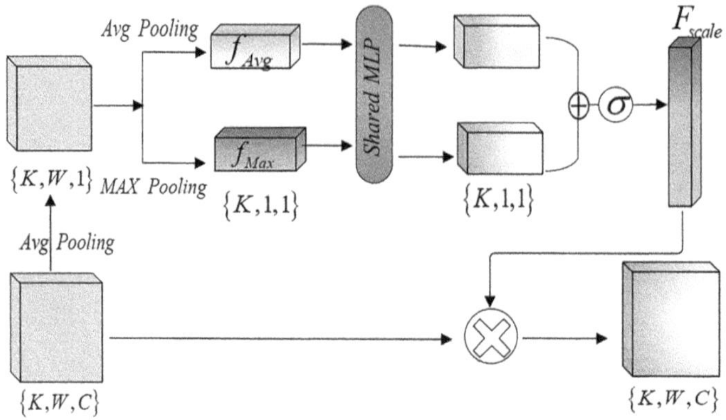

Fig. 3. The structure of DAAM

Where, K denotes the number of convolutional paths in the MDCM, W is the length of the input features, C is the number of output channels. First, the feature maps from different convolutional paths are concatenated to form a unified feature map $x \in \mathbb{R}^{k \times W \times C}$. Then, global average pooling is performed along the channel dimension to extract the average features for each channel. Next, both global max pooling and average pooling are applied to the feature map to generate two global feature vectors, f_{Avg} and f_{Max} ($f_{Avg}, f_{Max} \in \mathbb{R}^{K \times 1 \times 1}$), which are computed as follows:

$$f_{Avg} = F_{avg}\left(F_{avg}(x)\right) = \frac{1}{C \times W} \sum_{W}^{j=1} \sum_{C}^{k=1} x(jk) \tag{1}$$

$$f_{Max} = Favg_i \max_{j=1,2,\cdots,W} \frac{1}{C} \sum_{\max}^{\frac{k=1}{C}} \tag{2}$$

where, j and k represent the temporal axis and channel dimension, respectively.

Then, the vectors f_{Avg} and f_{Max} are each passed through a shared multilayer perceptron (MLP) to compute their respective attention scores, which are summed to enhance the representational capacity of the module. Subsequently, a Sigmoid function is applied to generate the multi-scale fused channel attention weights z ($z \in \mathbb{R}^{K \times 1 \times 1}$), which can be calculated as:

$$\begin{aligned}
z &= \sigma\left(\delta\left(\mathrm{MLP}\left(f_{avg}(V)\right) + \mathrm{MLP}(f_{max}())()\right)\right) \\
&= \sigma\left(\delta\left(W_1\left(W_0\left(f_{Avg}\right)\right) + W_1\left(W_0\left(f_{Max}\right)\right)\right)\right)
\end{aligned} \tag{3}$$

where $W_0 \in \mathbb{R}^{K/r \times K}$ and $W_1 \in \mathbb{R}^{K \times K/r}$ are the weight vectors of the MLP layers, r is the reduction ratio, δ represents the ReLU activation function, and σ denotes the activation function that transforms the attention scores into values between 0 and 1. Through this process, the importance of each convolutional path can be evaluated.

Next, a scaling operation $F_{scale}(\cdot)$ is applied to the input feature map x, where it is element-wise multiplied with the attention activation vector z along the channel dimension. The operation is defined as:

$$Y_{\text{scale}} = F_{\text{scale}}(X) = z \cdot X \tag{4}$$

(3) **Multi-scale Adaptive Attention Block**

The Multi-scale Adaptive Attention Block is the primary building block of the entire network. As shown in the figure, MAAB consists of a GroupNorm layer, a ReLU activation layer, a MDCM layer, a MDAA layer, and a 1D convolution layer. GroupNorm, as a normalization strategy, does not rely on batch size and normalizes the channels of each sample by groups. This makes it more suitable for multi-branch and shallow-channel architectures, helping to improve model stability and feature expression consistency. The use of GroupNorm and ReLU activation layers after convolution reduces the impact of overfitting and ensures that the activated outputs are sparse, which enhances computational efficiency (Fig. 4).

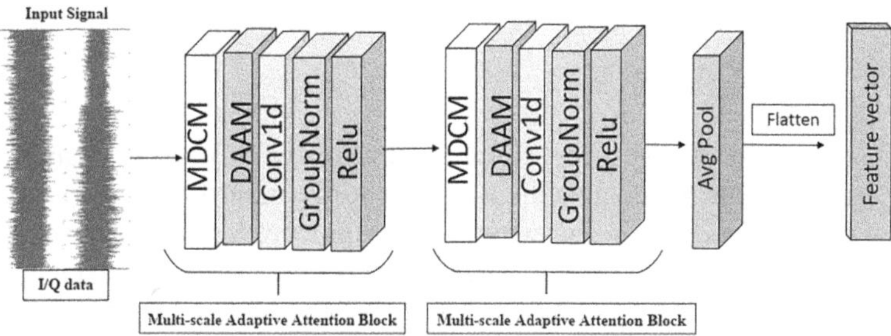

Fig. 4. The structure of MAAB

The primary purpose of applying convolution after multi-scale feature extraction is to further fuse features across different scales, improving the model's robustness and perception ability. Additionally, convolution helps to expand the receptive field, allowing the model to extract useful information from a broader context. Moreover, the convolution operation, with a stride of 2, reduces the size of the feature map by half while retaining as much useful information as possible. This operation also further learns the relationships between multi-scale features, effectively reducing information loss.

In our multi-scale domain-adaptive feature alignment network for radiation source signals, two DAAM blocks are stacked in series to progressively deepen the multi-scale feature expression and adaptive enhancement capabilities. The specific network structure is summarized in the table. The first MAAB focuses on the extraction and preliminary fusion of multi-scale features at the basic layer, capturing fine-grained structural information. The second MAAB further strengthens the modeling of high-level semantic features, enhancing feature representation through a larger receptive field and more complex channel dependencies. The feature dimension enhancement and spatial down-sampling between the two modules are achieved by convolution operations, which not only compress the feature map size but also elevate the abstraction level. The overall structure fully leverages the advantages of MAAB in local and global feature modeling, facilitating the efficient fusion of detailed information and contextual semantics, thus providing more informative and discriminative multi-scale representations for downstream tasks.

3.3 Domain-Invariance Learning Module

(1) Domain Adversarial Learning

Adversarial learning is a domain adaptation technique that introduces adversarial training to align feature distributions between domains. The core idea is to incorporate a domain discriminator into the model and train it in a way that encourages the extracted features from the source and target domains to become indistinguishable. In this manner, feature representations can be transferred from the source domain to the target domain. The adversarial learning process typically involves a feature extractor and a domain discriminator. To achieve accurate classification while learning domain-invariant features, the following optimization procedure is required:

First, the domain classification loss for each sample is computed using Eq. (5).

$$L_d^i(\theta_f, \theta_d) = L_d\left(G_d\left(G_f(x_i; \theta_f); \theta_d\right), d_i\right) \tag{5}$$

where, $G_f(\cdots; \theta_f)$ denotes the feature extractor with network parameters θ_f; $G_d(\cdots; \theta_d)$ epresents the domain discriminator with parameters θ_d; L_d is the domain classification loss function; d_i indicates the domain label for each sample, where the source domain is labeled as 0 and the target domain as 1; x_i denotes the input sample.

Next, the average domain classification loss for both source and target domain samples is computed, as shown in Eq. (6).

$$E(\theta_f, \theta_y, \theta_d) = -\lambda \left(\frac{1}{n_s} \sum_{i=1}^{n} L_d^i(\theta_f, \theta_d) + \frac{1}{n_t} \sum_{i=n+1}^{N} L_d^i(\theta_f, \theta_d) \right) \tag{6}$$

In the equation, E denotes the domain classification loss. n_s and n_t represent the number of source and target domain samples, respectively.

Then, through Eq. (7), the parameters θ_d are updated to maximize the domain discriminator loss. The goal is to encourage the feature extractor to learn domain-invariant features that confuse the domain discriminator. This process helps the model learn a balanced parameter, achieving both domain-invariant feature learning and accurate classification simultaneously.

$$\hat{\theta}_d = \arg\max E(\hat{\theta}_f, \theta_d) \tag{7}$$

Next, the classification loss generated by the domain discriminator is backpropagated to update the parameters of the feature extractor. The backpropagation minimizes the loss, thereby optimizing the objective. To maintain the backpropagation direction while maximizing the domain discriminator loss, a Gradient Reversal Layer (GRL) is introduced between the feature extractor and the domain classifier. This layer reverses the gradient during backpropagation, allowing the feature extractor to learn domain-invariant features while still enabling the domain discriminator to maximize its loss.

$$\theta_f \leftarrow \theta_f - \mu\left(-\lambda\frac{\partial L_d^i}{\partial \theta_f}\right) \tag{8}$$

where, λ is a weighting coefficient that controls the strength of the reversed gradient. It is usually gradually increased during training. μ is the learning rate.

Finally, the parameters of the domain discriminator are updated separately, as shown in Eq. (9).

$$\theta_d \leftarrow \theta_d - \mu\left(-\lambda\frac{\partial L_d^i}{\partial \theta_f}\right) \tag{9}$$

The domain adversarial method introduces an adversarial training mechanism, enabling the model to learn discriminative features shared between the source and target domains, thereby mitigating the domain shift problem to some extent. However, this method is prone to unstable optimization and insufficient adversarial signals during actual training, making it difficult to achieve precise alignment, especially when faced with complex distributions. To further enhance the stability and expressive power of feature alignment, the next section will introduce the MK-MMD method as a beneficial supplement to the domain adversarial mechanism.

(2) **Multi-Kernel Maximum Mean Discrepancy**

Adversarial learning implicitly aligns source and target domain features by training a discriminator, but it often falls into local optima and fails to capture fine-grained distribution differences. In contrast, MK-MMD explicitly measures and aligns distributions using higher-order statistics and multiple kernels, enabling more precise multi-scale feature alignment.

Let us denote the source domain samples as $\{x_i^s\}_{i=1}^n \sim P$ and the target domain samples as $\{x_j^t\}_{j=1}^m \sim Q$, To measure the distribution discrepancy between the source domain P and the target domain Q, this paper adopts MMD as a statistical distance metric. MMD is a non-parametric method based on kernel functions, which essentially compares the distance between the mean embeddings of two distributions in a Reproducing Kernel Hilbert Space (RKHS). The formal definition of MMD is given as:

$$\text{MMD}^2(P, Q) = \frac{1}{n}\sum_{i=1}^n \phi(x_i^s) - \frac{1}{m}\sum_{j=1}^m \phi(x_j^t)\Big\|_{\mathcal{H}}^2 \tag{10}$$

where, $\mathcal{H}$ denotes RKHS, $\phi(\cdot)$ epresents the feature mapping from the original feature space to the RKHS. $\|\cdot\|_{\mathcal{H}}$ denotes the norm in RKHS, the distance between vectors in this space.

This distance can be further expressed in terms of a kernel function as follows:

$$\text{MMD}^2(P, Q) = \mathbb{E}_{x,x'\sim P}\big[k(x, x')\big] + \mathbb{E}_{y,y'\sim Q}\big[k(y, y')\big] - 2\mathbb{E}_{x\sim P, y\sim Q}\big[k(x, y)\big] \tag{11}$$

The function $k(x, y)$ denotes the kernel function, and in this work, we adopt the Gaussian kernel, x, y represents the feature vector of any two points in the feature space. $\mathbb{E}_{x,x'\sim P}$ denotes the expected kernel value computed over two samples drawn from the source domain distribution, $\mathbb{E}_{y,y'\sim Q}$ denotes the expected kernel value computed over two samples drawn from the target domain distribution, $\mathbb{E}_{x\sim P,y\sim Q}$ denotes the cross-domain expectation between source and target domain samples.

Traditional MMD relies on a single kernel function, whose performance may be limited when dealing with distribution discrepancies at different scales. To address this limitation, we adopt MK-MMD, which introduces multiple Gaussian kernels with different bandwidths and combines them through a weighted sum, thereby enhancing the model's capability in distribution alignment. The multi-kernel combination is defined as shown in Eq. (12):

$$k(x, y) = \sum_{l=1}^{L} \beta_l \cdot \exp\left(-\frac{\|x - y\|^2}{2\sigma_l^2}\right) \tag{12}$$

where, L denotes the number of Gaussian kernels used, and $\|\cdots\|^2$ represents the squared Euclidean distance. The parameter σ_l denotes the bandwidth of the l-th Gaussian kernel, which controls the scale of the kernel function. A larger bandwidth σ_l enables the kernel to capture global feature alignments by covering a broader range, while a smaller bandwidth focuses on local discrepancies, facilitating fine-grained matching. The learnable weight β_l allows the network to dynamically adjust the importance of different scale kernels, thereby enabling adaptive multi-scale feature alignment.

In the actual model, assuming a batch size of n, and given that the source and target samples are concatenated, the kernel matrix K is computed using the above multi-kernel combination. The MK-MMD loss can then be formulated as:

$$\mathcal{L}_{\text{MK-MMD}} = \frac{1}{n^2} \sum_{i,j=1}^{n} K_{i,j}^{ss} + \frac{1}{n^2} \sum_{i,j=1}^{n} K_{i,j}^{tt} - \frac{2}{n^2} \sum_{i,j=1}^{n} K_{i,j}^{st} \tag{13}$$

where, $K_{i,j}^{ss}$, $K_{i,j}^{tt}$, $K_{i,j}^{st}$ represent the kernel values within the source domain, within the target domain, and between the source and target domains, respectively.

To address the instability and limited alignment of purely adversarial training, we introduce MK-MMD with multi-bandwidth Gaussian kernels to capture distribution discrepancies at multiple scales. By combining adversarial learning and MK-MMD, we build a hierarchical alignment strategy: adversarial learning ensures global distribution consistency, while MK-MMD provides fine-grained local alignment. This hybrid approach enhances cross-domain feature alignment and improves generalization.

4 Experimental

4.1 Experiment Setup

The experimental simulations were conducted using PyTorch on an RTX 4060Ti platform. A dataset containing wireless transmission signals from 10 different emitters was utilized, with a sampling rate of 80 MHz. Each emitter provides 1,000 signal samples, among which 800 were used for training and 200 for testing. The data are represented in I/Q format, and the source and target domains were collected under different transmission channel conditions. To verify and analyze the effectiveness of the proposed algorithm, four groups of experiments were conducted:1) A comparative experiment on recognition performance using different methods was conducted to validate the superiority of the proposed algorithm in cross-channel Wi-Fi signal identification.2) An analysis of individual performance differences was carried out to evaluate the robustness of the model under various SNR conditions.3) A sensitivity analysis of the feature extractor was performed to investigate the model's response to changes in signal conditions.4) An ablation study was designed to verify the necessity of each component in the proposed algorithm.

4.2 Comparison of Identification Performance of Different Methods

In this set of experiments, to accommodate the requirements of varying input sizes, 20% of the samples were randomly selected from the entire dataset. For each selected sample, signal segments were cropped from the beginning, middle, and end of the waveform. The lengths of the cropped segments were constrained within the range of [700, 1000], resulting in a dataset that includes both original-size and variable-size samples.

To evaluate the effectiveness of the proposed MAAB method in cross-domain identification, we conducted comparative experiments against several mainstream crossdomain recognition approaches, including Wasserstein [21], MSCNN [11], CVCNN [15], and Source Only. The ADAW method aligns domains using adversarial training and minimizes feature distribution discrepancies through Wasserstein distance. The MSCNN method employs a multi-layer feature extractor with varying convolutional kernels to learn multi-scale features and optimize domain-adaptive fingerprint features via adversarial training. The CVCNN method uses a complex-valued convolutional neural network to extract features from I/Q dual-channel complex signals. The Source Only method is trained on source domain data without domain adaptation (Fig. 5).

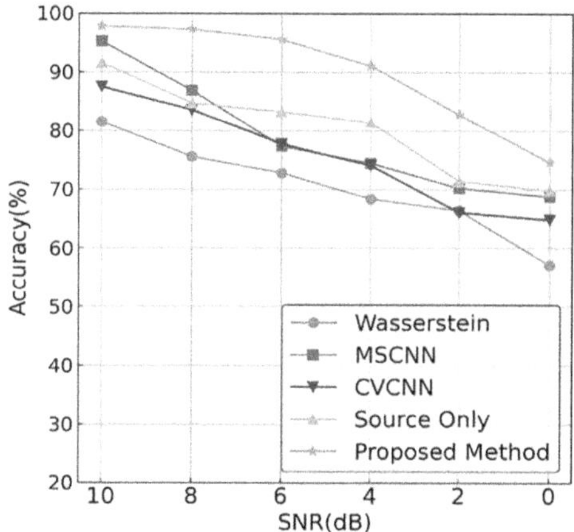

Fig. 5. Comparison of accuracy performance under different methods across various SNR.

The experimental results are shown in Fig. 6. Under the condition of SNR = 0 dB, MAAB achieves an accuracy of 74.60%, significantly outperforming other domain adaptation methods like ADAW and MSCNN. This improvement is due to the MDCM module in MAAB, which enhances the model's ability to learn multi-scale features. Additionally, the domain-invariant learning module improves domain adaptation, reduces the impact of noise, and strengthens feature extraction. Under the condition of SNR = 10 dB, MAAB reaches an accuracy of 97.80%. These results demonstrate that the MAAB method offers superior feature extraction and domain adaptation performance in complex noisy environments. They also validate the effectiveness of the MDCM module in learning cross-domain features of multi-scale emitters and highlight the importance of the domain-invariant learning module in reducing inter-domain discrepancies and mitigating noise interference.

4.3 Analysis of Individual Performance Variations

To further evaluate the robustness of the model under varying SNR conditions, tests were conducted with SNR levels gradually decreasing from 10 dB to 0 dB. The results indicate that as the SNR decreases, the model's performance gradually declines, with a more pronounced drop observed under lower SNR conditions. Specifically, when the SNR decreases from 10 dB to 4 dB, the accuracy remains above 90%, demonstrating the model's strong resilience to moderate levels of noise. However, as the SNR drops below 2 dB, the accuracy begins to decline rapidly, reaching only 74.60% at 0 dB. This phenomenon suggests that while the model exhibits strong robustness under high SNR environments, its recognition performance is somewhat affected under extremely low SNR conditions. Overall, the proposed method maintains good adaptability across a wide range of noise intensities (Table 1).

Table 1. The accuracy performance under different SNR.

SNR (dB)	Size range	Proportion (%)	Average accuracy	Declining accuracy
10	[700,1000)	20	97.80	–
8	[700,1000)	20	97.25	0.55
6	[700,1000)	20	95.55	1.7
4	[700,1000)	20	91.05	4.1
2	[700,1000)	20	82.75	8.3
0	[700,1000)	20	74.60	8.15

4.4 MAAB Sensitivity Analysis

Under a 10 dB SNR condition, a sensitivity analysis was conducted to evaluate the model's recognition performance across different data size ranges. The results show that as the data size decreases, the model's accuracy generally declines. In larger size ranges, such as [1000, 900), [900, 800), and [800, 700), the model maintains high and stable performance, with accuracy consistently above 97%, indicating the model's strong ability to extract and discriminate features when there is sufficient data. However, as the data size drops below 400, the accuracy decreases to approximately 88%-91%, and further drops to 85.25% in the [100, 0) range. This suggests that with fewer input features, the model extracts fewer discriminative features, which reduces its recognition capability. Overall, the model shows robust performance with larger data sizes but faces a performance bottleneck in scenarios with smaller data sizes. Future work may focus on improving the feature extraction and enhancement mechanisms for smaller sample sizes (Table 2).

Table 2. The accuracy within different data size ranges.

Size range	Proportion (%)	Average accuracy	Declining accuracy
[1000,900)	20	98.4	–
[900,800)	20	97.95	0.45
[800,700)	20	98.1	−0.15
[700,600)	20	97.3	0.8
[600,500)	20	96.6	0.7
[500,400)	20	96.0	0.6
[400,300)	20	88.05	7.95
[300,200)	20	88.50	−0.45
[200,100)	20	91.65	−3.15
[100,0)	20	85.25	6.4

Under the condition of consistent data size, we further investigated the impact of the proportion of different-sized data on model performance. The experimental results indicate that as the proportion of available training samples decreases, the model's accuracy exhibits a gradual decline. Overall, the accuracy drops from a maximum of 98.80 to 93.65% as the data proportion decreases, with a relatively small decrease. Moreover, the model maintains performance above 95% for most data proportions. This suggests that the model can fully learn the feature distribution when the sample size is sufficient, and even with a reduced amount of data, it retains strong recognition capability and robustness (Table 3).

Table 3. The accuracy at different proportions under the same size range.

Proportion	Size range	Average accuracy	Declining accuracy
0%	[700,1000)	98.80	–
10%	[700,1000)	98.30	0.5
20%	[700,1000)	97.80	0.5
30%	[700,1000)	97.40	0.4

(continued)

Table 3. (continued)

Proportion	Size range	Average accuracy	Declining accuracy
40%	[700,1000)	96.85	0.75
50%	[700,1000)	95.75	1.1
60%	[700,1000)	96.80	−1.05
70%	[700,1000)	95.70	1.1
80%	[700,1000)	95.90	−0.2
90%	[700,1000)	94.55	1.35
100%	[700,1000)	93.65	0.9

4.5 Ablation Study

We conducted an ablation study under different SNR conditions to analyze the impact of using domain adversarial training and MK-MMD in the implicit domain-invariant learning module on recognition performance. Under low SNR conditions, the performance without MK-MMD was worse than that without domain adversarial training. This indicates that MK-MMD is more effective for feature alignment. In high SNR conditions with better data quality, the recognition accuracy is higher without MK-MMD, and the impact of removing MK-MMD on model performance is relatively small, making the domain adversarial strategy more critical. When both modules are used together, the performance reaches its best, confirming the effectiveness of these two modules in the proposed method.

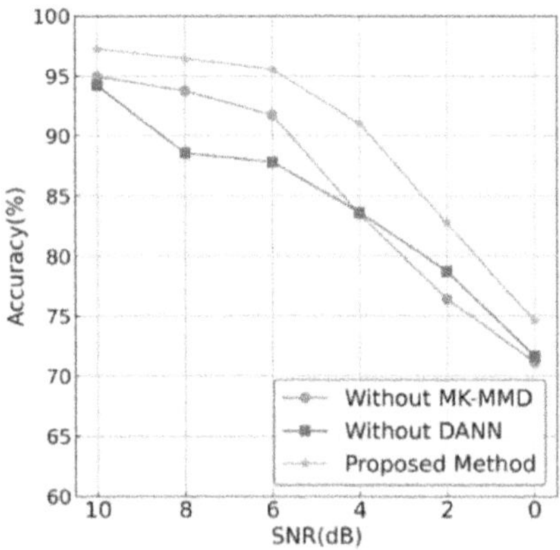

Fig. 6. Performance analysis of different modules in the domain-invariant learning module.

We conducted an ablation study under different SNR conditions to analyze the impact of using multi-scale feature extraction and the dynamic attention mechanism in the multi-scale radiation source signal cross-domain feature alignment module on recognition performance. Under various SNR levels, the recognition accuracy decreased when either of these two modules was removed. However, compared to removing DAAM, the removal of the MDCM module resulted in a more significant drop in accuracy, indicating that the MDCM module plays a more critical role in the multi-scale radiation source signal cross-domain feature alignment module. When both modules were used together, the performance was optimized, confirming the effectiveness of these two modules in the proposed method (Fig. 7).

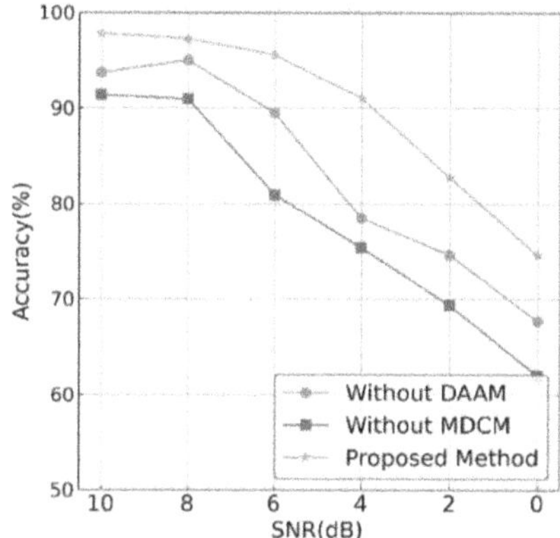

Fig. 7. The performance analysis of different modules in MAAB

5 Conclusions

In specific emitter identification tasks, due to factors such as device differences, changes in communication environments, and acquisition conditions, the time length, frequency, and sampling rate of signals often vary, resulting in scale inconsistency between different signals. This inconsistency exacerbates the challenges of cross-domain recognition, especially under conditions of frequency drift, channel noise, and dynamic environmental changes, where traditional methods have limited performance. To address this issue, this paper proposes a recognition method based on domain adaptation technology. It designs a MDCM to extract rich feature representations and introduces a dynamic adaptive attention mechanism to enhance the importance of features across different scales. Additionally, through MK-MMD distribution alignment and adversarial training strategies, the model's cross-domain robustness and environmental adaptability are significantly improved, providing an effective solution for SEI in dynamic and complex environments. Experimental results on real-world datasets show that the proposed method outperforms existing cross-domain methods across various SNR levels, addressing the limitations of traditional methods under scale inconsistency conditions and improving SEI recognition accuracy. Although the method performs excellently across most SNR ranges, recognition accuracy still decreases under extreme low SNR conditions, indicating that the model's feature extraction and alignment capabilities under strong noise interference need further enhancement. Future work will consider introducing pseudo-labels and dynamic feature enhancement mechanisms to further strengthen the model's robustness and generalization ability in extremely complex environments.

Acknowledgements. This research was supported by the Joint Fund of Zhejiang Provincial Natural Science Foundation of China under Grant LLSQN25F010002.

References

1. Lin, Y., Tu, Y., Dou, Z., et al.: Contour stella image and deep learning for signal recognition in the physical layer. IEEE Trans. Cogn. Commun. Netw. **7**(1), 34–46 (2020)
2. Liu, Y., Zhang, J.: Service function chain embedding meets machine learning: deep reinforcement learning approach. IEEE Trans. Netw. Serv. Manage. **21**(3), 3465–3481 (2024)
3. Talbot, K.I., Duley, P.R., Hyatt, M.H.: Specific emitter identification and verification, technology review **113**, 113–130 (2003)
4. Baldini, G., Steri, G., Giuliani, R.: Identification of wireless devices from their physical layer radio-frequency fingerprints. In: Encyclopedia of Information Science and Technology, Fourth Edition, pp. 6136–6146. IGI Global Scientific Publishing (2018)
5. Rehman, S.U., Sowerby, K.W., Coghill, C.: Radio-frequency fingerprinting for mitigating primary user emulation attack in low-end cognitive radios. IET Commun. **8**(8), 1274–1284 (2014)
6. Ding, L., Wang, S., Wang, F., et al.: Specific emitter identification via convolutional neural networks. IEEE Commun. Lett. **22**(12), 2591–2594 (2018)
7. Wang, W., Sun, Z., Piao, S., et al.: Wireless physical-layer identification: modeling and validation. IEEE Trans. Inf. Forensics Secur. **11**(9), 2091–2106 (2016)
8. Andrews, S., Gerdes, R.M., Li, M.: Towards physical layer identification of cognitive radio devices. In: 2017 IEEE Conference on Communications and Network Security (CNS), pp. 1–9. IEEE (2017)
9. Liu, C., Fu, X., Wang, Y., et al.: Overcoming data limitations: A few-shot specific emitter identification method using self-supervised learning and adversarial augmentation. IEEE Trans. Inf. Forensics Secur. **19**, 500–513 (2023)
10. Huang, K., Yang, J., Liu, H., et al.: Deep adversarial neural network for specific emitter identification under varying frequency. In: Bulletin of the Polish Academy of Sciences Technical Sciences (2021)
11. Liu, P., Guo, L., Zhao, H., et al.: A long time span-specific emitter identification method based on unsupervised domain adaptation. Rem. Sens. **15**(21), 5214 (2023)
12. Chen, J., Yu, L., Chen, Y., et al.: Prototype-driven unsupervised domain adaptation for specific emitter identification. IEEE Int. Things J. (2024)
13. Yin, L., et al.: Few-shot domain adaption-based specific emitter identification under varying modulation. In: 2023 IEEE 23rd International Conference on Communication Technology (ICCT), Wuxi, China, pp. 1439–1443 (2023)
14. Xiao, Z., Zhang, X., Sun, G., et al.: FTAN: feature transform and alignment network for cross-domain specific emitter identification. Sign. Process. **230**, 109800 (2025)
15. Wang, Y., Gui, G., Gacanin, H., et al.: An efficient specific emitter identification method based on complex-valued neural networks and network compression. IEEE J. Sel. Areas Commun. **39**(8), 2305–2317 (2021)
16. Liao, Y., Li, H., Cao, Y., et al.: Fast Fourier transform with multihead attention for specific emitter identification. IEEE Trans. Instrum. Meas. **73**, 1–12 (2023)
17. Wang, S., Zhang, Y., Sun, J., et al.: Attention-CNN-aided specific emitter identification method with limited radio frequency dataset. In: 2022 IEEE 22nd International Conference on Communication Technology (ICCT), pp. 1536–1540. IEEE (2022)
18. Ganin, Y., Ustinova, E., Ajakan, H., et al.: Domain-adversarial training of neural networks[J]. J. Mach. Learn. Res. **17**(59), 1–35 (2016)

19. Tzeng, E., Hoffman, J., Zhang, N., et al.: Deep domain confusion: Maximizing for domain invariance, arXiv preprint arXiv:1412.3474 (2014)
20. Sun, B., Saenko, K.: Deep coral: Correlation alignment for deep domain adaptation, Computer vision–ECCV 2016 workshops: Amsterdam, the Netherlands, October 8–10 and 15–16, 2016, proceedings, part III 14. Springer International Publishing, pp. 443–450 (2016)
21. Shen, J., Qu, Y., Zhang, W., et al.: Wasserstein distance guided representation learning for domain adaptation. In: Proceedings of the AAAI conference on artificial intelligence, pp. 1 (2018)
22. Wang, J., Zhang, B., Zhang, J., et al.: Specific emitter identification based on deep adversarial domain adaptation. In: 2021 4th International Conference on Information Communication and Signal Processing (ICICSP), pp. 104–109. IEEE (2021)
23. Ye, Y., Wang, C., Dong, H., et al.: Cross-session specific emitter identification using adversarial domain adaptation with wasserstein distance. In: 2022 26th International Conference on Pattern Recognition (ICPR), pp. 3119–3124. IEEE (2022)

Hierarchical Attention-Enhanced Transformer for Specific Emitter Identification in Complex Electromagnetic Environments

Zhengwei Xu[1], Zhilong Wang[1], Peiji Huang[1], Jun Chen[2,2(✉)], Chao Huang[2], and Zhenchuan Li[2]

[1] Henan Normal University, Xinxiang 453007, China
[2] ChengDu Fuyuanchen Technology Co., Ltd., Chengdu 610037, China
cdfyctc1@126.com

Abstract. This paper proposes a novel Specific Emitter Identification (SEI) method based on an improved Transformer architecture to address the challenges of low recognition accuracy and weak generalization in complex electromagnetic environments. Traditional SEI methods often struggle with dynamic signal variations and overlapping emitter characteristics. To overcome these limitations, we design a multi-head adaptive attention mechanism that dynamically adjusts the weights of temporal and spectral features in electromagnetic signals, enhancing the model's ability to capture discriminative fingerprint patterns. Furthermore, a hybrid convolutional-Transformer encoder is introduced to integrate local signal characteristics with global contextual dependencies.

Keywords: Specific emitter identification · Transformer · Multi-dimensional feature acquisition · Spatiotemporal features

1 Introduction

Specific Emitter Identification (SEI), a fundamental technology in wireless communications and electronic warfare (EW), has become a critical research focus for enhancing system security, reliability, and countermeasure capabilities [1]. With the rapid development of electronic warfare and complex communication systems, both the variety and complexity of signals have significantly increased. Consequently, the efficient identification and differentiation of individual emitters from massive signal datasets have emerged as a decisive factor in securing battlefield information superiority [2, 3]. However, conventional SEI methods predominantly rely on manual feature extraction, such as pulse amplitude, frequency, and phase, or model-based algorithms. While these methods perform adequately in simple signal environments with low noise, their performance deteriorates in complex electromagnetic environments (CEMEs) due to multipath effects and noise interference. Additionally, these methods fail to effectively capture spatiotemporal dependencies within emitter signals, leading to degraded identification performance under rapid signal variations or unstable channel conditions [4, 5].

C. Xu et al. (Eds.): MobiMedia 2025, LNICST 670, pp. 306–318, 2026.
https://doi.org/10.1007/978-3-032-16823-8_22

In recent years, artificial neural networks (ANNs) have gained prominence as a powerful technique, leading to major breakthroughs in fields such as language comprehension, visual interpretation, and speech analysis. Compared to traditional SEI methods, DL-based models can automatically extract discriminative features through hierarchical learning and fit complex SEI frameworks with minimal error rates [6]. These breakthroughs have established DL-based SEI methods as a major research focus in the field. Meanwhile, the Transformer model has gained widespread adoption in NLP and computer vision due to its superior temporal modeling and self-attention mechanisms [7] showing significant promise in signal processing and SEI tasks. However, despite its advantages in capturing spatiotemporal dependencies, the Transformer's feature extraction capabilities remain limited in complex electromagnetic environments (CEMEs), particularly in capturing fine-grained temporal-spatial information. This limitation compromises its recognition accuracy in time-varying channels and high-noise scenarios. Consequently, improving the Transformer's feature extraction robustness in complex environments has become a critical challenge in current SEI research.

To address the limitations of conventional methods and existing DL-based models, this paper proposes an improved Transformer architecture for SEI. The SEI method proposed in this paper overcomes conventional methods of SEI limitations by utilizing advanced deep learning techniques, which automatically extract complex features from raw signal data, rather than relying on manually engineered features. Moreover, By integrating multi-dimensional feature extraction and an enhanced Transformer structure, the proposed method effectively captures spatiotemporal dependencies in emitter signals and improves model robustness and recognition accuracy through global feature fusion.

2 Improved Transformer-Based SEI Methodology

Figure 1 illustrates the model framework of the Radiation Source Individual Recognition Method Based on the Improved Transformer, while Fig. 2 provides an expanded diagram of the same model framework. Specifically, pulse-level features and global features are extracted from emitter signals and subjected to normalization preprocessing. Subsequently, a spatial feature acquisition module and a temporal feature acquisition module hierarchically process the signals. An enhanced multi-head attention mechanism with dynamic weight adjustment is introduced in the Transformer architecture, allowing the model to dynamically adjust the weights of temporal and spectral features, improving its ability to capture discriminative spatiotemporal patterns. Finally, a global feature fusion module further strengthens the model's feature representation capability, thereby enhancing adaptability and recognition accuracy in complex environments.

2.1 Signal Preprocessing and Multi-dimensional Feature Extraction

Emitter signals inherently contain rich time-domain and frequency-domain information. To fully exploit these characteristics, this study extracts the following multi-dimensional features from raw signals. These features comprehensively describe emitter signal properties from diverse perspectives, providing enriched information for subsequent hierarchical processing and classification.

2.1.1 Pulse-Level Feature Extraction

Pulse-level features, extracted from individual signals, capture subtle emitter variations. Metrics such as pulse phase, rise time, and amplitude reveal detailed pulse structures that enable the discrimination of emitters with otherwise similar overall profiles. Nonetheless, these features may not fully characterize long-range dependencies or global signal behaviors, particularly under complex or noisy conditions. The specific extracted features are as follows:

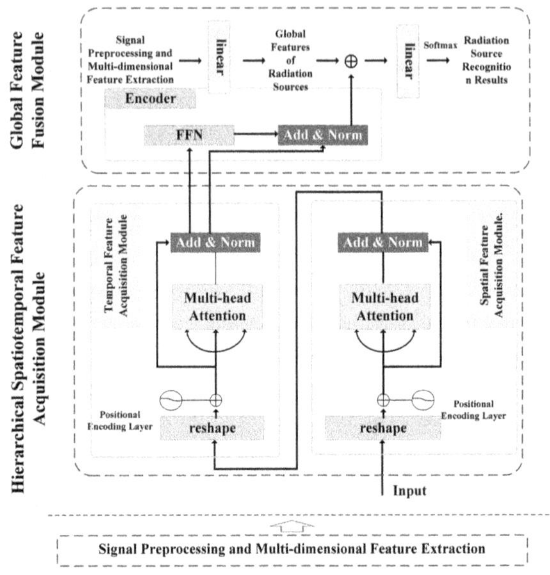

Fig. 1. Model framework of radiation source individual recognition method based on improved transformer

(1) Pulse Phase (Psum): The pulse phase is one of the important characteristics of pulse signals, representing the phase information of the signal. The calculation formula is:

$$Psum = angle(Xsum) \tag{1}$$

Here, $Xsum$ represents the sum of the pulse signals, and the function $angle$ is used to calculate the phase of the signal.

(2) Pulse Rise Time (PRT): The pulse rise time refers to the duration required for the pulse signal to increase from its minimum to maximum value. The formula for calculation is:

$$PRT = t_{end} - t_{start} \tag{2}$$

Here, t_{start} and t_{end} represent the pulse signal's start and end times, respectively.

(3) The pulse amplitude refers to the peak value of the pulse signal. The calculation formula is:

$$PA = \max(SigPulse) \tag{3}$$

Here, $SigPulse$ denotes the sequence of amplitudes of the pulse signal.

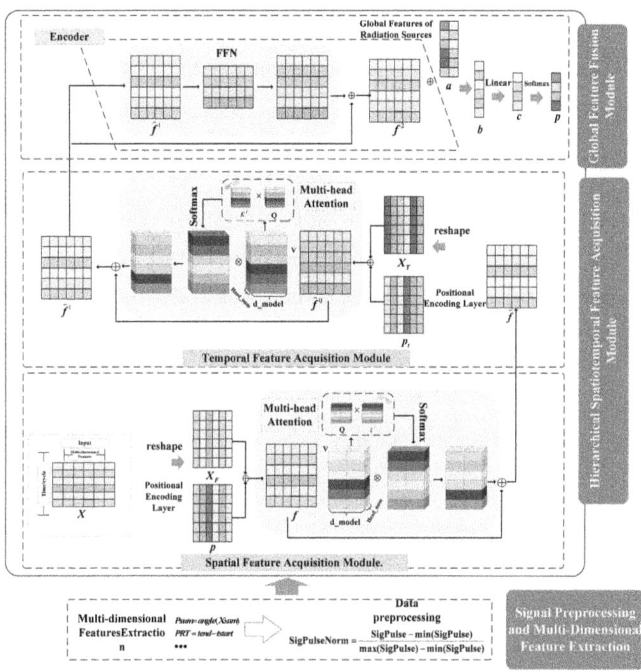

Fig. 2. Expanded diagram of radiation source individual recognition method based on improved transformer

(4) Pulse Inter-Phase Difference (DP): The pulse inter-phase difference represents the phase variation between adjacent pulses. The calculation formula is:

$$DP = \frac{\Delta P}{PRI} \tag{4}$$

Here, ΔP represents the phase difference between adjacent pulses, and PRI represents the pulse repetition interval.

2.1.2 Global Feature Extraction

Global features, extracted from the entire signal, encapsulate its overall characteristics. Metrics such as power spectral density (PSD) and amplitude probability distribution (APD) characterize the signal's strength and frequency attributes over its duration.

However, while these features offer a comprehensive view, they may lack the temporal resolution required to discern subtle inter-source differences when signals exhibit highly similar global properties. The specific features obtained are as follows:

(1) Amplitude Probability Distribution (APD): The amplitude probability distribution represents the probability distribution of the signal amplitude. The formula for calculation is:

$$APD = \{P_i\}, 1 \leq i \leq 100 \tag{5}$$

Here, P_i represents the probability of the signal amplitude being within the i-th interval, and N interval. The calculation formula is:

$$P_i = \frac{N_i}{N} \tag{6}$$

Here, N_i represents the number of times the signal amplitude falls within the i-th interval, and N represents the total number of sampling points.

(2) Power Spectral Density (PSD): The power spectral density represents the energy distribution of the signal in the frequency domain. The calculation formula is:

$$PSD = \frac{1}{N} \left| \sum_{n=0}^{N-1} x(n) e^{-j2\pi kn/N} \right|^2 \tag{7}$$

Here, $x(n)$ represents the time-domain signal, N represents the length of the signal, and k represents the frequency index.

2.1.3   Feature Normalization

To harmonize the dimensions across different features, the extracted features are normalized. The normalization formula is:

$$SigPulseNorm = \frac{SigPulse - \min(SigPulse)}{\max(SigPulse) - \min(SigPulse)} \tag{8}$$

Here, SigPulse represents the amplitude sequence of the pulse signal, and $\min(SigPulse)$ and $\max(SigPulse)$ represent the minimum and maximum values of the amplitude sequence, respectively.

2.1.4   Feature Fusion

Pulse-level and global features are integrated into a comprehensive multi-dimensional feature vector, capitalizing on both the fine details of individual pulses and the broader signal properties. This fusion significantly enhances classification accuracy by mitigating errors such as misidentification among closely related emitter sources, as demonstrated in subsequent experiments. The extracted pulse-level features are $Psum$, PRT, PA and DP, and the global features ar APD and PSD. The combined feature vector is:

$$X = [Psum, PA, DP, APD, PSD] \tag{9}$$

2.2 Hierarchical Spatiotemporal Feature Acquisition Module

After extracting the multi-dimensional features, an improved Transformer model is used for hierarchical spatiotemporal feature acquisition. This model introduces an enhanced multi-head attention mechanism with dynamic weight adjustment, which allows the model to adaptively assign different attention weights to temporal and spectral features. This dynamic adjustment enhances the model's ability to focus on the most relevant parts of the signal at each time step, improving its performance in capturing spatiotemporal dependencies. This module consists of a spatial feature acquisition module and a temporal feature acquisition module, which can effectively capture the spatiotemporal dependencies of emitter signals.

2.2.1 Spatial Feature Acquisition Module

① Embedding Layer:

The extracted pulse-level features, $Psum$, PRT, PA, DP and global features, APD and PSD, are converted into vector representations. Let the input features be X,

$X \in R^{F \times T}$, representing the time series of T steps from F sensors. For the input X, the data at T time steps can be regarded as the embedding of the sensor in the T-dimensional space, represented as:

$$X_F = [S_1, S_2, ..., S_F], S_i = \left[s_1^i, s_2^i, ..., s_T^i \right] \tag{10}$$

Here, F is the number of features, T is the number of time steps, and S_i represents the time series of the i-th feature.

② Positional Encoding Layer:

To preserve the sequential information of the time series, positional encoding is introduced. The result of the positional encoding for the multi-dimensional time series X can be represented as:

$$p_t = \begin{cases} p_i^{(2k)} = \sin(\frac{pos}{10000^{2k/d}}) \\ p_i^{(2k+1)} = \cos(\frac{pos}{10000^{2k/d}}) \end{cases} \tag{11}$$

Here, pos represents the position of the specific time point of the emitter signal feature S, in formula (11), the sum of $p_i^{(2k)}$ and $p_i^{(2k+1)}$ represents the positional encoding at position $pos.d$ represents the desired dimension after positional encoding. By using two different functions, the positional encoding gains diversity and expressive capability, enabling it to effectively capture the positional information correlation between different time points. The output of the positional encoding layer can be represented as:

$$f_t = p_t + X_F \tag{12}$$

③ Attention Layer:

The multi-head attention mechanism is configured to extract features from the spatial dimension as it enables the model to focus simultaneously on multiple feature representations from different positions, capturing the contributions of different sensors and applying weights to the embeddings of the multi-dimensional feature sequence X_F. The core formula is:

$$X_{F\prime} = X_F \odot W_S \tag{13}$$

$$Q_i = X_{F\prime}W_Q, \; K_i = X_{F\prime}W_Q, \; V_i = X_{F\prime}W_Q \tag{14}$$

$$SpatialAttention_i(X_{F\prime}) = Soft\max(\frac{Q_iK_i^T}{\sqrt{d_k}})V_i \tag{15}$$

Here, W_S serves as the spatial weight matrix to adjust the feature representations of each sensor. (Q_i, K_i, V_i) represents the query vector, key vector, and value vector for the i-th head, respectively. $SpatialAttention_i$ represents the spatial attention for the i-th head. The outputs of all heads are concatenated and integrated through a linear

$$f = \sum_{i=1}^{h} SpatialAttention_i(X_{F\prime})W_o^i \tag{16}$$

transformation to obtain the final spatial feature $f = [f_1, f_2, \ldots, f_T]$. In formula (16), W_o^i is the weight matrix for the linear transformation.

④ Residual Connection and Normalization Layer:

To mitigate the problem of vanishing gradients and speed up the training process, the Addition and Normalization layer is employed to process the features extracted by the attention mechanism. The formula is given as follows:

$$\widehat{f}_t = norm(f_t + c_t) \tag{17}$$

In summary, The result of the spatial feature acquisition process is:

$$\widehat{f} = \left[\widehat{f}_1, \widehat{f}_2, \ldots \widehat{f}_T\right] \tag{18}$$

2.2.2 Temporal Feature Acquisition Module

The temporal feature acquisition module consists of the encoding layer, positional encoding layer, multi-head attention layer, and Addition and Normalization layer, with the multi-head attention mechanism layer being the core of this module. Building on the results of the first layer of spatial feature acquisition, the contribution of the time dimension needs to be further explored. First, the encoding layer is used to encode the results from the spatial feature extraction module. Specifically, all features within a time step are considered as the embedding for that time step. The embedding process is as follows:

$$X_T = Out_F = [O_1, O_2, ..., O_F], O_j = \left[o_1^i, o_2^i, ..., o_T^i \right] \tag{19}$$

Then, since the time order information is missing, positional encoding is used to incorporate the relative positions into the sequence. Referring to formula (11), As the features along the time dimension play a vital role in prediction, the multi-head attention mechanism is designed to capture these features across various time steps, Which allows the model to simultaneously focus on multiple feature representations from different time steps, capturing the dynamic changes in the time series, and applying weights to the features in the time dimension. Using $\hat{f}^0 = X_T + P_{t-t}$ as the input, the result produced by the multi-head attention is calculated using formula (14) to obtain $M(Q, K, V) \in R^{T \times m}$. Finally, to avoid gradient vanishing, the Addition and Normalization layer is applied, and its calculation formula can be referenced from formula (17), with the output represented as $\hat{f}^1$.

2.2.3 Encoding Layer

The encoding layer comprises three key sub-layers: the Addition and Normalization layer, the Feedforward Neural Network (FFN) layer, and the linear mapping layer. These components process the deeply integrated spatiotemporal features from the multi-dimensional feature sequence, thereby improving the model's feature representation and enhancing overall performance.

(1) Feedforward Neural Network Layer and Addition and Normalization layer Layer:

In the Transformer encoder, alongside the multi-head self-attention mechanism, the FFN and Addition and Normalization layer layers play key roles. Thus, once the feature fusion is completed, these two layers must be incorporated. The FFN layer comprises two linear transformations and an activation function, with both input and output dimensions being d_model. The Addition and Normalization layer operation is applied according to formula (17).

2.3 Global Feature Fusion Module

After extracting the spatiotemporal features, this paper improves the model's classification performance by fusing the spatiotemporal features with the global features.

First, the original global features $(\hat{f}_1^{PSD}, \hat{f}_1^{APD})$ are passed through a fully connected layer, mapping them to the same dimension as the Transformer output features and introducing non-linearity into the features. The formula is as follows:

$$\hat{f}_2^{APD} = \text{Relu}\left(linear\left[\hat{f}_1^{APD} \right] \right) \tag{20}$$

$$\hat{f}_2^{PSD} = \text{Relu}\left(linear\left[\hat{f}_1^{PSD} \right] \right) \tag{21}$$

314   Z. Xu et al.

$$a = \left[\hat{f}_2^{APD}, \hat{f}_2^{PSD}\right] \tag{22}$$

Here, a represents the global features of the emitter.

Then, the spatiotemporal features are concatenated with the global features. The specific formula is as follows:

$$b = \hat{f}^2 \oplus a \tag{23}$$

To improve the feature representation capability even further, a fully connected layer is used to process the concatenated features b, resulting in the fused feature c. Then, the fused feature c is input into the classification layer, where the Softmax function outputs the probability p for each emitter category.

3 Simulation Experiment

In this study, we conducted signal recognition and classification experiments using both the WiSig dataset and the ORACLE dataset, both of which contain IQ signal samples collected in a Line-of-Sight (LOS) channel. Additionally, the hyperparameters used in their experiments are as follows: lr represents the learning rate, spatial-head refers to the number of spatial heads in the spatial feature extraction module of the hierarchical spatiotemporal feature acquisition module, temporal_head denotes the number of temporal heads in the temporal feature extraction module of the same hierarchical structure, and fc-dropout indicates the dropout rate for the neurons in the fully connected layer of the global feature fusion module.

The hyperparameters of wisig dataset oracle dataset

dataset	lr	Spatial-head	temporal_head	fc-dropout
wisig	0.001	3	4	0.5
oracle	0.001	1	1	0.5

3.1 WiSig Dataset Experiment

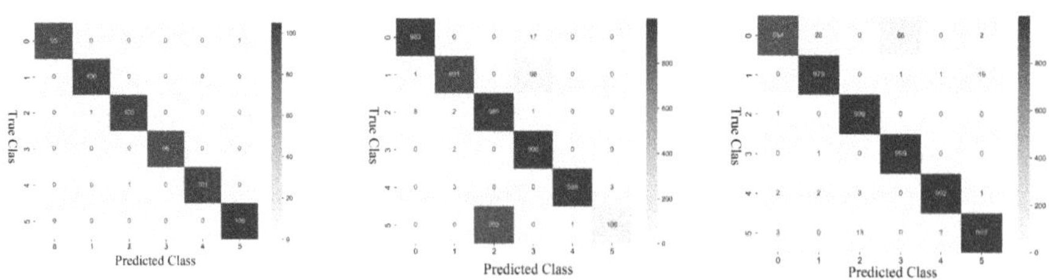

Fig.3. Experiment results on WiSig test set

The WiSig dataset was processed to correct for carrier frequency offsets and equalize the signals, making it suitable for evaluating SEI techniques under different channel conditions. The dataset consists of signal samples from 6 categories, with each sample having a dimension of 2 × 256 IQ data. The training set contains 900 samples per category, while the test set is divided into three subsets (T1, T2, and T3), each containing 1000 samples per category. The test sets correspond to different collection dates, representing various channel conditions. These subsets are designed to simulate real-world signal variations such as multipath effects, noise interference, and other dynamic channel characteristics that may be encountered in practical applications. Different channel conditions were applied during the simulation to further assess the effectiveness of the proposed SEI method. in dynamic wireless communication environments.

In the experiment, signal preprocessing and feature extraction were first performed. Pulse-level and global features from the WiSig dataset was used to improve the model's signal recognition capability. Then, an improved Transformer model was used to extract spatiotemporal features, further improving the classification accuracy of the signals. The training and test data were used for model training and evaluation. Specifically, the model's robustness was assessed by comparing its performance on the T1, T2, and T3 test subsets under different channel conditions. During training, model parameters were optimized to accommodate the characteristics of the WiSig dataset, and frequency offsets and noise were appropriately handled.

Figure 3 presents the test results of our proposed method on the three subsets. These subsets correspond to different channel conditions, which allows us to assess the model's performance under varying environments. The simulation results demonstrate that the improved Transformer-based SEI method performs excellently on the WiSig dataset,especially under varying channel conditions, where it effectively recognizes signals and maintains high classification accuracy. Compared to traditional methods, our approach shows stronger robustness and adaptability in handling frequency offsets and signal equalization. By comparing the test results under different channel conditions, the method's potential for application in complex wireless communication environments is proven, as it maintains a low misclassification rate and high efficiency even under varying channel interference. These results further confirm the effectiveness of the proposed SEI method in practical wireless communication and signal recognition applications.

3.2 ORACLE Dataset Experiment

This paper conducted signal recognition and classification experiments using the ORACLE dataset. The ORACLE dataset is a collection of IQ signal samples collected in a Line-of-Sight (LOS) channel, designed to simulate real-world wireless communication scenarios. The dataset includes two types of channel conditions: Static and Cross-channel. The static channel conditions are used for testing the model's performance under relatively stable channel characteristics, where the signal distribution in the test set closely matches the training set. In contrast, the cross-channel conditions simulate real-world scenarios where the channel characteristics differ from those seen during training, representing potential variations that the model must handle in practical applications.

This dataset includes signal samples from 16 categories, with each sample having a dimension of 2 × 6000 IQ data. The training set contains 300 samples per category,

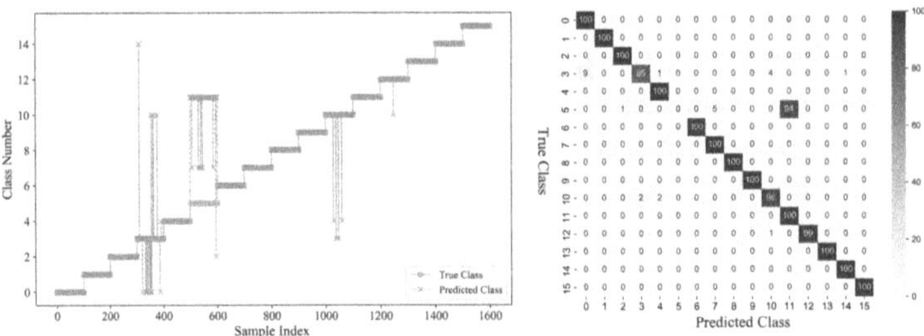

Fig. 4. Experiment results on ORACLE test set

and the test set includes both static and cross-channel conditions, with 100 samples per category in each condition. In the experiment, we first preprocessed the ORACLE dataset, extracting pulse-level and global features to enhance the model's recognition ability. Then, the improved Transformer model was used to extract spatiotemporal features, further increasing the signal classification accuracy.

During the simulation, we tested the model's performance under static and cross-channel conditions using the dataset. The results clearly indicate that the improved Transformer-based SEI method performs excellently, especially under cross-channel conditions. Despite the channel variations between the training and testing sets, the model still demonstrates strong signal recognition capabilities and maintains high classification accuracy. Figure 4 illustrates these experimental results, showing the model's robust adaptability and performance in environments with dynamic channel characteristics. The model effectively reduces misclassification rates while maintaining high accuracy across both static and cross-channel conditions, validating its applicability to diverse and challenging signal recognition tasks.

3.3 Model Stability Analysis and Feature Effectiveness

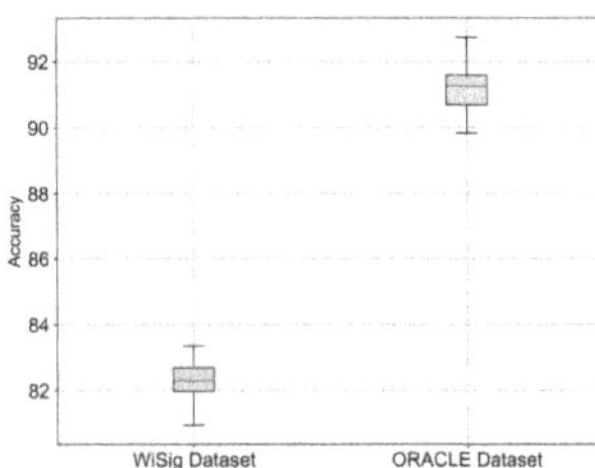

Fig 5 Stability analysis of accuracy for WiSig and ORACLE datasets

The box plot in Fig. 5 shows that the proposed model achieves high and stable prediction accuracy on both the WiSig and ORACLE datasets. The WiSig dataset has a narrow interquartile range, indicating consistent performance, with a standard deviation of 0. 5. In contrast, the ORACLE dataset shows slightly more variability, with a standard deviation of 0. 8, reflecting higher fluctuations in its accuracy. This higher variability

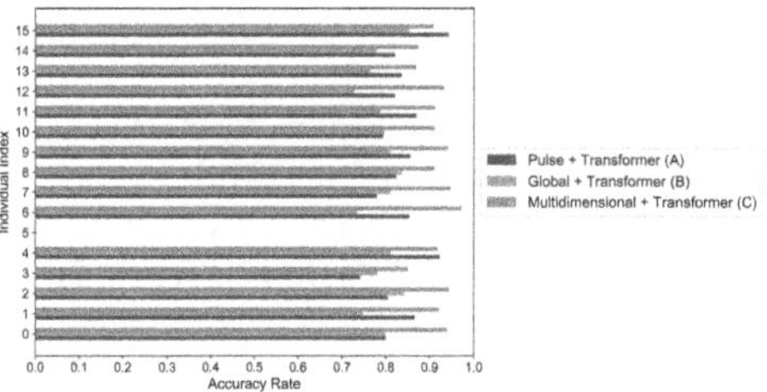

Fig.6. Accuracy for different feature

in the ORACLE dataset can be attributed to its more complex signal characteristics and the presence of diverse emitter categories collected under varying conditions, including dynamic and cross-channel scenarios. In comparison, the WiSig dataset has more stable channel conditions, which contributes to its relatively lower variability. Despite these differences, both datasets demonstrate high stability, with minimal outliers and close median values. Overall, the model exhibits reliable performance across different conditions.

Results of Fig. 6 suggest that multidimensional features combined with the Transformer network yield the highest identification accuracy in most individuals, as they offer a more complete representation of the signal's characteristics. It is also noted that individual 5 had zero accuracy rates across the three combinations, aligning with Sect. 2.3's findings, suggesting these combinations failed to capture essential identification patterns for individual 5. When pulse features and global features are used individually, there are still cases where misidentification occurs, especially with individuals like Individual 0 and Individual 6, whose recognition accuracy is lower in some trials. However, when multidimensional features are used, these issues are minimized, leading to an overall improvement in classification accuracy, Simultaneously, it also demonstrates that the two types of features play different roles in enhancing model performance.

4 Conclusion

The specific emitter identification approach, based on the enhanced Transformer presented in this paper, effectively overcomes the limitations of current methods in feature acquisition, spatiotemporal dependency modeling, and feature integration. By incorporating multi-dimensional feature extraction and an enhanced Transformer architecture, this method demonstrates good robustness and recognition performance in complex channel and noisy environments. Future research will further optimize the model architecture, explore more efficient training strategies, and extend to more practical application scenarios to promote the development of emitter identification technology.

References

1. Tu, Y., Lin, Y., Zha, H., et al.: Large-scale real-world radio signal recognition with deep learning. Chin. J. Aeronaut. **35**(9), 35–48 (2022)

2. Liu, C., et al.: A comprehensive survey on self-supervised learning for specific emitter identification. IEEE Commun. Surv. Tut. (2025)
3. .Li, J., Bi, D., Ying, Y., et al.: An improved algorithm for extracting subtle features of radiation source individual signals[J]. Electronics **8**(2), 246 (2019)
4. Liu, Y., Xiao, P., Wu, H., et al.: LPI radar signal detection based on radial integration of Choi-Williams time-frequency image[J]. J. Syst. Eng. Electron. **26**(05), 973–981 (2015)
5. Zhou, J., Zheng, S., Yu, X., Jin, X., Zhang, X.: Low probability of intercept communication based on structured radio beams using machine learning [J]. IEEE Access 169946–169952 (2019)
6. Qu, L., Yang, J., Huang, K., Liu, H.: Specific emitter identification based on one-dimensional complex-valued residual networks with an attention mechanism. Bull. Polish Acad. Sci. Technic. Sci. **69**(5), e138814 (2021)
7. Han, K., Wang, Y., Chen, H., et al.: A survey on vision transformer[J]. IEEE Trans. Pattern Anal. Mach. Intell. **45**(1), 87–110 (2022)

Research on Automatic Modulation Recognition Method Based on Knowledge Distillation*

Ruoyu Zhou, Zhuoran Cai$^{(\boxtimes)}$, and Guangda Xin

Yantai University, Yantai, Shandong, China
`zhouruoyu@s.ytu.edu.cn`, `caizhuoran@ytu.edu.cn`

Abstract. In communication systems, automatic modulation recognition facilitates the development of many critical signal processing applications, such as cognitive radio and spectrum sharing. However, the high computational cost and large model sizes pose significant obstacles for deploying traditional deep learning-based methods, especially in IoT networks and UAV-assisted systems. To resolve this matter, this paper proposes the method of knowledge distillation (KD), selecting the highly accurate Deep Residual Shrinkage Network (DRSN) as the teacher network and the lightweight ShuffleNetV2 as the student network. We specifically design a self-attention enhanced KD module: the self-attention layer is embedded after the 3rd convolutional block of both teacher and student networks, calculating attention weights via scaled dot-product attention to highlight critical features. The training process integrates an additional attention loss term (MSE between teacher and student attention weights) into the total loss function. Experiments on the RadioML2016.10A dataset indicate that the distilled network, while maintaining the low parameter count of the student network, achieves accuracy close to the teacher network.

Keywords: Deep learning · Automatic modulation classification · Knowledge distillation

1 Introduction

Automatic modulation recognition (AMR) is a significant aspect of communication signal processing, involving the automatic detection and identification of modulation types from received signals. Although traditional modulation recognition methods, such as feature-based techniques, have been extensively studied, these methods often require manual feature extraction [1] and complex algorithm

---

*Supported by organization x.

C. Xu et al. (Eds.): MobiMedia 2025, LNICST 670, pp. 319–332, 2026.
https://doi.org/10.1007/978-3-032-16823-8_23

tuning [12]. In the past few years, modulation recognition has seen the application of deep learning techniques, owing to their remarkable success in areas such as image and speech recognition.

T. O'Shea et al. [9] pioneered the use of deep learning in AMR and built a publicly available benchmark dataset to demonstrate that deep learning-based AMR methods are more efficient than manual methods. Meng et al. [7] used a multi-task training method, i.e., a network that performs both AMR and signal signal-to-noise-ratio identification tasks simultaneously, which enhances the robustness of the network and reduces overfitting. This method not only achieves modulation recognition but also effectively estimates the signal's SNR. He et al. [2] designed a deep residual network (ResNet) to avoid gradient vanishing and explosion through residual connections, continuously optimizing the parameters. Building on this, Zhang et al. [17] introduced hybrid attention into ResNet for improvement and applied it to wind turbine gearbox fault diagnosis. To address fault detection challenges in high-noise industrial settings, researchers led by Zhao proposed an enhanced diagnostic framework called Deep Residual Shrinkage Network (DRSN) [21], which integrates soft thresholding modules into ResNet's residual architecture for improved noise suppression. This adaptation enables automatic feature refinement through learned threshold parameters, effectively separating critical fault signatures from background interference during mechanical vibration analysis. Zhang et al. [20] proposed an improved version of DRSN, replacing the soft threshold with a leakage threshold to enhance model performance. Zhang et al. [19] introduced spatial domain attention into DRSN to capture the spatial dependencies of feature maps, constructing a hybrid attention mechanism that considers multiple channels. The enhanced DRSN has improved diagnostic accuracy in various noisy environments.

Although deep learning has exhibited outstanding performance across various domains, many mainstream network models typically require substantial computational power and storage capacity, making it challenging to deploy them on lightweight mobile devices. Consequently, model lightweighting has increasingly become a central topic in research exploration. Knowledge distillation (KD) has emerged as an efficient model compression technique, particularly through its teacher-student framework that transfers robust feature representations from complex to lightweight models. In 2015, Hinton et al. [3] formally proposed the KD technique, which transforms the prediction results of multiple models into soft targets for a single model, thereby transferring the knowledge of complex models to enable small models to achieve performance similar to that of large models. AT [15] transfers knowledge using multi-layer feature attention maps.

This paper explores the effective use of KD in the lightweight design of AMC networks. Specifically, we investigate how KD can achieve lightweight networks in AMC. The core contributions of this study can be encapsulated in the subsequent points:

1. In the AMC domain, we utilize DRSN as the teacher network for KD, leading to improved accuracy in the student network.

2. We analyze multiple KD methods and validate the student networks' overall classification accuracy on the RadioML2016.10A dataset under each method.
3. Experimental verification shows the self-attention-driven knowledge distillation model obtains 62% mean recognition accuracy, outperforming comparative approaches in noise-robust classification tasks. while using the fewest parameters compared to other network architectures.

2   Experimental Methods

2.1   Knowledge Distillation

KD is a commonly used model reduction method that enhances the performance and accuracy of lightweight student models by utilizing the output supervision information from teacher models, which contain a significant number of parameters and strong performance. The teacher model's outputs generate pedagogical knowledge assimilated by the student through distillation. This framework integrates both hard label supervision and the teacher's probabilistic soft targets for enhanced learning.

In the KD process, the teacher and student models are simultaneously trained using the same dataset to obtain output features. Soft label synthesis occurs through the teacher model's softmax distribution at a high temperature T with both networks classifiers respectively outputting the expression categories. The introduction of softmax temperature function helps to smooth the probability distribution of the predicted expressions, providing more class-specific information unique to the teacher network (Fig. 1).

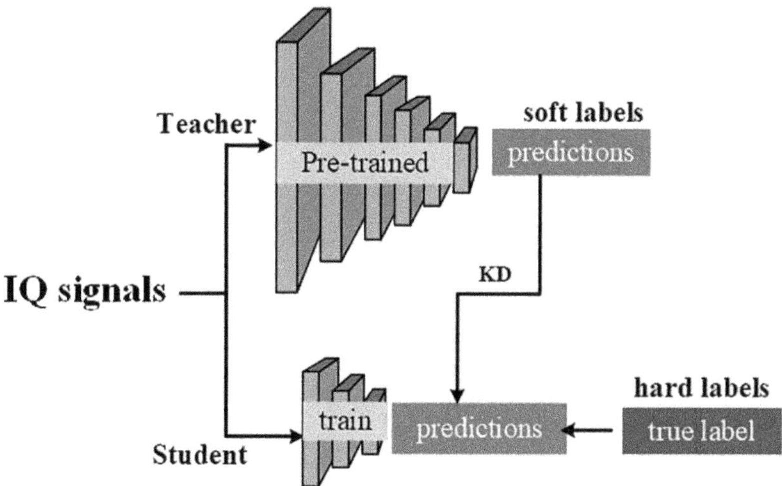

Fig. 1. The knowledge distillation process.

The total loss is obtained by a weighted average of two parts:

$$\mathcal{L}(g; R) = \alpha * \mathcal{F}\left(h, \rho\left(k_S; T = 1\right)\right)$$
$$+ \beta * \mathcal{F}\left(\rho\left(k_t; T = \tau\right), \rho\left(k_S, T = \tau\right)\right) \tag{1}$$

where g represents the input, R represents the parameters of the student model, h represents the true labels, $\mathcal{F}$ represents the cross-entropy loss function, ρ is the modified softmax loss function, and k_s and k_t respectively denote the logits of the student model and teacher model. Both α and β are hyperparameters.

(1) can be simplified as:

$$\mathcal{L} = \alpha \mathcal{L}_{soft} + \beta \mathcal{L}_{hard} \tag{2}$$

The two models process the transfer dataset in parallel, with the softmax probability distribution output by the teacher model used as soft labels. $\mathcal{L}_{soft}$ uses KL divergence as a criterion to evaluate the difference between the prediction results of the two models, i.e., the cross-entropy loss between the softmax output of the student model under the same temperature T condition and the soft labels.

$$L_{soft} = -\sum_{i}^{N} p_i^T \log(q_i^T) \tag{3}$$

where p_i^T denotes the softmax output value of the large model for the specific class i-th under the condition of temperature T, and q_i^T denotes the softmax output value of the small model for the specific class i-th under the same temperature condition.

$$p_i^T = \frac{\exp(t_i/T)}{\sum_k^N \exp(t_k/T)} \tag{4}$$

$$q_i^T = \frac{\exp(s_i/T)}{\sum_k^N \exp(s_k/T)} \tag{5}$$

where t_i represents the predictions of the teacher model output layer, s_i denotes the output layer predictions of the student model, with N representing the total number of labels.

$\mathcal{L}_{hard}$ is the difference between the predictions of the student model under the condition of $T = 1$ and the true labels of the expressions, calculated by the cross-entropy loss function.

$$L_{hard} = -\sum_{i}^{N} c_i \log(q_i^1) \tag{6}$$

where c_i represents the true label value for class ith, $c_i \in \{0, 1\}$ with positive labels taking the value 1 and negative labels taking the value 0. The equation for q_i^1 is as follows:

$$q_i^1 = \frac{\exp(s_i)}{\sum_k^N \exp(s_k)} \tag{7}$$

2.2   Deep Residual Shrinkage Network

A novel algorithm, DRSN, builds upon deep residual networks by embedding soft-thresholding as a nonlinear component within the network framework. This mechanism steers the network's focus toward non-core features using attention, filters out irrelevant ones using the soft-thresholding function, and preserves key features. As a result, the module efficiently extracts valuable information from noisy signals. It is primarily composed of three core components: Residual Shrinkage Building Units (RSBUs), attention mechanisms, and soft-thresholding. The RSBUs are the core structure of this network, primarily composed of soft-thresholding functions, attention mechanisms, and deep residual networks, as illustrated in Fig. 2. Specifically, each RSBU contains 2 convolutional layers (kernel size 3×3, 64 and 128 filters, respectively), a soft-thresholding layer with learnable threshold parameters, and a channel attention subnetwork (two fully connected layers with 128 and 64 neurons, followed by sigmoid activation).

Illustrated in Fig. 2, the subnetwork and soft-thresholding module are integrated into the RSBU. In the subnetwork, all input features are first taken the absolute value, global average pooling is later employed to summarize and obtain the key characteristics of the feature maps. In another path, the input features pass through two fully connected layers, followed by he values produced by the sigmoid function to obtain the scaling parameters, which range between 0 and 1.

The most crucial part of residual network is the residual unit. The introduction of residual networks targets the issue where gradients vanish or explode as networks become deeper, leading to slow learning or even an inability to update parameters and learn features, thus hindering the network from achieving good performance. This method alleviates the challenges of parameter optimization by adopting skip connections and can improve model performance while increasing network depth. The residual unit module, depicted in Fig. 3, consists of an input data represented as X and a residual function denoted as $F(X)$.

In signal processing, soft-thresholding is widely used as a standard technique for denoising, and its soft-thresholding function expression is given by (8).

$$
d_{out} = \begin{cases} d_{in} - \tau, & d_{in} > \tau \\ 0, & -\tau \leq d_{in} \leq \tau \\ d_{in} + \tau, & d_{in} < -\tau \end{cases} \tag{8}
$$

where d_{in} is input, d_{out} is output, τ is threshold.

This method first decomposes the input signal, then filters the decomposed signal using the soft-thresholding function, and finally reconstructs the signal. As indicated by (8), features with an absolute value less than τ are set to 0, while other features are adjusted towards 0, achieving the effect of "shrinkage". The introduction of attention mechanisms enables the automatic setting of the threshold value, avoiding errors caused by manually setting the threshold.

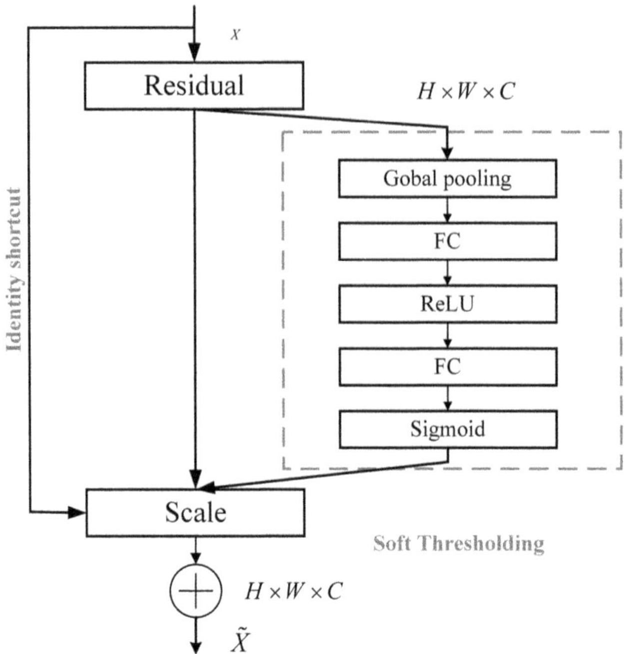

Fig. 2. The structure of RSBUs.

2.3 ShuffleNetV2

In this paper, ShuffleNetv2 [6] is employed as the student network in KD. In the modules of ShuffleNetv1 [18], 1x1 grouped convolutions are widely used, similar to the bottleneck layers in ResNet, which have different input and output channels. To address the shortcomings of v1, v2 introduces a new operation: channel shuffling. The specific configuration of ShuffleNetV2 in this study is as follows: 3 stages of ShuffleNet units, with each stage containing 3, 7, and 3 units, respectively; the first unit of each stage uses 3×3 depthwise separable convolution with stride = 2 (output channels 24, 116, 232, and 464 for each stage) and 1×1 convolution (groups = 2) for feature fusion; the channel split ratio is 1:1 for all units.

The unit module of ShuffleNet V2 is illustrated in Fig. 4. In the first unit of ShuffleNet V2, the input feature map is separated into two branches through channel split. The left branch adopts the identity mapping method, while the right branch consists of 3 convolutional operations. After channel shuffling, the channels are randomly played to exchange information between different groups. In the second unit of ShuffleNet V2, both branches simultaneously branch the input features. The left branch contains two different convolutional operations, while the structure of the right branch is identical to the first unit, but the movement interval in the depthwise separable convolution in both branches is two. Then, the outputs of the two branches of the second unit are combined through

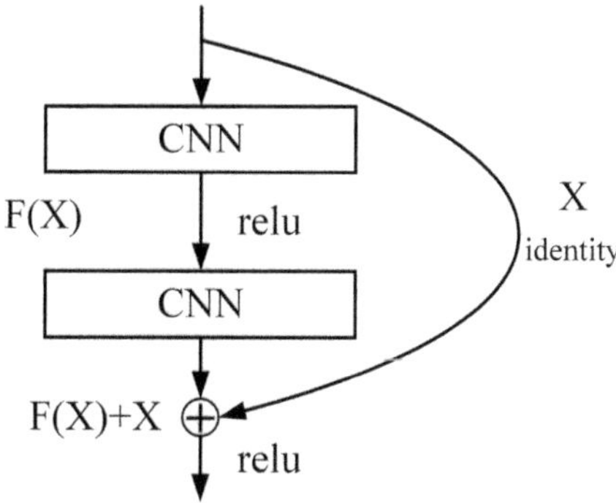

Fig. 3. The structure of residual unit module.

the concat operation, doubling the amount of channels, thereby strengthening the network's capacity for feature extraction. Finally, a channel shuffle operation is performed. ShuffleNet V2's unit design reduces computation through grouped convolutions and integrates features fully through channel shuffling, ensuring complete decorrelation between input and output channels.

3   Simulation

3.1   Dataset

The experiment utilizes the RadioML2016.10A dataset, an open-source dataset provided by DeepSig Inc. This dataset comprises 11 modulation schemes, including 8 digital modulation types (8PSK, QAM64, BPSK, GFSK, QAM16, CPFSK, QPSK, 4PAM) and 3 analog modulation types (WBFM, AM-DSB, AM-SSB). The signal-to-noise ratio (SNR) varies between $-20\,\mathrm{dB}$ and $18\,\mathrm{dB}$, in $2\,\mathrm{dB}$ increments. To simulate a more realistic channel environment, included in the dataset are factors such as additive white Gaussian noise rate offset, fading effects, center sampling, and frequency offset.

The experiment is conducted on a GeForce GTX 3060 GPU, utilizing the PyTorch 1.11 framework with Python 3.9 environment. The training is set for 80 epochs with a learning rate of 0.001.

3.2   Comparision with Different Methods

We use DRSN as the teacher network and ShuffleNetV2 as the student network, employing the basic KD method for experimentation.

Figure 5 depicts the accuracy comparison among DRSN, ShuffleNetV2, and ShuffleNetV2 after KD. The results indicate that DRSN, as the teacher network, exhibits better recognition accuracy. The accuracy of ShuffleNetV2 starts to diverge significantly from the teacher network at $-8\,\mathrm{dB}$. However, after KD, the accuracy of ShuffleNetV2 improves compared to the original ShuffleNetV2,

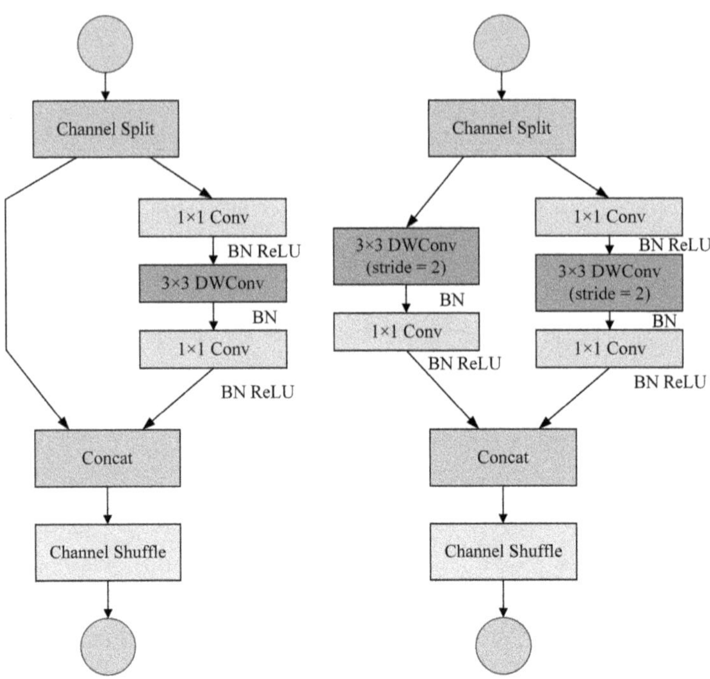

Fig. 4. Structure of ShuffleNet V2 units.

especially between $-8\,$dB and $2\,$dB, where it surpasses the original network. Beyond $2\,$dB, the accuracy gradually stabilizes and remains comparable to the original network. These results substantiate that KD can enhance the recognition accuracy of the network while preserving its original architecture. Table 1 provides a comparison of the parameters, average accuracy, and highest accuracy among the three models on the RML2016.10A dataset.

Table 1. Comparision of parameters and accuracy under the Rml2016.10A dataset.

Model	Parameters	Average accuracy
DRSN	3,261,643	**0.627**
ShuffleNeV2	108,355	0.528
KD	**108,355**	0.610

According to Table 1, after KD, although the accuracy of the network has decreased by 1.7% compared to the DRSN, it has increased by 2.8% on average compared to the ShuffleNeV2 while having only 1/30 of the parameters of the DRSN. Therefore, KD significantly reduces the parameter count of the network while keeping the teacher network's accuracy intact.

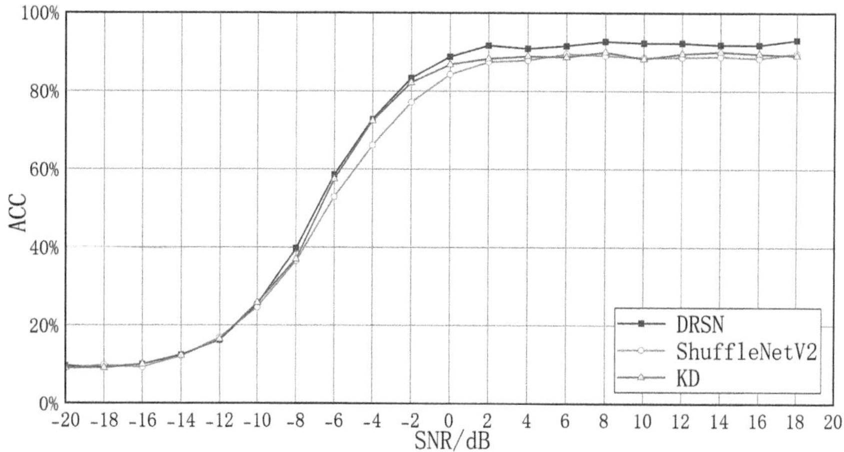

Fig. 5. Comparison of network accuracy after KD.

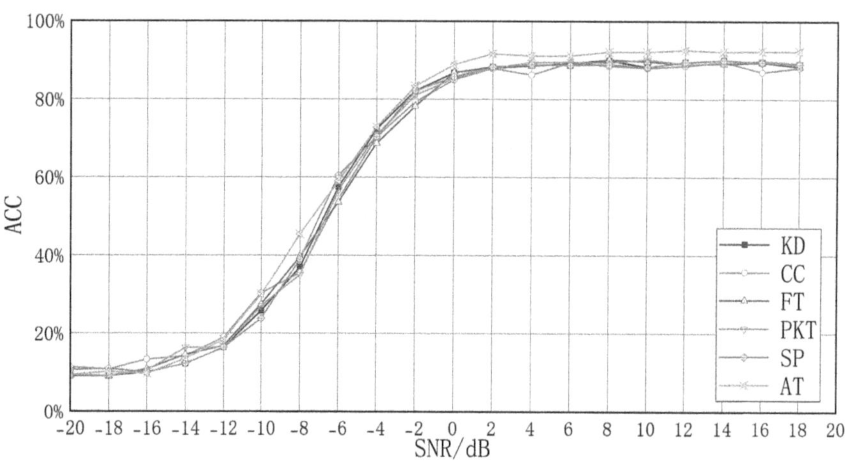

Fig. 6. The comparison of different methods.

However, based on the results obtained from the conventional distillation method, the highest accuracy is comparable to that of the student network. Therefore, we will conduct experiments comparing with other distillation methods: KD [3], CC [11], FT [4], PKT [10], SP [14].

Figure 6 presents the accuracy comparison based on the distillation methods. It can be observed that all distillation methods improve the accuracy of the student network. However, the distillation method based on self-attention mechanism exhibits closer performance to the teacher network across all SNRs. These results demonstrate that the distillation method based on self-attention mechanism is more suitable for distilling DRSN into ShuffleNetV2.

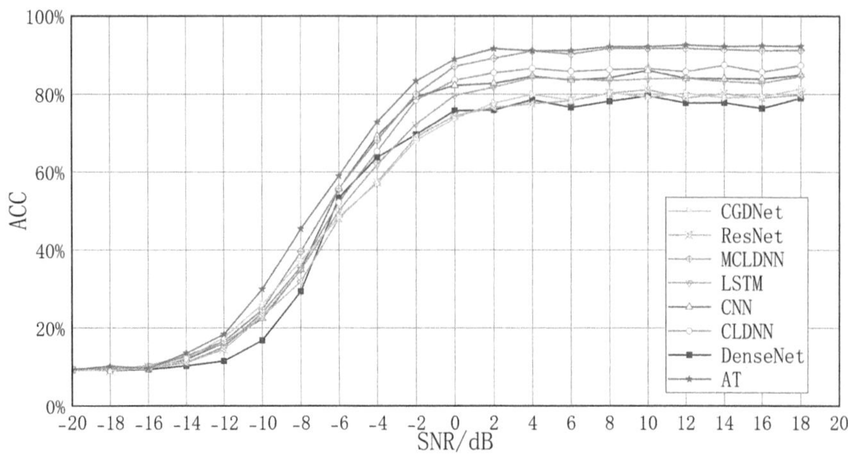

Fig. 7. SNR-accuracy performance comparison of AMR models on RadioML2016.10A dataset.

Figure 7 compares the accuracy of the distilled ShuffleNetV2 with the currently popular CGDNet [8], CLDNN [5], DenseNet [13], ResNet [2], CNN [13], LSTM [16], and MCLDNN [16] networks. As shown in Fig. 7, the distilled ShuffleNetV2 network achieves good performance across all SNRs. Figure 7 shows the SNR-Accuracy Performance Comparison of AMR Models on the RadioML2016.10A Dataset. As observed in Fig. 7, the performance of all models exhibits a positive correlation with SNR. In the low SNR range (below −5 dB), the accuracy of each model is relatively low and remains close, mainly due to the severe noise interference masking the signal characteristics. When SNR exceeds 0 dB, the AT model begins to show obvious advantages, with its accuracy increasing rapidly and eventually reaching over 0.8, which is 5%–10% higher than other models. This indicates that the AT model has stronger noise robustness and feature extraction capability, especially in high SNR environments.

The comparison of parameter count, average accuracy, and highest accuracy of models on the RadioML2016.10A dataset is shown in the table below:

From Table 2, it can be observed that the distilled ShuffleNetV2 based on the self-attention mechanism not only has the fewest parameters but also achieves higher average accuracy and highest accuracy compared to other networks. The AT model has the smallest number of parameters, which is only 1/30 of ResNet and DenseNet, achieving the lightweight goal. Meanwhile, its average accuracy ranks first, 0.01 higher than MCLDNN, which has the second-highest accuracy. This fully demonstrates that the knowledge distillation method effectively transfers the knowledge of the teacher network to the student network, realizing the balance between model lightweight and performance retention. This indicates that our proposed lightweight model achieves better recognition performance with the least number of parameters, providing a new solution for practical deployment on lightweight devices.

Table 2. Comparative analysis of model size and recognition performance on RadioML2016.10A dataset.

Model	Parameters	Average accuracy
CGDNet	124,933	0.54
ResNet	3,098,283	0.53
MCLDNN	406,199	0.61
LSTM	201,099	0.56
CNN	858,123	0.57
CLDNN	517,643	0.58
DenseNet	3,282,603	0.52
AT	**108,355**	**0.62**

3.3   The Classification Accuracy of the KD

From Fig. 8, it is evident that at $SNR = 0\,dB$, the recognition accuracy of other signals tends to be 1, but there is significant confusion between BPSK and PAM4, with only 35% of BPSK accurately identified. Although the confusion is somewhat alleviated at $SNR = 18$ dB, it remains substantial. This could be attributed to the influence of various noise and interference in the dataset, resulting in confusion between these two signals already during recognition by the teacher network. This confusion is not effectively addressed when distilled into the student network.

The underlying reason for such persistent confusion lies in the structural similarities between BPSK and PAM4 in both time and frequency domains. BPSK encodes information through binary phase shifts ($0°$ and $180°$), while PAM4 uses four distinct amplitude levels for quaternary transmission. In low-SNR environments (like 0 dB), noise distorts phase coherence for BPSK and blurs amplitude boundaries for PAM4, making their feature distributions overlap significantly. Even at higher SNR ($18\,dB$), residual noise or signal fading can still reduce the discriminative gap, as both modulation types retain simple waveform patterns that lack complex frequency components for clear differentiation.

However, other networks manage to accurately identify easily confused signals such as AM-DSB and WBFM, as well as QAM16 and QAM64, without confusion.

4   Conclusions and Future Work

In this article, we use knowledge distillation as a method for network lightweighting. We validate the experimental method using the RML2016.10A dataset. The recognition results demonstrate that ShuffleNetV2, with only 1/30 of the parameters of DRSN, achieves a recognition accuracy only 1.7% lower than that of DRSN, and 8.2% higher than the original network model. We then compared various knowledge distillation methods, and the results indicate that the

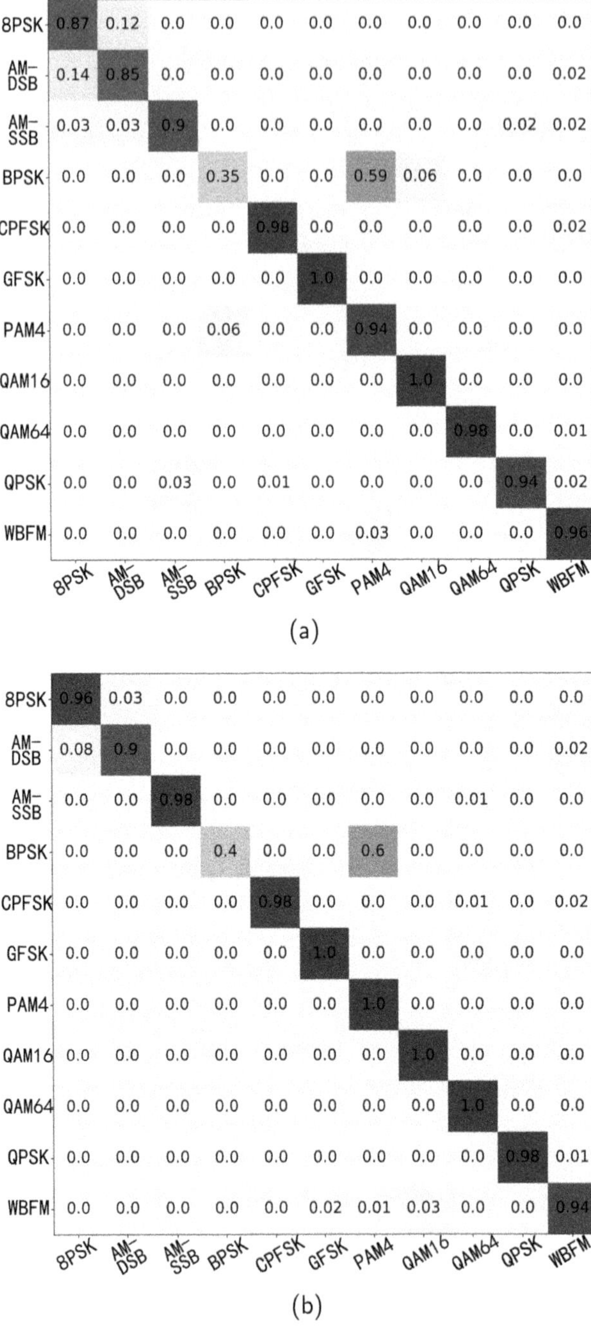

(a)

(b)

Fig. 8. Classification accuracy of modulated signals using KD: (a) SNR = 0 dB (b) SNR = 18 dB.

knowledge distillation method based on the self-attention mechanism achieves an average recognition rate of 62%, the highest among the methods tested. Finally, the ShuffleNetV2 network, derived from KD based on the self-attention mechanism, achieves the highest recognition accuracy while using the fewest parameters compared to other networks.

To further enhance the reliability of the proposed model, future work should include an evaluation on an additional dataset such as RadioML2018.01A. This dataset, which features a more diverse range of modulation types and channel conditions compared to RadioML2016.10A, would serve as a valuable testbed for assessing the model's generalization capabilities. Conducting such an experiment could reveal how the model performs when exposed to previously unseen modulation schemes and more complex noise environments, providing critical insights into its potential for real-world applications.

References

1. Azzouz, E., Nandi, A.: Procedure for automatic recognition of analogue and digital modulations. IEE Proc. Commun. **143**(5), 259–266 (1996)
2. He, K., Zhang, X., Ren, S., Sun, J.: Deep residual learning for image recognition. In: Proceedings of the IEEE Conference on Computer Vision and Pattern Recognition, pp. 770–778 (2016)
3. Hinton, G.: Distilling the knowledge in a neural network. arXiv preprint arXiv:1503.02531 (2015)
4. Kim, J., Park, S., Kwak, N.: Paraphrasing complex network: network compression via factor transfer. In: Advances in Neural Information Processing Systems, vol. 31 (2018)
5. Liu, X., Yang, D., El Gamal, A.: Deep neural network architectures for modulation classification. In: 2017 51st Asilomar Conference on Signals, Systems, and Computers, pp. 915–919. IEEE (2017)
6. Ma, N., Zhang, X., Zheng, H.T., Sun, J.: Shufflenet v2: practical guidelines for efficient CNN architecture design. In: Proceedings of the European Conference on Computer Vision (ECCV), pp. 116–131 (2018)
7. Meng, F., Chen, P., Wu, L., Wang, X.: Automatic modulation classification: a deep learning enabled approach. IEEE Trans. Veh. Technol. **67**(11), 10760–10772 (2018)
8. Njoku, J.N., Morocho-Cayamcela, M.E., Lim, W.: CGDNet: efficient hybrid deep learning model for robust automatic modulation recognition. IEEE Netw. Lett. **3**(2), 47–51 (2021)
9. O'shea, T., Hoydis, J.: An introduction to deep learning for the physical layer. IEEE Trans. Cogn. Commun. Netw. **3**(4), 563–575 (2017)
10. Passalis, N., Tefas, A.: Learning deep representations with probabilistic knowledge transfer. In: Proceedings of the European Conference on Computer Vision (ECCV), pp. 268–284 (2018)
11. Peng, B., Jin, X., Liu, J., Li, D., Wu, Y., Liu, Y., Zhou, S., Zhang, Z.: Correlation congruence for knowledge distillation. In: Proceedings of the IEEE/CVF International Conference on Computer Vision, pp. 5007–5016 (2019)
12. Ramezani-Kebrya, A., Kim, I.M., Kim, D.I., Chan, F., Inkol, R.: Likelihood-based modulation classification for multiple-antenna receiver. IEEE Trans. Commun. **61**(9), 3816–3829 (2013)

13. Tekbıyık, K., Ekti, A.R., Görçin, A., Kurt, G.K., Keçeci, C.: Robust and fast automatic modulation classification with CNN under multipath fading channels. In: 2020 IEEE 91st Vehicular Technology Conference (VTC2020-Spring), pp. 1–6. IEEE (2020)
14. Tung, F., Mori, G.: Similarity-preserving knowledge distillation. In: Proceedings of the IEEE/CVF International Conference on Computer Vision, pp. 1365–1374 (2019)
15. Vaswani, A.: Attention is all you need. In: Advances in Neural Information Processing Systems (2017)
16. Xu, J., Luo, C., Parr, G., Luo, Y.: A spatiotemporal multi-channel learning framework for automatic modulation recognition. IEEE Wirel. Commun. Lett. **9**(10), 1629–1632 (2020)
17. Zhang, K., Tang, B., Deng, L., Liu, X.: A hybrid attention improved resnet based fault diagnosis method of wind turbines gearbox. Measurement **179**, 109491 (2021)
18. Zhang, X., Zhou, X., Lin, M., Sun, J.: Shufflenet: an extremely efficient convolutional neural network for mobile devices. In: Proceedings of the IEEE Conference on Computer Vision and Pattern Recognition, pp. 6848–6856 (2018)
19. Zhang, X., Wang, Y., Wei, S., Zhou, Y., Jia, L.: Multi-scale deep residual shrinkage networks with a hybrid attention mechanism for rolling bearing fault diagnosis. J. Instrum. **19**(05), P05015 (2024)
20. Zhang, Z., Li, H., Chen, L., Han, P.: Rolling bearing fault diagnosis using improved deep residual shrinkage networks. Shock. Vib. **2021**(1), 9942249 (2021)
21. Zhao, M., Zhong, S., Fu, X., Tang, B., Pecht, M.: Deep residual shrinkage networks for fault diagnosis. IEEE Trans. Industr. Inf. **16**(7), 4681–4690 (2019)

Model Mutation-Based Adversarial Example Detection Method for Automatic Modulation Classification

Sicheng Zhang[1], Chen Yang[1], Jiangzhi Fu[1(✉)], Yun Lin[1], Peixian Zhao[2], and Cong Liu[2]

[1] College of Information and Communication, Harbin Engineering University, Harbin, China
{2015080325,yangchen,fujiangzhi,linyun}@hrbeu.edu.cn
[2] The 54th Research Institute of CETC, Shijiazhuang, Hebei, China
{xiaochenghome,liuconggd}@163.com

Abstract. The electromagnetic spectrum is a key national strategic resource, and intelligent electromagnetic spectrum monitoring is largely dependent on reliable automatic modulation classification. Although deep neural networks excel in automatic modulation classification tasks, their susceptibility to adversarial examples brings systemic risks. Existing defense methods show limitations in handling electromagnetic signals: feature reconstruction-based approaches incur high computational costs, while robust training degrades performance on benign examples. To alleviate the above issues, this paper proposes Model Mutation-based Adversarial Example Detection method (MMAED). This method uses sensitivity to changes in the boundaries of decision models to detect adversarial examples. Specifically, the innovation involves four lightweight mutation operators that create diverse mutated models. Integrated with layer freezing and adaptive threshold selection, our method distinguishes adversarial examples from normal ones through label variation analysis. Evaluations of the RML2016.10a dataset show the superior detection accuracy of MMAED against multiple attacks compared to feature-based methods. Our proposed approach effectively identifies adversarial examples in modulation recognition systems by analyzing their distinctive responses across mutated models, offering practical defense against adversarial threats.

Keywords: Automatic modulation classification · Adversarial attack · Adversarial defense · Adversarial examples detection · Model mutation

Supported by the National Natural Science Foundation of China under Grant 62201172.

1 Introduction

As a vital strategic resource in the era of information, the electromagnetic spectrum serves as the fundamental carrier of modern communication systems, public safety operations, and intelligent Internet of Things networks. Its efficient management and reliable monitoring have become key concerns in the development of critical national infrastructure. Automatic Modulation Classification (AMC) models are the core component of spectrum situation awareness, anti-interference communication system, and intelligent spectrum management [1]. Electromagnetic signal examples exhibit unique physical characteristics that challenge conventional feature engineering methods to establish accurate analytical models.

The literature indicates that the accuracy of traditional AMC models is particularly insufficient, especially under complex electromagnetic environmental conditions [2]. In recent years, AMC models based on deep learning (DL) have made significant breakthroughs, especially in feature extraction architecture and cross-domain generalization capability. However, studies have shown that adversarial examples are made to trick classification models by carefully designing optimization algorithms that superimpose imperceptible perturbations onto the original signal. Although nearly indistinguishable from genuine examples perceptually, these maliciously perturbed inputs can induce deep neural networks to produce entirely erroneous classification results with high confidence [3]. Sadeghi et al. [4] first demonstrated that adversarial examples can significantly reduce the signal recognition performance of AMC models. Lin et al. [5] systematically studied adversarial attack methods by injecting adversarial perturbations into input signals, and experiments showed that adversarial examples can significantly reduce the recognition performance of AMC models. Zhang et al. [6] further proposed a spectrum focused frequency domain adversarial perturbation generation strategy that enhances cross-channel robustness while maintaining stealthiness.

Existing defense research against adversarial examples in deep learning models primarily follows two technical paradigms. The first one focuses on model robustness enhancement, which aims to improve adversarial robustness of AMC models through modified training processes or architectural innovations. Han et al. [7] demonstrated significant accuracy improvements against C&W attacks through their robustness enhancement framework. Bao et al. [8] developed a more resilient classification model through optimized adversarial training algorithms. Zhang et al. [9] introduced DIBAD, which is a decoupling adversarial defense method based on the information bottleneck. It innovatively transforms adversarial defense in spectrum security into mutual information optimization in feature space. The second one is the adversarial example detection method. This type of method does not directly interfere with model parameters, but instead recognizes adversarial examples by analyzing the distribution characteristics of the input examples in the feature space or the internal activation pattern of the model. Xu et al. [10] designed a detection strategy by extracting and fusing multiple signal features. Han et al. [11] designed the detection autoencoder and used reconstruction errors and convolutional neural networks to distinguish deep features.

Although both methods can improve the adversarial robustness of AMC models to some extent, robustness enhancement methods often sacrifice the classification performance of normal examples. In contrast, detection methods provide greater flexibility and scalability, enabling defense against unknown attack types without compromising the performance of the original model. Most existing studies in the electromagnetic signal domain suffer from computationally intensive feature analysis. These limitations result in high training costs and suboptimal detection performance for adversarial example detection models. To address these challenges, this paper proposes Model Mutation-based Adversarial Example Detection method (MMAED). Due to the fact that most adversarial examples are located near the decision boundary, this method distinguishes between normal examples and adversarial examples by statistically analyzing the changes in their categories. The method employs four lightweight mutation operators to construct a mutated model ensemble, integrating inter-layer freezing strategies in signal feature spaces and optimal threshold selection mechanisms to achieve highly sensitive detection of adversarial perturbations.

2 Related Work

2.1 Adversarial Attack

Szegedy et al. [3] first discovered that applying specially designed minor perturbations to neural network inputs could induce models to produce high confidence erroneous predictions, with these misclassified instances termed adversarial examples. Inspired by the proven effectiveness of adversarial attacks in image classification, Sadeghi et al. [4] demonstrated that DL-based AMC models are similarly vulnerable to adversarial example attacks in modulation classification tasks. Lin et al. [5] systematically investigated the impact of adversarial attack methods on modulation recognition, quantitatively measuring the effectiveness of such attacks against signals. Their experimental results confirmed that deep neural network-based modulation recognition systems are highly vulnerable to adversarial interference. Simultaneously, they proposed a visionary framework for establishing an adversarial attack-defense platform tailored to electromagnetic signal recognition models.

In wireless communication scenarios, adversarial examples can be defined as malicious inputs generated by applying carefully designed minor perturbations to original signals, with the intent of causing deep learning models to produce erroneous classification results with high confidence. Given that traditional adversarial attacks suffer significant performance degradation after wireless channel transmission, Zhang et al. [6] proposed a channel-robust class-specific spectrum-focused frequency adversarial attack method for modulation signal classification models. Concurrently, Bai et al. [12] developed a multi-scale discriminative attack method for modulated signals, which constrains intermediate layer activations through multilayer activation interruption loss to prevent adversarial examples from retaining deep features of original signals. However, most existing adversarial attack methods operate under white-box assumptions, which is an overly idealized premise that creates the illusion of easily compromising DL systems. Addressing this limitation, Qi et al. [13] introduced a detection-tolerant black-box adversarial attack method specifically for DL-based AMC systems, experimentally demonstrating over 20% improvement in adversarial example transferability across target models.

2.2   Adversarial Defense

With the rapid advancement of adversarial attack techniques, the security of deep learning models faces increasingly severe threats, driving researchers to propose diverse defense strategies primarily categorized into model robustness enhancement and adversarial example detection. For example, Han et al. [7] developed an adversarial defense framework based on ensemble learning that improves the robustness of modulation signal recognition systems against attacks by integrating multiple heterogeneous DL models. Concurrently, Bao et al. [8] introduced a genetic algorithm in adversarial training, optimizing adaptive weights specific to the layer of neural networks. Zhang et al. [9] implemented the Hilbert-Schmidt Independence Criterion to achieve secure feature decoupling, significantly improving the robustness of the modulation recognition model by constraining statistical dependencies between informative features and adversarial perturbations.

However, these methods often require substantial training costs and exhibit limited generalization capabilities, struggling to address unknown attack types. Compared to detection approaches, robustness enhancement strategies inevitably compromise classification accuracy on benign examples. To mitigate this trade off, Xu et al. [10] proposed a radio frequency signal adversarial example detection method based on multi-feature fusion, establishing a multidimensional anomaly detection index system through joint analysis of Constellation Diagram (CD) characteristics and Local Intrinsic Dimension (LID) characteristics, thereby enhancing detection rates. Han et al. [11] designed a defense framework integrating adversarial example detection and recovery for signal recognition networks. They proposes a dual-channel defense framework that integrates two sequential mechanisms: a feature perturbation-based detection module for identifying anomalous signals, followed by adversarial example restoration via a generative adversarial network.

3   Methodology

This section introduces the research motivation, the AEDM-MM detection framework and the core algorithm in turn. This paper is inspired by an adversarial example interpretability study based on manifold boundaries. The model mutation algorithm is used to continuously change the high-dimensional manifold boundaries, amplify the difference in label change rate between normal examples and adversarial examples, providing a new paradigm for adversarial example detection in dynamic electromagnetic environments.

3.1 Motivation

The emergence of adversarial examples is fundamentally rooted in manifold learning theory, in which the deep neural network approximates the decision boundary to a high-dimensional manifold geometry. Adversarial examples generated by input spatial perturbations are mainly concentrated near the boundaries of these manifolds because they are sensitive to directional gradients orthogonal to the data distribution. This spatial proximity enables minute adversarial displacements to traverse through the critical manifold partitions, using the geometric sensitivity represented by the hierarchical features of the deep neural network, while maintaining the perceptual fidelity in the original domain. Szegedy et al. [3] identified that the vulnerability of adversarial examples stems from the local linearity of models near manifold boundaries, where minor perturbations can induce cross-manifold misclassification. Hendrycks et al. [14] further validated through principal component analysis that adversarial examples exhibit statistically distinct properties from original examples, demonstrating significantly higher variance in principal components near high-dimensional manifold boundaries. Han et al. [15] systematically reviewed current interpretability research on adversarial examples from three perspectives, including model-centric, data-centric, and hybrid viewpoints, while highlighting limitations in this field.

These studies collectively reveal that deep neural network training processes yield decision boundaries that are predominantly flat across most regions but hypersensitive to input variations near boundary areas, where even imperceptible perturbations can trigger erroneous decisions. Consequently, implementing model mutations alters the position or geometry of decision boundaries, inducing drastic categorical shifts in adversarial examples clustered near these boundaries. Building on these theoretical foundations, this paper proposes MMAED method, using the Label Change Rate (LCR) to quantify the rate of change in example categories, as illustrated in Fig. 1.

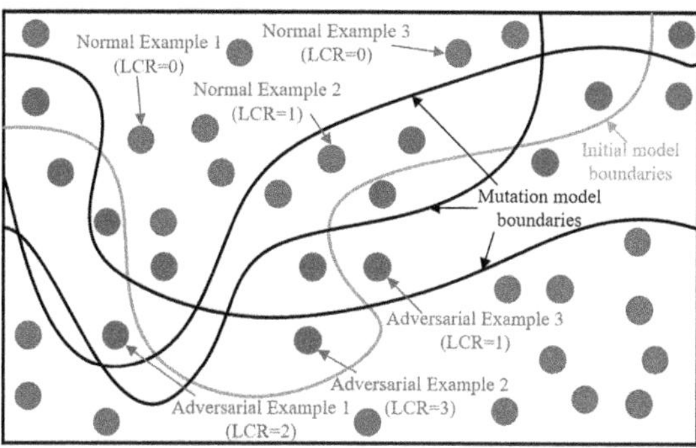

Fig. 1. Changes in decision boundary affect LCR of examples

3.2 MMAED Detection Framework

The MMAED detection framework achieves efficient adversarial example detection through multistage collaborative optimization and model decision boundary change strategy. As illustrated in Fig. 2, its core workflow initiates with adversarial example diversity generation and model mutation, progresses through quantitative analysis of LCR, and culminates decision-making via threshold optimization.

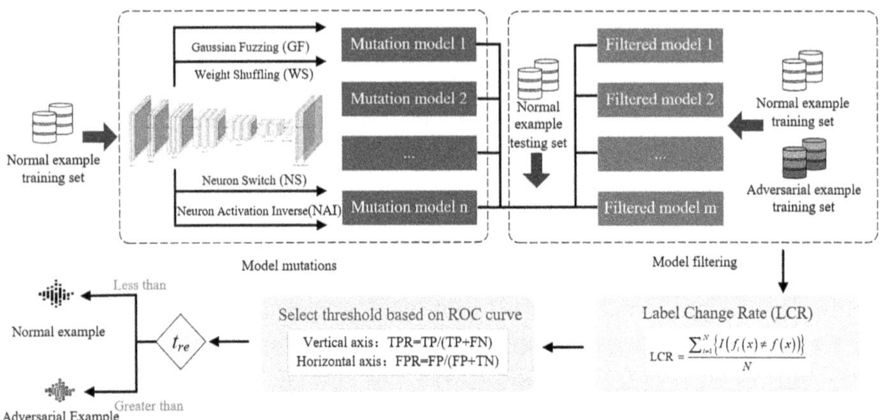

Fig. 2. The framework of MMAED method

The proposed method initializes by training a deep neural network model on the original example training dataset as the baseline, followed by generating a mutated model ensemble using four distinct algorithms. To address computational and storage challenges posed by large-scale mutated models, a front-rear layer freezing strategy is implemented during mutation, which retains fixed parameters for the first two convolutional layers while exclusively mutating deeper network components. Subsequently, the double filtering mechanism constructed a high-quality subset of variation models: first, the classification accuracy threshold was enforced to eliminate models with poor performance, which were less than 80% of the benchmark performance. Secondly, confidence interval verification is applied to eliminate statistical outliers to ensure the prediction consistency of the whole integration. Then, the LCR of original examples and adversarial examples is calculated in the mutated model ensemble. Finally, the framework integrates the Receiver Operating Characteristic (ROC) curve-driven optimization with dynamic adaptive mechanisms to determine optimal detection thresholds, establishing a robust adversarial example detection system. Through theoretical innovation and engineering design, this framework provides an efficient and scalable defense paradigm for intelligent communication security in complex electromagnetic environments.

3.3   Model Mutation Algorithm

In traditional software testing, mutation testing has been widely adopted to assess the quality of program components. However, software testing for DL systems is fundamentally distinct from conventional software testing paradigms. Consequently, software testing techniques for DL systems require substantial adaptations of conventional mutation testing methodologies. In this section, we propose four model-level mutation algorithms tailored for DL systems, employing mutation operators to directly alter the structural configurations and parametric attributes of DL models.

(1) Gaussian Fuzzing (GF): GF reduces the transferability of adversarial examples by injecting Gaussian noise into model weights, thereby disrupting attackers' precise reliance on weight distributions. Applying the GF mutation operator, the perturbed weight matrix becomes:

$$W' = W + \epsilon, \epsilon \sim \mathrm{N}\left(0, \sigma^2\right), \tag{1}$$

where W denotes the original weight matrix, ϵ represents Gaussian distribution noise with mean value of 0 and variance of σ^2. Typically, the standard deviation parameter σ is configured to confine weight perturbations within a range centered at W, though the range can be adjusted, with corresponding changes in probability coverage. This algorithm injects randomized Gaussian noise into the weight parameters of a specific model layer, inducing minor perturbations to weight values while preserving the model's classification performance without significant degradation. Gaussian noise interferes with the ability of attackers to generate effective transferable adversarial examples through fuzzy adversarial examples, which usually depend on the gradient direction in the weight space where they conduct gradient based attacks.

(2) Weight Shuffling (WS): Weights quantify the significance of inter-neuronal connections and directly govern the decision logic of deep neural networks. WS disrupts spatial or channel-wise correlations among weights by shuffling the element order within a specified layer's weight matrix. Let During mutation, the matrix is first flattened into a one-dimensional vector $\vec{w} = [w_1, w_2, \cdots, w_{m \times n}]$, then randomly permuting the element order to generate a perturbed vector:

$$\vec{w'} = \mathrm{Permute}(\vec{w}), \tag{2}$$

Finally, the perturbed vector is reshaped to its original dimensions:

$$\vec{w} = \mathrm{Reshape}\left(\vec{w'}, m, n\right), \tag{3}$$

where m and n represent the length and width of the weight matrix respectively. This algorithm preserves the numerical distribution of weights while disrupting their spatial positional relationships. Since adversarial examples often exploit specific weight patterns to craft perturbations, weight randomization prevents attackers from predicting weight permutations, thereby reducing the success rate of transfer attacks.

(3) Neuron Switch (NS): In feedforward neural networks, outputs from neurons in the preceding layer propagate to the subsequent layer. Randomly swapping two neurons within a layer alters the weight vectors and network connectivity pathways. Consider a layer with N neurons, where two neuron indices i and j are randomly selected. The NS mutation operation is defined as:

$$W_i' = W_j, W_j' = W_i,\tag{4}$$

where W_i denotes the weight vector of the i-th neuron. Adversarial examples rely on specific neuronal activation patterns to execute attacks. By swapping the weight parameters of two neurons, this operation alters their response patterns during forward propagation, thereby disrupting their intended activation pathways and ultimately invalidating adversarial attacks.

(4) Neuron Activation Inverse (NAI): Activation functions, as critical components of neural networks, enable the comprehension and learning of complex nonlinear relationships. NAI modifies feature representations by inverting either the sign of neuronal activation values or the nonlinear function itself at a specified layer. For instance, the Rectified Linear Unit function exhibits fundamentally distinct behaviors between activated and non-activated states. The NAI operation is defined as:

$$a_k' = \begin{cases} -a_k & , \text{if } a_k > 0 \\ 0 & , \text{otherwise} \end{cases},\tag{5}$$

where a_k denote the activation value of a neuron in layer k. The inversion operation can be formulated as:

$$a_k' = 1 - \sigma(x),\tag{6}$$

where $\sigma(x) = 1/(1 + e^{-x})$ is the activation function. The activation state of neurons can be manipulated through sign inversion of neuronal outputs prior to applying the activation function, thereby creating diversified mutated activation patterns. This inversion operation disrupts the anticipated feature responses of neural networks while significantly enhancing the difficulty of executing adversarial attacks.

The substantial computational overhead and storage costs arising from numerous mutated models necessitate an innovative front-rear layer freezing strategy to reduce computational burdens while enhancing optimization efficiency. By freezing parameters in the initial convolutional layers and restricting mutations to subsequent network layers, this method retains the basic feature extraction ability of the early layer, while significantly reducing the resource expenditure, all of which will not affect the model performance or generalization ability. Specifically, we designed a training protocol that freezes the first two convolutional layers by setting their weights as non-trainable parameters, while exclusively optimizing deeper layers.

3.4   Calculation of LCR

Given an example x with its true label $y = f(x)$ assigned by the trained base deep neural network model f, when we obtain an ensemble of N mutated models F, where the predicted label of input x on the i-th mutated model is denoted as , LCR of example x is defined as follows:

$$\mathrm{LCR} = \frac{\sum_{i=1}^{N} \{I\left(f_i(x) \neq f(x)\right)\}}{N}, \tag{7}$$

where $I(\cdot)$ denotes the indicator function that takes the value 1 if the label $f_i(x)$ predicted by the i-th mutated model differs from the label $f(x)$ assigned by the base model.

3.5   Optimal Threshold Selection

This paper proposes a threshold selection method based on ROC curve. The approach evaluates classifier performance under varying thresholds and identifies the optimal threshold to maximize detection efficacy for adversarial examples. In ROC analysis, the horizontal axis represents the False Positive Rate (FPR), while the vertical axis corresponds to the True Positive Rate (TPR). As the threshold adjusts, the model's output probabilities shift accordingly, both TPR and FPR dynamically change, resulting in distinct shapes of the ROC curve. Ideally, we aim to select a threshold that maximizes the TPR while minimizing the FPR. To achieve this, this study selects the point on the ROC curve that is closest to the upper-left corner, which represents the optimal detection performance. The distance metric is calculated as:

$$\tau_{\mathrm{best}} = \arg\min_{\theta} \sqrt{(1 - \mathrm{TPR}(\theta))^2 + \mathrm{FPR}(\theta)^2}, \tag{8}$$

where θ denotes the decision threshold, and the optimization objective is to minimize the Euclidean distance between the selected operating point and the ideal upper-left corner. By employing this strategy, the identified optimal threshold significantly enhances both detection accuracy and robustness against adversarial examples.

4   Experimental Settings and Results Analysis

This section elaborates on the dataset, model selection, experimental results, and analysis. First, the proposed MMAED framework is benchmarked against comparison methods. Subsequently, its performance is rigorously evaluated under diverse adversarial attack conditions, demonstrating superior robustness. Finally, ablation studies validate the efficacy of the LCR metric and mutation operators in adversarial example detection.

4.1 Dataset and Experimental Settings

The experiments employ the RML2016.10a dataset [16], a public benchmark widely used in wireless signal modulation recognition, which covers 11 common modulation types including BPSK, 8PSK, QPSK, 16-QAM, 64-QAM, AM-DSB, AM-SSB, CPFSK, GFSK, 4-PAM, and WBFM. To investigate adversarial robustness under extreme noise conditions, we specifically focus on examples with a 0 dB SNR where the noise power equals the original signal power, establishing a challenging yet practical scenario for adversarial example generation and model robustness evaluation. The dataset is split into training and test sets with an 8:2 ratio to ensure rigorous validation.

The experiments employ the DeepConvNet architecture [17], adapted for adversarial example generation and model mutation on the RML2016.10a modulation dataset. To address the fundamental differences between wireless signal processing and conventional image domains, we implement structural optimizations including layer configuration refinement, network parameter adjustment, weight initialization modification, and input signal reshaping into a 2×128 tensor format. Performance evaluation adopts five key metrics: The Area Under the Receiver Operating Characteristic (AUROC), Accuracy (ACC), Precision (PRE), False Alarm Rate (FAR), and Missing Detection Rate (MDR).

4.2 Adversarial Example Detection Performance Comparison

This experiment uses gradient based and optimization based adversarial attack methods to generate five different types of adversarial examples, namely FGSM, PGD, BIM, C&W and DeepFool. To comprehensively evaluate the advancement of MMAED, this study compares it with two mainstream detection methods: the Adversarial Example Detection method based on fusion of Constellation Diagram features and Local Intrinsic Dimensional characteristics (AED-CD+LID) [10], and the Adversarial Example Detection method based on AutoenCoder Reconstruction Error (AED-ACRE) [11]. AUROC is adopted as the evaluation metric, with comparative results illustrated in Fig. 3.

As evidenced by the results, MMAED demonstrates significantly superior adversarial example detection performance compared to both baseline methods across five attack scenarios. For gradient-based attacks, FGSM, PGD, BIM, MMAED achieves AUROC scores of 0.9823, 0.9938, and 0.9791, surpassing AED-CD+LID by 4.11%, 10.17%, and 6.35%, and outperforming AED-ACRE by 6.96%, 6.22%, and 5.87%, respectively. While AED-CD+LID and AED-ACRE exhibit acceptable performance against these attacks, their limitations in handling sophisticated gradient perturbations highlight the advancements of MMAED. Against optimization-based attack, DeepFool, C&W, MMAED attains AUROC values of 0.9862 and 0.8215, exceeding AED-CD+LID by 6.41% and 8.55%, and AED-ACRE by 15.33% and 9.94%, respectively. The fundamental superiority of MMAED stems from its four mutation operators that systematically alter model boundaries: Gaussian blur operator injects adaptive Gaussian noise into weight matrices to disrupt attackers' precise parameter dependency;

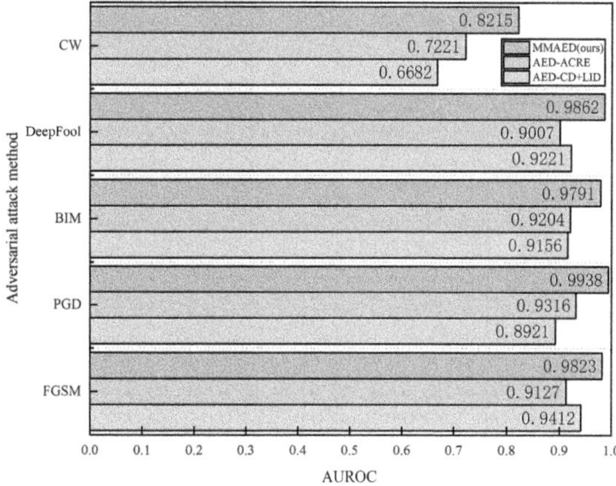

Fig. 3. Comparative analysis of MMAED and comparison detection methods

weight randomization operator permutes weight elements to break spatial correlations; neuron switching operator exchanges weight vectors to modify feature propagation paths; activation inversion operator flips activation function polarities to perturb nonlinear responses. In contrast, AED-CD+LID suffers from insufficient representation of iterative perturbations in constellation diagram features, while AED-ACRE faces generalization deficits against emerging attack patterns due to autoencoder reconstruction constraints, both exhibiting critical detection bottlenecks in complex electromagnetic environments.

4.3   Performance Analysis of the MMAED Detection Method

In real-world communication systems where adversaries generally operate without knowledge of model architectures or parameters, a scenario modeled through black-box attack simulations, the evaluation of detection algorithms must prioritize practical applicability. To this end, we evaluate the robustness of MMAED under both white-box and black-box threat models against two major adversarial example categories: gradient-based attacks, FGSM, PGD, BIM, and optimization-based attacks, C&W, DeepFool. The evaluation framework employs four critical metrics: ACC, PRE, FAR, and MDR. As systematically demonstrated in Fig. 4, these multidimensional measurements reveal fundamental insights into the method's operational reliability across threat landscapes.

As shown in Fig. 4, MMAED demonstrates superior detection efficacy under white-box attacks compared to black-box conditions, with performance improving as the Disturbance Intensity (DI) increases. Figure 4(a) and (b) reveal that under white-box attacks, the proposed method achieves 82.25% detection accuracy against FGSM adversarial examples at DI = 0.1, while exceeding 90.22% accuracy for PGD and BIM attacks. When DI rises to 0.5, detection accuracy and precision for all three gradient-based attacks surpass 97.60%. Under black-box settings, gradient-based attacks yield approximately 69.74% detection accuracy

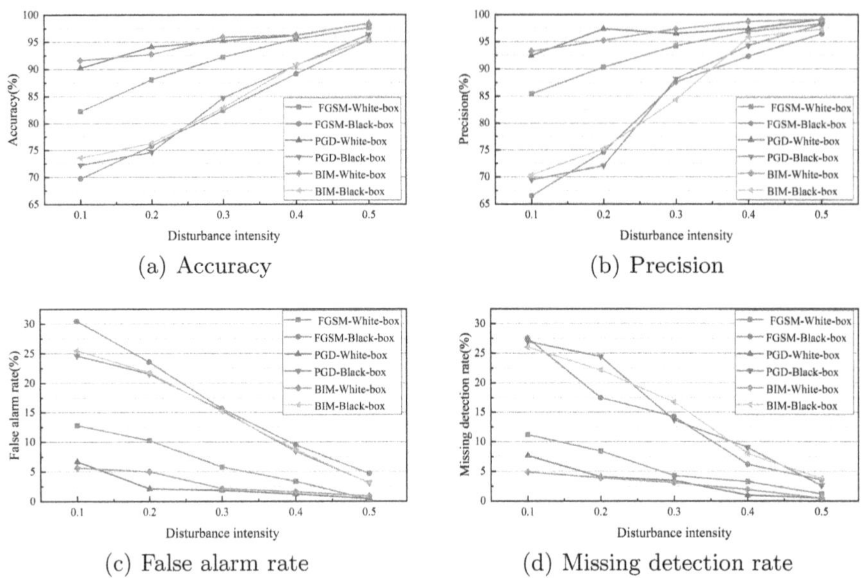

Fig. 4. MMAED detection effect for gradient-based adversarial attacks

at DI $= 0.1$, but accuracy and precision exceed 95.32% at DI $= 0.5$. Figure 4(c) and (d) indicate false alarm and miss rates below 1.22% for white-box attacks and under 4.67% for black-box scenarios at DI $= 0.5$. These results conclusively validate the method's effectiveness in detecting gradient-based adversarial examples across varying threat models.

As shown in Table 1, under white-box conditions, MMAED achieves a detection accuracy of 68.96% against C&W attacks, while demonstrating detection accuracy and precision exceeding 92.45% with false alarm and miss rates below 6.73% for DeepFool attacks. Compared to white-box scenarios, adversarial example detection under black-box conditions shows a noticeable performance decline: the method attains 59.81% detection accuracy against C&W attacks and maintains 82.56% or higher accuracy and precision for DeepFool attacks. These results confirm the ability of MMAED to detect adversarial examples based on optimization.

Table 1. MMAED detection effect for optimization-based adversarial attacks.

Attack method	Attack conditions	ACC (%)	PRE (%)	FAR (%)	MDR (%)
C&W	White-box	68.96%	70.29%	26.45%	24.68%
DeepFool	White-box	92.45%	95.33%	6.73%	5.86%
C&W	Black-box	59.81%	62.19%	33.17%	31.86%
DeepFool	Black-box	82.80%	82.56%	16.52%	14.69%

4.4 Validation of LCR Effectiveness

To validate the effectiveness of LCR to distinguish adversarial examples, the experiment calculates LCR values for both normal and adversarial examples using 200 screened mutated models generated with equal proportions of four mutation operators. As shown in Table 2, the first column specifies the mutation operator type, the second column presents the average LCR with 90% confidence intervals for 1,000 randomly selected normal examples from the test set, while the remaining columns display the average LCR values for 1,000 adversarial examples generated by five attack methods.

Table 2. Average LCR of normal and adversarial examples under 200 mutation models.

Mutation operator	No attack	FGSM	PGD	BIM	C&W	DeepFool
Gaussian fuzzing	0.1251	0.6815	0.6929	0.6439	0.3986	0.5869
Weight shuffling	0.2244	0.5660	0.5475	0.5263	0.3802	0.5097
Neuron switch	0.1806	0.4835	0.4738	0.4046	0.2883	0.4646
Neuron activation inverse	0.1162	0.5072	0.5281	0.5442	0.3625	0.5284

As evident from Table 2, substantial LCR differentials exist between benign and adversarial examples: three gradient-based attack methods exhibit discrepancies exceeding 0.3, C&W attacks show a differential of approximately 0.15, and DeepFool achieves differentials consistently above 0.28. These findings demonstrate conclusively that LCR serves as an effective discriminator for adversarial example identification.

4.5 Performance Evaluation and Comparative Analysis of Mutation Operators

To investigate whether combining four mutation operators provides performance improvements over single-operator implementations, this study evaluates individual mutation operators and compares them with MMAED using the Area Under the AUROC metric, with results presented in Fig 5.

As demonstrated in Fig. 5, MMAED consistently outperforms all single mutation operators across adversarial attack scenarios. Under C&W attacks, significant AUROC disparities emerge: MMAED achieves an AUROC of 0.8215, surpassing NAI, NS, WS, and GF by 5.61%, 10.41%, 8.25%, and 8.13%, respectively. Against DeepFool attacks, MMAED attains a 0.9862 AUROC, exceeding NAI, NS, WS, and GF by 5.34%, 6.54%, 5.10%, and 4.14%. For BIM attacks, MMAED achieves 0.9791 AUROC, with comparator methods all approaching or exceeding 0.97, confirming strong gradient attack adaptability of mutation techniques. PGD attack detection further confirms the superiority of MMAED,

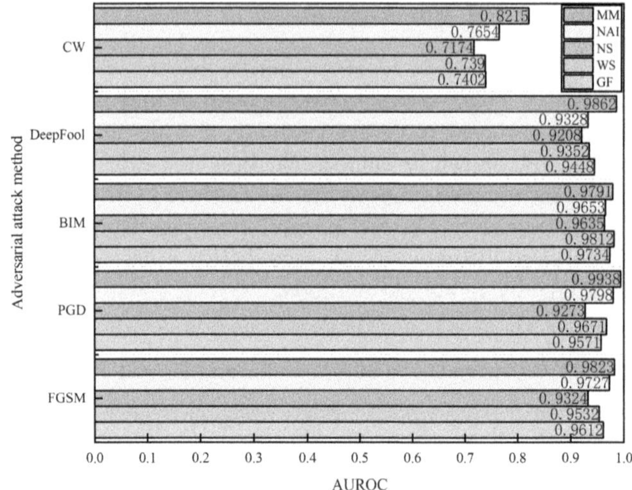

Fig. 5. Comparison of detection effects of MMAED and single operator mutation method.

with an AUROC of 0.9938, marginally higher than FGSM performance. Under FGSM attacks, MMAED maintains optimal detection capability, its AUROC = 0.9823, outperforming NAI, NS, WS, and GF by 0.96%, 4.99%, 2.91%, and 2.11%, respectively.

5   Conclusion

This paper effectively alleviated the threat of adversarial examples to deep learning models in signal modulation recognition by proposing the MMAED detection framework. The method employs Gaussian blur and weight randomization mutation operators to disrupt the dependency of attackers on prior knowledge of target models, thereby significantly enhancing the LCR capability for adversarial example identification. A front-rear layer freezing strategy during mutated model generation reduces computational overhead, while integrated model screening and threshold optimization mechanisms improve classification accuracy for both benign and adversarial examples. The experiment has demonstrated the superiority of MMAED, achieving 10.17% and 15.33% higher detection accuracy than its counterparts, with particularly strong efficacy against gradient-based and optimization-based adversarial example generation paradigms.

References

1. Lin, Y., Tu, Y., Dou, Z., et al.: Contour Stella image and deep learning for signal recognition in the physical layer. IEEE Trans. Cogn. Commun. Netw. **7**(1), 34–46 (2020)
2. Huynh-The, T., Pham, Q.V., Nguyen, T.V., et al.: Automatic modulation classification: a deep architecture survey. IEEE Access 142950–142971 (2021)
3. Szegedy, C., Zaremba, W., Sutskever, I., et al.: Intriguing properties of neural networks. arXiv preprint arXiv:1312.6199 (2013)
4. Sadeghi, M., Larsson, E.G.: Physical adversarial attacks against end-to-end autoencoder communication systems. IEEE Commun. Lett. **23**(5), 847–850 (2019)
5. Lin, Y., Zhao, H., Ma, X., et al.: Adversarial attacks in modulation recognition with convolutional neural networks. IEEE Trans. Reliab. **70**(1), 389–401 (2020)
6. Zhang, S., Fu, J., Yu, J, et al.: A channel-robust class-universal spectrum-focused frequency adversarial attacks on modulated classification models. IEEE Trans. Cogn. Commun. Netw. **10**(4), 1280–1293 (2024)
7. Han, C., Qin, R., Wang, L., et al.: Adversarial defense method based on ensemble learning for modulation signal intelligent recognition. Wireless Netw. **29**(7), 2967–2980 (2023)
8. Bao, Z., He, J., Zhang, C., et al.: OATGA: optimizing adversarial training via genetic algorithm for automatic modulation classification. In: GLOBECOM 2023-2023 IEEE Global Communications Conference, pp. 6073–6078. IEEE (2023)
9. Zhang, S., Yang, Y., Zhou, Z., et al.: DIBAD: a disentangled information bottleneck adversarial defense method using Hilbert-Schmidt independence criterion for spectrum security. IEEE Trans. Inf. Forensics Secur. **19**, 3879–3891 (2024)
10. Xu, D., Yang, H., Gu, C., et al.: Adversarial examples detection of radio signals based on multifeature fusion. IEEE Trans. Circuits Syst. II Express Briefs **68**(12), 3607–3611 (2021)
11. Han, C., Qin, R., Wang, L., et al.: Adversarial example detection and restoration defensive framework for signal intelligent recognition networks. Appl. Sci. **13**(21), 11880 (2023)
12. Bai, J., Ge, C., Xiao, Z., et al.: A multiscale discriminative attack method for automatic modulation classification. IEEE Trans. Inf. Forensics Secur. **20**, 294–308 (2024)
13. Qi, P., Jiang, T., Yuan, X., et al.: Detection tolerant black-box adversarial attack against automatic modulation classification with deep learning. IEEE Trans. Reliab. **71**(2), 674–686 (2022)
14. Hendrycks, D., Gimpel, K.: Early methods for detecting adversarial images. arXiv preprint arXiv: 1608.00530 (2016)
15. Han, S., Lin, C., Shen, C., et al.: Interpreting adversarial examples in deep learning: a review. ACM Comput. Surv. **55**(14s), 1–38 (2023)
16. O'Shea, T.J., Corgan, J., Clancy, T.C., et al.: Convolutional radio modulation recognition networks. In: Engineering Applications of Neural Networks: 17th International Conference (EANN), pp. 213–226 (2016)
17. Schirrmeister, R.T., Springenberg, J.T., Fiederer, L.D.J., et al.: Deep learning with convolutional neural networks for EEG decoding and visualization. Hum. Brain Mapp. **38**(11), 5391–5420 (2017)

Joint Optimization Scheduling of UAV Spectrum Resources Based on an Improved Multi-Objective Optimization Algorithm

Yingbo Liu[1], Liangtian Wan[1(✉)], Yuan Tian[1], Lu Sun[2], and Xianpeng Wang[3]

[1] School of Software, Dalian University of Technology, Dalian 116620, China
32317042@mail.dlut.edu.cn, {wanliangtian,tianyuan_ca}@dlut.edu.cn
[2] Department of Communication Engineering, Institute of Information Science Technology, Dalian Maritime University, Dalian 116026, China
sunlu@dlmu.edu.cn
[3] School of Information and Communication Engineering, Hainan University, Haikou 570228, China
wxpeng2016@hainanu.edu.cn

Abstract. To address the challenge of efficient spectrum resource utilization by unmanned aerial vehicles (UAVs) in interference-prone environments, this study optimizes UAV bandwidth allocation, frequency selection, and power distribution while ensuring solution diversity and uniformity. A multi-objective optimization model for joint spectrum resource allocation is proposed, along with an enhanced multi-objective evolutionary algorithm incorporating adaptive hybrid crossover and constraint repair strategies. The developed algorithm is applied to spectrum resource allocation problems, featuring an adaptive crossover mechanism and a constraint repair strategy to guarantee solution feasibility. Experimental results demonstrate that the proposed method effectively optimizes UAV spectrum resource allocation schemes, significantly improving anti-interference performance. Furthermore, it not only maintains convergence but also enhances the diversity and feasibility of the solution population distribution.

Keywords: spectrum resource · anti-interference performance · multi-objective optimization

1 Introduction

In recent years, with the rapid expansion of unmanned aerial vehicle (UAV) applications, particularly in complex electromagnetic environments such as urban dense communication scenarios, the efficient utilization of spectrum resources has faced unprecedented challenges[1]. Existing research indicates that

C. Xu et al. (Eds.): MobiMedia 2025, LNICST 670, pp. 348–360, 2026.
https://doi.org/10.1007/978-3-032-16823-8_25

the exponential growth of electromagnetic interference sources has led to significant fragmentation characteristics in available spectra [2], posing severe challenges to resource allocation in UAV communication systems. Effective spectrum resource optimization algorithms can not only significantly enhance UAV communication capabilities [3] but also improve their robustness in interference-prone environments [4].

Current research on UAV spectrum resource optimization primarily confronts two critical challenges: (1) Severe electromagnetic interference has resulted in notable spectrum fragmentation, substantially increasing the complexity of resource allocation[5]; (2) The high-density deployment of UAVs within limited frequency bands has led to serious co-channel interference issues [6]. To address these challenges, academia has proposed single-objective and multi-objective optimization approaches. Literature [7] introduced a spectrum allocation scheme based on an improved Chimp Optimization Algorithm (ChOA). This algorithm simulates the social hierarchy and collaborative hunting mechanisms of chimpanzee groups, achieving enhanced allocation efficiency in dynamic spectrum environments. Compared to traditional algorithms, the improved ChOA demonstrates faster convergence and is suitable for large-scale real-time spectrum demands. Literature [8] employed an improved Wolf Swarm Algorithm (WSA) for spectrum resource optimization. By reconstructing the leading wolf guidance strategy and group collaboration mechanism, it improved spectrum utilization while reducing inter-channel interference. Literature [9] proposed an Indicator-Based Multi-Objective Evolutionary Algorithm (MOEAs) that utilizes quantitative metrics such as Hypervolume (HV) and Inverted Generational Distance (IGD) to effectively balance multi-dimensional objectives like spectral efficiency and energy consumption control. Literature [10] introduced an adaptive constrained multi-objective optimization method based on problem-type classification (PTO-CMOEA), enhancing the algorithm's convergence, feasible solution ratio, and Pareto front coverage in complex constrained scenarios.

The main contributions of this paper are reflected in the following two aspects:

(1) A multi-UAV resource allocation model for fragmented spectrum conditions is proposed, with dual optimization objectives of data transmission time and anti-interference performance.

(2) An improved multi-objective genetic algorithm framework is designed. By incorporating an adaptive hybrid crossover strategy and a discrete variable constraint repair mechanism, the algorithm dynamically adjusts solution legality and population diversity. Experimental results demonstrate that the proposed algorithm effectively enhances performance in discrete optimization problems.

2 Modeling of Spectrum Resource Allocation Problem

2.1 Environment Model

For different scenario types, this paper establishes a spectrum resource allocation model under strong interference conditions based on real-world scenarios. The spectrum resource space is modeled as follows: multiple interfered frequency bands exist, resulting in fragmented available frequency segments. A horizontal coordinate system is used to represent electromagnetic interference zones, available spectrum regions, and allocated spectrum areas. The scenario involves multiple unmanned aerial vehicles (UAVs) performing data transmission tasks while multiple radiation sources create interference in the environmental spectrum resources. The resource space model is illustrated in the accompanying in Fig. 1.

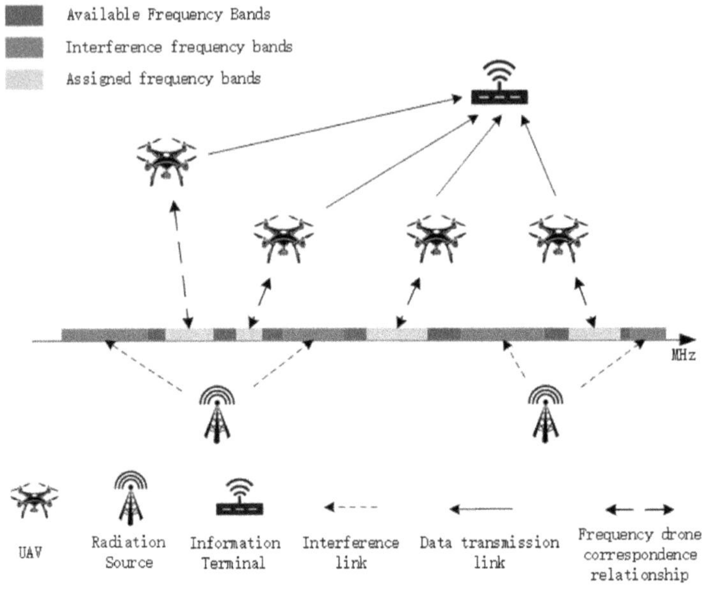

Fig. 1. The resource space model

Available Frequency Bands. Multiple non-contiguous available spectrum segments are formed between interfered frequency bands. The total number of available spectral intervals is denoted as m and the set of available spectral intervals is defined as $F = \{F_1, F_2, \ldots, F_j, \ldots, F_m\}$, Each interval $F_i = [f_{i_{start}}, f_{i_{snd}}]$ specifies the lower and upper frequency bounds of an available spectral segment, where $f_{i_{start}}$ and $f_{i_{end}}$ represent its lower and upper frequency bounds, respectively.

2.2 Resource Allocation Model and Multi-Objective Optimization Model

This section presents the calculation of UAV transmission time and anti-jamming performance metrics under self-interference and heterogeneous data transmission sizes in jamming environments, as well as the formulation of a joint resource optimization problem for UAV operations.Consider a swarm system comprising n unmanned aerial vehicles (UAVs), formally represented as the set $E = \{E_1, E_2, \ldots, E_j, \ldots, E_n\}$.

(1) Constraints. During UAV data transmission, both transmit power and bandwidth allocation must comply with device specifications while being constrained by available frequency segments. Notably, all UAVs operating within the same available frequency segment must select non-overlapping center frequencies.

The operating bandwidth range of UAV E_j must satisfy its inherent limitations:

$$C_1 : b_{j_{\min}} \leq b_j \leq b_{j_{\max}} \tag{1}$$

where $b_{j_{\min}}$ represents the minimum allowable bandwidth and $b_{j_{\max}}$ denotes the maximum allowable bandwidth for UAV E_j .

The transmit power p_j of UAV E_j must remain within its operational power range:

$$C_2 : p_{j_{\min}} \leq p_j \leq p_{j_{\max}} \tag{2}$$

where $p_{j_{min}}$ indicates the minimum transmit power and $p_{j_{max}}$ specifies the maximum transmit power for UAV E_j.

When operating within frequency segment F_i, UAV E_j must fully occupy the allocated spectrum:

$$C_3 : f_{i_{\text{start}}} \leq f_j - \frac{b_j}{2} \cup f_j + \frac{b_j}{2} \leq f_{i_{\text{end}}} \tag{3}$$

where $f_{i_{start}}$ and $f_{i_{end}}$ represent the starting and ending frequencies of segment F_i respectively, and f_j denotes the center frequency of UAV E_j.

For any two UAVs E_j and E_k operating in the same frequency segment F_i, their spectral allocations must satisfy:

$$C_4 : (f_j + \frac{b_j}{2}) \leq f_k - \frac{b_k}{2} \| (f_k + \frac{b_k}{2}) \leq f_j - \frac{b_j}{2} \tag{4}$$

where f_j and f_k are the center frequencies, and b_j and b_k are the bandwidth allocations of UAVs E_j and E_k respectively.

(2)Total Transmission Time. During UAV data transmission, the transmission time is jointly determined by the UAV's bandwidth and transmit power, and is influenced by the varying data volumes transmitted by UAV. The total transmission time, denoted as T, can be calculated using the following formula:

$$T = \sum_{j=0}^{n} \left(\frac{M_j}{b_j \cdot \log_2(1 + S/N)} \right) \tag{5}$$

In the formulation, n denotes the total number of UAVs in the system, M_j represents the data volume transmitted by the j-th UAV, and S/N indicates the Signal-to-Noise Ratio (SNR) of the operational environment. Due to the complex electromagnetic interference in UAV operational environments, where interference levels vary across frequency bands, a computational model for SNR is introduced to simulate realistic conditions:

$$S/N = \frac{P_j}{P_{\text{noise}} + P_{\text{interference}}} \tag{6}$$

where P_{noise} is the environmental noise power within the current operational band, and $P_{interference}$ is the aggregate interference power from other devices operating in the same frequency band.

(3) Anti-Interference Performance. During operation, UAVs are subject not only to external interference but also to mutual interference with other UAVs sharing the same frequency band. To quantify this intra-system interference, the concept of frequency separation is introduced. For a UAV located at the edge of a frequency band, interference calculation is required only from one adjacent UAV. For instance, when a UAV operates at a center frequency f_j, and its neighboring UAV operates at f_{j-1}, the frequency separation metric is defined as:

$$\left(\frac{1}{|f_j - f_{j-1}|}\right)^{\alpha} \tag{7}$$

where α is a tunable exponent that adjusts the impact of frequency separation on interference intensity.

By incorporating this metric, the interference between adjacent UAVs across all frequency bands is aggregated. For each UAV, interference from one adjacent UAV is considered (except for the first and last UAVs in a band, which interact with only one neighbor). The total anti-interference performance metric H_{total} is formulated as:

$$\begin{aligned}
H_{\text{total}} = \sum_{i=1}^{m} \Bigg(& \sum_{u=2}^{\nu-1} \Bigg(\left(\frac{1}{|f_u - f_{u-1}|}\right)^{\alpha} \cdot p_u \cdot p_{u-1} \\
& + \left(\frac{1}{|f_u - f_{u+1}|}\right)^{\alpha} \cdot p_u \cdot p_{u+1} \Bigg) \\
& + \left(\frac{1}{|f_1 - f_2|}\right)^{\alpha} \cdot p_1 \cdot p_2 \\
& + \left(\frac{1}{|f_\nu - f_{\nu-1}|}\right)^{\alpha} \cdot p_\nu \cdot p_{\nu-1}
\end{aligned} \tag{8}$$

where ν represents the number of UAVs operating on a specific frequency band F_i, while m denotes the total number of available frequency bands within the operational spectrum. The center frequency of the u-th UAV is defined as f_u, and its corresponding transmit power is denoted by p_u. For adjacent UAVs within the same frequency band, the center frequencies of the preceding and succeeding UAVs relative to the u-th UAV are f_{u-1} and f_{u+1}, respectively, with their transmit powers represented as p_{u-1} and p_{u+1}.

(4)Problem Formulation. In summary, this paper transforms the problem of drone resource allocation into a multi-objective optimization problem.

$$Minimize(T, H_{total}) \tag{9}$$

3   Improved Multi-Objective Algorithms

With the increasing scarcity of electromagnetic spectrum resources[11,12], intelligent optimization algorithms have garnered widespread attention and application in the field of spectrum resource allocation [13,14]. In multi-objective optimization problems based on continuous variables, traditional crossover and mutation operations for continuous variables can effectively enhance population convergence performance. However, when dealing with mixed-variable optimization problems that involve both continuous variables and discrete constrained variables, their search efficiency significantly deteriorates. This paper proposes an enhanced multi-objective evolutionary algorithm based on an adaptive hybrid crossover strategy and discrete variable constraint repair mechanism. By adjusting the selection probabilities of search operators and parameter configurations, the algorithm significantly improves global exploration and local exploitation capabilities in the solution space. The specific improvements are as follows. This paper proposes an enhanced multi-objective evolutionary algorithm based on an adaptive hybrid crossover strategy. The algorithm incorporates an adaptive hybrid crossover mechanism and a discrete variable constraint repair mechanism to improve the convergence, uniformity, and diversity of population solutions. The specific improvements are as follows.

3.1   Genetic Evolution Process

Adaptive Mixed Crossover Mechanism. The proposed strategy dynamically selects either arithmetic crossover or an innovative ranked recombination approach based on constraint satisfaction conditions, effectively addressing optimization problems involving both continuous and discrete/constrained variables. Two parent individuals are defined as:

$$\mathbf{x}_1 = (\mathbf{x}_1^c, \mathbf{x}_1^d), \quad \mathbf{x}_2 = (\mathbf{x}_2^c, \mathbf{x}_2^d) \tag{10}$$

where $\mathbf{x}^c \in \mathbb{R}^n$ represents continuous variables, and $x^d \in \mathbb{R}^n$ (or $\mathbb{Z}^n$) denotes discrete or constrained variables. The adaptive crossover operator employs a constraint-based decision mechanism:

$$\text{Cross}_d(\mathbf{x}_1^d, \mathbf{x}_2^d, \mu) = \begin{cases} \mu \mathbf{x}_1^d + (1-\mu)\mathbf{x}_2^d & \text{if } \forall ii \ \mathbf{x}_{1,ii}^d, \mathbf{x}_{2,ii}^d \in C_1 \vee C_2 \\ \text{SortRecombine}(\mathbf{x}_1^d, \mathbf{x}_2^d) & \text{otherwise} \end{cases} \tag{11}$$

where $\mu \in (0,1]$ is a random weight vector. When arithmetic crossover violates constraints, the algorithm switches to the sorted recombination mechanism, proceeding as follows:

Parent Vector Sorting.

$$x_1^{d,\text{sorted}} = \text{sort}(x_1^d), \quad x_2^{d,\text{sorted}} = \text{sort}(x_2^d) \tag{12}$$

Adaptive arithmetic crossover is performed in the sorted domain:

$$\begin{cases} \mathbf{y}_1^{d,sorted} = \text{AdaptiveCross}(\mathbf{x}_1^{d,sorted}, \mathbf{x}_2^{d,sorted}, \mu) \\ \mathbf{y}_2^{d,sorted} = \text{AdaptiveCross}(\mathbf{x}_2^{d,sorted}, \mathbf{x}_1^{d,sorted}, \mu) \end{cases} \tag{13}$$

where the adaptive crossover operator is defined as:

$$\text{AdaptiveCross}(\mathbf{u}, \mathbf{v}, \mu)_i = \begin{cases} \mu u_{ik} + (1 - \mu)v_{ik} & \text{if } \exists j \text{ s.t.} u_{ik}, v_{ik} \in F_j \\ u_i & \text{otherwise} \end{cases} \tag{14}$$

The crossover results are mapped back to their original order using inverse sorting:

$$\begin{cases} y_1^d = \text{argsort}^{-1}(\mathbf{x}_1^d, \mathbf{y}_1^{d,\text{sorted}}) \\ y_2^d = \text{argsort}^{-1}(\mathbf{x}_2^d, \mathbf{y}_2^{d,\text{sorted}}) \end{cases} \tag{15}$$

The final offspring are generated as:

$$\mathbf{y}_1 = (\mathbf{y}_1^c, \mathbf{y}_1^d), \quad \mathbf{y}_2 = (\mathbf{y}_2^c, \mathbf{y}_2^d) \tag{16}$$

Discrete Variable Constraint Violation Repair Strategy. For the issue of constraint violations during crossover and mutation operations involving discrete variables, this paper proposes an out-of-bounds repair strategy based on dual-factor weight allocation. When a frequency variable f_j violates C_3 and C_4, the system first calculates the remaining allocatable length R_i for each candidate constraint F_i within the feasible constraint set F. The calculation formula is defined as follows:

$$R_i = L_i - \sum_{\vartheta \in \mathcal{I}_k} b_\vartheta \tag{17}$$

where L_i represents the total allocatable length permitted by constraint F_i, $\mathcal{I}_k$ denotes the set of frequency points currently allocated within F_i and b_ϑ indicates the bandwidth occupied by the ϑ-th frequency point. To optimize frequency band selection, a weight function ζ_i is designed for all candidate constraints $F_i \in F$ to quantify the priority of each candidate constraint. The function is defined as follows:

$$\zeta_i = \xi \cdot \frac{R_i}{R_{\max}} + (1 - \xi) \cdot \frac{1}{1 + d_i} \tag{18}$$

where $R_{\max}$ represents the maximum remaining capacity in set F, $\xi \in [0, 1]$ denotes the balancing coefficient used to control the trade-off between resource utilization and distance cost, and d_i indicates the distance between the currently out-of-bounds variable and the center point of F_i. The system selects the frequency band F_ζ with maximal weight ζ_i as the target range and generates a new compliant frequency point f_j' through uniform stochastic sampling:

$$f_j' \sim \mathcal{U}\left(F_{\zeta_{start}} + \frac{b_j}{2}, F_{\zeta_{end}} - \frac{b_j}{2}\right) \tag{19}$$

3.2   Algorithm Framework

The proposed AHC-DR-NSGA-II algorithm follows the basic framework of NSGA-II, with key modifications(as shown in algorithm1).

Algorithm 1 Basic framework of AHC-DR-NSGA-II

1: Initialize random population
2: **for** each generation **do**
3:      Evaluate solutions
4:      Rank by non-domination (Pareto fronts)
5:      Compute crowding distance
6:      Select parents (tournament selection)
7:      Create offspring (Adaptive Constraint-Aware Crossover + mutation)
8:      Discrete Variable Repair Strategy
9:      Combine parents and offspring
10:      Select new population (elitism)
11: **end for**
12: **return:** best solutions (first Pareto front)

The AHC-DR-NSGA-II algorithm proposed in this paper improves the convergence, uniformity, and diversity of population solutions by using an adaptive hybrid crossover mechanism and a discrete variable constraint repair mechanism.

The adaptive mixed crossover function is shown in algorithm 2.

Algorithm 2 Adaptive Constraint-Aware Crossover

1: **input:** Parent individuals $x_1 = (x_1^c, x_1^d)$, $x_2 = (x_2^c, x_2^d)$, weight $\mu \in [0, 1]$
2: **output:** Offspring individuals y_1, y_2
3: **Continuous variable crossover:**
4: $y_1^c \leftarrow \mu x_1^c + (1 - \mu)x_2^c$
5: $y_2^c \leftarrow \mu x_2^c + (1 - \mu)x_1^c$
6: **Discrete variable crossover:**
7: **if** $\forall i \ x_{1,i}^d, x_{2,i}^d \in C_1 \cup C_2$ **then**   ▷ Constraint check
8:      $y_1^d \leftarrow \mu x_1^d + (1 - \mu)x_2^d$
9:      $y_2^d \leftarrow \mu x_2^d + (1 - \mu)x_1^d$
10: **else**
11:      $x_1^{sorted} \leftarrow \text{Sort}(x_1^d)$ ▷ Sort-Recombine mechanism
12:      $x_2^{sorted} \leftarrow \text{Sort}(x_2^d)$
13:      $y_1^{sorted} \leftarrow \text{AdaptiveCross}(x_1^{sorted}, x_2^{sorted}, \mu)$
14:      $y_2^{sorted} \leftarrow \text{AdaptiveCross}(x_2^{sorted}, x_1^{sorted}, \mu)$
15:      $y_1^d \leftarrow \text{InverseArgsort}(x_1^d, y_1^{sorted})$
16:      $y_2^d \leftarrow \text{InverseArgsort}(x_2^d, y_2^{sorted})$
17: **end if**
18: **Combine outputs:**
19: $y_1 \leftarrow (y_1^c, y_1^d)$
20: $y_2 \leftarrow (y_2^c, y_2^d)$

The adaptive crossover operation is shown in the algorithm3.

Algorithm 3 AdaptiveCross(u, v, μ)

1: **for** each element k **do**
2:     **if** $u_k, v_k \in F_j$ **then**
3:         $w_k \leftarrow \mu u_k + (1 - \mu)v_k$
4:     **else**
5:         $w_k \leftarrow u_k$ ▷ Keep parent value
6:     **end if**
7: **end for**
8: **return:** w

The discrete variable repair strategy is shown in the algorithm 4.

Algorithm 4 Discrete Variable Repair Strategy

1: **input:**
    Violated variable f_j with bandwidth b_j
    Feasible constraint set $F = \{F_1, \ldots, F_n\}$
    Balancing coefficient $\xi \in [0, 1]$
2: **output:** Repaired variable f_j' satisfying constraints
3: Calculate remaining capacity $\forall F_i \in F$:
4: **for** each $F_i \in F$ **do**
5:     $R_i \leftarrow L_i - \sum_{\vartheta \in \mathcal{I}_k} b_\vartheta$
6: **end for**
7: $R_{\max} \leftarrow \max(\{R_i\}_{i=1}^n)$
8: Compute selection weights:
9: **for** each $F_i \in F$ **do**
10:     $d_i \leftarrow \text{distance}(f_j, \text{center}(F_i))$
11:     $\zeta_i \leftarrow \xi \cdot \frac{R_i}{R_{\max}} + (1 - \xi) \cdot \frac{1}{1+d_i}$
12: **end for**
13: Select optimal band:
14: $F_\zeta \leftarrow \text{argmax}_{F_i} \zeta_i$
15: Generate compliant value:
16: $f_j' \leftarrow \text{SampleUniform}(F_\zeta^{\text{start}} + \frac{b_j}{2}, F_\zeta^{\text{end}} - \frac{b_j}{2})$
17: **return:** f_j'

---

4   Experimental Design

4.1   Parameter Setting

According to the the characteristics of multi-objective evolutionary algorithms, this paper selects the MOWOA, AHC-NSGA-II, NSGA-II-GLS algorithms, along with the proposed AHC-DR-NSGA-II algorithm, to conduct simulation experiments on spectrum resource optimization under interference [15, 16]. The relevant parameter settings of the algorithms are listed in Table 1.

Table 1. The Parameters of The Experimental Algorithm.

Parameter	Note	Value
D	Number of drones	20
N	population size	100
M	Number of optimization	2
max FE	Maximum number of function evaluations	10000
p_c	crossover probability	0.7
max p_m	mutation probability	0.3

4.2 Experimental Results

This section presents realistic experimental results and in-depth analysis of the proposed algorithm for joint optimization of spectrum resources in interference-prone environments.

Figure 2 presents the population solution distribution diagrams obtained from 30 independent runs (100 iterations each) of four multi-objective optimization algorithms: AHC-DR-NSGA-II, AHC-NSGA-II, NSGA-II-GLS, and MOWOA, for spectrum resource allocation in interference environments. The results demonstrate that: (1) all algorithms effectively optimize the two objective functions of the spectrum allocation problem; (2) regarding Pareto front approximation, AHC-DR-NSGA-II and AHC-NSGA-II exhibit superior performance–their solution sets not only achieve better distribution uniformity but also demonstrate enhanced global search capability, effectively preventing premature convergence. Notably, the AHC-DR-NSGA-II algorithm maintains superior population diversity while obtaining non-dominated solution sets with higher precision.

To provide a more comprehensive comparison of the performance of multi-objective optimization algorithms, this paper conducts statistical analysis on the hypervolume (HV) index values obtained by four algorithms in the joint optimization problem of spectrum resource allocation. As illustrated in Fig. 3, the average HV values achieved by the four algorithms over independent runs are presented. The results demonstrate that the AHC-DR-NSGA-II algorithm attains the highest HV value for the obtained solutions after completing 100 iterations.

5 Conclusion

To investigate the joint optimization of electromagnetic spectrum resources in interference environments, a multi-UAV spectrum resource allocation model under fragmented spectrum conditions was adopted. This model quantifies the impact of band interference and mutual interference among UAVs on transmission rates and anti-jamming effectiveness, making the spectrum resource allocation model for UAVs in interference environments more aligned with real-world scenarios.

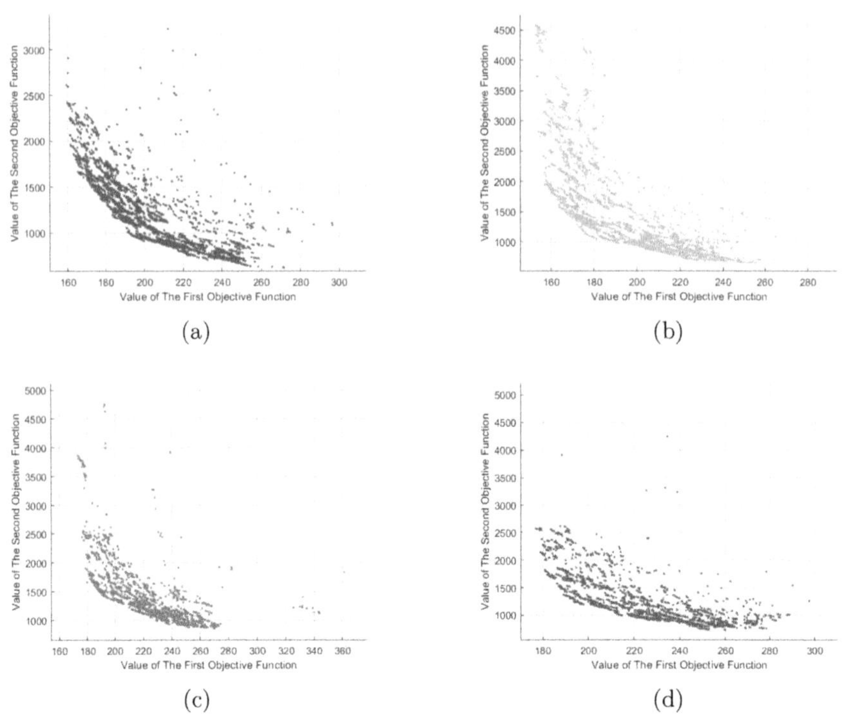

Fig. 2. The Distribution of The Solutions by (a) AHC-DR-NSGA-II (b) AHC-NSGA-II (c) NSGA-II-GLS (d) MOWOA

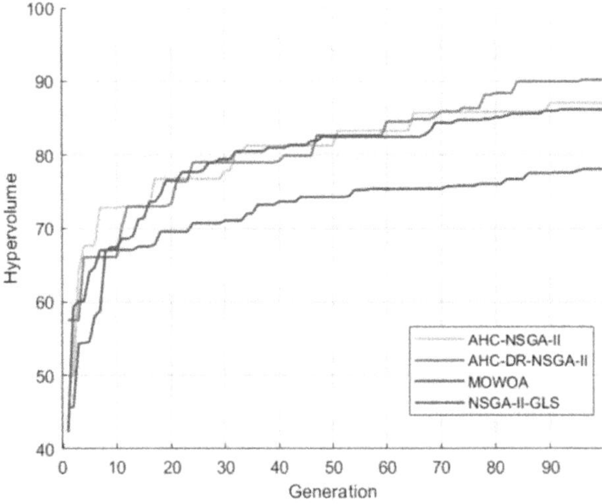

Fig. 3. The Maximum Vector Angle Priority Principle

To address the multi-objective optimization problem, this paper proposes an AHC-DR-NSGA-II algorithm, which incorporates an adaptive hybrid crossover strategy and a discrete variable constraint repair mechanism to adjust population diversity and enhance the algorithm's global search capability. Analysis of experimental results and evaluation metrics demonstrates that the proposed AHC-DR-NSGA-II algorithm exhibits superior optimization performance.

Acknowledgment. This work is supported by National Natural Science Foundation of China (62571080), Fundamental Research Funds for the Central Universities (3132025248).

References

1. Yongjun, X., Gui, G., Gacanin, H., Adachi, F.: A survey on resource allocation for 5g heterogeneous networks: current research, future trends, and challenges. IEEE Commun. Surv. Tutorials **23**(2), 668–695 (2021)
2. Kaur, M., Kakar, S., Mandal, D.: Electromagnetic interference. In: 2011 3rd International Conference on Electronics Computer Technology, vol. 4, pp. 1–5 (2011)
3. Zhang, J., Zeng, Y., Zhang, R.: Spectrum and energy efficiency maximization in uav-enabled mobile relaying. In: 2017 IEEE International Conference on Communications (ICC), pp. 1–6 (2017)
4. Zhou, L., Chen, X., Hong, M., Jin, S., Shi, Q.: Efficient resource allocation for multi-uav communication against adjacent and co-channel interference. IEEE Trans. Veh. Technol. **70**(10), 10222–10235 (2021)
5. Tsiropoulos, G.I., Dobre, O.A., Ahmed, M.H., Baddour, K.E.: Radio resource allocation techniques for efficient spectrum access in cognitive radio networks. IEEE Commun. Surv. Tutorials **18**(1), 824–847 (2016)
6. Khuwaja, A.A., Zheng, G., Chen, Y., Feng, W.: Optimum deployment of multiple uavs for coverage area maximization in the presence of co-channel interference. IEEE Access **7**, 85203–85212 (2019)
7. Huo, X., Li, K., Jiang, H.: Spectrum allocation algorithm based on improved chimp optimization algorithm. In: Li, J., Zhang, B., Ying, Y. (eds.) 6GN for Future Wireless Networks, pp. 69–78. Springer Nature Switzerland, Cham (2024)
8. Cao, C., Li, K.: Spectrum allocation algorithm based on improved wolf swarm algorithm. In: 2022 9th International Conference on Dependable Systems and Their Applications (DSA), pp. 1000–1001 (2022)
9. Falcón-Cardona, J.G., Coello Coello, C.A.: Indicator-based multi-objective evolutionary algorithms: a comprehensive survey. ACM Comput. Surv. (CSUR) **53**(2), 1–35(2020)
10. Wagner, M., Neumann, F.: A fast approximation-guided evolutionary multi-objective algorithm. In: Proceedings of the 15th Annual Conference on Genetic and Evolutionary Computation, pp. 687–694 (2013)
11. Staple, G., Werbach, K.: The end of spectrum scarcity [spectrum allocation and utilization]. IEEE Spectr. **41**(3), 48–52 (2004)
12. Struzak, R., Tjelta, T., Borrego, J.P.: On radio-frequency spectrum management. URSI Radio Sci. Bull. **2015**(354), 11–35 (2015)
13. Mallikarjuna Gowda, C.P., Vijayakumar, T.: Analysis and performance evaluation of pso for spectrum allocation in crn. In: 2021 International Conference on Innovative Practices in Technology and Management (ICIPTM), pp. 119–124 (2021)

14. Zhang, K., Zhiwei, X., Yen, G.G., Zhang, L.: Two-stage multiobjective evolution strategy for constrained multiobjective optimization. IEEE Trans. Evol. Comput. **28**(1), 17–31 (2024)
15. Kumawat, I.S., Nanda, S.J., Maddila, R.K.: Multi-objective whale optimization. In: Tencon 2017-2017 IEEE Region 10 Conference, pp. 2747–2752. IEEE (2017)
16. Zhang, Z., Lu, B.: Improving nsga-ii by a local search strategy with gaussian mutation. In: 2021 40th Chinese Control Conference (CCC), pp. 1628–1633 (2021)

Multi-UAV Spectrum Scheduling Algorithm Under Incomplete Conditions Based on NSGA-II

Liangtian Wan[1]([✉]), Wenxuan Nie[1], Lu Sun[2], and Xianpeng Wang[3]

[1] School of Software, Dalian University of Technology, Dalian 116620, China
wanliangtian@dlut.edu.cn, 2606324899@mail.dlut.edu.cn
[2] Department of Communication Engineering, Institute of Information Science Technology, Dalian Maritime University, Dalian 116026, China
sunlu@dlmu.edu.cn
[3] School of Information and Communication Engineering, Hainan University, Haikou 570228, China
wxpeng2016@hainanu.edu.cn

Abstract. This study investigates- the spectrum allocation problem for multiple unmanned aerial vehicles(multi-UAVs) systems operating under uncertain environmental interference, aiming to balance mission effectiveness and energy efficiency. An enhanced NSGA-II optimization framework is proposed, integrating a Gaussian incomplete interference model with an innovative partially mapped crossover(PMX) interval crossover mechanism. The methodology establishes a dual-objective optimization paradigm that simultaneously maximizes task utility and minimizes communication power consumption through Pareto optimality analysis. Experimental results demonstrate that the proposed approach significantly outperforms conventional methods in interference mitigation and energy conservation, achieving substantial improvements in spectrum utilization efficiency under dynamic conditions. The core contributions lie in two aspects: (1) a probabilistic interference prediction model addressing environmental uncertainty, and (2) a diversity-preserving evolutionary operator design that enhances solution convergence. This work provides a theoretically grounded framework for resource-constrained UAV network deployments in complex electromagnetic environments.

Keywords: UAV swarm · spectrum scheduling · incomplete interference · NSGA-II · PMX interval crossover

1 Introduction

The rapid proliferation of unmanned aerial vehicles (UAVs) in applications such as surveillance, disaster response, and logistics has intensified the demand for efficient spectrum resource management in multi-UAVs systems [1,2]. However,

C. Xu et al. (Eds.): MobiMedia 2025, LNICST 670, pp. 361–373, 2026.
https://doi.org/10.1007/978-3-032-16823-8_26

the dynamic and uncertain nature of real-world electromagnetic environments—characterized by incomplete interference information, time-varying channel conditions [3], and stringent frequency orthogonality constraints—poses significant challenges to existing spectrum scheduling algorithms. Recent research in multi-UAV spectrum scheduling has explored diverse strategies to address dynamic interference and resource allocation challenges. Zhang et al. [4]proposed a cooperative spectrum sensing framework for cognitive UAV networks, leveraging multi-UAV collaboration to enhance detection accuracy in static environments. However, their approach lacks adaptability to incomplete interference scenarios with uncertain spatiotemporal dynamics. In mission-critical applications, Liao et al. [5] introduced a joint mission planning and spectrum optimization method, balancing task completion time and communication reliability, yet their model assumes deterministic interference patterns, limiting robustness under partial observability. Chen et al. [6,7] developed coalition formation games to jointly optimize task assignment and spectrum allocation in heterogeneous UAV networks, demonstrating improved fairness and scalability. While effective in small-scale systems, their methods struggle with high-dimensional discrete frequency assignments and real-time adaptability. For interference coordination, Shen et al. [8] combined trajectory control and power allocation to minimize mutual interference, achieving significant performance gains but requiring centralized coordination—a limitation in decentralized UAV swarms. Machine learning techniques have also been investigated. Shamsoshoara et al. [9] employed multi-agent reinforcement learning for distributed spectrum sharing, enabling autonomous decision-making in dynamic environments. However, their framework demands extensive training data and lacks theoretical guarantees for constraint satisfaction. Addressing uncertainty awareness, Shi et al. [10] recently integrated U-Net architectures with probabilistic modeling to enhance spectrum sensing reliability, marking progress toward handling incomplete interference information. Despite these advances, critical gaps persist: (1) Existing crossover operators in evolutionary methods (e.g., [4,6]) frequently violate spectral orthogonality constraints ($|f_i - f_j| \geq \Delta_f$), necessitating post-hoc repairs; (2) Most approaches [5,8,9] assume full knowledge of interference parameters, overlooking real-world incomplete conditions.

This article has the following main contributions:

(1) A Gaussian-based incomplete interference model is proposed to characterize environmental uncertainty, explicitly capturing the stochastic distribution of interference intensity and frequency preferences. Unlike deterministic models, this framework enables adaptive spectrum allocation by dynamically updating interference likelihood estimates, even when critical parameters (e.g., interference source locations) remain partially unknown.

(2) PMX interval crossover is designed to enforce conflict-free spectrum scheduling. By inheriting feasible frequency segments from parent solutions and resolving overlaps through interval-aware conflict checks, the operator eliminates spectral collisions during genetic operations. This avoids cross repair steps and reduces computational overhead while maintaining structural validity.

2   System Modeling

2.1   Environment Model

Let D denote the mission area for UAV operations, where multiple neutral electromagnetic devices and radiation sources are distributed. These neutral entities may generate interference to both the communication links and telemetry/control links of our UAVs. The system comprises M UAVs, represented by the set $V = \{V_1, V_2, \ldots, V_M\}$ Fig. 1.

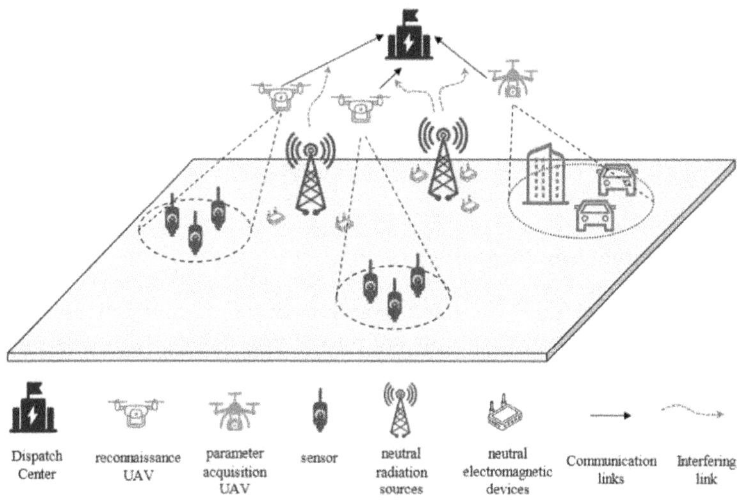

Fig. 1. The environment model

2.2   Incomplete Interference Model

(1) Distribution of Environmental Interference Given the presence of numerous neutral emitters and jammers in operational scenarios where UAVs perform tasks, we assume mutual independence among neutral emitters. Due to the time-varying nature of environmental conditions, interference links exhibit temporal dynamics. UAVs must conduct spectrum scheduling and execute missions under incomplete interference information. Let σ_e denote the concentration level of environmental interference, where μ_e represents the frequency preference of environmental interference. Based on the Central Limit Theorem, the aggregated environmental interference affecting UAVs is assumed to follow a Gaussian distribution:

$$f_c(x) = \frac{1}{\sqrt{2\pi}\sigma_e} \exp\left(-\frac{(x - \mu_e)^2}{2\sigma_e^2}\right) \tag{1}$$

(2) Single-UAV Interference Exposure Level The interference experienced by UAVs during mission execution is correlated with their operational bandwidth and transmission power. Specifically, wider bandwidth usage increases susceptibility to environmental interference, while lower transmission power may similarly elevate vulnerability. Consequently, the environmental interference affecting an individual UAV can be formulated as:

$$F_I\left(B^{ic}\right) = \alpha\left(\frac{P_f}{P_i}\right) \exp\left(-\frac{\left(E(f_c(x)) - B^{ic}\right)^2}{2\sigma'}\right) \tag{2}$$

where α represents the basic strength of the environmental interference effect, P_f represents the average interference power of the environment, P_i represents the power of our i-th drone, $f_c(x)$ represents the Gaussian distribution expression followed by the center frequency of the interference, B^{ic} represents the center frequency of our i-th drone, and σ' represents the frequency variance of the interference signal.

2.3   Communication Model

The Air-to-Ground (A2G) channel model between unmanned aerial vehicles (UAVs) and ground control stations comprises two distinct propagation modes: Nonlinear-of-Sight (NLOS) and Linear-of-Sight (LOS) links. NLOS links occur when physical obstructions block the direct transmission path, introducing additional path loss through multipath reflections and diffraction, whereas LOS links maintain unobstructed propagation with minimal signal attenuation, thereby ensuring superior communication quality. In practical UAV deployment scenarios, partial obstructions frequently induce stochastic transitions between LOS/NLOS states. Consequently, the design of UAV-assisted communication systems must account for the probabilistic nature of hybrid LOS-NLOS channels, necessitating the integration of a probabilistic model that jointly considers both propagation modes.

The hybrid Air-to-Ground (A2G) channel incorporates both LOS and NLOS propagation modes. The expected path loss is formulated as:

$$\overline{PL} = PL_{\mathrm{LOS}} \cdot P(\mathrm{LOS}, \theta) + PL_{\mathrm{NLOS}} \cdot P(\mathrm{NLOS}, \theta) \tag{3}$$

where PL_{LOS} and PL_{NLOS} denote path loss for LOS/NLOS links, $P(\mathrm{LOS}, \theta) + P(\mathrm{NLOS}, \theta) = 1$ ensures probability normalization.

The LOS probability follows a sigmoidal relationship with elevation angle:

$$P(\mathrm{LOS}, \theta) = \frac{1}{1 + a\exp[-b(\theta - a)]} \tag{4}$$

where a, b is the Environment-dependent coefficients (terrain type and carrier frequency), $\theta = \frac{180}{\pi}\sin^{-1}\left(\frac{H}{d}\right)$ is the Elevation angle, H is the UAV altitude, d is the Horizontal distance

The path loss components for each mode are defined as:

$$PL = \Lambda_{\text{free}} + \eta = \begin{cases} \dfrac{1}{\eta_{\text{LOS}}} \left(\dfrac{4\pi f_c d}{c} \right)^{-\beta}, & \text{LOS} \\[3mm] \dfrac{1}{\eta_{\text{NLOS}}} \left(\dfrac{4\pi f_c d}{c} \right)^{-\beta}, & \text{NLOS} \end{cases} \tag{5}$$

where $\Lambda_{\text{free}} = \left(\dfrac{4\pi f_c d}{c} \right)^{-\beta}$ is the loss of the path in free space, η is the additional loss of the path, $\eta_{\text{LOS}}, \eta_{\text{NLOS}}$ is the additional attenuation factors, β is the exponent of the path loss, f_c is the carrier frequency, c is the speed of light The final ensemble path loss combines both modes:

$$\overline{PL} = \frac{1}{\eta_{\text{LOS}}} \left(\frac{4\pi f_c d}{c} \right)^{-\beta} P(\text{LOS}, \theta) + \frac{1}{\eta_{\text{NLOS}}} \left(\frac{4\pi f_c d}{c} \right)^{-\beta} P(\text{NLOS}, \theta) \tag{6}$$

During communication between UAVs and ground control stations, the presence of noise and interference impacts signal quality. The SINR is defined as:

$$SINR = \frac{p_k}{PL\sigma^2} \tag{7}$$

where p_k is the Transmission power of the UAV, $\frac{1}{PL}$ is the Channel gain between the UAV and ground control station, σ^2 is the Additive white Gaussian noise (AWGN) power at the receiver.

2.4 Multi-Objective Optimization Model

(1) Task Benefits In practical scenarios, two distinct mission types are considered: reconnaissance missions and sensor parameter collection missions. For reconnaissance missions, the mission effectiveness primarily depends on the number of targets detected by the radar. Specifically, higher radar sensitivity equipped on the reconnaissance UAV enhances its capability to capture weak signals, thereby improving target detection performance. The reconnaissance effectiveness is formally defined as follows:

$$S_a^i = \frac{P_a^i G_a G_r c^2 \overline{PL}}{(4\pi R_{\max} \bullet B_a^{ic})^2} \frac{in_a}{B_a^i \bullet F_I(B_a^{ic})} \tag{8}$$

For sensor parameter collection missions, the mission effectiveness is primarily influenced by the data transmission rate of the UAV. Specifically, the higher the data volume transmitted within the same timeframe, the greater the mission effectiveness. The effectiveness of parameter acquisition tasks is formally defined as follows:

$$R_b^i = B_b^i \log_2(1 + SINR) \tag{9}$$

In the system model, $F_I()$ denotes the environmental interference value affecting our UAVs. The transmission power of the i-th reconnaissance UAV is represented by P_a^i. The bandwidth length assigned to the i-th reconnaissance and parameter acquisition UAV are B_a^i and B_b^i, respectively. The operational center frequencies to the i-th reconnaissance UAV are B_a^{ic}. The key parameters of the system include G_a for the gain of the radar antenna, G_r for the gain of the receiver antenna, c for the speed of light and R_{max} for the maximum range of reconnaissance. The interference-to-sensitivity conversion coefficient,in_a, characterizes the relationship between environmental interference and degradation of sensor performance. Let w_a denote the weight assigned to reconnaissance missions, and w_b represent the weight for sensor parameter collection missions.n_a and n_b are the number of reconnaissance UAVs and the number of parameter acquisition UAVs, respectively The total utility function is mathematically formulated as follows:

$$E_{total} = w_a \sum_{i=1}^{n_a} S_a^i + w_b \sum_{i=1}^{n_b} R_b^i \tag{10}$$

(2) Communication Power Consumption In electromagnetic spectrum scheduling, only the communication power consumption of UAVs is considered, with other energy expenditures excluded from the scheduling process. The communication power consumption is proportional to both the data transmission volume and the allocated transmit power. Let p_k denote the communication power of the i-th UAV. The corresponding communication energy consumption E_{nc} is formulated as:

$$E_{nc} = P_k B_k \log_2\left(1 + SINR\right) \tag{11}$$

(3) Problem Formulation. For algorithm consistency, take the reciprocal of optimization objective 1. In summary, this paper transforms the spectrum scheduling for multi-UAV systems under incomplete interference conditions into a multi-objective optimization problem:

$$\begin{cases} \min E'_{total} = \frac{1}{E_{total}} \\ \min E_{rc} = P_k B_k \log_2\left(1 + SINR\right) \end{cases} \tag{12}$$

3 Improved IC-NSGA-II Algorithms

In the domain of communication resource allocation for unmanned aerial vehicles (UAVs), frequency points discrete variables constrained by strict orthogonality requirements pose unique challenges for optimization algorithms [11]. Traditional implementations of the NSGA-II algorithm, which rely on arithmetic or single-point crossover operators, encounter significant limitations when applied to such discrete and highly constrained problems [12]. Arithmetic crossover, which linearly combines parental frequency points (e.g., $\alpha f_1 + (1-\alpha)f_2$), risks generating offspring frequencies that overlap with existing allocations, violating spectral orthogonality constraints and introducing inter-channel interference. Additionally, crossover operations may produce solutions outside predefined frequency bounds (e.g., $f_{\min} \leq f \leq f_{\max}$), necessitating computationally intensive repair mechanisms to enforce feasibility. Furthermore, the inherent conflict-free nature of frequency allocation, governed by constraints such as $\|f_i - f_j\| \geq \Delta_f$, is poorly preserved by conventional crossover methods, leading to widespread infeasible offspring and degrading algorithmic convergence. These limitations collectively underscore the inadequacy of generic crossover strategies in high-dimensional discrete optimization spaces, emphasizing the need for specialized operators tailored to the structural and spectral constraints of UAV communication systems.

3.1   PMX Interval Crossover Algorithm

To address the limitation of traditional crossover methods in preserving feasible structural characteristics inherited from parent individuals, this paper proposes an innovative PMX Interval Crossover Algorithm.

The PMX Interval Crossover operator, an enhanced variant of PMX, demonstrates significant efficacy in discrete frequency allocation problems with strict spectral constraints. By integrating interval-aware conflict checks during crossover, the operator inherently avoids spectrum overlaps, ensuring compliance with bandwidth requirements ($|f_i - f_j| \geq B$) without post-repair mechanisms. The operator preserves structural validity by inheriting contiguous frequency segments from parent solutions, maintaining high-quality schemata while balancing exploration and exploitation through adjustable segment lengths. Furthermore, PMX's permutation-based design naturally aligns with discrete frequency indices, circumventing the feasibility issues inherent to continuous blending operators like arithmetic crossover. These features collectively enable efficient navigation of high-dimensional search spaces while adhering to orthogonality constraints, making PMX Interval Crossover Algorithm particularly suited for UAV spectrum scheduling where interference avoidance and computational efficiency are critical.

3.2   Algorithm Framework

The basic framework of NSGA-II algorithm is described in algorithm 1, which is similar to the basic framework of multi-objective evolutionary algorithms.

Algorithm 1 NSGA-II Algorithm

1: **input:** population size N, p_c, p_m, max generations $G_{\max}$
2: **output:** non-dominated solutions
3: Initialize population P_0 with size N
4: $g \leftarrow 0$
5: **repeat**
6:     Evaluate objectives for P_g
7:     Rank solutions using non-dominated sort
8:     Calculate crowding distance
9:     Select parents using tournament selection
10:     Generate offspring via crossover and mutation
11:     Combine parents and offspring
12:     Select new population P_{g+1} based on rank and crowding
13:     $g \leftarrow g + 1$
14: **until** $g = G_{\max}$
15: **return** first non-dominated front of P_g

Specifically, the crossover operation in Step 10 of Algorithm 1 is modified to PMX interval crossover. The steps of the PMX interval crossover algorithm are outlined as follows:

Algorithm 2 PMX Interval Crossover Algorithm

1: **Input:**
2:     Parent frequency lists: $P_1 = [f_1^1, \ldots, f_N^1]$, $P_2 = [f_1^2, \ldots, f_N^2]$
3:     Fixed bandwidth: B
4:     Number of devices: N
5: **Output:** Offspring frequency lists O_1, O_2
6: Initialize offspring:
7:     $O_1 \leftarrow P_1$, $O_2 \leftarrow P_2$
8: Randomly select crossover region indices s, e where $1 \leq s < e \leq N$
9: Exchange segments:
10:     $O_1[s : e] \leftarrow P_2[s : e]$, $O_2[s : e] \leftarrow P_1[s : e]$
11: **for** each $i \notin [s, e]$ **do**
12:     **if** no conflict between $P_2[i]$ and O_1 **then**
13:         $O_1[i] \leftarrow P_2[i]$
14:     **end if**
15:     **if** no conflict between $P_1[i]$ and O_2 **then**
16:         $O_2[i] \leftarrow P_1[i]$
17:     **end if**
18: **end for**
19: **return** O_1, O_2

Algorithm 3 Conflict Detection

1: **function** CONFLICT($S, f_{\text{new}}, B, \text{skip\_idx}$)
2:     **for** each $j \neq \text{skip\_idx}$ **do**
3:         **if** $|f_{\text{new}} - S[j]| < B$ **then**
4:             **return** True
5:         **end if**
6:     **end for**
7:     **return** False
8: **end function**

---

4   Experimental Design

4.1   Parameter Setting

According to the characteristics of multi-objective evolutionary algorithms, this paper selects NSGA-II-GLS [13], NSGA-II [14],NSPSO [15] algorithms and the IC-NSGA-II algorithm proposed in this paper to conduct simulation experiments on electromagnetic spectrum scheduling of multi-UAVs under incomplete interference. The relevant parameter settings of the algorithm are shown in Table 1.

Table 1. The Parameters of The Experimental Algorithm.

Parameter	Note	Value
D	Number of UAVs	20
N	population size	50
M	Number of optimization	2
max FE	Maximum number of function evaluations	10000
p_c	crossover probability	0.8
max p_m	mutation probability	0.2

4.2   Experimental Results

This section gives the comparative experimental results and experimental analysis of the algorithm for the spectrum scheduling for multi-UAV systems under incomplete interference conditions.

Figure 2 presents the distribution of solution populations obtained from 30 independent experiments conducted on IC-NSGA-II, NSGA-II-GLS, NSGA-II, and NSPSO after 100 iterations. The results demonstrate that most multi-objective optimization algorithms effectively optimize the two objectives of wireless sensor network deployment in underground spaces. Regarding solution diversity, IC-NSGA-II and NSGA-II-GLS outperform other algorithms, exhibiting

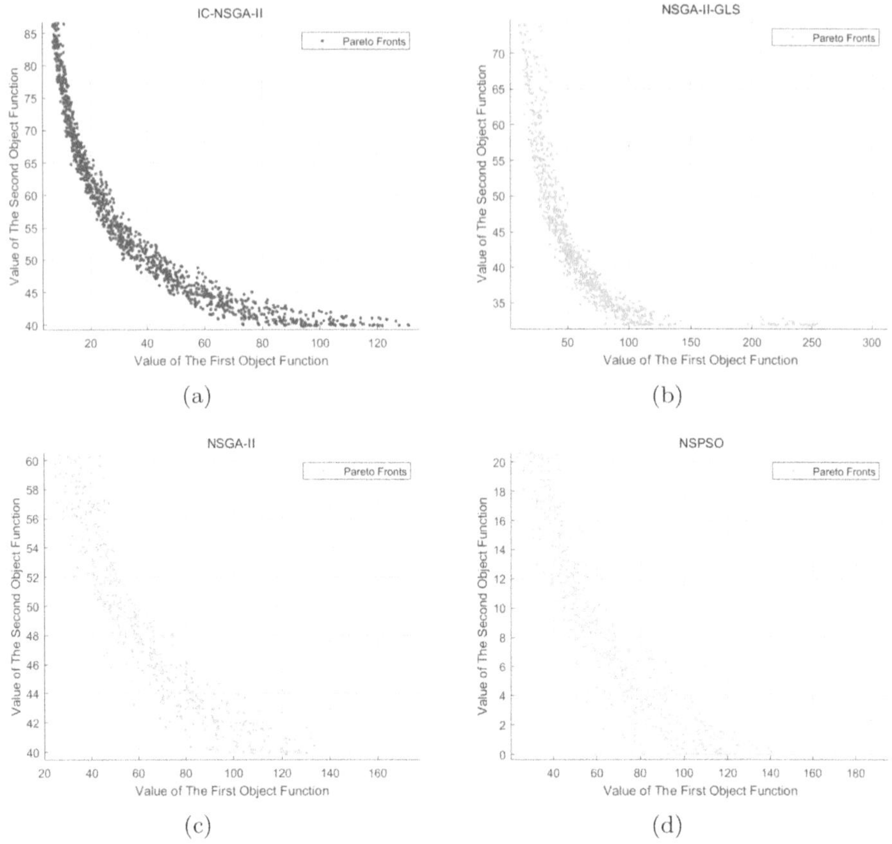

Fig. 2. The Distribution of The Solutions by (a) IC-NSGA-II (b) NSGA-II-GLS (c) NSGA-II (d) NSPSO

more uniformly distributed solutions and ultimately retaining a greater number of non-dominated solutions.

For a comprehensive performance evaluation of multi-objective optimization algorithms, this study statistically analyzes the Hypervolume (HV) metric values achieved by four algorithms in wireless sensor network deployment optimization. Figure 3 displays the average HV values obtained from 30 independent runs of each algorithm. The results show that IC-NSGA-II achieves superior performance, attaining HV values above 96 after 100 iterations—the highest among all compared algorithms. Furthermore, IC-NSGA-II consistently maintains higher HV values than other algorithms throughout the entire evolutionary process, demonstrating superior capabilities in both convergence and diversity preservation.

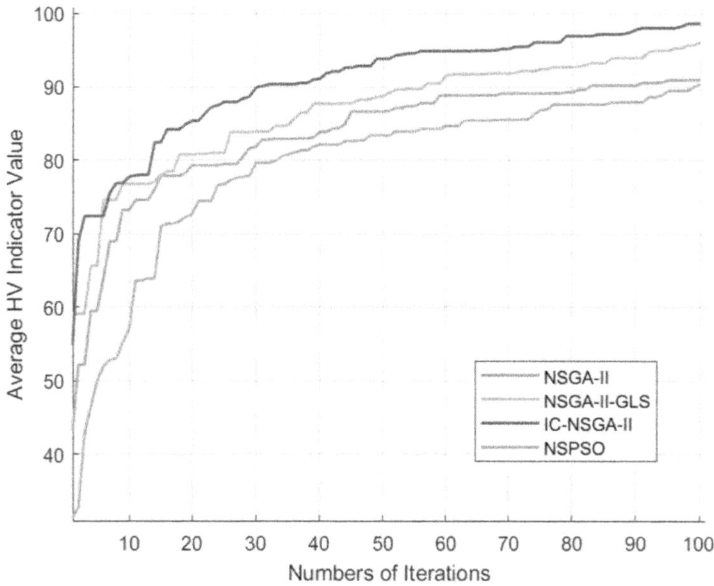

Fig. 3. The Maximum Vector Angle Priority Principle

5   Conclusion

For the study of UAV spectrum scheduling under incomplete interference conditions, the probability of visible and non visible links is comprehensively considered to evaluate the path loss of signals, making the spectrum scheduling of unmanned aerial vehicles in complex electromagnetic environments more realistic. In order to solve multi-objective optimization problems under incomplete conditions, this paper proposes an IC-NSGA-II algorithm that uses an improved PMX Interval Crossover technique. Through real-time detection and repair of frequency band conflicts, the algorithm strictly satisfies the frequency band orthogonality constraint while ensuring the diversity of the solution set, thus balancing the uniformity and diversity of the distribution of solutions in the population. Through the analysis of experimental results and HV indicators, it can be seen that the IC-NSGA-II algorithm proposed in this paper is superior to traditional multi-objective optimization algorithms in terms of convergence and solution distribution, and the optimization performance is significantly improved.

Acknowledgment. This work is supported by National Natural Science Foundation of China (62571080), Fundamental Research Funds for the Central Universities (3132025248).

References

1. Mohsan, S.A.H., Othman, N.Q.H., Li, Y., Alsharif, M.H., Khan, M.A.: Unmanned aerial vehicles (uavs): practical aspects, applications, open challenges, security issues, and future trends. Intell. Service Robot. **16**(1), 109–137 (2023)
2. Mohamed, N., Al-Jaroodi, J., Jawhar, I., Idries, A., Mohammed, F.: Unmanned aerial vehicles applications in future smart cities. Technol. Forecast. Soc. Chang. **153**, 119293 (2020)
3. Wen, Q.: An overview of the study of the complexity of the complex electromagnetic environments. In: 2015 8th International Symposium on Computational Intelligence and Design (ISCID), vol. 1, pp. 245–250. IEEE (2015)
4. Zhang, H., Da, X., Hu, H.: Multi-uav cooperative spectrum sensing in cognitive uav network. In: Proceedings of the 5th International Conference on Communication and Information Processing, pp. 273–278 (2019)
5. Liao, N., He, P., Yihang, D., Zhang, Yu., Chen, Y., Liang, T.: Joint mission planning and spectrum resources optimization for multi-uav reconnaissance. IET Commun. **17**(3), 324–335 (2023)
6. Chen, J., Qihui, W., Yuhua, X., Qi, N., Guan, X., Zhang, Y., Xue, Z.: Joint task assignment and spectrum allocation in heterogeneous uav communication networks: a coalition formation game-theoretic approach. IEEE Trans. Wireless Commun. **20**(1), 440–452 (2020)
7. Chen, J., Qihui, W., Yuhua, X., Qi, N., Fang, T., Liu, D.X.: Spectrum allocation for task-driven uav communication networks exploiting game theory. IEEE Wirel. Commun. **28**(4), 174–181 (2021)
8. Shen, C., Chang, T.-H., Gong, J., Zeng, Y., Zhang, R.: Multi-uav interference coordination via joint trajectory and power control. IEEE Trans. Signal Process. **68**, 843–858 (2020)
9. Shamsoshoara, A., Khaledi, M., Afghah, F., Razi, A., Ashdown, J.: Distributed cooperative spectrum sharing in uav networks using multi-agent reinforcement learning. In: 2019 16th IEEE Annual Consumer Communications & Networking Conference (CCNC), pp. 1–6. IEEE (2019)
10. Shi, J., Wu, J., Chong, J., Yang, Z.: Collaborative spectrum sensing for multi-uav system: a u-net approach with uncertainty awareness. IEEE Trans. Veh. Technol. (2025)
11. Ma, H., Zhang, Y., Sun, S., Liu, T., Shan, Yu.: A comprehensive survey on nsga-ii for multi-objective optimization and applications. Artif. Intell. Rev. **56**(12), 15217–15270 (2023)
12. Verma, S., Pant, M., Snasel, V.: A comprehensive review on nsga-ii for multi-objective combinatorial optimization problems. IEEE Access **9**, 57757–57791 (2021)
13. Zhang, Z., Lu, B.: Improving nsga-ii by a local search strategy with Gaussian mutation. In: 2021 40th Chinese Control Conference (CCC), pp. 1628–1633. IEEE (2021)

14. Deb, K., Pratap, A., Agarwal, S., Meyarivan, T.A.M.T.: A fast and elitist multiobjective genetic algorithm: Nsga-ii. IEEE Trans. Evol. Comput. **6**(2), 182–197 (2002)
15. Liu, Y.: A fast and elitist multi-objective particle swarm algorithm: Nspso. In: 2008 IEEE International Conference on Granular Computing, pp. 470–475. IEEE (2008)

Author Index

© ICST Institute for Computer Sciences, Social Informatics and Telecommunications Engineering 2026
Published by Springer Nature Switzerland AG 2026. All Rights Reserved
C. Xu et al. (Eds.): MobiMedia 2025, LNICST 670, pp. 375–376, 2026.
https://doi.org/10.1007/978-3-032-16823-8

R
Ruxin, Zhi   3

S
Si, Guangzhen   288
Siheng, Zhao   3
Song, Boyang   277
Sun, Lu   348, 361
Sun, Yan   77

T
Tian, Qiao   277
Tian, Yuan   348
Tu, Hanxiang   133

W
Wan, Liangtian   348, 361
Wang, Bin   47
Wang, Junyi   265
Wang, Juzhen   288
Wang, Meiyu   235, 288
Wang, Qi   35
Wang, Shihao   193
Wang, Wei   177
Wang, Xianpeng   348, 361
Wang, Yu   26
Wang, Yubo   193
Wang, Zhaoqing   112
Wang, Zhilong   306
Wu, Shunan   61, 77, 221
Wu, Wenjie   251
Wu, Xiangyu   47
Wu, Zewen   235

X
Xia, Tianhao   177
Xin, Guangda   319
Xu, Dongwei   177
Xu, Zhengwei   161, 209, 306
Xuan, Qi   177
Xue, Ye   17

Y
Yan, Zhen   112
Yang, Chen   333
Yang, Yu   144
Yang, Zilong   144
Ye, Fang   133, 265
Yin, Peng   35
Yulong, Wang   3

Z
Zhan, Xu   3
Zhang, Guangyuan   112
Zhang, Linzhi   17
Zhang, Sicheng   277, 333
Zhang, Xiaoshuai   112
Zhang, Yan   91
Zhao, Jing   251
Zhao, Peixian   333
Zheng, Zhiwen   112
Zhou, Haotian   35
Zhou, Ruoyu   319
Zhu, Haifeng   144
Zou, Hongyu   288

GPSR Compliance
The European Union's (EU) General Product Safety Regulation (GPSR) is a set
of rules that requires consumer products to be safe and our obligations to
ensure this.

If you have any concerns about our products, you can contact us on

ProductSafety@springernature.com

In case Publisher is established outside the EU, the EU authorized
representative is:

Springer Nature Customer Service Center GmbH
Europaplatz 3
69115 Heidelberg, Germany